COMPARATIVE CONSTITUTIONALISM AND GOOD GOVERNANCE IN THE COMMONWEALTH

The central role that good, effective and capable governance plays in the economic and social development of a country is now widely recognised. Using the Commonwealth countries of eastern and southern Africa (the ESA states) as the basis for discussion, this book analyses some of the key constitutional issues in the process of developing, strengthening and consolidating the capacity of states to ensure the good governance of their peoples. Utilising comparative material, the book seeks to draw lessons, both positive and negative, about the problems of constitutionalism in the region and, in doing so, critically addresses the legal issues involved in seeking to make constitutions 'work' in practice.

John Hatchard is Visiting Professor of Law at The Open University and General Secretary of the Commonwealth Legal Education Association. He is Joint Editor of the *Journal of African Law*. He has lived and worked in Africa for many years and has held senior positions on the law faculty at both the University of Zambia and University of Zimbabwe.

Muna Ndulo is Professor of Law at the Cornell Law School and Director of the Institute for African Development in the University. He was formerly Professor of Law and Dean of the School of Law, University of Zambia and Director of the Law Practice Institute of the Council of Legal Education in Zambia. He has served as Legal Officer, United Nations Commission on International Trade Law. He has worked on elections and political transformation in several countries. He was Chief Political Adviser to the Special Representative of the UN Secretary General for South Africa and Head of the United Nations Mission in South Africa, Chief Legal Adviser, United Nations Mission to East Timor and Legal Officer with United Nations Mission in Kosovo.

Peter Slinn is Director of the Diplomacy Programme at the School of Oriental and African Studies, University of London and adjunct Professor of Law, University of Notre-Dame. He is Vice-President of the Commonwealth Legal Education Association, Joint General Editor of the *Law Reports of the Commonwealth*, and a member of the Executive Committee of the Commonwealth Lawyers' Association and the Trustee Committee of the Commonwealth Human Rights Initiative.

COMPARATIVE CONSTITUTIONALISM AND GOOD GOVERNANCE IN THE COMMONWEALTH

An Eastern and Southern African Perspective

JOHN HATCHARD

MUNA NDULO

PETER SLINN

CAMBRIDGE
UNIVERSITY PRESS

CAMBRIDGE UNIVERSITY PRESS
Cambridge, New York, Melbourne, Madrid, Cape Town, Singapore, São Paulo, Delhi

Cambridge University Press
The Edinburgh Building, Cambridge CB2 8RU, UK

Published in the United States of America by Cambridge University Press, New York

www.cambridge.org
Information on this title: www.cambridge.org/9780521118293

First published 2004
This digitally printed version 2009

A catalogue record for this publication is available from the British Library

Library of Congress Cataloguing in Publication data
Hatchard, John.
Comparative constitutionalism and good governance in the Commonwealth: an Eastern and Southern African perspective / John Hatchard, Muna Ndulo, Peter Slinn.
p. cm.
Includes bibliographical references and index.
ISBN 0 521 58464 7
1. Constitutional law – Africa, East. 2. Constitutional law – Africa, Southern. 3. Constitutional law – Commonwealth countries. 4. Africa, East – Politics and government. 5. Africa, Southern – Politics and government. 6. Commonwealth countries – Politics and government.
I. Ndulo, Muna. II. Slinn, Peter. III. Title.
KQC522 H68 2004
342.6802 – dc22 2003055751

ISBN 978-0-521-58464-7 hardback
ISBN 978-0-521-11829-3 paperback

CONTENTS

PREFACE

This book has been some years in gestation. Conceived in an era of optimism after the almost miraculous constitutional transition in South Africa and the emergence of a new democratic dispensation in other countries of eastern and southern Africa, our offspring has emerged from the delivery room in the summer of 2002 in an atmosphere clouded by serious threats to the practice of good governance in the region. The world's press is full of pessimistic stories of the breakdown of the rule of law in Zimbabwe, once heralded as a model for African development, and of the regional prospect of disastrous famines exacerbated by evidence of governmental corruption and incompetence. We hope to throw some light, from our particular legal perspective, on Africa's continuing quest for sustainable good governance and development.

In the process of writing, we have incurred many debts of gratitude to our fellow workers in the field of law and policy in Commonwealth Africa and to the institutions which have sustained us during our collective labours. It would be invidious to identify particular individuals, other than to record our warm appreciation of the support and forebearance of Ms Finola O'Sullivan, Ms Jenny Rubio and their colleagues of the Cambridge University Press and of the patience of our respective families. In general we have been able to include materials available to us as of 1 August 2002, although we have been able to make some reference to the *Report of the Constitution of Kenya Review Commission*, which appeared in mid-September 2002.

John Hatchard, Muna Ndulo and Peter Slinn

CASES

CONSTITUTIONS

Constitution of Malawi 1994

Constitution of Namibia 1990

STATUTES

OTHER INSTRUMENTS

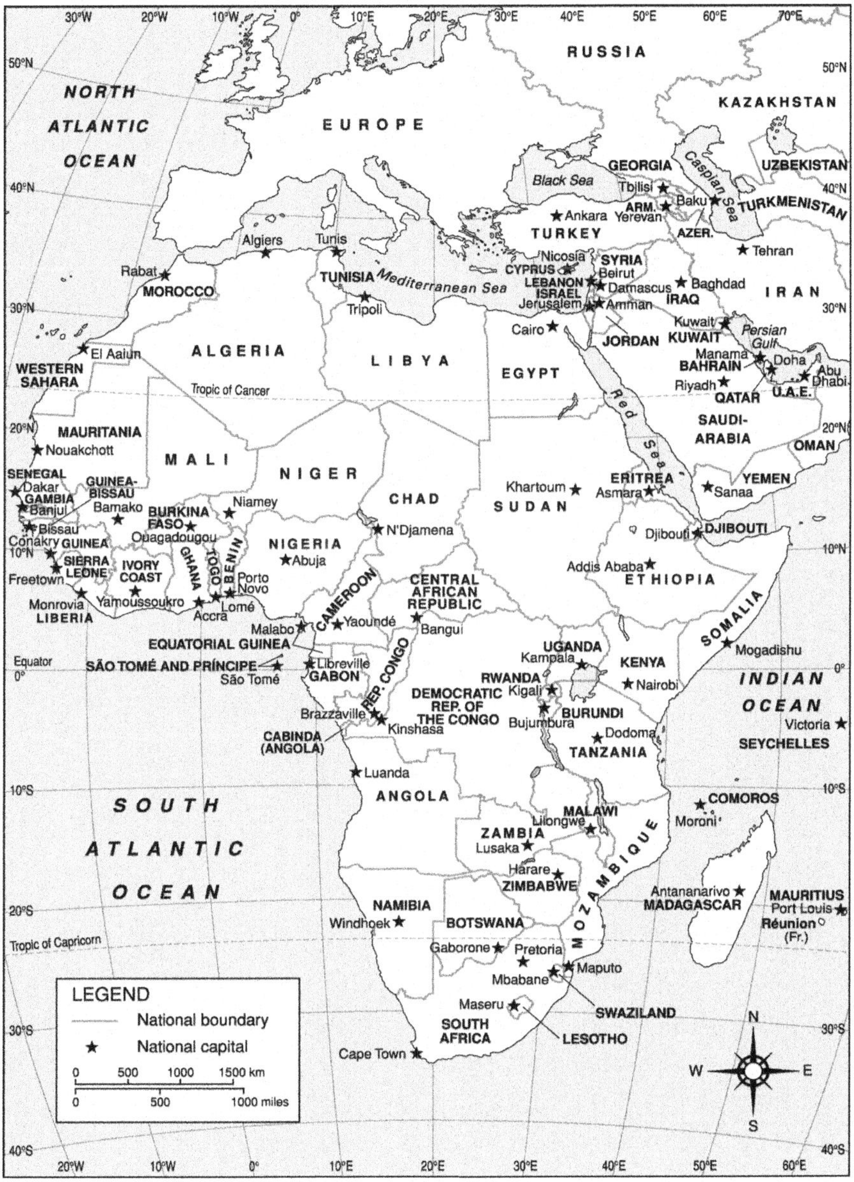
RUSSIA
EUROPE
KAZAKHSTAN
NORTH ATLANTIC OCEAN
GEORGIA
Caspian Sea
UZBEKISTAN
Black Sea
Tbilisi
ARM.
Yerevan
Baku
TURKMENISTAN
Ankara
TURKEY
AZER.
Tehran
Algiers
Tunis
Rabat
MOROCCO
TUNISIA
Mediterranean Sea
Nicosia
CYPRUS
SYRIA
Beirut
LEBANON
ISRAEL
Damascus
Baghdad
IRAN
Jerusalem
Amman
IRAQ
Tripoli
Cairo
Kuwait
Persian Gulf
JORDAN
KUWAIT
El Aaiun
ALGERIA
LIBYA
EGYPT
Manama
BAHRAIN
Doha
Abu Dhabi
WESTERN SAHARA
Riyadh
QATAR
U.A.E.
Tropic of Cancer
Red Sea
SAUDI-ARABIA
MAURITANIA
Nouakchott
OMAN
MALI
NIGER
SENEGAL
Dakar
GAMBIA
Banjul
GUINEA-BISSAU
Bamako
Niamey
CHAD
Khartoum
SUDAN
ERITREA
Asmara
YEMEN
Sanaa
BURKINA FASO
Ouagadougou
Bissau
Conakry
GUINEA
N'Djamena
Djibouti
DJIBOUTI
NIGERIA
Abuja
SIERRA LEONE
Freetown
IVORY COAST
GHANA
TOGO
BENIN
Porto Novo
Addis Ababa
ETHIOPIA
Monrovia
LIBERIA
Yamoussoukro
Accra
Lomé
CAMEROON
CENTRAL AFRICAN REPUBLIC
Malabo
Yaoundé
Bangui
SOMALIA
EQUATORIAL GUINEA
UGANDA
Kampala
Mogadishu
KENYA
Equator
SÃO TOMÉ AND PRÍNCIPE
São Tomé
Libreville
GABON
REP. CONGO
RWANDA
Kigali
Nairobi
INDIAN OCEAN
DEMOCRATIC REP. OF THE CONGO
Brazzaville
Kinshasa
Bujumbura
BURUNDI
Dodoma
Victoria
SEYCHELLES
CABINDA (ANGOLA)
TANZANIA
Luanda
ANGOLA
COMOROS
Moroni
SOUTH ATLANTIC OCEAN
MALAWI
Lilongwe
ZAMBIA
Lusaka
MOZAMBIQUE
Harare
ZIMBABWE
Antananarivo
MADAGASCAR
MAURITIUS
Port Louis
Réunion (Fr.)
NAMIBIA
Windhoek
BOTSWANA
Gaborone
Pretoria
Tropic of Capricorn
Maputo
Mbabane
Maseru
SWAZILAND
SOUTH AFRICA
LESOTHO
Cape Town
LEGEND
National boundary
National capital
0 500 1000 1500 km
0 500 1000 miles
N
W
E
S
30°W 20°W 10°W 0° 10°E 20°E 30°E 40°E 50°E 60°E 70°E
50°N 40°N 30°N 20°N 10°N 0° 10°S 20°S 30°S 40°S
20°W 10°W 0° 10°E 20°E 30°E 40°E 50°E 60°E

Introduction

We are conscious that there are many pitfalls in writing a book of this kind. They were pointed out over thirty years ago by the authors of a pioneering work on public law and political change in Kenya.[1] Our project is in a sense even more ambitious in that we deal not with one state but eleven eastern and southern African states (the ESA states). Even the title caused us much difficulty. It is to be hoped that readers will get beyond a textual analysis of expressions which raise some difficult questions. What is 'constitutionalism'? What is 'good governance'? What are the boundaries of 'eastern and southern Africa'? What is the relevance of the Commonwealth?

De Smith's view of the concept of constitutionalism is firmly set in a western liberal democratic mould:

> The idea of constitutionalism involves the proposition that the exercise of governmental power shall be bounded by rules, rules prescribing the procedure according to which legislative and executive acts are to be performed and delimiting their permissible content – Constitutionalism becomes a living reality to the extent that these rules curb the arbitrariness of discretion and are in fact observed by the wielders of political power, and to the extent that within the forbidden zones upon which authority may not trespass there is significant room for the enjoyment of individual liberty.[2]

This definition has been characterised as 'minimalist' by one of Africa's most distinguished academic lawyers, noting that western constitutionalism was often argued to be representative of a foreign element

[1] Preface to Y. P. Ghai and J. P. W. B. McAuslan, *Public Law and Political Change in Kenya*, Oxford, Oxford University Press, 1970: 'There are so many reasons for not writing a book on the public law of an African state, not least that much of the subject matter . . . tends to be somewhat ephemeral.' It is particularly fitting that we close this study with a reference to the Report of the Constitution of Kenya Review Commission, chaired by Professor Ghai, p. 324.

[2] S. A. de Smith, *The New Commonwealth and its Constitutions*, London, Stevens, 1964, p. 106.

which had no place in African tradition, history or practice.[3] This latter perspective led to a 'developmental' argument in favour of authoritarianism: no fetter should be placed on the exercise of state power in the interests of the development of the masses. At the heart of this book lies the issue of the extent to which the exercise of arbitrary power may be limited by constitutional and other means so as to ensure the good government of the people.

'Good governance' is another much used but ill-defined concept. 'Good governance is more than putting constitutional limits to the power of the government.'[4] The adjective 'good' perhaps is merely there for emphasis, for while 'government' may be good or bad, 'governance' in the modern language of the development industry implies 'the conscious management of regime structures with a view to enhancing the legitimacy of the public realm'.[5] As it was put in the World Bank's report which marked that institution's damascene conversion to the importance of governance issues in the quest for sustainable development,

> Underlying the litany of Africa's development problem is a crisis of governance. By governance is meant the exercise of political power to manage a nation's affairs . . . [Appropriate economic policies must] go hand-in-hand with good governance – a public service that is efficient, a judicial system that is reliable and an administration that is accountable to the public.[6]

Africa's quest is thus for a golden triptych of good governance → constitutionalism → sustainable development.

The boundaries of the study are comprised by the anglophone Commonwealth countries of eastern and southern Africa (the ESA states): Botswana, Kenya, Lesotho, Malawi, Namibia, South Africa, Swaziland,

[3] Issa G. Shivji, 'State and Constitutionalism: a New Democratic Perspective', in Issa G. Shivji (ed.) *State and Constitutionalism*, Harare, Zimbabwe, Sapes 1991, pp. 28–9.

[4] Ali A. Mazrui, 'Constitutional Change and Cultural Engineering: Africa's Search for New Directions', in J. Oloka-Onyango (ed.) *Constitutionalism in Africa: Creating Opportunities, Facing Challenges*, Kampala, Fountain Publishers, 2001, p. 22.

[5] Goran Hyden and Michael Bratton *Governance and Politics in Africa*, Boulder, CO, Lynne Reinner Publishers, 1993 p. 7, quoted in a helpful synthesis by H. W. O. Okoth-Ogendo, 'Governance and Sustainable Development in Africa', in K. Ginther, E. Denters and P. de Waart (eds.) *Sustainable Development and Good Governance*, Dordrecht, Kluwer, 1995, p. 107.

[6] World Bank, *Sub-Saharan Africa: from Crisis to Sustainable Growth*, Washington, DC, World Bank 1989, pp. 60 and xii. See also Peter Slinn, 'Constitutional orders and sustainable development: the Southern African experience and prospects', in Ginther, Denters and de Waart *Sustainable Development*, p. 165.

Tanzania, Uganda, Zambia and Zimbabwe.[7] Our collective expertise lies in these countries and we have all taught comparative constitutional law in diverse places. Whilst it is appropriate to draw some useful comparisons, the intention is not to undertake a comparative analysis of the texts of the constitutions of the ESA states, but rather to draw lessons, both positive and negative, from the experience of these countries in the development of constitutionalism in the region. In doing so, we address critically the legal issues involved in seeking to make constitutions 'work': for example, the protection of the constitutional order from being undermined by 'unconstitutional means' through the undue influence or involvement in government of the military or by 'constitutional means' through executive abuse of power.

The Commonwealth in our view is a vital component of the constitutionalism agenda for the ESA states. Representing an international organisation which is comprised of fifty-four countries from all parts of the globe, both developed and developing, but which lacks the threat of super-power dominance, Commonwealth Heads of Government Meetings (CHOGM) have adopted and frequently endorsed a statement of fundamental political values. The Commonwealth Principles including 'the inalienable right [of citizens] to participate by means of free and democratic political processes in framing the society in which they live', were first adopted at the Singapore CHOGM in 1971.[8] The Harare Commonwealth Declaration of 1991 explicitly linked the advancement of the Commonwealth's fundamental political values with promoting sustainable development.[9] CHOGM in Australia in 2002 re-affirmed a shared commitment to 'democracy, the rule of law, good governance, freedom of expression and the protection of human rights'.[10] Moreover, the Commonwealth Ministerial Action Group on the Harare

[7] Mozambique, although a Commonwealth ESA state, is omitted on the grounds that it is a Lusophone country with a radically different constitutional tradition. We have not dealt in any detail with the complex story of South Africa's transition, about which a vast literature already exists, although the post apartheid constitutional order demands frequent attention. Zimbabwe is included, although after this book went to press, Zimbabwe withdrew from the Commonwealth. This was in response to the decision of Commonwealth Heads of Government in December 2003 at their Meeting in Abuja, to extend Zimbabwe's suspension from the Councils of the Commonwealth imposed in March 2002. See chapter 1 at p. 11. All references to the number of Commonwealth member states in this book should take into account this situation.

[8] The Declaration of Commonwealth Principles, Singapore, 22 January 1971.

[9] Harare Commonwealth Declaration, 20 October 1991.

[10] Coolum Declaration of Commonwealth Heads of Government, 5 March 2002. Significantly, a reference to freedom of expression appeared for the first time in this series of Declarations.

Declaration (CMAG) was established in 1995 to deal with serious or persistent violations of the principles contained in that Declaration.[11]

While no study of Africa can ignore the historical context, the emphasis here is on the contemporary constitutional scene.[12] 'Contemporary' may be defined for this purpose as the era ushered in by the wind of constitutional change which blew through Africa in the early 1990s. This wind proved too strong for the *de jure* one-party state regimes which had been a particular feature of the SEA states and even proved strong enough to topple the very *apartheid* system from the parliamentary ramparts of which Harold Macmillan had identified that earlier wind of change blowing through the continent some forty years before.[13]

We are conscious of our limitations as constitutional lawyers. We do not seek to offer an analysis of the political economy of the region. However we hope that this book will be of interest not only to fellow constitutional lawyers but to all those interested in confronting Africa's twenty-first century challenges. We hope to make a useful contribution to the analysis of the successes and failures of African development in the region in so far as these may be attributable to matters within our focus – to the problem of tailoring appropriate constitutional clothes to fit the body politic in a way which promotes the good governance which is now accepted as a prerequisite for sustainable development.

[11] Millbrook Commonwealth Action Programme on the Harare Declaration issued by Heads of Government at Millbrook, New Zealand, 1995, Commonwealth Secretariat.

[12] The importance of the historical background is illustrated by the discussion of the colonial legacy and one-party states, see chapter 2.

[13] Peter Slinn, 'A fresh start for Africa? New African Constitutional Perspectives for the 1990s' [1991] 35 *Journal of African Law* 1.

1

The democratic state in Africa: setting the scene

Setting the scene: Africa's record

It is appropriate to begin with some general reflections upon Africa's successes and failures in the field of governance since independence and upon the future of democracy on the continent in the new millennium. Africa, with a land area three times the size of the United States and a population in excess of 600 million people, is both the least developed and, in terms of natural resources, the most endowed continent in the world.[1] With its vast mineral, oil, water, land and human resources, the continent has the ability to attain sustainable development, that is to say 'increasingly productive employment opportunities and a steadily improving quality of life for all its citizens'.[2] Yet millions of Africans live in acute poverty, have no access to safe drinking water and are illiterate.[3] The ambiguity in Africa's position is revealed with particular clarity in relation to food production. In pre-colonial times, the continent was self-sufficient in this

[1] World Bank, 'Accelerated Development in Sub-Saharan Africa: an Agenda for Action', Washington DC, World Bank, 1981; Organisation of African Unity (OAU), *The Lagos Plan of Action for the Implementation of the Monrovia Strategy for the Economic Development of Africa*, adopted by the Second Extraordinary Assembly of the OAU Heads of State and Government Devoted to Economic Matters, Lagos, Nigeria, 28–9 April, 1980.

[2] *World Bank, Sub-Saharan Africa: from Crisis to Sustainable Growth*, Washington, DC, World Bank, 1989; Julius Nyerere, 'Africa Exists in the Economic South,' *Development and Social Economic Progress* 41(3)(1988), 7–8; United Nations Economic Commission for Africa (UNECA), *Africa Alternative Framework to Structural Adjustment Programs for Socio-Economic Recovery and Transformation* (E/ECA/CM.15/6/Rev.3).

[3] This is emphasised by the Human Development Index contained in the United Nations Human Development Report 2001 which measures the achievement of 163 countries world wide in terms of life expectancy, educational attainment and adjusted real income. It reveals that forty of the fifty-four worst performing countries are found in sub-Saharan Africa and these include all the ESA states, with the exception of South Africa. For a discussion of Africa's economic situation, see generally, Adebayo Adedeji, 'The Leadership Challenge for Improving the Economic and Social Situation of Africa', paper presented at the Africa Leadership Forum, 24 October – 1 November, 1988, Ota, Nigeria; and A. Y. Yansane (ed.) *Prospects for Recovery and Sustainable Development in Africa*, Westport, CT Greenwood Press, 1996.

area. Now, however, many African countries are dependent upon external food supplies. On the face of it, the inability of the African continent to feed itself is paradoxical, since one of its chief assets is its huge agricultural potential. Further it has all the conditions for becoming one of the world's major food baskets.[4]

Unfortunately, Africa lacks the domestic capital necessary to translate its enormous wealth into realisable benefits for its people and it has failed to attract sizable foreign investment to fill the gap. While, for example, African countries have put in place a myriad of investment codes in an effort to attract foreign capital, they receive only some 5 per cent of all direct foreign investment flowing to developing countries.[5] Furthermore, about half of this investment goes into oil and mineral production and most of it to a few countries such as South Africa, Nigeria, Angola and Botswana; this in spite of the fact that investments made in Africa consistently generate high rates of return.[6]

At the root of the problem is the world-wide perception of Africa as an unstable, poorly governed, conflict- and poverty-ridden continent that cannot guarantee the safety of foreign investments.[7] Several researchers have tested the impact of political stability, or conversely, political risk, on foreign direct investment flows. They found that a major factor cited by investors to explain their decision not to invest in a particular country was political instability.[8] Certainly Africa's political instability has

[4] Karl Lavrencic, 'Food for Africa', *New African* 137, 90, February 1979.

[5] United Nations Conference on Trade and Development, *Foreign Investment in Africa*, UNCTAD/DTCI/19, Current Studies, Series A, No. 28, 1995, p. 3.

[6] For example, the average annual return on book value of US direct investment in Africa is nearly 28 per cent compared with 8.5 per cent for US direct investment worldwide. See *United States Direct Investment in Africa*, Southern African Development Community – USA, Trade and Investment publication, Washington DC, 1998, p. 4.

[7] Since 1970, more than thirty-two wars have been fought in Africa, the vast majority of them intra-state in origin. In 1996 alone fourteen of the fifty-three countries of Africa were afflicted by armed conflicts, accounting for more than half of all war-related deaths worldwide and resulting in more than 8 million refugees, returnees and displaced persons. See United Nations, *Secretary-General's Report to the United Nations Security Council*, New York, United Nations, September 1998. See also Ted Robert Gurr and Barbara Harff, *Ethnic Conflict in World Politics*, Westview Press, Boulder, CO, 1994, at 13. However, Africa also suffers from the fact that the image of the continent is poor even in areas such as corruption where the actual situation is perhaps better than that prevailing in some other regions.

[8] Yair Aharon, *Foreign Investment Decision Process*, Cambridge, MA, Harvard University Press, 1966; E. I. Nwogugu, *Legal Aspects of Foreign Investment in Developing Countries*, Manchester, Manchester University Press, 1965.

exacted a huge cost on its development efforts. In its 1989 report on Sub-Saharan Africa the World Bank concluded that '. . . underlying the litany of Africa's development problems is a crisis of governance'. The report continued:

> By governance is meant the exercise of political power to manage a nation's affairs. Because countervailing power has been lacking, state officials in many countries have served their own interests without fear of being called to account. The leadership assumes broad discretionary authority and loses its legitimacy. Information is controlled, and voluntary associations are co-opted or disbanded. This environment cannot readily support a dynamic economy.[9]

The answer to the development quagmire therefore lies in establishing just and honest government. The starting point is examining the obstacles to achieving and sustaining this goal.

To a large extent the problems are rooted in the past. The continent has suffered a painful history that includes some of the worst human tragedies: slavery, colonialism and apartheid. As a direct result, when African countries won independence they faced formidable constraints to development. These included an acute shortage of skilled human resources, political fragility and insecurity rooted in ill-suited institutions. This legacy will continue to hamper development for decades to come. Yet Africa should be able to draw lessons, strength and determination from them. The serious problems should generate a predisposition to engage in a fundamental re-examination and re-direction rather than despair. Any avoidance of an unpromising future requires the transcending not only of the unfavourable indicators for the decades immediately ahead, but also the unhelpful inheritance from the past.

If issues of governance are resolved, Africa can become one of the fastest growing regions in the world. Just and honest government can result in the adoption of policies that will resolve the constraints that hinder sustained economic development. It is now acknowledged that after years of decline, some African economies are beginning to experience significant growth[10] and that parts of the continent are slowly becoming an attractive 'emerging

[9] World Bank Report, Sub-Saharan Africa *From Crisis to Sustainable Development*, 1989, Washington, DC.

[10] World Bank, *Annual Report, 1997*, World Bank, Washington, DC, 1997. See also World Bank, *World Development Report 1999/2000: Entering the Twenty-First Century*, World Bank, Washington, DC.

market' and investment opportunity.[11] But this fragile progress can easily be reversed and therefore needs consolidation. There is much to be done to translate the recent improvements into sustainable progress that will have a positive impact on the lives of everyone.

Not since independence have both the hopes and the challenges been simultaneously so great. Yet in reality whilst some African countries may be doing quite well, most Africans are not.[12] Africa remains host to the largest population of refugees and displaced persons on any continent. Too many people are trapped in conditions of grinding poverty, face violence and abuse daily and suffer under corrupt regimes. They are condemned to live their lives in squatter settlements or rural slums with inadequate sanitation, schooling and health facilities and to endure a police force and criminal justice system that seemingly does little to address their needs. All this contributes to conflict, instability and misery.[13] States must also pay particular attention to the experiences of poverty and address and respond to the legal problems that adversely affect the lives of the poor, e.g. corruption, governmental lawlessness and institutional failure.

Criticism might be levelled here that this broad approach runs the danger of over-generalising the problems and the solutions applicable to individual countries. In fact one can make a strong case that African countries, though a mix, share common problems in relation to governance and development. They all face high levels of illiteracy, disease and poor infrastructure, are virtually all multi-ethnic in composition and most of their people live in grinding poverty. In other words, they are all struggling with the challenges of economic development and nation building.

[11] As Douglas Anglin has observed: 'Africa, long the poor cousin of a resurgent Asia is beginning to emerge from under its shadow. The continent's long-heralded renaissance is at last capturing the imagination of the world and in the process contributing to a new and more positive image as well as providing fresh momentum for constructive change' (D. Anglin, 'Conflict in Sub-Saharan Africa', Bellville, Centre for Southern African Studies, 1997).

[12] See, 'Africa Growth and Opportunity Act: a Cursory Appraisal', Africa Faith and Justice Network, September 1997. See also, 'Letter from Several African-Americans to Members of the US Senate urging modifications of the US–Africa Bill', 13 May, 1998. In it the authors point out the devastating social impact on Africans of the structural adjustment programmes being pursued by the World Bank and the IMF.

[13] In fact as Anglin ('Conflict', at p. 6) has observed, Africa has arguably slipped into one of the most violent phases of its post independence history 'with political struggles spilling across borders as states interfere militarily in their neighbours' affairs in ways once uncommon'. He cites the conflicts in Congo (now the Democratic Republic of the Congo), Rwanda, Burundi and Lesotho where neighbouring states have intervened in internal conflicts.

Many of Africa's problems are the result of an inability to create 'capable states'.[14] A capable state, in this context, is one characterised by transparency, accountability, the ability to enforce law and order fairly throughout the country, respect for human rights, the effective sharing of resources between the rural and urban populations, a limited role in the market economy, the creation of a predictable, open and enlightened policy-making environment and the working in partnership with the private sector, the media and organs of civil society.[15] In addition, the acceptance of competitive politics and the maintenance of a bureaucracy imbued with a professional ethos and committed to acting in furtherance of the public good is required.[16] These characteristics enable a state to effectively perform its role of developing the country and bringing about a better life for its people.

For these to occur, the rule of law must prevail. Political pluralism cannot prosper until effective legal institutions are established. In order to function effectively, a legal system must include not only relevant and up-to-date laws, but also an efficient institutional infrastructure for the design and administration of the law. The national constitution is the most important legal instrument here. Thus, part of the answer to the present predicament lies in the development of constitutions that can stand the test of time and that deliberately structure national institutions engaged in the management of the country in such a way as to ensure the creation of a capable state.

The central role that good, efficient and capable governance plays in the economic and social development of a country is now widely recognised.[17] This was emphasised in 1991 by the Commonwealth,[18] a voluntary association of fifty-four sovereign independent states that includes

[14] Apolo Nsibambi, 'The Interface among the Capable State, the Private Sector and Civil Society in Acquiring Food Security', Keynote paper at the Conference on Building for the Capable State in Africa, Institute for African Studies, Cornell University, 24–8 October, 1997.

[15] Patricia Armstrong, 'Human Rights and Multilateral Development Banks: Governance Concerns in Decision Making', 88 *American Society of International Law Proceedings*, 271.

[16] See Nsibambi, 'Interface', at p. 14.

[17] See, UNISA 'Deliberations of African Governance Forum, organised in the context of the United Nations System-wide Special Initiative on Africa' (UNISA), 11–12 July, 1997, New York. See also World Bank, *Development Report, 1997*, World Bank, Washington, DC, 1997.

[18] These comprise all those with direct or indirect colonial ties with Britain along with the 'special' case of Mozambique. For full details of the work of the Commonwealth see J. Hatchard (ed.), *Directory of Commonwealth Law Schools 2003–2004*, Cavendish Publishing, London, 2002, pp. 49–82.

the eleven ESA states. In the 1991 Harare Commonwealth Declaration,[19] which established its guiding principles, Commonwealth Heads of Government pledged:

> [T]he Commonwealth *and our countries* to work with renewed vigour, concentrating especially on the following areas:
> * the protection and promotion of the fundamental political values of the Commonwealth
>   – democracy, democratic processes and institutions which reflect national circumstances, the rule of law and the independence of the judiciary, just and honest government;
>   – fundamental human rights, including equal rights and opportunities for all citizens regardless of race, colour, creed or political belief . . .
> * extending the benefits of development within a framework of respect for human rights; . . .' (our emphasis).[20]

That just and honest government takes time to develop and that at the meeting the concept was treated with little respect by many heads of government is well illustrated by noting the names of some Heads of African Delegations who 'pledged' their countries to uphold the Declaration. They included Dr Hastings Banda, the Life President of Malawi, as well as the leaders of four other *de jure* one-party states.[21] Military governments were also well represented by the presence of (using their official titles) HE Major-General Elias Phisoana Ramaema, Chairman of the Military Council of Lesotho, HE General Ibrahim Babangida, President of Nigeria and Hon. Paul Obeng, Member of the Provisional National Defence Council (Prime Minister) of Ghana.

Whilst practice and theory were clearly far apart in 1991, the Declaration's importance is that it has provided and continues to provide a benchmark upon which to judge the ESA states performance on principles to which that they themselves have voluntarily agreed. Evidence of the Declaration's increasing significance lies in the fact that any country

[19] For the context and significance of the Declaration see Alison Duxbury 'Rejuvenating the Commonwealth: the Human Rights Remedy' (1997) 46 ICLQ 344.

[20] The UN General Assembly has also recognised that democracy and transparent and accountable governance and administration in all sectors of society are indispensable foundations for the realisation of social and people-centred sustainable development and that governments in all countries should provide and protect all human rights and fundamental freedoms, including the right to development, bearing in mind the interdependent and mutually reinforcing relationship between democracy, development and respect for human rights: Resolution 50/225 of 19 April 1996.

[21] Plus the 'no-party' state of Uganda.

seeking entry or re-entry into the organisation must comply with its provisions.[22] Further, military intervention into government now leads in the first instance to the suspension of that member state from participation in the Councils of the Commonwealth and ultimately to suspension from the organisation itself.[23] The willingness of the Commonwealth to take action against member states with civilian governments which are responsible for 'substantial and persistent' breaches of the Harare Declaration is reflected in the decision in March 2002 to suspend Zimbabwe (ironically the home of the Harare Declaration) from the Councils of the Commonwealth. This followed the Commonwealth Election Observer Group's findings that the 2002 presidential election was marred by a high level of politically motivated violence and that 'the conditions in Zimbabwe did not adequately allow for a free expression of the will of the electors'.[24]

It is against this background that the book sets out to examine the experiences of the eleven ESA states.

[22] This rubric was included after the 1995 entry of Cameroon into the Commonwealth. At that time, the rubric was that a prospective member should be 'in the process of' complying with the Declaration. Concern at Cameroon's continuing poor human rights record brought about the change. What constitutes 'compliance' is determined by Commonwealth Heads of Government.

[23] This approach was agreed to by Commonwealth Heads of Government in 1995 in the *Millbrook Commonwealth Action Programme on the Harare Commonwealth Declaration*. It is overseen by the Commonwealth Ministerial Action Group (CMAG) that consists of senior ministers from around the Commonwealth who meet regularly to assess progress in those states which have been referred to them for scrutiny. CMAG's ultimate power is to recommend that a state be suspended from the Commonwealth. For details of the work of CMAG see fn19 above and pp. 244 and 323.

[24] See *Marlborough House Statement on Zimbabwe*, 19 March 2002, paragraphs 3 and 8. The decision to suspend was taken by the Commonwealth Chairpersons' Committee on Zimbabwe, a body mandated to do so by Commonwealth Heads of Government. The Committee comprised the President of South Africa, Thabo Mbeki, and the President of Nigeria, Olusegun Obasanjo, as well as John Howard, the Australian Prime Minister. See also n. 7 on p. 3 above.

2

Constitutions and the search for a viable political order

A constitution enjoys a special place in the life of any nation. It is the supreme and fundamental law that sets out the state's basic structure including the exercise of political power and the relationship between political entities and between the state and the people. As the former Chief Justice of South Africa, Justice Ismail Mohammed, once observed, a constitution is not simply a statute which mechanically defines the structures of government and the relations between the government and the governed, but it is:

> [A]mirror reflecting the national soul, the identification of the ideals and aspirations of a nation; the articulation of the values binding its people and disciplining its government.[1]

It also shapes the organisation and development of a society both for the present and for future generations. As the Preamble to the Constitution of Uganda 1995 puts it:

> WE THE PEOPLE OF UGANDA COMMITTED to building a better future by establishing a socio-economic and political order through a popular and durable national Constitution . . . DO HEREBY. . . solemnly adopt, enact and give to ourselves and our posterity, this Constitution of Uganda.

This notion is in sharp contrast to that of the colonial period and much of the immediate post-colonial period. This chapter therefore examines the history of constitutionalism in the ESA states prior to 1990 and traces the reasons for the making of new constitutions in the 1990s.

[1] *State v. Acheson* 1991 (2) SA 805 (Nm) at p. 813 A-B. Van der Vyer has also observed that '. . . superimposed constitutional formulae, or constitutional arrangements that . . . do not address the real causes of discontent, are sure to generate their own legitimacy crisis' (J. van der Vyer, 'Constitutional Options for Post-Apartheid South Africa' (1991) 40 *Emory Law Journal* 745, 822). See also Ziyad Motala, *Constitutional Options for a Democratic South Africa: a Comparative Perspective*, Howard University Press, Washington, DC, 1995, p. 1.

The colonial legacy

Traditional African society had its own system of social and political organisation with built-in checks and balances. As Davidson has noted, a 'well-built polity had to be a participatory polity. No participation had to mean no stability. This indispensable participation therefore formed the hearthstone of statesmanship.'[2] This was lost with the advent of colonialism, as African societies experienced protracted economic and social changes. At the Berlin Conference of 1884, the colonial powers partitioned the continent into territorial units. African kingdoms, states and communities were arbitrarily divided,[3] unrelated areas and peoples were arbitrarily joined together whilst united peoples were torn apart. The era of colonialism initiated and that of independence consummated a dynamic process of disruption in tribal organisation and tribal life. Unlike in pre-colonial Africa, the financial, political and military security of African societies no longer depended upon traditional organisations and custom. There was a departure from agrarian self-subsistence communities to a money economy dependent on the capitalist economic system. With such fundamental changes, the human institutions governing African societies also had to change. The foremost act of disruption was the unification of ethnic communities under the umbrella of colonial states created pursuant to the Berlin Conference. Within such entities, the colonial authorities exercised overriding powers of political control regardless of traditional systems of governance.[4] Dislocation of African peoples from their lands and communities continued throughout the colonial period as the needs of the colonial economy expanded, further undermining any tribal economy or social organisation that were left in place after the initial establishment of colonial rule.[5]

[2] B. Davidson, *The Black Man's Burden*, James Currey, London, 1993, at p. 225.

[3] For example in 1890, Lord Salisbury, the British Prime Minister remarked at a dinner that followed the conclusion of the Anglo-French Convention which established spheres of influence in West Africa: 'We have been engaged in drawing lines upon maps where no white man's foot ever trod; we have been giving away mountains and rivers and lakes to each other, only hindered by the small impediment that we never really knew exactly where the mountains and rivers and lakes were' (M. Mukuwa Wa Mukua, 'Why Redraw the Map of Africa? A Moral and Legal Inquiry' (1995) 16 *Michigan Journal of International Law* 1135 quoting J. C. Anene, *The International Boundaries of Nigeria 1865–1960*, Humanities Press, New York 1970, at p. 3).

[4] See R. Rotberg, *The Rise of Nationalism in Central Africa: the Making of Malawi and Zambia, 1873–1964*, Harvard University Press, Cambridge, MA, 1965, at p. 303; R. Hall, *Zambia*, Praeger, New York, 1964; and J. B. Ojwang, Rural Dispute Settlement in Kenya (1975–8) 7–10 Zambia Law Journal 63.

[5] Okoth Ogendo, 'Property Systems and Social Organisation in Africa: an Essay on the Relative Position of Women under Indigenous and Received Law', in P. Takirambudde

Colonial rule was philosophically and organisationally elitist, centralist and absolute and left no room for either constitutions or representative institutions. The colonial administration not only implemented policy, it made it as well. As Seidman has noted, 'the authoritarian principle of colonial government was marked by its dominant theory of the exercise of power'.[6] Authoritarian forms of government everywhere expressed their character by giving relatively unfettered discretion to 'the man on the spot'. This philosophy of government was expressed in law principally by rules that gave almost unlimited discretion to colonial officials, and the absence of formal controls over its exercise.[7] As colonial rulers sought expedient collaborators, they distorted or destroyed pre-colonial governance systems by creating or encouraging arrangements such as indirect rule, which made local chiefs more despotic and created new ones (warrant chiefs) where none had previously existed.[8] Culturally, colonialism divided Africa into two societies: the *traditional culture* found in the rural areas where the great majority of the people lived and which was largely outside the framework of colonial elitism and the *modern culture* found in urban areas. The urban economy and culture was the link between the metropolitan country and the colony in the export of raw materials.[9] Colonial economic policies kept African economies small, excessively open, dependent and poorly integrated.[10] The result was a colonial state characterised by a huge gap in the standard and quality of life between the rural and urban areas.[11]

(ed.), *The Individual under African Law*, University of Swaziland, Mbabane, 1982, p. 47. See also K. Bentsi-Enchil, 'Do African Systems of Land Tenure Require a Special Terminology?', Reprint Series No. 7 North Western University Program of African Studies, 1966.

6 R. Seidman, 'Law and Stagnation in Africa', in M. Ndulo (ed.), *Law in Zambia*, East African Publishing House, Nairobi, 1984, p. 271 at p. 285.

7 *Ibid.*, at p. 285.

8 See generally, A. J. Wills, *An Introduction to the History of Central Africa*, Oxford, Oxford University Press, 1973; L. F. G. Anthony, *The Story of Northern Rhodesia*, Humanities Press, New York, 1953; L. H. Gann, *The Birth of a Plural Society, the Development of Northern Rhodesia Under the British South Africa Company, 1894–1914*, Greenwood Press, Westport CT, 1958; and L. H. Gann, *History of Northern Rhodesia*, Humanities Press, New York, 1964.

9 R. Seidman, 'Drafting for the Rule of Law: Maintaining Legality in Developing Countries' (1987) 12 *Yale Journal of International Law* 85.

10 *Ibid.*, at p.87.

11 B. O. Nwabueze, 'Our March to Constitutional Democracy' (1989), Guardian Lecture, 24 July 1989. Also published in *Law and Practice, Journal of Nigerian Bar Association* (NBA) August 1989, 19–38.

That is not to say that colonial officials were uninterested in governance issues. In British Africa, 'indirect rule' was professed by its advocates to offer a genuine alternative to western-style forms of democratic governance. Moreover, under the post-World War II Labour government led by Clement Attlee, a new generation of colonial officials sought to reinvent the British Empire in Africa as an instrument of development and good governance through a process of 'African advancement', embracing economic, social and political change.[12]

The making of the independence constitutions

> Britain in the 1960s was hustled and harried out of most of her old colonies. In the 1950s, the Sudan, Gold Coast and Malaya had been the only ones to escape. In the 1960s, it became quite suddenly a stampede.[13]

By the late 1960s, British rule had come to an end in eastern and southern Africa (apart from the fleeting restoration of 'lawful government' in Southern Rhodesia from December 1979 until April 1980) in a welter of constitution-making. Teams of lawyers in the Colonial Office in Whitehall and in the territories themselves toiled over ever more complex drafts. At the apogee of the process, the pace of constitutional change was rapid with independence coming in quick succession to Tanganyika (1961), Uganda (1962), Kenya (1963), Zanzibar (1963), Northern Rhodesia (1964) and Malawi (1964). These were followed by Botswana (1966), Lesotho (1966) and Swaziland (1968). Southern Rhodesia also obtained a new constitution in 1961, although independence was to be long delayed by the rebellion of 1965. It is easy to assume that the constitutions emerged from a 'scissors and paste' process whereby the 'Westminster model' imposed by Whitehall was put in place willy-nilly by the departing colonial rulers, essentially indifferent to local conditions and susceptibilities. This assumption is made easier in the wider imperial context for the Colonial Office was also engaged in similar exercises in West Africa, the West Indies, Malta and the 'Far East'.

Obviously, there was a rush and the pressure of work was intense. The Colonial Office in its last years sustained a level of activity unimaginable to those familiar with the leisurely pace of the 1930s, when, so far as Africa

[12] J. M. Lee, *Colonial Development and Good Government: a Study of the Ideas Expressed by the British Official Classes in Planning Decolonisation 1939–1964*, Oxford University Press, Oxford, 1967.

[13] B. Porter, *The Lion's Share*, Longman, London, 1996 3rd edn., p. 342.

was concerned, the complexities of the governing theory of indirect rule attracted philosophical analysis and missionary enthusiasm. As far as the texts of the independence constitutions were concerned there were many similarities, particularly, for example, as to the wording of the Bill of Rights and on the basic provisions relating to the judiciary.[14] The colonial office clearly saw no point in re-inventing the wheel each time. However, the bulky files relating to the transfer of power, now open for inspection in the Public Records Office (PRO) in London reveal both the meticulous care taken over the smallest details and the extent of the consultations which took place between the Colonial Office and local ministers and officials.[15]

This may be illustrated by reference to a key issue in the process of the making and re-making of constitutions: the headship of state and the disposition of executive power. Eight countries within the compass of this book attained independence between 1961 and 1968. Tanganyika (1961), Uganda (1962), Kenya (1963) and Malawi (1964) all initially adopted the Queen as head of state under a 'Westminster export model' constitution with a Prime Minister and Cabinet. Each then moved relatively rapidly to adopt a republican form of government.[16] Zambia (1964) and Botswana (1966) proceeded straight to an executive presidency. Lesotho (1966) and Swaziland (1968) became constitutional monarchies each with its own traditional ruler as head of state (as briefly did Zanzibar in 1963). It might be supposed that the retention of the Queen as Head of State was favoured by the British government which resisted local pressure for republican status. The PRO records, however, tell a very different story. For example, in July 1963, the British government became aware that the

[14] The remarkable history of the Colonial Office's conversion, of truly damascene proportions, to bills of rights as part of the independence apparatus for the African colonies is related in A. W. Brian Simpson, *Human Rights and the End of Empire*, Oxford University Press, Oxford, 2001.

[15] Compare the views of G. W. Kanyeihamba, *Constitutional Law and Government in Uganda*, East Africa Literature Bureau Nairobi, Uganda,' 1975, p. 56 and R. Seidman, 'Perspectives on Constitution-Making: Independence Constitutions of Namibia and South Africa' (1987) 3 *Lesotho Law Journal* 45.

[16] Tanganyika in 1962, Kenya in 1964 and Malawi in 1966. In 1963 in Uganda the Queen was replaced by the Kabaka of Buganda as 'Supreme Head of the State of Uganda'. The country did not formally become a republic until after the 'prime-ministerial coup' of 1966 by Milton Obote. The precedent had been set by Ghana which, in 1957, became the first British colony in Africa to attain independence. In 1960, Ghana became a republic, the Prime Minister, Kwame Nkrumah, assuming office as executive president. Nigeria retained the Queen as head of state at independence in 1960, but became a republic in 1963 with a non-executive president.

Kenyan government, now led by Jomo Kenyatta as Prime Minister under a constitution providing for internal self government, wished to retain the Queen as Head of State after independence. The assumption on the British side was that Kenya would become a republic, soon to be merged into a federal republic of East Africa, consisting of Kenya, Tanganyika (which was already a republic after retaining the Queen for one year) and Uganda (which was about to follow suit in adopting a republican status). However, the prospective creation of a Kenyan Republic and the consequent need to devise a method of selection of the head of state raised difficulties. These were not in respect of the British government but within the ranks of Kenyan politicians to whom the short-term retention of the monarchy became attractive. As a Colonial Office official minuted on the 'Head of State' file, 'the British government would not be disposed to agree that the Queen should be made a convenience of in this way'. However the Governor, Malcolm MacDonald, himself a former dominions secretary, seemed disposed to go along with the urgings of Kenyatta who also wished MacDonald to stay on as Governor-General. Eventually, after a secret tea-time meeting between MacDonald, Kenyatta and Ronald Ngala, the Kenya African Democratic Union party leader, the views of local politicians prevailed and the way was cleared for Kenyan independence in December 1963.[17] In the following year, Malawi achieved independence with the Queen remaining as Head of State and with the incumbent governor, Sir Glyn Jones, staying on as Governor-General. Again the British government acquiesced with the wishes of Prime Minister Hastings Banda even though the latter made it clear that this was purely a matter of convenience for six to twelve months.[18] It was hardly surprising therefore that British ministers and officials grasped eagerly at the desire of Kenneth Kaunda, the Prime Minister of Northern Rhodesia (Zambia), for immediate republican status upon independence even though the Governor, Sir Evelyn Hone, who had developed a warm relationship with Kaunda, had

[17] Correspondence in CO 822/3117 in the UK Public Records Office. MacDonald wrote almost plaintively to the Secretary of State in a secret despatch of 9 September 1963, 'I shall do my best to persuade Kenyatta that it would be more seemly for them to become a republic unless they intend to remain [a monarchy] for a number of years but I think it extremely unlikely that I shall have any success.' Kenya became independent on 12 December 1963 and a republic one year later.

[18] Correspondence in DO/183/60. Matters relating to Malawian independence were this time dealt with not by the Colonial Office but the Central African Office set up by British Prime Minister, Harold MacMillan, in effect to oversee the dissolution of the Federation of Rhodesia and Nyasaland. In fact Malawi became independent on 6 July 1964 and a republic two years later.

recommended the retention of the monarchy for a considerable period in order to bolster the morale and confidence of the (expatriate) civil servants and the British community.[19]

The decisive influence of locally elected nationalist leaders on the independence constitutions was not confined to the question of the monarchy. The drafting of the Kenyan Constitution itself was the product of a lengthy consultation exercise involving detailed discussions in 1962–3 in the Kenya Council of Ministers (which had an elected African majority).[20] In Nyasaland (Malawi), once internal self-government had been conceded in 1963, officials in London accepted that Prime Minister Hastings Banda would have a decisive influence on the drafting of the new constitution on matters such as the appointment of the Chief Justice, retention of appeals to the Privy Council and the procedure for constitutional amendment.[21] As for the composition of the Public Service Commission, one official acknowledged:

> The Public Service Commission is one of the more considerable and conspicuous bees in Dr Banda's bonnet. He does not like it and will only be prepared to allow it to exist more or less on his own terms.[22]

The picture that emerges from the British Government records is a corrective to the traditional view, reflected in the secondary literature, that Whitehall imposed the independence constitutions with little or no regard for local conditions and without adequate consultations locally. In the cases of Kenya, Malawi and Zambia, discussed above, with the granting of internal self-government, their democratically elected nationalist leaders, Kenyatta, Banda and Kaunda, had a crucial role in the shaping of the independence constitutions. Indeed on key issues such as the retention of the monarchy, the entrenchment of a Bill of Rights, executive powers,

19 Correspondence in DO/183/70. Kaunda was named in the Constitution as first president when Northern Rhodesia became independent as the Republic of Zambia on 24 October 1964. He remained president until 1991 confounding the pessimism of one Central African Office official who wrote: 'My own private fear is that Dr Kaunda's trouble is that he is too moderate and reasonable for his own good and that those very qualities that make him so admired by Western observers may be working for his downfall' (Jamieson to Whitley, 2 March 1964).

20 See Webber/Steel correspondence in CO 822/3105.

21 Correspondence in DO/183/60.

22 Minute from Neale to Whitley, Central African Office, 8 November 1963. Secretary of State Butler reluctantly accepted: '. . . the position that matters is non-negotiable: no firmer entrenchment of minority rights and no freedom of service commissions from political control' (Correspondence in DO/183/60).

the independence of service commissions and the procedure for constitutional amendment, their voices were decisive. It is, of course, arguable that British officials were not primarily concerned with the implanting of genuine democracies but with a smooth hand-over of power to local leaders who would then be free to indulge their more autocratic inclinations. Officials were aware of events in Ghana where, by January 1964, Dr Nkrumah had secured approval by referendum for the establishment of a one-party state and were under no illusions that a similar path might be followed in other parts of Commonwealth Africa. However the Ghana precedent was not considered to be a basis for attempts to restrict executive power under the new constitutions of the ESA states.[23]

The next wave of constitution-making

Many governments that emerged after independence soon became undemocratic, over-centralised and authoritarian. Predictably, political monopolies led to corruption, nepotism and abuse of power. Presidents (or Kings) replaced the colonial governor in fact and in deeds. This often led to the emergence of repressive one-party systems of government with the constitution being amended or re-made to reflect the new reality.[24] With these systems, power came to be concentrated in the head of government. This left little or no space for alternative challenges, questions or

[23] The proposed provision in the Malawian Constitution that the Chief Justice should be appointed by the Governor-General solely on the advice of the Prime Minister 'may seem open to question in the light of recent events in Ghana but it is out of the question that Nyasaland would accept restrictions higher than standard' (Tennant CAO, 9 January 1964, DO/183/60). Immediately after independence, Governor-General Jones attempted to dissuade Dr Banda from introducing a Preventive Detention Act. As an official gloomily noted, the existing Public Security Ordinance 'provides everything that a government would reasonably need by way of detention powers . . . However, it may not be good enough for a "one-party state"', (Minute to Watson, 31 July 1964). In fact Malawi was already a *de facto* one-party state before independence in that elections scheduled for May 1964 did not take place because only the Malawi Congress Party had nominated candidates who were all elected unopposed. See D. Nohlen, M. Krennerich and B. Thibaut, *Elections in Africa: a Data Handbook*, 1999, Oxford University Press, Oxford, p. 548. This handbook is a mine of statistical information about elections in the countries under review in this book.

[24] C. Gertzel, C. Baylis and M. Szeftel, *The Dynamics of the One-Party State in Zambia*, Manchester, Manchester University Press, 1984. Also A. Yusuf, 'Reflections on the Fragility of State Institutions in Africa', *African Yearbook of International Law*, vol. 2, 1994, pp. 2–8; L. Zimba, 'The Origins and Spread of One-Party States in Commonwealth Africa, their Impact on Personal Liberties: a Case Study of the Zambian Model', in M. Ndulo (ed.), *Law in Zambia*, East African Publishing House, Nairobi, at 113.

control from below.[25] Dissent, for which there had always been a secure and honoured place in traditional African society, came to be viewed with ill-concealed hostility, almost as if it was treason. Other political parties, even if originally formed around national agendas, generally tended to lead to ethnically based bodies that made African states ungovernable.[26] One-party or military rule was often regarded as a viable and sometimes desirable solution to the ethnically based parties in Africa's new modern states.[27] Ultimately, the Party supplanted the machinery of the state and the differences between the two became blurred.[28] The independence constitutions themselves were amended or replaced and the draconian colonial security laws retained or even strengthened in order to provide the basis for this 'executive terrorism'.

The summary by the Nyalali Commission on the constitutional position in Tanzania under the one-party state is equally applicable elsewhere: (i) one-party rule had largely undermined the participation of citizens in governance; (ii) the ruling party had transformed itself from a political party to a state party monopolising all politics; (iii) various civil organisations, non-governmental organisations and other pressure groups had fallen under the hegemonic control of the party; (iv) repressive colonial laws had not only been retained but expanded; (v) the Bill of Rights had been significantly undermined by the presence of numerous clawback clauses; (vi) the judiciary had often been interfered with and had its right to act independently infringed upon; (vii) the division of power between the executive, judiciary and legislature had been lopsidedly weighted in

[25] I. G. Shivji, *The State and the Working People in Tanzania*, Codestria Book Services, Dar es Salaam, 1985, p. 10.

[26] Thus Museveni's main justification for his 'Movement system' in Uganda is that political parties form on the basis of ethnicity. He observes that one of the biggest factors weakening Africa is tribalism and other forms of sectarianism and that in African politics tribalism is always emphasised: see Y. Museveni, *What is Africa's Problem?*, University of Minnesota Press, Minneapolis, MN, 1992, p. 42. The UN Secretary-General has observed that this is compounded by the fact that the framework of colonial laws and institutions which most states inherited were designed to exploit local divisions, not to overcome them. See, 'Causes of Conflict and the Promotion of Durable Peace and Sustainable Development in Africa', Report of the Secretary-General to the Security Council, 1998.

[27] S. Mubako, 'Single Party Constitution–a Search for Unity and Development' (1973) 5 *Zambia Law Journal* 67; Republic of Zambia, *Report of the National Commission on the Establishment of a One-Party Participatory Democracy in Zambia* (the Chona Commission), Lusaka, Zambia, 1972.

[28] Gertzel, Baylis and Szeftel, *Dynamics of the One-Party State*; J. M. Mwanakatwe, *The End of the Kaunda Era*, Multimedia, Lusaka, Zambia,1994, p. 101. See further discussion in chapter 5.

favour of the executive and especially the office of the President; (viii) the absolute power of the state party meant it overshadowed the legislature; and (ix) the Constitution was full of very serious shortcomings, contradictions and inconsistencies.[29] To these one may add two other features: the development of widespread corruption on the part of public officials and preferential access to power and resources determined by religious, ethnic or geographical considerations. The result was what Oruka has called 'uncivil republics' whereby the average man or woman enjoyed few freedoms and one where 'those who stand up to speak for them are easily silenced or wiped out by the tools of legal terrorism'.[30]

So the independence constitutions failed to work '. . . not so much because of a failure by Africans to learn the lesson of parliamentary government: rather the lesson of authoritarian colonial rule was taught and learnt too well'.[31] Thus was created a litter of incapable and failed states. Such political rigidity shut off the springs of activity in the people. As Obasanjo has observed 'the men and women of spirit who are the leaven of every society either began to go into exile in foreign countries or withdrew into stultifying private life; to their loss yes, but to the even greater loss of society at large'.[32]

The result of all this was unprecedented economic decline and mismanagement, resulting in unimaginable poverty and a growing economic divide between the urban and rural areas. Even today the rural areas often remain neglected, marginalised and impoverished. The dreams of prosperity following independence and self-rule became the nightmare of insecurity and poverty.[33] The 1970s and 1980s can rightly be characterised as the lost decades for good governance.[34]

[29] See Nyalali Commission Report, *Report of the Presidential Commission on Single Party or Multiparty System in Tanzania*, Government Printer, Dar es Salaam, 1991, vol. 1, paras. 229–38.

[30] H. O. Oruka, *Punishment and Terrorism in Africa*, Nairobi, East African Publishing House, 1985, pp. 117–18.

[31] Quoted by P. Slinn, 'A Fresh Start for Africa? New African Constitutional Perspectives for the 1990s' (1991) 35 *Journal of African Law* 1, at p. 6.

[32] Paper presented at the Africa Leadership Forum, 'The Leadership Challenge for Improving the Economic and Social Situation of Africa', Ota, Nigeria, 24 October–1 November 1988. Sadly the exodus of such persons continues although it is now often economic considerations rather more than political ones that are the cause.

[33] T. M. Shaw, *Alternative Futures for Africa*, Westview Press, Boulder, CO, 1982, p. 93.

[34] Paper presented at the African Leadership Forum, 'The Leadership Challenge for Improving the Economic and Social Situation of Africa', 24 October–1 November 1988, Ota, Nigeria.

The new winds of change

The ending of the Cold War, the Harare Commonwealth Declaration's influence and pressure from international donors through the linking of economic aid with good governance, all played a key part in bringing about constitutional changes in the 1990s that were unmatched since the ending of colonialism.[35] Such conditions now began to support local people who had for years advocated democratic reform but who had received little backing from the international community.

Despite their previous experiences, faith in the existence of a single written document as the charter for the exercise of political power was retained.[36] Zambia, Malawi and Lesotho all ended the one-party era by introducing new constitutions that provide for a multi-party state, free and fair elections, a wide-ranging Bill of Rights and oversight bodies such as an Office of the Ombudsman and/or a Human Rights Commission. Elsewhere, both Kenya and Tanzania amended their constitutions and returned to a multi-party state.[37] Uganda's efforts to deal with its own turbulent past also saw the making of a new constitution.[38] Only Botswana retained its independence 'Westminster model' constitution virtually intact. Zimbabwe has ostensibly done the same though in reality the constant amendments to the 1979 document means that it bears little relationship to the original. The sole 'casualty' remains the Constitution of Swaziland which was abrogated in 1973 by King Sobhuza II and the Kingdom remains an absolute monarchy with the current monarch, King Mswati III, continuing to legislate by decree.[39]

[35] As Reyntjens (F. Reyntjens 'The Winds of Change: Political and Constitutional Evolution in Francophone Africa' (1991) 35 *Journal of African Law* 44) observes, virtually no country was left untouched by the wave of political reforms. See also A. K. Wing, 'Towards Democracy in a New South Africa, a Review of Ziyad Motala, Constitutional Options for A Democratic South Africa: a Comparative Perspective' (1995) 16 *Michigan Journal of International Law*, 689 and Slinn, 'A Fresh Start for Africa?', p. 102.

[36] This despite the criticism 'Many African constitutions are irrelevant': a view expressed by R. Green, 'Participatory Pluralism and Pervasive Poverty: Some Reflections', 1989 *Third World Legal Studies* 21 at p. 47.

[37] In 2000 work commenced on a new constitution for Kenya by the Constitution of Kenya Review Commission. For full details see www.kenyaconstitution.org.

[38] Uganda retains the 'movement political system' which has individual merit as the basis for election to political office: see article 70 Constitution of Uganda. In a referendum in 1999, the Ugandan people voted to retain the system.

[39] This despite moves to introduce a new constitution, including the setting up of a Constitutional Review Commission in 1996. Its report was presented to the King in 2000 but never published. For a fuller discussion on the monarchies, see chapter 5.

Two notable additions to the constitutional scene during the 1990s were Namibia and South Africa with both adopting constitutions that are designed to address the challenges resulting from the misrule of previous minority racist governments. The dramatic effect of the new 'winds of change' was that one-party states became an historical anachronism so that at the 1999 Commonwealth Heads of Government Meeting in Durban, South Africa, every ESA state, save Swaziland, was represented by a democratically elected Head of Government.

Design and content of the ESA constitutions

According to Wheare, a constitution should contain 'the very minimum, and that minimum to be rules of law'.[40] In contrast to the trend in francophone Africa, this is not the case in the ESA states. Here the documents have always been long, elaborate and technical and reflect the British tradition that a statute should be as exhaustive as possible and that the drafting must leave as few ambiguities as possible.

In terms of content, as noted earlier, the independence constitutions were based on the Westminster export model, albeit with significant local variations.[41] The basic features of this model were that it: (i) provided for at least one chamber in the legislature to be freely elected through universal adult suffrage; (ii) made provision for a recognised opposition; (iii) provided for executive power to be vested in the Head of State but largely exercised by a Cabinet of ministers headed by a Prime Minister chosen from the party (or parties) having the support of the majority of members in the elected chamber and answerable to that chamber; (iv) included an entrenched Bill of Rights; and (v) incorporated a set of constitutional conventions.[42] In practice the Westminster model still rules 'from its grave' for in their design and structure the new constitutions of the 1990s show a remarkable resemblance to the original independence constitutions of thirty years before.

Some scholars have criticised the current constitutional arrangements on the grounds that they follow too closely Western models of governance and the Westminster export model in particular, rather than African

[40] K. C. Wheare, *Modern Constitutions*, London, Sweet and Maxwell, 1966, pp. 33–4.

[41] See generally W. Dale, 'The Making and Re-Making of Commonwealth Constitutions' (1993) 42 ICLQ 67.

[42] On the issue of the continuing validity of such conventions, see the discussion in chapter 5, pp. 57–8.

ideals of governance.[43] Whilst such criticism may have some application to the original constitutional documents (although as the earlier discussion indicates, even this is not wholly justified) that is not necessarily the case given the new constitutions' autochthonous nature. Besides, while transplanting European models into Africa might be problematic, the motives of some of those who advocate 'African solutions to Africa problems' are often suspect. Many post-independence dictatorships and indeed the African one-party system of governance in, for example, Zambia, Kenya and Tanzania were justified on the grounds that they were a variant of democracy best suited to the peculiar African circumstances, and, at the same time, a natural facilitator for economic growth and the promoter of national unity.[44] Today it is clear that such justifications had little to do with 'African concepts of governance' and more to do with the consolidation of political power through the elimination of all political opposition.[45]

Thus it is incorrect to say that such documents are inappropriate in the African context. The constitutional structures and theory bequeathed at independence are still largely accepted and acceptable as providing the basis for national development. Further, such documents seek to put into practice the principles enshrined in the Harare Commonwealth Declaration and which the ESA states have pledged themselves to support.

Producing a new constitution is not enough. A serious search for viable constitutional arrangements must begin with a recognition of certain fundamental issues that the document must address. One is the need to encourage national unity or cohesion to generate social and political

[43] Howard, in commenting on the issue of cultural relativism, social change and human rights, concludes that during five centuries of contact between Africa and the western world, social changes have been introduced that have increasingly undermined any social structure or cultural uniqueness Africa might once have possessed (R. Howard, *Human Rights in Commonwealth Africa*, Rowman and Little Field, Totowa, NJ, 1986, p. 16). Yansane observes that colonialism destroyed many indigenous institutions by transforming non-European societies into European replicas (A. Yansane, *Prospects for Recovery and Sustainable Development in Africa*, Greenwood Press, Westport, 1996, at p. 7).

[44] See, for example, Zimba, 'Origins and Spread of One-Party States', p. 119. In Kenya the post-colonial government justified the one party state on the basis that '[W]e seek out the modern constitutional form most suited to our traditional needs . . . Our people have always governed their affairs by looking to an elected council of elders . . . headed by their own chosen leader, giving them strong and wise leadership. That tradition – which is an Africanism – will be preserved in this new constitution' (see Ojwang, *Constitutional Development in Kenya*, p. 79.

[45] S. Mubako, 'Zambia's Single-Party Constitution: a Search for Unity and Development' (1973) 5 *Zambia Law Journal* 67.

power that is strong enough to enable the diverse peoples that make up each state to achieve purposes of well-being and development that are beyond their reach as separate units. Given the intensity of the attachment of many people to ethnicity, accommodating the often vast ethnic diversity in states is an enormous challenge. As experience has shown, the problem of ethnicity can be a considerable destabilising factor to the democratic process. As President Museveni has observed:

> Uganda and most other African countries in black Africa are still pre-industrial societies and they must be handled as such. Societies at this stage of development tend to have a vertical polarisation based mainly on tribe and ethnicity. This means that people support some one because he belongs to their group, not because he puts forward the right policies.[46]

Constitutions must deal with this situation sensitively, by actively seeking to assume the fears and apprehensions of minority groups, meeting their legitimate demands and involving them, in a meaningful fashion, in the political system and in nation building. In some cases there is a similar need to accommodate different religious beliefs.[47]

Whilst recognising that even the most progressive of constitutions cannot alone resolve all of the ills of society,[48] a constitution that aspires to be legitimate, progressive, authoritative and to be accepted as the fundamental law must also address the following issues: (a) regulating and limiting the powers of government, and providing mechanisms to secure the efficacy of such limitations; (b) ensuring political pluralism so that there is no hindrance in the flow and exchange of alternative ideas; (c) providing for the political accountability of political leaders on the basis of openness, probity and honesty; (d) ensuring that government is required to seek the mandate of the people at regular intervals through elections that are executed and administered by independent electoral authorities and in accordance with fair electoral laws; (e) ensuring that the fundamental rights of the people are fully protected; (f) providing for the elimination of all

46 *Ibid.*, at p. 187.

47 It follows that including in a constitution a proclamation that the country is a 'Christian' or 'Islamic' state is unhelpful: see, for example, the Preamble to the Constitution of Zambia 1991.

48 As Gloppen has observed: '. . . neither ethnic conflict, nor (and even less so) problems of poverty, inequality, and violence, are solved by enacting a constitution, not even if the ideal constitution could be found. Some constitutional structures provide more adequate frameworks, however, within which these problems may be addressed. This is what is critical in this whole matter of constitution-making' (Siri Gloppen, *South Africa: the Battle over the Constitution*, Ashgate, Aldershot, 1997, pp. 264–5).

forms of discrimination, and especially that against women; (g) ensuring that disputes, including those concerning the constitutionality of legislation and government acts are adjudicated impartially by regular ordinary courts that are independent of the protagonists; (h) ensuring that the ordinary laws applied in the execution of governance and adjudication of disputes are made in conformity with the provisions of the constitution and in accordance with the procedure for law-making prescribed therein; (i) encouraging the functioning of a non-partisan public service; and (j) acknowledging the role and importance of civil society in national affairs, for without this it is doubtful whether good governance can take and secure roots.[49]

Overview

The new winds of change of the 1990s brought fundamental political and constitutional changes throughout sub-Saharan Africa. Yet in many countries the advances in democracy, though real, remain fragile. The tragedies in Rwanda, Sierra Leone, Somalia, Liberia and the Democratic Republic of Congo graphically illustrate the horrendous consequences of failed constitutional arrangements and the fact that we must not become complacent and assume that the transition to democracy, constitutionalism and the rule of law is irreversible. The 1998 political crisis in Lesotho that led to the complete breakdown of law and order and the military intervention of South African and Botswana forces emphasises that the ESA states are not necessarily immune from such problems.

States need to establish stable political and constitutional orders that promote development and aid the fight against poverty, hunger, disease and ignorance, while also guaranteeing citizens the rule of law and equal protection of the law.[50] To respond successfully to the needs of its people and realise their dreams of rapid economic development, states must apply careful thought and inquiry to the proper organisation of political, economic and administrative institutions. Such arrangements must

[49] For an elaboration of some of these issues see 'Building Constitutional Order in Sub-Saharan Africa', *Third World Legal Studies*, 1988. See also *Proceedings of the International Round Table on Democratic Constitutional Development*, CSIR, Pretoria, South Africa, 17–20 July 1995.

[50] K. Bentsi-Enchil, 'Civitas de Africana: Realizing the African Political Dream' (1965) 2 *Zambia Law Journal* 65; Y. Museveni, *Sowing the Mustard Seed: the Struggle for Freedom and Democracy in Uganda*, Macmillan, London, 1997, p. 188.

ensure that governmental authority is exercised in a predictable, responsible, transparent and legally regulated way to the satisfaction of civil society.[51] A constitution can play a pivotal role here by establishing viable mechanisms and institutions within which to conduct the business of governance and thereby foster an environment where peace and development can flourish.

[51] R. Meyer, Republic of South Africa, Debates of the Constitutional Assembly, 24 January to 20 February 1995, No.1, p. 14.

3

Devising popular and durable national constitutions: the new constitutions of the 1990s

The new 'winds of change' in the 1990s brought about dramatic constitutional changes throughout the ESA region. So much euphoria; so much hope. But the question remains as to whether the new constitutions are autochthonous, popular and durable documents that can help give people 'a better future by establishing a socio-economic and political order . . . based on the principle of unity, peace, equality, democracy, freedom, social justice and progress'.[1]

The answer depends upon many factors, not the least of which being the political will to make constitutionalism take root in the ESA states. The starting point, however, is to examine the adoption of a national constitution through a process which can affect fundamentally the document's substance and legitimacy. This is the focus here. It is argued that the process must come from the integration of ideas of the major stake-holders in the country including the government, political parties, both within and without Parliament, organs of civil society and individual citizens. It follows that the process is one which the government should neither control nor unduly influence nor should it be a merely formal technical exercise. But it involves the making of a complex bargain between the various stake-holders with often fiercely contested political trade-offs. Further the process must be transparent, i.e. it must be undertaken in full view of the country and the international community.[2] Such a process provides the best opportunity for a state to adopt an autochthonous,

[1] Preamble to the Constitution of Uganda 1995. 'Autochthonous' is used in the sense of 'home-grown', the process of the enactment of a constitution reflecting the wishes of the local people. With the possible exception of Namibia, constitutions of the ESA states are not autochthonous in the formal sense for their pedigree is traceable to colonial instruments. See Sir William Dale, *The Modern Commonwealth*, Butterworths, London, 1983, p. 108.

[2] A. Johnson, S. Shezi and G. Brandshaw, *Constitution-Making in the New South Africa*, Leicester University Press, Leicester, 1993; and 'Proceedings of the International Round Table on Democratic Constitutional Development', CSIR Conference Facility, Pretoria, South Africa, 17–20 July 1995, p. 3.

popular and durable constitution. This is crucial for establishing an *ethos of constitutionalism*, i.e. a recognition by the people that it is 'their constitution' upon which they were consulted and which they endorse, that it contains provisions from which they derive demonstrable benefits that are worth defending, and that it encourages in both the governed and governors alike a habit of compliance and respect for its provisions.

Making the new constitutions

Seeking the people's views

On the face of it, the key to making an autochthonous constitution is to consult the people on its contents. This approach has several advantages, in particular its inclusiveness can help raise public awareness of the constitution-making process and enhance the chances of addressing in the new document issues of importance to the people.[3] Typically a commission of inquiry is established with commissioners soliciting the people's views at public meetings throughout the country on possible constitutional arrangements. It then produces a report to the drafters of the new constitution.

The constitution-making process in Uganda is instructive. In an effort to address past horrors and to establish constitutional stability, the National Resistance Movement Government upon its assuming power in 1986 gave 'the people of Uganda an opportunity to make their new Constitution'. A twenty-one member Constitutional Commission was established that toured the country obtaining the public's views through a series of seminars, workshops, debates and discussions.[4] Efforts to sensitize the public to pertinent constitutional issues were spearheaded by a user-friendly publication entitled *Guidelines on Constitutional Issues.*[5] As a result, the Commission received 25,542 submissions and, based on these, it proceeded to produce a draft constitution. The draft was then submitted to a popularly elected Constituent Assembly that enacted it as

[3] Such an approach is potentially time consuming and expensive although it is an exercise that is likely to attract foreign donor assistance. For example, the Mwanakatwe Commission in Zambia was funded by USAID.

[4] It also gathered views from many Ugandans residing abroad. This provides an important lesson as most of the ESA states have large numbers of nationals, many of them highly skilled, living outside of the country.

[5] It was 'written in a clear and simple manner in order to assist Ugandans understand the relevant constitutional issues and to enable them to contribute actively to the making of the new constitution' (Uganda Constitutional Commission, 1991, Kampala, 1).

the Constitution of Uganda 1995.[6] The result is a document that, although controversial in some respects,[7] still seemingly commands considerable public support. The Constitution has also led to the establishment of significant new institutions, such as the Uganda Human Rights Commission, and has helped bring constitutional and economic stability to the country.

In practice, the effectiveness of constitutional commissions hinges upon their independence and their mandate. Zambia's constitution-making experience is helpful here. In 1972 the first constitutional commission, the Chona Commission, held countrywide public meetings on the proposed new constitution. In practice its work was undermined by two factors: firstly, the government announcement that the country would change from a multi-party state to a one-party state;[8] secondly, the fact that the Commission reported to the President who was then able to vet its recommendations. Indeed the Commission's main recommendations aimed at placing safeguards on the exercise of presidential power were swiftly rejected by President Kaunda.[9] So the ensuing 1973 Constitution of Zambia was essentially a creation of the ruling political elite. Following another failed constitution commission in 1991,[10] a new political organisation, the Movement for Multi-Party Democracy (MMD) undertook to promote constitutional debate designed to lead to a constitution that would be above partisan politics and which strengthened democracy and the protection of human rights.[11] Instead, upon gaining power, the MMD established a seven-person task force within the Ministry of Legal Affairs chaired by the Attorney-General to review the constitution. Heavy criticism forced the government to accept that it was unwise to leave a task of

[6] A similar process was used in the making of the current Constitution of Lesotho.

[7] Particularly on retaining the Movement system: see chapter 6.

[8] This was in response to a serious challenge for political power posed to the ruling party, UNIP, by the newly formed United Peoples Party (UPP): see S. V. Mubako 'Zambia's single party constitution: a search for unity and development' (1973) 5 *Zambia Law Journal* 67.

[9] In particular the proposal for the introduction of a two-term limit for the President and direct elections for Central Committee members of the ruling party.

[10] When political change became inevitable in 1991, another constitutional commission toured the country obtaining people's views on the shape of the new constitution. On this occasion both the government and the opposition parties rejected the commission's recommendations. After protracted negotiations between them had failed to produce any agreement, church leaders organised a national conference and mediated the dispute. As a result, the 1991 Constitution was agreed to by all political parties and was subsequently enacted into law by parliament. Significantly, there was no public debate on the document nor was it approved in a national referendum.

[11] *The Third Republic Alternative: a Bulletin for Social-Economic Change*, No.1, June 1991.

this magnitude in the hands of a committee under the chairmanship of its principal legal adviser[12] and so appointed a constitutional commission, the Mwanakatwe Commission. As before it toured the country extensively and its report made many important recommendations which, if adopted, would have greatly strengthened democracy in the country.[13] It also recommended that in order to achieve the maximum consensus, the Constitution should be adopted by a constituent assembly comprising representatives of all political parties in the country. Sadly the MMD government chose to adopt the same 'pick and choose' tactics as its predecessor. It ignored or rejected many of the commission's most important recommendations and had its preferred version adopted by the government-dominated legislature. So constitutional stability remains elusive with opposition parties continuing to dispute the 1996 constitutional amendments on the grounds that the text does not reflect the views of the Zambian people and that the constitution-making process was manipulated by the ruling party.[14]

The constitutional commissions in Zambia were essentially an exercise in futility because they reported directly to government which then was free to reject any or all of their recommendations. As regards the Mwanakatwe Commission's report, the MMD Government defended its actions in a pamphlet published in response to widespread public criticism of its 'pick and choose' tactics.[15] It argued that according to the 'constitutional practice in the Commonwealth, an independent commission of this kind was required to submit its proposals to the government which has the power and freedom to reject, accept, amend or note the proposals'. The assertion is spurious for whilst some Commonwealth states have employed the undemocratic 'pick and choose' method it is not a typical Commonwealth practice. Furthermore, it should not become one because it cannot result in the production of a popular and durable constitution.[16]

[12] M. Ndulo and R. Kent, 'Constitutionalism in Zambia: Past, Present and Future' (1996) 40 *Journal of African Law* 256 at p. 271.

[13] For details see *ibid.*

[14] See, Report, *Citizen's Convention on the Draft Constitution*, Lusaka, Zambia, 1996. See also Human Rights Watch, 'Africa, Zambia and Human Rights in the Third Republic', Human Rights Watch, New York, 1996, p. 13.

[15] Ministry of Legal Affairs, *Constitutional Reform 1996: the Public Debate – Adopting the Constitution: Topic 1 The Constituent Assembly* Ministry of Legal Affairs, Lusaka, 1996.

[16] In Tanzania in 1999, the government-appointed Kisanga Committee, having visited every district in the country, delivered an 800 page report to the President on constitutional reform. Without publishing the report, the President made it clear that he would disregard any recommendations which conflicted with 'the views of the people', although perhaps

The Zimbabwean experience also illustrates the manner in which a government can use a commission to ostensibly consult with the people on constitutional reform whilst, in reality, ensuring that it retains control of the process. Here the President established a Constitutional Commission (CC) in 1998 using his powers under the Commission of Inquiries Act. This had two significant consequences. Firstly, he was able to determine the Commission's size and make-up. As a result it comprised 500 members, the great majority of whom were supporters of the ruling party ZANU(PF).[17] Secondly, it enabled the President to adopt the 'pick and choose' approach as the Commission's mandate was to submit a report to him with recommendations on a new constitution and, as in Zambia, the President was under no legal obligation to accept any or all of the recommendations.

The work of the hugely expensive commission was also 'seriously hampered by its ridiculously unwieldy size', a fact seemingly admitted by even the Commission's Chairman.[18] Why the President deemed it necessary to create such a large number of commissioners is not clear. Seemingly it was some kind of presidential 'overkill' designed to ensure a favourable report.[19] Certainly the Commission's final draft was never put to a vote but was forced through at a plenary session with the Chairman declaring the draft constitution adopted 'by acclamation' despite a number of dissenting voices.[20]

Although the Commission undertook an impressive and wide-ranging consultation exercise throughout the country, its work (and report) was undoubtedly tainted by the public's perception that it was a government-oriented body. Even then, the draft constitution submitted by the

one should read here 'the views of the President'. As a result, constitutional change in the country has stalled. See, C. M. Peter, 'Constitution-making in Tanzania', in K. Kibwana, C. M. Peter and N. Bazaara, *Constitutionalism in East Africa: Progress, Challenges and Prospects in 1999*, Fountain Press, Nairobi, 2001, at p. 29.

17 A point emphasised by the inclusion of all 150 members of parliament, all bar three being supporters of the ruling party.

18 Noted by Bartlett J. in *Mushayakarara v Chidyausiku NO* 2000 (1) ZLR 248 at p. 251. The chairman of the Commission was a High Court judge, Mr Justice Godfrey Chidyausiku. Thereafter he was rapidly appointed Judge President (head of the High Court), then, in March 2001, Acting Chief Justice and, in June 2001, Chief Justice.

19 According to one senior government source, the reasons for including all MPs was to ensure a 'Yes' vote in the referendum on the new constitution (Private communication to John Hatchard, July 1999).

20 As there was no formal procedure for voting including the necessary majority required to adopt the report, the Chairman was seemingly within his rights to act in this manner, however inappropriate this may appear.

Commission still did not satisfy the President.[21] Despite prior assurances to the contrary,[22] a few weeks later the *Government Gazette* published what were termed 'Corrections and Clarifications' to the document. It is worth setting out the explanation for the reasons for the changes which were widely published in the national press:

> It is common cause that any *draft* is by definition subject to improvement by way of grammatical and factual corrections as well as linguistic clarifications in order to avoid any doubt about the meaning of what is in the draft. The corrections and clarifications below were done on the basis of the records of the Commission as contained in the Commission's Committee minutes and published in the Commission's 1 437 page Special Report. It's all there for the asking and there is nothing new because the record is public and therefore speaks for itself.
>
> Only people with literacy problems or hidden political agendas will find it difficult to tell the otherwise clear difference between corrections and clarifications on the one hand and amendments on the other. Don't be misled.

In spite of the rhetoric, the 'Corrections and Clarifications' made several significant changes of substance to the recommendations in the Constitutional Commission's report.[23] Yet it was the amended version that was put to the people in the subsequent referendum. The President's power to place before the electorate whatever document he wished was made clear following a legal challenge by some constitutional commissioners to the referendum on the ground that the draft constitution had not been properly adopted. In rejecting the submission, Bartlett, J. in the Zimbabwe High Court stated:

> [The President] is not, in my view, required to put before the voters a constitution approved by the Constitutional Commission. *He is entitled to put forward any draft constitution he so wishes* to ascertain the views

[21] At the later ZANU(PF) Congress he reportedly described the section dealing with land acquisition as drawn up by the Constitutional Commission as 'stupid'. See, *Financial Gazette*, 6 January 2000.

[22] For example, commissioners were reportedly assured by the chairman of the Commission that the new constitution they would formulate would not be tampered with. See, 'New Constitution Will Reflect Findings', *The Herald*, 31 August 1999, p. 1.

[23] These included providing for the compulsory acquisition of agricultural land for resettlement without compensation; compulsory military service; and the prohibition on same-sex marriages. The Constitutional Commission was never formally consulted on these changes.

> of the voters. It may or may not be considered unwise to make changes to a document produced by a body specifically set up to produce a draft constitution, but it is certainly not unlawful.[24]

Developing an effective procedure to prevent the manipulation of the constitution-making process by those in political power is a considerable challenge. The experiences of Zambia and Zimbabwe demonstrate that such commissions can have a meaningful role only if they are themselves independent and report to, or are part of, a demonstrably independent constitution-making body. Further ensuring that a broad spectrum of the people discuss and voice their opinions on the country's future constitution is essential. This is particularly challenging in that, if given no proper guidance, people making submissions to the commission often tend to talk about their grievances and dissatisfaction with the present government rather than address constitutional issues. Questions of relevance and weight to be attached to individual submissions are also glossed over providing a perfect opportunity for the government to manipulate the constitution-making process. Besides, as the Zimbabwe experience illustrates, with the thousands of submissions, an average lawyer can easily write any number of versions of a constitution and find justification in the submissions made to the commission for each one of them.

The lessons are clear. A constitutional commission of this nature must be fully representative of society, must take into account the concerns of the widest possible segment of the population, must be transparent in its work, and, to make such consultations meaningful, must properly structure its methods of consultation.[25] In addition, its subsequent report and draft constitution must not be subject to unilateral executive interference.[26]

Utilising comparative experiences

Access to comparative experience is particularly useful during a constitutional review process as it provides a wide range of information on possible options and lessons on what to do (and what *not* to do). Where local expertise is limited, calling on international legal experts to provide appropriate comparative material and analysis is helpful.

[24] Our emphasis. *Mushayakarara v Chidyausiku NO* 2000 (1) ZLR 248, at p. 252.

[25] It was on this basis that the Constitution of Kenya Review Commission undertook its work in 2000–2. See further www.kenyaconstitution.org.

[26] See also the discussion on the South African constitution-making process below.

This approach was adopted in Zimbabwe in 1999 in an apparent effort to provide legitimacy to the process. Here the Constitutional Commission invited international constitutional experts 'to exchange ideas and experiences with commissioners and to provide comments and a critique of the draft constitution'.[27] In reality this was always an unlikely scenario, especially given the fact that the experts only came a few days before the Commission finished its work and by that time it was too late for them to have any impact.[28] The Constitution of Kenya Review Commission has adopted a far better approach by seeking expert advice on key aspects of constitutional reform. For example in 2002 it established an Advisory Panel made up largely of senior judicial figures from the ESA region[29] and charged with advising the Commission 'on constitutional reforms regarding the Kenya Judiciary'.[30]

Adopting the new constitution

The next question is how best to involve the people in the adoption of the new constitution so as to give it maximum legitimacy. Being the supreme law the document must not be adopted using the same procedures as that for passing ordinary legislation.[31] In practice, debate has focused on whether adopting a constitution is the legislature's function (albeit with the requirement for a special majority or procedure) or that of a separate constituent assembly. In either case some states also require approval of the document by the people in a national referendum. Some have argued that the adoption of the constitution by a separate constituent assembly is unnecessary, as the matter is best left to the legislature.[32] Whether or

[27] See letter of invitation from the Chairman of the Commission to the experts. One of the present authors accepted the invitation, another did not.

[28] An added complication was that, even at that stage, there was no draft document available for them to examine.

[29] Justice George Kanyeihamba from the Supreme Court of Uganda chaired the Panel with other members drawn from the Court of Appeal of Tanzania, the Constitutional Court of South Africa and the Court of Appeal for Ontario.

[30] Their 'Report of the Advisory Panel of Commonwealth Judicial Experts' is a highly disturbing critique of the state of the Kenyan judiciary but makes some invaluable recommendations for the constitution-makers.

[31] See, for example, the 'Report of the Constitutional Review Commission', Government of the Republic of Zambia, Lusaka, 1995, p. 64.

[32] A point made by the Zambian Government in respect of the making of the 1996 Constitution. See Mwanakatwe Constitutional Review Commission Supplement, Republic of Zambia, Government Paper, No. 1 of 1995.

not the legislature has power to enact a constitution is not the issue. The real question is how to ensure that the people's sovereign will on which the edifice of democracy rests occupies centre stage in the process of producing a legitimate, credible and enduring constitution.[33]

In practice the most popular approach in the ESA states is to have the national legislature double up as a constituent assembly. For example, in Namibia, the independence constitution of 1990 was drawn up by a constituent assembly comprising members of the seven political parties that had mustered sufficient support in the United Nations-supervised elections.[34] Although based on a draft produced by the South West Africa Peoples Organisation, which won most seats in the general election, crucially the results gave no political party the necessary two-thirds majority required to adopt the constitution alone. Thus the minority parties played an important part in the constitution's preparation and as a result there was consensus as to the final document. Indeed the Namibian Constitution is widely regarded as something of a model constitution and has been extremely influential in developing a high regard for fundamental rights and freedoms in the country.[35] Even so, it is worth noting that the process was criticised for precluding any true popular participation. For example, the National Union of Namibian Workers, the country's trade union federation, called for the promotion of public debate on the draft constitution and the press expressed concern at the seeming lack of a genuine attempt on the part of the Constituent Assembly to involve the public in finalising the Constitution.[36] Arguably, however, such criticism was unwarranted since through the general election the people had mandated the Constituent Assembly to draw up the new constitution.

Uganda provides a useful example of the convening of a separate Constituent Assembly to adopt the constitution. Here the idea that the National Resistance Council should draw up the new constitution proved controversial, particularly as it was not a directly elected body and so

[33] B. O. Nwabueze, *Constitutionalism in the Emergent States*, London: Hurst, 1973, at p. 305.

[34] It was understood in the election that voters were electing people to draw up the constitution.

[35] For a useful discussion on the process see D. Van Wyk, 'The Making of the Namibian Constitution: Lessons for Africa' (1990) *Comparative and International Law Journal of Southern Africa* 341. See also John Hatchard and Peter Slinn, 'Namibia: the Constitutional Path to Freedom' (1990) 10 *International Relations* 137, at pp. 144–6.

[36] See *The Namibian* 11 and 19 January 1990 and the discussion in Hatchard and Slinn, 'Namibian', pp. 145–6. For a helpful account of the development of the 1995 Constitution of Malawi, see A. Peter Mutharika, 'The 1995 Democratic Constitution of Malawi' (1996) 40 JAL 205, esp pp. 207–9.

did not enjoy a popular mandate. As a result, elections to a Constituent Assembly were authorised by the Constituent Assembly Statute 1993. These were successfully held in April 1993 and mandated a popularly elected Constituent Assembly of 214 members to adopt the Constitution. These members were joined by representatives from, amongst others, the army, trades unions, political parties, youth and the disabled, together with thirty-nine women (one from each district). Indeed one notable aspect was the involvement of women and women's groups throughout the entire process. After sixteen months of sometimes acrimonious debate, the Constituent Assembly adopted the new constitution which was promulgated in October 1995.

The constitution-making process in South Africa is instructive for, whilst it inevitably included some unique features, it again emphasises the importance of building a broad-based consensus on the terms of the new constitution. Here there were two phases: firstly, developing the interim constitution and, secondly, adopting the permanent or final constitution. The two phases were required because those involved in drawing up the interim constitution were, of necessity, not elected to their positions as a result of any free and fair elections. Thus it was thought desirable that the final constitution should be adopted by a 'credible body properly mandated to do so in consequence of free and fair elections based on universal adult suffrage'.

The negotiating process leading to the making of the interim Constitution of 1994 took place through the Multi-party Negotiating Forum (MPNF). Attended by delegates from twenty-six parties and political groups that spanned the political spectrum, all groups participated on the basis of formal equality and decisions were taken on the basis of 'sufficient consensus'.[37] The whole process was notable for the participants' willingness to reach a consensus through compromise which led to agreement on the transitional process, the terms of the interim Constitution and a date for elections. Given the country's political history and the fears on the African National Congress's (ANC) part that it might not have the support of the, predominantly white, security forces it was agreed to establish a government of national unity which would govern the country on a coalition basis functioning under the interim constitution.[38] A

[37] The decision to invite all political parties was taken because, in the absence of free and fair elections, there was no way of determining their respective popular support.

[38] This ensured that there was a party in government which they supported. The matter was first mooted in an article in the *African Communist* by the South Africa Communist Party

Constitutional Assembly, elected by universal adult suffrage would then act as the constitution-making body. It was to be composed of members from both houses of Parliament and, when sitting as a constitutional assembly, to meet under a different leadership from that of Parliament and have its own rules of procedure.[39]

At the MPNF Negotiations, it was agreed that the permanent constitution would be drawn up in accordance with constitutional principles adopted by the Forum. The '34 Constitutional Principles', as they became known (although in reality they covered many more issues), were the key to the adoption of the final Constitution. As the preamble to the interim constitution put it:

> **AND WHEREAS** in order to secure the achievement of this goal, elected representatives of all the people of South Africa should be mandated to adopt a new Constitution in accordance with a solemn pact recorded as Constitutional Principles.

To ensure the new constitution complied with the Constitutional Principles the process called for an independent determination by the Constitutional Court. As section 71(2) of the interim Constitution provided:

> The new constitutional text passed by the Constitutional Assembly, or any provision thereof, shall not be of any force and effect unless the Constitutional Court has certified that all the provisions of such text comply with the Constitutional Principles . . .

The drafting of the permanent Constitution of South Africa followed a more structured approach to make public consultation more meaningful. In developing the document, a democratically elected Constitutional Assembly met to draw up a draft constitution. Within the framework of the Constitutional Assembly, an Independent Panel of Constitutional

chairman Joe Slovo in what were termed 'sunset clauses'. As a result, he came under strong attack from the left wing of the ANC until Nelson Mandela gave him his full support. As Hamill has pointed out, there was an irony in the conciliatory role played by Slovo who had long figured as a 'demon' of the highest rank in white mythology. See James Hamill, 'The Crossing of the Rubicon: South Africa's Post-Apartheid Political Process 1990–1992' (1995) 12(3) *International Relations* 9–37. See further John Hatchard and Peter Slinn, 'The Path towards a New Order in South Africa' (1995) 12(4) *International Relations* 1–26 at pp. 5–6.

[39] See 'The Process of Drafting South Africa's New Constitution', paper delivered by Hassen Ebrahim, Executive Director of the Constitutional Assembly, International Round Table on Democratic Constitutional Development, CSIR Conference Facility, Pretoria, South Africa, 17–20 July 1995.

Experts and a Constitutional Committee were established to facilitate both the process of negotiations and the process of drafting sections of the constitution. The Constitutional Committee was designed as the negotiating and co-ordinating structure of the Constitutional Assembly. They further established a management committee to attend to the procedural aspects of the constitution-making process. The drafting was based on the work of six theme committees set up by the Constitutional Assembly as part of the structure to facilitate public participation in the exercise.[40] The six themes were the character of a democratic state; the structure of government; the relationship between levels of government; fundamental rights; the judiciary and legal systems; and specialised structures of government.[41] The committees' task was to gather, collate and refine the views of the political parties and the public on specific issues and submit them to the constitution-making body. A technical Committee consisting of specialists in particular fields supported each Committee. This approach gave the ensuing debate structure along constitutional themes. The Constitution's draft articles as approved by the theme Committees, after discussion in the Constitutional Committees, were then forwarded to the Constitutional Assembly.

An important lesson applied here was that in order to facilitate consideration of the draft articles, it is preferable to accompany them with commentaries that analyse the various aspects of the constitution, highlighting options and identifying problems and difficulties that might be incurred in applying the various suggested provisions. Only when completed should the document be subjected to public scrutiny and analysis in a forum such as a constitutional assembly that has been elected specifically to elaborate the constitution. The existence of a draft serves to limit the parameters of discussion to constitutional issues and helps prevent the hi-jacking of the process by the political elite.[42]

On 8 May 1996 the Constitutional Assembly adopted the new Constitution. Particularly significant is the fact that the Assembly adopted consensus as a way of making decisions and there was never any voting as a way of adopting any provision. The document was then duly referred to the Constitutional Court. In undertaking its task of certification, the Court

[40] See, Republic of South Africa, *Debates of the Constitutional Assembly*, 24 January–20 February 1995, Cape Town, at p. 3.

[41] Ebrahim, 'Process of Drafting South Africa's New Constitution', at pp. 1–5.

[42] In fairness, the Zimbabwe Constitutional Commission also worked through a series of theme committees but this process was undermined by the pro-government bias of the majority of its membership and the fact that it reported directly to the President.

invited political parties and any other body or person wishing to object to any of its provisions on the grounds that they did not comply with the overall constitutional principles, to submit a written objection (the latter being restricted to 1,000 words). In the event, objections were submitted on behalf of five political parties and eighty-four private individuals and groups. A right of audience was granted to the political parties as well as twenty-seven other bodies or persons. On 6 September 1996 the court delivered its judgment in *Certification of the Constitution of the Republic of South Africa, 1996*.[43] It recognised that the new constitution represented a 'monumental achievement', particularly given the circumstances of South Africa, and concluded that the document complied with the overwhelming majority of the Constitutional Principles requirements. However it identified several areas for re-consideration by the Constitutional Assembly before it could certify the Constitution. Having addressed these concerns, the Final Constitution received presidential assent on 18 December, 1996. The complex process represented a high-risk strategy and could well have unravelled on a number of occasions. However, the willingness on all sides to work together towards developing consensual documents meant that, in fact, the process proved remarkably successful.

Securing the people's approval in a referendum

Approving a constitution through a national referendum encourages the full participation of the people who can give it their formal 'seal of approval'.[44] The process can also generate wide publicity and engender full public debate thus increasing the chances of the document receiving the sort of critical and objective consideration that it deserves. Further a referendum can also counterbalance a presidential or government-inspired document being approved by a compliant parliament or constituent assembly.[45]

However, the February 2000 referendum on the draft constitution in Zimbabwe illustrates some of the pitfalls associated with the process. Here the referendum was merely a consultative exercise as the President was under no legal obligation to abide by the referendum result.[46] Government

[43] 1996 (10) BCLR 1253 (CC).

[44] A point emphasised by D. Butler and A. Ranney (eds.), *Referendums: a Comparative Study of Practice and Theory*, American Enterprise Institute for Public Policy Research: Washington DC: 1978, at p. 226.

[45] See for example, the discussion on the position in Zambia in chapter 4.

[46] As noted earlier, he had the final word on the contents of the draft and, in any event, the constitution was to be formally adopted by the government-dominated parliament.

manipulation of the process quickly became apparent for in the weeks leading up to the referendum the state controlled media launched an intensive publicity campaign in support of a 'Yes' vote. At the same time, it was seemingly less prepared to allow air time to those campaigning for a 'No' vote.[47] Further, the significant number of Zimbabweans living abroad were denied the right to participate due to 'logistical' problems,[48] whilst arrangements for holding the referendum were left in the hands of the Electoral Commission, whose independence was a matter of concern for many of those supporting a 'No' vote.[49]

A related question is whether, given its importance, a special majority is needed for a referendum.[50] The usefulness of such a device is neatly illustrated by the 1992 experience of the Seychelles. Here it was agreed that the adoption of the draft Constitution required a 60 per cent affirmative vote in a referendum. The unsatisfactory nature of the constitution-making process led to opposition groups claiming that the draft document would perpetuate one-party rule[51] and the referendum gave them an opportunity to campaign strongly for a 'No' vote. Their cause was assisted by the influential Catholic church which opposed the provision in the draft document permitting abortion. In the event the referendum produced only a 53.7 per cent affirmative vote and, as a result, the Constitutional Commission resumed its work, but this time with all parties participating. A new and thoroughly revised bi-partisan document was later put to the people in a second referendum and received a 73.6 per cent affirmative vote.

Referenda inevitably have their own drawbacks. In particular the actual wording of the question(s) may greatly influence the result; they are expensive and time-consuming;[52] and some consider them too 'formal

[47] It eventually took a court order to obtain such access.

[48] See comments of the Registrar-General in *Zimbabwe Independent*, 11 February 2000. He added that the constitutional commission had consulted Zimbabweans abroad during the outreach programme.

[49] Despite these efforts, the draft was rejected by 697,754 votes to 578,210. There is little doubt this was because the referendum was largely seen as a means of registering a vote of no-confidence in the President rather than a popular judgment upon the proposals themselves. Herein lies an inherent problem with a referendum: there may be many reasons for 'No' votes.

[50] For example, in the 2000 Zimbabwe referendum, only some 25 per cent of those eligible to vote actually did so.

[51] See J. Hatchard, 'Re-establishing a Multi-Party State: some Reflections from the 1992 Constitutional Developments in the Seychelles' (1993) 31 *Journal of Modern African Studies* 601, at p. 606.

[52] Although this might actually act as a useful deterrent to frequent constitutional amendment exercises.

and static'.[53] Certainly these are important concerns but the experience of Zimbabwe and the Seychelles amply demonstrates that they can play a key role in ensuring that the wishes of the President/government remain subordinate to those of the people.[54]

Overview

Because a constitution is 'a mirror reflecting the national soul' getting the adoption process 'right' is crucial. If this is done, the resultant document has a chance of becoming and remaining a popular and durable constitution, i.e. one that is above partisan politics, that can help develop an ethos of constitutionalism and that reflects the values enshrined in the Harare Commonwealth Declaration.

On the face of it, the constitution-making and re-making process of the 1990s was ostensibly designed to achieve this goal. Closer examination reveals the unwillingness of some governments to recognise the basic principle that the Constitution belongs to the people and that they must be intimately involved in its creation and adoption. The consequences of failing to involve the people is amply demonstrated by the ongoing constitutional uncertainty in Zambia and Zimbabwe. Overall, the ideal is that stated by the Ugandan Constitutional Commission:

> The People themselves must be involved in the formulation and adoption of their Constitution because . . . a Constitution imposed on the people by force cannot be the basis of a stable and peaceful Government of the people.[55]

[53] This represented the views of Nigerian government when rejecting the recommendations of the Constitution Review Committee for a referendum on a new constitution in 1988. See J. S. Read, 'Nigeria's New Constitution for 1992: the Third Republic' (1991) 35 *Journal of African Law* 174, at pp. 175–6.

[54] As is discussed in the next chapter, the need for a referendum can also act as a deterrent against government efforts to force through constitutional amendments.

[55] *Guidelines on Constitutional Issues*, Uganda Constitutional Commission, 1991, p. 1.

4

Perfecting imperfections: amending a constitution

Safeguarding a constitution against retrogressive amendments[1] is of paramount importance for otherwise:

> A constitution, which is to some extent a device for *preserving* certain states of affairs, might become a device for *undermining* the very states of affairs it is designed to preserve.[2]

This has led some to argue for an unamendable constitution.[3] Attractive as it may appear at first sight, it overlooks the crucial fact that however rigorous the procedure for its making, a constitution may still contain imperfections or become outdated. As George Washington himself noted in 1787: 'The warmest friends and the best supporters the [United States] Constitution has do not contend that it is free from imperfections; but they found them unavoidable and are sensible that if evil is likely to arise there from, the remedy must come hereafter.'[4] Further, as Justice Khanna of the Indian Supreme Court has noted, no generation has a monopoly on knowledge that entitles it to bind future generations irreversibly, and a constitution that denies people the right of amendment invites attempts

[1] Distinguishing between a constitutional 'amendment' and the 'making' of a constitution is not always easy. For example, in Zambia almost the entire 1991 Constitution was 'amended' by a 1996 constitutional amendment Act (Act 18 of 1996) (see below). Such a scenario also raises the applicability of the basic structure doctrine (also discussed below).

[2] Mark Brandon, 'The "Original" Thirteenth Amendment and the Limits to Formal Constitutional Change', in Sanford Levinson (ed.), *Responding to Imperfection: the Theory and Practice of Constitutional Amendment*, Princeton University Press, Princeton, NJ, 1995, p. 215 (emphasis in the original). See also John Hatchard, 'Undermining the Constitution by Constitutional Means: some Thoughts on the New Constitutions of Southern Africa' (1995) 27 *Comparative and International Law Journal of Southern Africa* 21.

[3] For example, John Locke's draft of the 1669 Fundamental Constitutions of Carolinas provided that 'these fundamental constitutions shall be and remain the sacred and unalterable form and rule of government . . . forever': quoted in Levinson, *Responding to Imperfection*, at p. 4. See also the discussion on the Namibian Constitution (below).

[4] Quoted in Levinson, *Responding to Imperfection*, at p. 1.

at extra-legal revolutionary change.[5] In short, 'a constitution that will not bend will break'.[6]

Further we must not forget that an unscrupulous executive may seek to make a constitution unamendable for its own political ends. For example, the Constitution of Ghana 1979 came into effect following the handover of power by the Armed Forces Revolutionary Council to a civilian government. Shortly before promulgating the Constitution, the Council inserted certain so-called unamendable 'Transitional Provisions', the net effect of which was to ensure that neither the incoming administration nor the courts could disturb certain decisions taken by the Council. This struck at the balance of the whole document itself and provoked a storm of protest from both within and without Parliament against the deprivation of the people's inherent right to amend any constitutional provision under which they were democratically governed.[7]

It follows that there is an 'inherent right' to amend a constitution in order to 'perfect imperfections' and to strengthen its provisions where necessary. Indeed providing for a regular constitutional review process is, in itself, useful.[8] More problematic is determining the appropriate procedure for constitutional amendments and whether there are certain fundamental constitutional provisions that should remain 'unamendable'.

The amendment procedure

Being the supreme law, a constitution is not subject to amendment in the same manner as an Act of Parliament. Yet devising an appropriate

[5] See *Kesavananda v State of Kerala* AIR 1973, S.C. 1461, pp. 1849 and 1850.

[6] K. C. Wheare, *Modern Constitutions*, 1966, Sweet and Maxwell, London, p. 33.

[7] The situation was never resolved because at the height of the national debate on the subject, the Government and Constitution were overthrown in another military coup. The Constitution of Ghana 1969 also had provisions that were declared unalterable for all time. These included matters such as the supremacy of the Constitution, judicial power to interpret and enforce the Constitution and a specific provision that 'Parliament shall have no power to pass a law establishing a one-party state'. This constitution lasted little more than two years before the country experienced yet another military takeover.

[8] Section 135 of the Constitution of Malawi empowers the Law Commission to 'review and make recommendations regarding any matter pertaining to this Constitution'. A constitutional review was undertaken in 1998 to deal with some of the 'rough edges' and 'technical irregularities' in the 1995 document. Civil society groups, the Electoral Commission and government ministries all made representations to the Commission which also had the benefit of several 'technical papers' provided by constitutional experts. See 'Report of the Law Commission on the Technical Review of the Constitution', 35(58) *Government Gazette*, 16 November 1998.

amendment procedure is not easy.[9] An over-rigid process may prevent or deter efforts to strengthen constitutional provisions. A 'weak' amendment procedure creates the danger of the document's wholesale amendment by an unscrupulous government intent on increasing executive power.

The Westminster export model provided for a specially enhanced parliamentary majority (SEPM) (normally a two-thirds majority of all members of Parliament) coupled with a requirement to publish the Bill in the *Government Gazette* not less than thirty days before the final parliamentary vote. This was seemingly based on the view that Parliament was the 'guardian of the constitution' and thus best suited to take responsibility for approving constitutional amendments. Although still widely used in the ESA states, the SEPM procedure has two major defects. Firstly, practice has shown that legislatures are generally ill-suited to playing a guardianship role.[10] Secondly, it is anomalous that despite the replacement of parliamentary supremacy by the supremacy of the constitution,[11] an exclusively parliamentary process is used to amend the 'supreme law'. The experience of Zimbabwe illustrates these problems.

The Zimbabwe experience

Since independence in 1980, sixteen separate amendment Acts (all of which made multiple constitutional changes) have entirely re-shaped the Constitution of Zimbabwe. Given the circumstances of its birth, some amendments were inevitable and entirely desirable.[12] The same cannot be said for others. Thus constitutional amendments have, amongst other things, sought to oust the jurisdiction of the courts,[13] prevented the Supreme Court from hearing a case relating to fundamental rights provisions and overturned the court's decisions thereon.[14] For example, in

[9] See, for example, the views of Amissah, J.P. in the Court of Appeal (Botswana) in *Dow v Attorney-General* in [1992] LRC (Const) 623 at p. 632.

[10] For a discussion on improving the effectiveness of legislatures see chapter 7 below.

[11] As Gubbay C. J. put it in *Chairman of the Public Service Commission v Zimbabwe Teachers Association* [1997] 1 LRC 479: 'Zimbabwe unlike Great Britain is not a parliamentary democracy. It is a constitutional democracy. The centrepiece of our democracy is not a sovereign parliament but a supreme law – the Constitution' (p. 490).

[12] For example, the removal of the parliamentary seats reserved for non-Africans.

[13] Constitution of Zimbabwe Amendment (No 12) Act, 1993, section 2 of which amended section 16(1)(e) of the Constitution.

[14] Section 24 of the Constitution gives the Supreme Court original jurisdiction to 'hear and determine' issues relating to fundamental rights and to 'make such orders . . . and give such directions as it may consider appropriate for the purpose of enforcing or securing the enforcement of the Declaration of Rights'.

1990 in *S v Chileya*[15] the Supreme Court asked for full argument on the issue of whether the use of hanging constituted inhuman or degrading treatment or punishment contrary to section 15(1) of the Constitution and a date was set down for the hearing. The response of government was immediate. Shortly before the hearing, a constitutional amendment Bill was published which included a provision specifically upholding the constitutionality of executions by hanging.[16] The Minister of Justice, Legal and Parliamentary Affairs informed Parliament that any holding to the contrary 'would be untenable to government which holds the correct and firm view . . . that Parliament makes the laws and the courts interpret them'. He added that the abolition of the death sentence was a matter for the executive and legislature and that 'government will not and cannot countenance a situation where the death penalty is *de facto* abolished through the back door . . .'[17] As discussed below, there was little parliamentary debate on this aspect of the Bill and members overwhelmingly approved the measure.

A further example concerns the well-known case of the *Catholic Commission for Justice and Peace in Zimbabwe v Attorney-General.*[18] Here the Supreme Court held that the dehumanising factor of prolonged delay, viewed in conjunction with the harsh and degrading conditions in the condemned section of the holding prison, meant that executing four condemned prisoners would have constituted inhuman and degrading treatment contrary to section 15(1) of the Constitution. The court directed that the death sentences be replaced by sentences of life imprisonment. It also gave a series of directions on the procedure for dealing with condemned prisoners and suggested that petitions of mercy should be dealt with expeditiously by the executive with three months being a possible time-frame. The landmark decision was later followed by the Judicial Committee of the Privy Council[19] and received warm approval from commentators.[20] Yet it drew a critical response from the government and within weeks the Constitution of Zimbabwe Amendment (No. 13) Act 1993 was passed which retrospectively exempted the death penalty from

[15] Case number SC 64/90 (unreported).

[16] This later became section 15(4) of the Constitution.

[17] *Parliamentary Debates*, 6 December 1990. [18] 1993 (4) SA 239.

[19] *Pratt and Morgan v Attorney-General for Jamaica* [1993] 4 All ER 769.

[20] See, for example, W. A. Schabas '*Soering*'s Legacy: the Human Rights Committee and the Judicial Committee of the Privy Council Take a Walk Down Death Row' (1994) 43 ICLQ 913. It is also worth noting that Zimbabwean government's public criticism of the judgment ceased after the decision in *Pratt and Morgan* (above).

the scope of section 15(1). Once again members of Parliament overwhelmingly approved the Bill.

The Zimbabwean experience highlights the problem of centring the amendment procedure on the legislature[21] for having had the first twenty years of independence dominated by one political party, the two-thirds parliamentary majority had proved of no practical value as a check against retrogressive constitutional amendments.[22] Of course it is arguable that the ruling party's overwhelming parliamentary majority demonstrated that it enjoyed the popular support necessary to pass such amendments. But this overlooks the reality of a dominant-party state where the Party seeks to exercise complete control over members of Parliament with the resultant rubber-stamping of all constitutional amendments. Further, it is questionable whether all members of Parliament are able and/or prepared to undertake a critical and informed view of proposed constitutional changes. For example, in the parliamentary debate on the 1993 Act in Zimbabwe, the few members of Parliament who did speak seemingly did not understand the Supreme Court decision in the *Catholic Commission* case and believed its effect was to abolish the death penalty itself.[23] Indeed just one member managed to state and analyse the ruling accurately.[24] Regrettably, members were not assisted by the Minister of Justice, Legal and Parliamentary Affairs who informed them that the decision 'allowed the de facto abolition of the death sentence by the judiciary' and that the judgment:

> . . . was to the effect that from the day a person is sentenced to death by the High Court, three months should be the maximum. If three months pass before he is executed . . . then there is a delay, which in the opinion of the Supreme Court, vitiates the execution.[25]

As noted above, that was *not* the Supreme Court's ruling. Parliament's failure to appreciate the importance of the constitutional amendment

[21] It also demonstrates the limitations on the judicial power to 'develop' constitutional rights.

[22] In fact in the three years of its operation, the interim Constitution in South Africa, which contained a similar provision to that in Zimbabwe, was amended no less than ten times and gave effect to numerous individual amendments.

[23] Just twenty-six of the 150 members made any contribution to the debate on the Second Reading and, seemingly, only five of these were not in favour of the Bill although their contributions on the matter were not always very clear. Thus one member asserted that 'the proposal should be supported and we should remove [the] death sentence for the democratic development of our nation', Mr Nyashanu, *Parliamentary Debates*, 28 September 1994.

[24] See the contribution of Mr Malunga in *Parliamentary Debates*, 22 September 1994.

[25] *Parliamentary Debates*, 22 September 1994.

process was also demonstrated when the final vote on the amendment Bill was nullified and then retaken because of an oversight that it required a two-thirds majority. Such actions do not reflect well on the role of parliamentarians of

> not allowing amendments to fundamental rights provisions in the Constitution to be rushed through Parliament. The people should expect their Parliamentarians to consider with great care the implications of any measures which will have the effect of diluting fundamental rights provisions. The people expect Parliament to uphold fundamental rights and not to acquiesce in a process which weakens these rights.[26]

In addition, constitutional amendment Bills typically contained multiple changes that may well account for the inadequate discussion and consideration of some provisions. For example, the provision pre-empting the Supreme Court from hearing the appeal in *Chileya* was included in a Bill that also amended the highly sensitive and emotive land provisions. In their eagerness to discuss the land issue, members almost entirely neglected to consider the death sentence issue.[27]

Overall, these (and other) amendments have transformed the Zimbabwean constitution into an effective executive dictatorship with the legislature merely playing a rubber-stamp function. Such a situation fatally exposes the weakness of the special parliamentary majority procedure.[28]

Strengthening the parliamentary safeguard

The SEPM procedure's continued popularity is evidenced by its retention for all constitutional amendments in Zimbabwe, Zambia and Kenya, and as part of the amendment process in Lesotho and Malawi. Surprisingly, the constitution-making process in several of these states included little debate on the amendment provisions. This was in sharp contrast to South Africa where the issue took on considerable importance.

[26] See the Editorial entitled 'A Regrettable Amendment' in *Legal Forum* 6, 1994, 1–2.

[27] It might also be noted that one of the provisions in the draft constitution that was rejected by the electorate in the referendum of 2000 concerned compulsory acquisition of land. Despite this, a constitutional amendment providing exactly the same provision was then passed by the ZANU(PF) dominated parliament.

[28] For a fuller account see John Hatchard, 'The African-Zimbabwe Constitution: a Model for Africa?' (1991) 35 Journal of African Law 79. Similar criticism has been leveled against constitutional amendments in Tanzania. See C. M. Peter, 'Constitution-making in East Africa', in K. Kibwana, C. M. Peter and N. Bazaara, (eds.), *Constitutionalism in East Africa: Progress, Challenges and Prospects in 1999,* Fountain Press, Nairobi, 2001, p. 29–31.

As noted in the previous chapter, before coming into force, the South African Constitutional Court was required to certify that the final constitution complied with the Constitutional Principles contained in the interim Constitution. During the certification process, the Court specifically identified the constitutional amendment provisions for reconsideration by the Constituent Assembly. The inclusion of the SEPM procedure was extraordinary particularly because, as the Association of Law Societies (ALS) noted, it meant that although the Constitutional Court was required to check the new constitutional text against the Constitutional Principles, the provision left

> Parliament free the following day (by a mere two-thirds majority) to amend the new Constitution in a way which violated the Constitutional Principles and thus upset the compromises so carefully negotiated.[29]

The Court itself focused on the requirement in Constitutional Principle XV that the amendment procedure must provide for 'special procedures involving special majorities' and decided that the relevant section did not satisfy that Principle. The Constituent Assembly was thus required to re-visit the matter and eventually approved an amended provision that reinforced the specially enhanced parliamentary majority procedure and this was then accepted by the Constitutional Court.[30]

Essentially the problem is that whilst constitution-makers have rightly recognised that a consensual approach to constitutional amendments is necessary, most have seemingly ignored the fact that the SEPM approach is not always a practical mechanism for achieving this goal since it fails to take into account the common scenario of one political party or body dominating the legislature. There is also no consensus on what constitutes the 'appropriate' special majority: a two-thirds majority,[31] a 65 per cent majority,[32] a 75 per cent majority,[33] or a 100 per cent affirmative

[29] See ALS written submissions to the Constitutional Court, 31 May 1996, paras 3.2–3.3. Of course in the 1994 general election the ANC had fallen just short of a two-thirds parliamentary majority but an agreement with another smaller parliamentary party was (and remains) possible.

[30] See *Certification of the Amended Text of the Constitution of the Republic of South Africa, 1996* in [1997] 1 BCLR 1. The revised section is discussed below.

[31] As required for amending parts of the Constitutions of Zambia and Lesotho.

[32] As required for amending the Constitution of Kenya.

[33] As required in South Africa for amending the 'Founding Provisions' and the section providing for constitutional amendment: otherwise, only a two-thirds majority is required: see section 74 Constitution of South Africa 1996.

vote.[34] Alternative procedures towards obtaining a consensual approach need exploring. If parliament remains the preferred forum for making constitutional amendments, two possibilities might be considered.

One possibility requires that constitutional amendment Bills receive all-party parliamentary support, i.e. the majority of the members of the ruling party together with the majority of the members from the main minority party (or parties).[35] The procedure has several advantages. Firstly, it involves a wider range of political opinion by directly including minority parties in the amendment process. Secondly, it may improve the level of parliamentary debate as the Government must persuade more than just its own parliamentary supporters on the merits of the proposed amendment. Thirdly, the approach emphasises that the constitution is above partisan politics. Curiously the effect of this method is to reduce the number of parliamentary votes required to pass a constitutional amendment Bill. But actual numbers are not so important here for its value lies in encouraging a genuine consensual approach that the SEPM procedure generally lacks.

A second possibility involves including the second parliamentary chamber in the amendment process. Since 1990, such chambers have reappeared in a number of constitutions and are often given a role in the amendment process. Indeed in some cases, the second chamber enjoys a veto power over an amendment Bill. This is the position in South Africa where a constitutional amendment Bill requires the supporting vote of representatives from at least six (out of the nine) provinces in the upper house as well as a special majority in the lower house.[36] In Namibia in the event of the second chamber (the National Council) rejecting the Bill, the President *may* make the amendment Bill the subject of a national referendum.[37] In practice the usefulness of the safeguard largely depends upon the representative nature of the upper chamber.[38]

Whilst such procedures may encourage a consensual approach to constitutional amendments, the continuing weakness of minority

[34] As required in Zimbabwe for the amending of certain provisions during the first ten years after independence.

[35] A threshold of perhaps 5 per cent of the parliamentary seats is desirable for a minority party to enjoy this right.

[36] See s.74(1)–(3) A weaker and less useful procedure is found in Lesotho where the upper chamber, the Senate, merely has a delaying power. See section 85(2) Constitution of Lesotho.

[37] Art. 132(3)(a). This wording leaves unclear the circumstances in which the President can exercise his/her discretion. A duty to hold a referendum following disagreement between the two chambers would avoid the uncertainty.

[38] In any event, most ESA states have a uni-cameral legislature.

parliamentary parties,[39] the widespread unrepresentative nature of parliaments themselves and the strict hegemony of the ruling party creates doubts as to the ability of legislatures to act as the 'guardian of the Constitution'. It is time to consider alternative approaches.

Approval through a constituent assembly

Under this system substantive constitutional amendments are approved by a specially elected constituent assembly whose membership represents a genuine cross-section of civil society. In other words, since popular participation in the constitution-making process is the ideal, the constitution-amendment process should follow the same pattern. Though at first sight this appears expensive and time consuming, the procedure allows for full public participation in and consultation on the amendment debate.

Of course it is an inconvenient procedure if the amendment itself is of a minor nature. Here the Constitution of Malawi provides a helpful solution as the Bill may be passed with a two-thirds majority of the National Assembly when the Speaker of the National Assembly certifies that the 'amendment would not affect the substance of [*sic*] effect of the Constitution'.[40]

Approval through a national referendum

The people's right to direct involvement in the constitutional amendment process is recognised in several ESA constitutions that stretch back as far as the 1966 Constitution of Botswana. The current Constitution of Malawi, for example, provides that any amendment to the 'Fundamental Principles' or human rights provisions in the Constitution requires a simple parliamentary majority *provided* that the proposed amendment receives the support of the majority of those voting in a national referendum.

[39] Witness the efforts, so far seemingly largely fruitless, of the Commonwealth to support the operation of minority parties. See, for example, 'Democracy and Good Governance: Challenges, Impediments and Local Solutions in Africa', Paper prepared by the Commonwealth Secretariat for the Roundtable of Heads of Government of Commonwealth Africa on Democracy and Good Governance in Africa, Gaborone, Botswana, 23–27 February 1997 at p. 6, in particular, the Opening Remarks of the Commonwealth Secretary-General at pp. 2–4. See further the discussion in chapter 6.

[40] See ss.195–7. Of course this begs the question as to the meaning of 'substance or effect'. This might well lead to considerable controversy and, in the last resort, the Speaker's ruling might well be the subject of judicial review.

Lesotho has adopted a similar approach in which a constitutional amendment Bill cannot be submitted to the King for assent unless, between two and six months after parliamentary approval of the Bill, it is approved in a national referendum.[41] In Uganda, the amendment of a fundamental constitutional provision requires approval in a national referendum as well as a special parliamentary majority.[42]

Reinforcing the parliamentary role is attractive as it encourages governments to think twice before seeking amendments to fundamental constitutional provisions. For example, in 1996 the Zambian Government sought to amend the 1991 Constitution. A two-thirds parliamentary majority was required for any amendment save for those relating to any of its fundamental rights provisions that required approval by a national referendum.[43] Whilst the government could rely on a compliant legislature to replace the rest of the 1991 Constitution, it seemingly did not believe it enjoyed sufficient public support to make changes to the Bill of Rights and did not pursue the matter.

Publicising the proposed amendment(s)

To allow for public comment, the Constitutions of Zimbabwe, South Africa and Zambia, amongst others, require the text of any constitutional amendment Bill to be published in the *Government Gazette* for public comment for thirty days before the first reading in the legislature.[44] There are some refinements: thus in South Africa the National Assembly cannot vote on a constitutional amendment Bill within thirty days of its introduction/tabling in the Assembly.[45]

Whether such 'special procedures' make a constitution less vulnerable to amendment is questionable and this may have persuaded some constitutional drafters to favour holding a national referendum instead. Even

[41] Chapter VII of the Constitution of Lesotho. This is only in respect of the amendment of certain key constitutional powers: see s.85(3).

[42] See Chapter 18, Constitution of Uganda. In the case of Botswana, three referenda have been held since 1987. These covered issues such as reducing the voting age from 21 to 18 years and changes to the structure and conditions of service of the judiciary.

[43] See art. 79(3) Constitution of Zambia 1991.

[44] See art. 79(2) Constitution of Zambia 1991 and s.52 Constitution of Zimbabwe. In South Africa, the person or committee introducing the amendment Bill must submit any written comments received from the public and the provincial legislatures to the Speaker for tabling in the National Assembly: see s.74(6) Constitution of South Africa.

[45] S.74(7). Elsewhere, the period of notice is sometimes extended: for example to three months in The Gambia.

so, a 'cooling-off' period at least provides a check on over-hasty constitutional amendments. In particular, it is a potentially useful means of stimulating public awareness, for allowing human rights commissions to comment on the Bill and for civil society to engage in dialogue with the government.[46]

To enhance its value, wide publicity of the Bill is essential and it is not enough to merely publish it in the official government organ. Effective dissemination requires that proposed amendments are published in the major news media including those in the indigenous languages. A useful precedent is found in Zimbabwe, albeit on a different issue. Here any compulsory purchase of land must be signified by a notice published once in the *Government Gazette* and twice 'in a newspaper circulating in the area in which the land is to be acquired is situated and in such other manner as the acquiring authority thinks will best bring the notice to the attention of the owner'.[47]

'Protecting perfection': preventing any weakening of fundamental constitutional provisions

Prohibiting retrogressive constitutional amendments

As noted earlier, the rationale for constitutional amendments is the need to 'perfect imperfections' or to strengthen constitutional protections. But suppose certain provisions are considered 'perfect': for example, where the fundamental rights and freedoms provisions in a constitution specifically entrench the universal and 'inalienable' rights set out in international human rights documents. What of the scenario where a proposed amendment will fundamentally change the whole balance of the constitution by dramatically increasing executive power and/or establishing a one-party state? Should the current constitutional provisions remain unamendable in these circumstances?

Article 131 of the Namibian Constitution addresses such problems by prohibiting the repeal or amendment of any constitutional provision in so far as this '. . . diminishes or detracts from the fundamental rights and freedoms contained in [the Constitution] . . .' Thus fundamental rights

46 This is well illustrated by the critical response from human rights NGOs in Zimbabwe in 1997 to plans to amend the constitution to abolish the right of a non-citizen husband to reside in Zimbabwe with his citizen wife. As a result of their pressure, changes were made to the resultant constitutional amendment Bill.

47 Land Acquisition Act 1992, s.5. The section itself was rendered ineffective following the illegal farm invasions.

can be strengthened ('perfecting imperfections') but not weakened (protecting 'perfection'). This approach clearly has the advantage of avoiding any repetition of the Zimbabwean experience discussed earlier. Of course, what constitutes 'perfection' is debatable and may vary from time to time in line with changes in public attitudes. Thus, a totally inflexible model could introduce serious constitutional tensions. In the Namibian context, for instance, this might occur where, despite overwhelming public support for the re-introduction of capital punishment, such a move was rejected on the ground that it was not constitutionally permissible.[48]

Article 131 is unique to Namibia and its inflexibility is problematic. Even so, its value lies in the protection of rights that are generally accepted as 'non-derogable' in international and regional human rights instruments. Other than these, a constitution should retain some flexibility for however 'perfect' it may appear at the time of its drafting, some amendment may become appropriate in the future. This means that the need to provide a satisfactory amendment procedure remains paramount.

Protecting the basic structure of the constitution

With most ESA states retaining the specially enhanced parliamentary majority procedure and ruling parties enjoying a two-thirds majority in several of them, a repeat of the Zimbabwean experience is not unlikely. A constitution's vulnerability to retrogressive amendment raises the issues of judicial involvement in tackling 'political' questions and protecting fundamental constitutional provisions.

Such involvement occurred in the well-known Indian case of *Kesavananda v State of Kerala*.[49] Here a majority of the Indian Supreme Court held that the basic institutional structure of the state must remain intact and thus Parliament could not amend the Constitution's essential or basic structure, even through a formal constitutional amendment process, because this would amount not just to its amendment but to its replacement by a new document.[50]

[48] Article 6 of the Namibian Constitution prohibits, amongst other things, the imposition of the death sentence. The article itself is protected from amendment by article 131.

[49] AIR 1973, S.C. 1461. See also the Bangladeshi case of *Chowdury v Bangladesh* 41 DLR (AD) 1989, 165.

[50] For a useful discussion see D. G. Morgan, 'The Indian Essential Features Case' (1981) 30 ICLQ 307. Later developments are chronicled by M. Abraham, 'Judicial Role in Constitutional Amendment in India: the Basic Structure Doctrine', in M. Andenas (ed.), *The Creation and Amendment of Constitutional Norms*, 2000, London: British Institute of International and Comparative Law, 195.

Whilst no ESA court has yet openly adopted this reasoning,[51] the response to the Chileya affair in Zimbabwe is interesting. At the opening of the High Court in February 1991, the Chief Justice launched a thinly veiled attack on the amendments to section 15. He asserted that there were certain basic principles enshrined in the Declaration of Rights that were not subject to curtailment and which the courts would seek to protect. In doing so he was seemingly preparing the ground to adopt the basic structure doctrine.[52] This is a high-risk strategy as it will almost certainly provoke a confrontation between the judiciary and the executive, with the latter being the likely victor.[53] Given the establishment of an appropriate amendment procedure, the matter becomes academic. Yet when, for example, an executive dictatorship can be introduced through piecemeal amendments of a constitution with the legislature being willing collaborators, the judiciary may be the only body capable of acting as the 'guardians of the constitution'. In such cases, the judiciary may have the right and duty to intervene and utilise the basic structure doctrine.

Overview

Many constitutions in the ESA states have proved fragile documents and their fate has often been one of abrogation, derogation and retrogressive amendment. This chapter has highlighted the importance of protecting constitutions by establishing effective formal procedural safeguards against their being 'undermined' through constitutional amendment.

The question now is who are the 'guardians of the constitution'? One striking feature of the post-1990 Constitutions is that many still place

[51] Although the basic structure doctrine gained favour, albeit as *obiter*, in the judgment of Mahomed D. P. in *Premier, KwaZulu-Natal and Others v President of the Republic of South Africa and Others* 1996 (1) SA 769 (CC), paras 45–8.

[52] He returned to the same theme some years later arguing that if the structural pillars of the Constitution are damaged or destroyed the 'whole constitutional edifice will crumble. Therefore it is the duty and function of the judiciary to protect the Constitution against such damage. How else can courts seek to ensure that their expansive interpretations of human rights provisions are neither over-ridden nor disrespected?' See A. R. Gubbay, 'The Role of the Courts in Zimbabwe in Implementing Human Rights, with Special Reference to the Application of International Human Rights Norms', in *Developing Human Rights Jurisprudence*, volume 8 2001, London: Interights/Commonwealth Secretariat, at p. 52.

[53] Indeed the day following the handing down of the *Kesavananda* judgment, it was announced that Sikri C. J., one of the majority who has upheld the doctrine, was to retire. Against all tradition, his successor was named as Ray J. who was the most senior member of the minority in the case: see Morgan, 'Indian Essential Features Case', at pp. 335–6.

their faith in parliamentarians. This despite the fact that there is little to suggest that this is justified. In reality, the key is ensuring that any constitutional amendment is legitimised in the eyes of the people, thereby maintaining public confidence in the entire document. In other words, it is the people themselves who are the 'guardians of the constitution' and it is they who must consent to any proposed amendment of *their* constitution. Perhaps this is best achieved by means of a double-locking mechanism, i.e. requiring that any substantive constitutional amendment must (i) either be supported by a special parliamentary majority or approved by a fully representative constituent assembly; and (ii) receive public backing in a national referendum. Such an approach also has the benefit of ensuring that the judiciary is not dragged into the political arena by being forced to play the role of the failsafe 'guardians of the constitution'.

5

Presidentialism and restraints upon executive power

> Presidentialism in . . . Africa has tended towards dictatorship and tyranny, not so much because of its great power as because of insufficient constitutional, political and social restraint upon that power . . .[1]

The exercise of presidential power

Like others the world over, constitutions in the ESA states typically provide for an executive arm of government with specific powers and responsibilities. Yet the necessity for government creates its own problems and in particular the problem of how to limit the arbitrariness inherent in government and to ensure that its powers are used for the good of society. In any political system, whilst the executive is often the major initiator and executor of public policies it also has the potential for operating as a super-ordinate branch of the political system with tentacles that stultify the other branches.

A president heads the executive branch of government in all the ESA states, with the exception of Lesotho and Swaziland.[2] As Head of State, Head of Government and Commander in the Chief of the armed forces, the president necessarily enjoys considerable constitutional powers and duties. Responsibilities include assenting to Bills; convening and presiding over Cabinet meetings; appointing and dismissing Cabinet and other ministers; exercising the power of pardon and the prerogative of mercy; and declaring a state of emergency.[3] Further, to the extent that presidential powers are not expressly enumerated and defined by the Constitution, it appears that in a number of cases, he/she has retained those derived from the ancient common law prerogatives of the Crown. Indeed the drafters of

[1] B. O. Nwabueze, *Presidentialism in Commonwealth Africa*, Hurst, London, 1974, at p. 1.

[2] These monarchies merit separate treatment and are dealt with below at page 93.

[3] Other presidential functions usually include the maintenance of law and order; executing laws enacted by the legislature; determining policy; directing and controlling departments of state, their activities and staff; pure administration; protecting and preserving the properties, instrumentalities and finances of the government and co-ordinating government activities.

the independence constitutions took care expressly to ensure their transmission.[4] In the case of South Africa the prerogatives of the Crown were preserved for the State President under the 1961 and 1983 constitutions. However, the extent to which they have been retained by the president under the new constitutional dispensation, which is designed to make a clean break from a discredited Westminster tradition, is unclear and has been the subject of some division of academic and judicial opinion.[5]

The exercise of presidential power is not unlimited for the incumbent is constitutionally bound to abide by, uphold and safeguard the Constitution and the laws of the state as well as to promote the welfare of all citizens. Typically, a constitution also sets out the manner in which presidential power is to be exercised and any limits on the president's freedom of action. The challenge is to enable the incumbent to carry out his/her duties as effectively as possible whilst remaining subject to appropriate and meaningful safeguards on the exercise of that power. The need to limit and control presidential power has philosophical roots in the notions of democracy which emphasise that the government has no right to govern save with the consent of the governed and that a government must not be allowed to be too powerful, otherwise it is liable to abuse its powers.

At independence, most ESA states made an attempt to blend Westminster-style Cabinet government with an American version of presidential power. In the case of Botswana and Zambia the functions of

[4] Thus section 18 of the Zambian Independence Order, 1964 (to which the Constitution of Zambia was scheduled) provided: 'Where under any law in force in Northern Rhodesia immediately before the commencement of this Order any prerogatives or privileges are vested in Her Majesty those prerogatives or privileges shall, from the commencement of this Order, vest in the President.' Transitional provisions to the same effect were included when subsequent constitutions were brought into force. In the case of Zimbabwe, the President expressly retains prerogative powers: see s.31H(3) Constitution of Zimbabwe and the discussion in P. Slinn, 'Zimbabwe Achieves Independence' (1980) *Commonwealth Law Bulletin* 1038 at p. 1056. Given its very different constitutional history, the prerogative powers have no relevance to Namibia.

[5] In the view of the Constitutional Court, 'There are no powers derived from the royal prerogative which are conferred upon the President other than those enumerated in section 82(1) [section 84(2) of the 1996 Constitution]' per Goldstone J. in *Hugo v President of South Africa* [1998] 1 LRC 662 at p. 681. Earlier academic opinion suggested that the President had retained common-law powers as part of existing law in so far as their exercise was not inconsistent with the Constitution. For a full discussion of this complex issue, see G. Devenish, *A Commentary on the South African Constitution*, Butterworths, Durban, 1998, pp. 155–7.

head of state and chief executive were fused in the office of President immediately. Almost all the ESA states that had adopted the model of a non-executive president soon followed suit. Seemingly uneasy with the demands and challenges of the office, presidents began seeking to develop a constitutional order that would weaken or remove constraints on the exercise of their power. Thus through their replacement and/or amendment, constitutions came to provide for a very strong executive president. Lacking sufficient countervailing safeguards to secure an effective balance of power, the Cabinet, legislature and judiciary tended to become subordinate to the executive leaving presidents to act with little or no restraint under a system that, in practice, often equated with authoritarianism.

As Mugabi Kiai observed in 1996 with respect to Kenya:

> A striking historical feature that has emerged from post-colonial Kenya is the perception of the presidency as an immensely powerful institution. Indeed this office has been so powerful that the two successive Presidents in Kenya's post independence era have been the alpha and omega of the social, political, economic and cultural life of the nation. Except in very few instances, it is impossible for any undertaking to take root in Kenya without the President's good will.[6]

Abuses of such power remain commonplace. For instance, in the period after 1999, the Zimbabwean government incited so-called war veterans to invade and seize farms without due process of law. The President and his political allies broke the laws whose passage they had engineered through Parliament, ignored court orders and denigrated the very judges who sought to assert the rule of law. As the Supreme Court noted:

> Wicked things have been done and continue to be done. They must be stopped. Common law crimes have been, and are being, committed with impunity. Laws made by Parliament have been flouted by the Government. The activities of the past nine months must be condemned.[7]

[6] Mugabi Kiai, 'Presidential Directives vis-à-vis Democracy, Human Rights and the Rule of Law: a Paradox', in K. Kibwana, Chris Maina Peter and Joseph Olaka-Onyango (eds.), *In Search of Freedom and Prosperity: Constitutional Reform in East Africa*, Claripress, Nairobi, 1996, p. 267.

[7] The decision of the Full Bench of the Supreme Court of Zimbabwe in *Commercial Farmers' Union v Minister of Lands, Agriculture and Resettlement* (Unreported, Supreme Court of Zimbabwe, S-132-2000). In *Commercial Farmers' Union v Commissioner of Police* (Unreported, HH-3544-2000), the High Court declared the invasion of commercial farms illegal

It follows that the composition and powers of the various organs of government and their relationship with the President and with each other is critical to the operation of a democratic state.[8] In a constitutional democracy, arrangements must be geared towards maximising checks and balances among the organs of government, and securing the independence of institutions so that they can act as an effective check on each other. Traditional accountability mechanisms and institutions exist in the form of an independent judiciary that hears and determines matters involving the interpretation of the constitution, a legislature that scrutinises both primary and secondary legislation and calls for presidential accountability, and independent commissions that deal with issues such as judicial and other public appointments as well as the oversight of elections. Offices of the ombudsman which address issues of maladministration within the public service, anti-corruption commissions and human rights commissions that have extensive powers to promote and protect human rights have been added to improve accountability.

Ensuring that the exercise of presidential power is subject to effective scrutiny and safeguard lies at the heart of any current discussion on good governance. Thus in this and the following chapters we examine the nature of presidential power and the critical question of whether, in reality, there are sufficient checks and balances on its exercise in the constitutional arrangements of the ESA states. The mere formal divisions in a constitution afford no conclusive evidence of the actual effect of those checks and balances. Rather these have to be judged in the context of the entire constitutional system.

Election and tenure of the president

An appropriate starting point is the manner in which the electoral process and tenure provisions can be used as accountability mechanisms.

and ordered the police to evict the unlawful occupiers from the land within twenty-four hours. The court also ordered the Police Commissioner and his officers to disregard any executive instruction if that instruction prevented the police from effecting the evictions. These orders were not complied with by the police on the basis of a lack of resources and that any attempt to do so would 'ignite the powder-keg'. However, at a subsequent hearing, the High Court refused to modify the orders as to do so 'would not be upholding its sworn duty – to uphold the law of Zimbabwe', *Commissioner of Police v Commercial Farmers' Union* [2001] 2 LRC 85 at p. 106. For a detailed account of the executive lawlessness in Zimbabwe see, *Justice in Zimbabwe*, Report of the Legal Resources Foundation, Harare, 2002.

[8] Nwabueze, *Presidentialism*, at pp. 12 and 14.

Electoral process

The direct election of a president who is both head of state and head of government remains popular in many of the ESA states.[9] The real significance of election by the people lies in the fact that it gives the president an independent right to govern. In contrast, a president who is elected by the legislature derives his or her right to govern from that body. Here the popular election is for members of the legislature who then elect the President and there is no separate direct presidential election. This is the position in, for example, South Africa.[10]

The issue of whether a president should be directly or indirectly elected is a complex one. In divided societies it may be preferable to elect presidents indirectly through parliament. Shugart and Carey identify three problems in relation to an electoral process where a president is directly elected: temporal rigidity, majoritarian tendencies and dual democratic legitimacy.[11] 'Temporal rigidity' refers to a presidential term of office that is fixed and difficult to change. This means that, unlike the Westminster system where a prime minister can be removed at any time as a result of a parliamentary vote of no confidence, a directly elected president can only be removed constitutionally during his/her term of office on grounds of incapacity or by a complex process of impeachment.[12]

'Majoritarian tendencies' refers to the possibility of a president being elected on a minority vote by a simple majority over a number of other candidates. For example in the 2001 Zambian presidential election, the successful candidate obtained just 29 per cent of the votes. This is hardly a resounding mandate for the new President and for constitutional stability. Such a problem is overcome by requiring that a successful candidate obtain an absolute majority of the electoral votes. However, this approach is by no means universal and in recent years both Tanzania and Zambia have

[9] I.e. Namibia, Uganda, Malawi, Tanzania, Zambia, and Zimbabwe. In Kenya, following the attainment of republican status in 1964, the successful presidential candidate was required to be an elected member of Parliament and his/her term of office was linked to that of the National Assembly. See J. Ojwang, *Constitutional Development in Kenya: Institutional Adaptation and Social Change*, Nairobi: ACTS, 1990, p. 79. The parliamentary and presidential elections remain linked with the successful presidential candidate requiring to be an elected member of the National Assembly: see s.5(3)(f) Constitution of Kenya. A somewhat similar approach is adopted in Botswana: see s.32 Constitution of Botswana.

[10] See s.86(1) Constitution of South Africa.

[11] M. Shugart and J. Cary, *Presidents and Assemblies: Constitutional Design and Electoral Dynamics*, Cambridge University Press, Cambridge 1992, pp. 28–43.

[12] Ibid., at p. 29. See below for a detailed discussion of impeachment proceedings.

replaced the absolute majority system by the first past the post system on the ground that it avoids the expense of a second round of elections. A second round of voting is surely a small price to pay to avoid an unfortunate outcome such as that in Zambia.[13] Another concern is that the simple majority system makes a directly elected president more susceptible to being pressured into ethnic or regional exclusivity for he/she may have an incentive to offer special privileges to their own ethnic or regional groups as a means of ensuring re-election.[14] This can be addressed, to some extent, however, by requiring a minimum level of national support for the successful candidate.[15] 'Dual democratic legitimacy' arises when both Parliament and the President are 'popularly elected' in that both can claim a unique popular mandate. This may encourage presidents to interpret their mandate as distinct from that of members of Parliament and as entitling them to dominate Parliament,[16] or at least prevail in the event of conflict between the two institutions.

A further concern is that in a multi-ethnic society without a history of stable democracy, there is no assurance that the losers of a direct presidential election will accept defeat in what amounts to a zero-sum game. Two examples from outside the ESA states highlight this problem. In the case of Angola, Reid blames the 1994 collapse of peace plans and the resultant bloody conflict largely on the country's presidential system. She observes that because José Eduardo Dos Santos and Jonas Savimbi were vying for the presidency, which was the only prize worth having, Savimbi would inevitably resume his violent struggle after losing the election.[17] Again in 1992 in Congo (Brazzaville), Sassou Nguesso succumbed to popular

13 Compare the provisions of article 34 of the Constitution of Zambia 1991 and its replacement by the 1996 Constitutional Amendment Act.

14 Nwabueze, *Presidentialism*, at p. 17.

15 For example, in Kenya a successful presidential candidate must receive a minimum of 25 per cent of the valid votes cast in at least five of the eight provinces: s.5(3)(f) Constitution of Kenya.

16 Nwabueze, *Presidentialism*, at p. 29.

17 Ann Reid, *Conflict Resolution in Africa: Lessons from Angola*, INR Foreign Affairs Brief, Bureau of Intelligence and Research, U.S. Department of State, Washington DC (April 1993). Indeed it was only after the death of Savimbi in 2002 that hopes for a lasting peace in the country were raised. Campbell also notes that in Nigeria, the all-or-nothing structure of the 1993 presidential election made it easy for the military to succeed in annulling the election before the final results had been officially announced. Unsuccessful candidates had no immediate stake in the political outcome, and many readily acquiesced in the annulment of the election in the hope of being able to run again (Ian Campbell, 'Nigeria's Failed Transition: 1993 Presidential Elections' (1994) 12 *Journal of Contemporary African Studies* 182).

pressure and permitted multi-party presidential elections. After losing the election, he became obsessed with ousting his successor, Pascal Lissouba, and mounted a military campaign against him until he succeeded in regaining power in June 1998.[18] This scenario is less likely to happen in a situation where a president is elected by Parliament as such an arrangement is conducive to formal and informal power-sharing arrangements. Even without grand coalition requirements, minority parties can hope to influence the choice of president and the composition of the Cabinet, particularly where no one party has a clear parliamentary majority.[19]

Overall, it is significant that perhaps the most radical and innovative constitution of the 1990s, that of South Africa, follows this arrangement. Here Parliament, at its first sitting after its election, and whenever necessary to fill a vacancy, must elect a woman or man from among its members to be the President. Upon election, the person ceases to be a member of the National Assembly.[20] As one South African commentator has noted:

> The Constitution moves closer to the *German model of Chancellor* government in which Parliament gives its imprimatur to the leader of the executive.[21]

For countries that have adopted a proportional representation system, the parliamentary election of a president has the further advantage of demonstrating national support for the President.

Tenure of and qualification for office

The presidential constitutions introduced after independence in the 1960s placed no limit on the number of terms an individual might serve. As a result President Nyerere in Tanzania, President Kaunda in Zambia, President Moi in Kenya and President Banda in Malawi were each able to enjoy more than twenty years in office.[22] President Mugabe of Zimbabwe still displays similar longevity.

[18] D. Anglin, 'Conflict in Sub-Saharan Africa 1997–1998', Centre for Southern African Studies, Bellville, South Africa 1997.

[19] Siri Gloppen, *South Africa: the Battle Over the Constitution*, Ashgate, Aldershot, 1997, at pp. 217–18.

[20] Ss.86(1) and 87 Constitution of South Africa.

[21] A. Venter, 'The Executive: a Critical Evaluation', in B. de Villiers (ed.), *Birth of a Constitution*, Juta, Kenwyn, 1994, p. 177.

[22] Sir Seretse Khama served as President of Botswana from independence in 1966 until his death in 1980 having been elected by Parliament on three occasions. His successor, Sir Ketunile Masire, elected in 1980, resigned voluntarily in 1998.

The office of President is too important a position in any country to be monopolised for too long by one individual. Experience shows that many long-serving presidents have used the constitution and other means to entrench their hold on political power and that this is a recipe for stagnation and the development of autocratic rule. The lifting of curbs on political activity can then produce some interesting results, as demonstrated by the electoral performance of some long-serving presidents following the return of multi-party democracy to their countries. For example, in Zambia in 1988, Kenneth Kaunda obtained a 95.5 per cent 'Yes' vote in the last 'Yes/No' presidential election under the one-party state. In 1991, he obtained 24.2 per cent of the votes in a straight fight with Frederick Chiluba. Malawi provides another example. In 1994 Hastings Banda, who had never even submitted himself for election as president under the one-party state,[23] came second with 33.5 per cent of the votes in a four-horse race in the first competitive presidential election.[24]

A further consideration is that however popular and constitutionally minded the incumbent president may be, it does not mean that this will always be the case, as the deliberate undermining of the rule of law in recent years in Zimbabwe by the long-serving (and formerly much admired) President Mugabe so starkly illustrates. In addition, no one can guarantee that any successor to a model president will be equally constitutionally minded. It follows that the challenge is to provide a framework that not only encourages but also ensures that political power is restrained and does not remain in the hands of one individual for a lengthy period of time. Herein lies the importance of restricting a person to a maximum of two terms in office. This ensures a regular change in the political leadership and is further designed to prevent an oligarchy developing. As Mubako also suggests, a limit on the presidential term of office 'would teach a . . . nation to depend on the strength of its institutions rather than on the chance occurrence of a good leader'.[25] Arguably, this is such a fundamental provision that it forms part of the 'basic structure' of the state and is therefore not subject to amendment.[26]

[23] He had been declared President for life by acclamation at the Malawi Congress Party convention in 1970.

[24] In Kenya, Daniel Arap Moi, previously elected unopposed in 1979, 1983 and 1988, obtained only 36.6 per cent of the votes in the first contested presidential election in 1992. Even so, the opposition vote was split between seven other candidates, so there was no transfer of power.

[25] S. V. Mubako, 'The Constitution of the Republic of Zambia', unpublished paper, 1972, p. 16.

[26] See the discussion in chapter 4 on *Kesavananda v State of Kerala* AIR 1973, SC 1461. In 1972 a 'third way' was recommended by the Chona Constitutional Review Commission in

Certainly in the SEA constitutions drafted in the 1990s the trend has been to limit presidents to a maximum of two terms in office. Yet presidents still seek to extend their time in power. Thus President Nujoma in Namibia was able to bring about a constitutional amendment that allowed him to seek a further term in office,[27] whilst in 2001 the then Zambian President, Frederick Chiluba made a determined, albeit unsuccessful, attempt to do likewise. In 2002 President Bakili Muluzi of Malawi was also engaged in ultimately unsuccessful efforts to run for a third term. Such presidential actions are particularly disappointing in that, whilst their original elections were seen as ushering in a new era of democratic accountability with a limit on the presidential tenure of office as a key ingredient, their desire to cling to power was seemingly undiminished.

The formal qualifications for office in terms of citizenship and age might be thought to be uncontroversial. However the qualifications issue has been used as a political weapon. Thus for the purposes of the 1996 elections in Zambia, the citizenship requirement was extended to disqualify persons whose parents were not born in Zambia. This was widely condemned and was seen as aimed at the former president, Kenneth Kaunda, whose parents were born in Malawi.[28] The Namibian Constitution, by contrast, simply provides that 'every citizen of Namibia by birth or descent' is eligible for election.[29] There is no consensus as to the minimum age for election as president and this ranges between thirty to forty years. This is unexceptional and is intended to avoid youthful persons ascending to the

Zambia in which a president would be eligible for an unlimited number of five year terms provided that not more than two terms were held consecutively ('Report of the National Commission on the Establishment of a One-Party Participatory Democracy in Zambia', Lusaka, 1972, para. 48). This device has little merit in that it encourages former presidents to linger on the political stage.

27 Thus ensuring that he can serve fifteen years in office. The constitutional amendment only affected the position of the incumbent and all future presidents will be restricted to two terms of office (unless and until they too engineer a constitutional amendment). Arguing in favour of the third term, SWAPO, the ruling party in Namibia since independence in 1990, asserted that the two term rule only applied to a directly elected president and that Nujoma had not been directly elected in 1990.

28 See Constitution of Zambia, 1996, art. 34(3). When President Chiluba was elected for a second term, this provision was used to mount a constitutional challenge to his election. See *Lewanika v Chiluba* [1999] 1 LRC 138. This kind of 'tit for tat' constitutional litigation is in the interests of no one and is extremely wasteful of scarce judicial time. As Ngulube C. J. was constrained to point out (at p. 143), the hearings in this complex case involving over 100 witnesses had occupied the Supreme Court for the greater part of the period between February 1997 and January 1998. The complexity of the matter meant that judgment was not delivered until November 1998.

29 Art. 28(3).

office of president.[30] Some constitutions also set a maximum age for presidential candidates. This has the considerable advantage of setting a finite limit to the tenure of one person in the absence of any other restrictions and avoids a senile president hanging on to power.[31]

The President, Vice-President and Cabinet

The starting point for any discussion on the exercise of presidential power is the relationship between the President and his/her Vice-President[32] and Cabinet.

The Vice-President

The Vice President is second in command of the executive and acts as president in the absence of the incumbent. An abiding problem in many ESA states is that the constitutional position of the Vice-President is weak for he/she almost invariably holds office at the pleasure of the President. The seeming desire on the part of many heads of state to prevent a clear successor emerging (and thus a potential rival for power) leads to the perception that often many vice-presidents are appointed more for their loyalty than their competence.[33]

In practice, the constitutional role of the Vice-President throughout the ESA states is ill defined with the principal function being to assist the President and/or to exercise such functions as may be conferred upon him/her by the President, the Constitution or by an Act of

[30] It may also help avoid a family dynasty in which a youthful son or daughter replaces their father as the chief executive. That this can occur is illustrated by the elevation of the youthful Joseph Kabila to the presidency of the Democratic Republic of Congo in succession to his murdered father. Of course in this case neither men were popularly elected.

[31] Of course this discriminates against elderly candidates, for example veteran politicians who may not have had an opportunity to previously participate in free and fair elections. Indeed such a provision might also have excluded Nelson Mandela from becoming the South African president.

[32] In Namibia a similar function is fulfilled by the Prime Minister. See arts. 34(1) and 36 Namibian Constitution. In South Africa the office-holder is known as the Deputy President: see s.91 Constitution of South Africa.

[33] An alternative model is found in Malawi where the prospective President and Vice-President stand for election as a team with the Vice-President only being forced from office by a formal impeachment process. See ss.80(4) and 86(1) Constitution of Malawi. It remains to be seen how this will affect the role and prestige of the Vice-President. Certainly the role of the Vice-President remains that of an assistant to the President. See s.79 Constitution of Malawi.

Parliament.[34] Typically, the Vice-President's sole express constitutional function is the right to preside over Cabinet meetings in the temporary absence of the president.[35] The reality is therefore that the Vice-President is in no position to play any effective restraining role on the head of state, either from a constitutional or political point of view.

The Cabinet

Given the history of presidential dictatorship in the region, it is clear that the Cabinet, as an institution, has made little meaningful contribution to the accountability process. This is well illustrated by the experience of Zambia under the presidency of Kenneth Kaunda. Here Kaunda developed a practice of appointing special assistants, even labelling some 'ministers'. These individuals appeared more important and closer to the President than Cabinet ministers themselves.[36] The situation of ministers was even worse in Zambia under the one-party system for, through the doctrine of party supremacy over all other organs of state, the Cabinet was subordinated to the party, a fact that greatly compromised its policy-making powers. The highest forum for the formulation of policy became the party congress and this led to the concept of the 'Party and its Government'.[37] Indeed the Central Committee of the ruling party, UNIP, eventually appropriated the powers and prerogatives once traditionally enjoyed by the Cabinet. Power as re-arranged meant that elected officials, especially Cabinet ministers, did not have the final say on policy formulation.[38] From a democratic perspective, this essentially deprived citizens of the right to influence the course of policy by way of lobbying

[34] Article 108(3) Constitution of the Republic of Uganda for instance, provides that the Vice-President shall deputise for the President as and when the need arises, and perform such functions as may be assigned to him or her by the President or may be conferred on him by the Constitution.

[35] This may be further complicated by the appointment of several Vice-Presidents, often for politically expedient motives, as has occurred in South Africa and Zimbabwe.

[36] M. Ndulo and R. Kent, 'The Constitutions of Zambia' (1998) 30 *Zambia Law Journal* 7.

[37] In the Constitution of Zambia 1973 which introduced the one-party state, the Constitution of the United National Independence Party was even annexed thereto 'for information' (art. 4(2)).

[38] See especially article 47(a)(b)(c) of the Constitution of Zambia 1973 which was added by Act 22 of 1975. Article 47(c)(1) provided: 'The Central Committee shall formulate the policy of the Party and the Government and shall be responsible for advising the President with respect to the policy of the Party and the Government . . .' Article 47(c)(2) then provided: 'Where a decision of the Central Committee is in conflict with a decision of the Cabinet, the decision of the Central Committee shall prevail.' The supremacy of the

elected officials and reduced the Cabinet role to merely advising the President on the implementation of policies made by the Party.[39] This meant that the government was no longer responsible to Parliament but to the Party. Parliament's role was accordingly severely restricted and became a mere sub-committee of the Central Committee as its members were controlled by internal Party disciplinary procedures.[40] Parliament became less crucial in debating national issues and could only question government ministers on policy implementation as policies, once decided by the Party, were not subject to parliamentary debate. So accountability, which is so critical to democratic rule, was eclipsed as authoritarianism took centre stage. As the 1995 Mwanakatwe Constitutional Review Commission later observed, 'the supremacy of the party was a veiled cover for a powerful and autonomous president who merged the mobilization power of the party together with the instruments and material resources of government to near totalitarian proportions'.[41]

Under the new multi-party constitutions of the 1990s, the model of a Cabinet consisting of the President, Vice-President and Ministers appointed by the President from members of the legislature remains commonplace.[42] The Cabinet's effectiveness as a safeguard on the exercise of presidential power depends upon several factors, including its constitutional role and the scope for independent action by Cabinet Ministers.

Constitutional role of the Cabinet

The formal constitutional requirement for the Cabinet is intended to minimise the possibility of personal government and to operate as a safeguard on the President. As Kenneth Kaunda once put it, establishing a Cabinet in the Commonwealth African presidential constitutions sought to ensure that, by subjecting him/her to its advice and influence, the President

Party was further reflected in the composition of the Cabinet over which the Secretary-General of the Party presided in the absence of the President: art. 50(2), Constitution of Zambia 1973.

39 J. Mwanakatwe, *The End of the Kaunda Era*, Multimedia, Lusaka, 1994, p. 103.

40 For an excellent modern example, see the disciplinary action taken by ZANU(PF) against one of its members of Parliament, Dzikamai Mavaire, for daring to criticise the President in the legislature. This case is discussed further in chapter 7.

41 'Report of the Constitutional Review Commission', Lusaka, 1995, p. 7.

42 The exception is in Malawi which has adopted a presidential-style system where ministers do not have to be members of the legislature but must be available to Parliament to answer queries or participate in debates on the content of government policies. See s.96(e), Constitution of Malawi.

'would not be able to assume dictatorial power'.[43] Thus collective consultation and responsibility are seen as more likely to have a restraining effect on the President especially as it is harder to ride roughshod over determined opposition from the Cabinet than from an individual minister. A president who does so faces a heavier political responsibility in the event of any failure or mistake, and may provoke the resignation of some ministers and a consequent undermining of the unity of the administration as well as a possible loss of public support and confidence.

In Botswana, Kenya, Tanzania, Zambia and Malawi, the Cabinet's major constitutional role is to advise the President on government policy and such matters as are referred to it by the President. The aim is to bring the collective wisdom of all members to bear upon matters of state, but without depriving the head of state of the decision-making power or the authority to reject the views of ministers when he/she thinks fit. Of course, it is not practicable for every presidential decision to be based on the advice of the Cabinet, although it might be argued that the existence of a requirement to consult the Cabinet implies an intention that the President is not to govern without its restraining and moderating influence. This means that the President should have regular and frequent meetings with the Vice-President and Ministers in order to obtain their advice on general policy and to co-ordinate government activities. When consultation occurs it must go beyond merely giving information or approving a decision already taken for it implies an opportunity to express an opinion, to criticise any proposal the President may bring and to offer advice. The opinion, criticism or advice needs genuine consideration by the President when making a decision. In reality, however, under an autocratic president, the Cabinet is not an effective check in such a system for if the incumbent refuses to accept their advice, ministerial options are very limited.

Innovative approaches are necessary to encourage genuine consultation. Several possibilities are worth noting. The Cabinet's constitutional position is apparently most strongly entrenched in Namibia, where the executive power vests jointly in the President *and the Cabinet*.[44] In Zimbabwe, under the independence constitution, in the exercise of his/her

[43] Colin Legum (ed.), *Zambia, Independence and Beyond: the Speeches of Kenneth Kaunda*, Nelson, London, 1966, p. 834. As noted earlier, when President of Zambia, Kaunda himself did not practise what he preached.

[44] Article 27(2), Constitution of Namibia. However, article 27(3) goes on to provide that, in exercising his/her executive functions, the President is only obliged to act *in consultation with* the Cabinet.

functions, the President was required to act on the advice of the Cabinet or of a minister (almost invariably the Prime Minister) acting under the authority of the Cabinet. The move to the executive presidency in 1987 retained this basic structure. Section 31H(5) of the Constitution provides that in general, in the exercise of his/her functions the President 'shall act on the advice of the Cabinet'. Independent presidential action is permitted in respect of the dissolution or prorogation of Parliament; the appointment or the removal of a Vice-President, provincial governors or any minister or deputy minister; the appointment of the twelve appointed members of Parliament; and certain other appointments. Subject to these important exceptions, the President is bound by a Cabinet decision in exactly the same way as any other minister. On the face of it, section 31H(5) represents a remarkable restriction on the exercise of presidential power. Some have argued that this restriction is illusory because Cabinet ministers still hold office at the pleasure of the President and thus the Cabinet cannot in reality act as a check or restraint on the excesses of the head of state.[45] Regrettably, this view has proved accurate as an extreme form of presidential dictatorship in Zimbabwe has developed. Yet, arguably, this has more to do with the unwillingness or inability of other Cabinet members to utilise their powers effectively and does not undermine the principle that in such circumstances the Cabinet can act as a potential check on presidential power.[46]

Another approach is to set out how presidential/executive power is to be exercised. This is exemplified in the South African Constitution where section 85(2) provides that the President exercises the executive authority, together with the other members of the Cabinet, by (a) implementing national legislation except where the Constitution or an Act of Parliament provides otherwise; (b) developing and implementing national policy; (c) co-ordinating the functions of state departments and administrations; (d) preparing and initiating legislation; and (e) performing any other executive function provided for in the Constitution or in national legislation. Crucially, section 101(1) then provides that the President's decision

[45] See, for example, W. N'Cube and S. Nzombe, 'The Constitutional Reconstruction of Zimbabwe: Much Ado about Nothing?' (1987) 5 *Zimbabwe Law Review* 2, at p. 13.

[46] The Constitution is now silent as to the effect of a presidential refusal to comply with a Cabinet decision. Previously the President was entitled to request that any Cabinet advice be reconsidered and, in general, it was only after the same advice was again tendered that it became necessary to implement the decision. This provision is now repealed. No doubt a major rupture of relations between the President and Cabinet would lead to a Cabinet re-shuffle, provided the President was politically able to pursue such a policy.

must be in writing if it (a) is taken in terms of legislation; or (b) has legal consequences. Further another Cabinet member must countersign a written decision by the President if that decision concerns a function assigned to that other Cabinet member.[47]

Independence of action for Cabinet ministers

Cabinet ministers are appointed by the President, invariably serve at the President's pleasure and exercise such governmental responsibility, including the administration of any department of government, as the incumbent may assign. In such circumstances, it is perhaps unrealistic to expect individuals to seek to challenge presidential wishes and dictates. Yet as a former Minister of Justice in Zimbabwe once argued, 'Ministers are not nonentities, particularly when clothed with the collective responsibility vested in them . . . Political realities prevent presidents from having a completely free hand in appointing or dismissing ministers.'[48] The argument contains some merit since individual ministers may enjoy strong personal support in the legislature or in parts of the country. In addition, the need to balance various regional groupings in the Cabinet may also restrict presidential freedom of action.

Recent examples suggest that presidential dictates still prevail even in the most serious of cases. Thus in South Africa in 2000, President Mbeki took what, to the overwhelming majority of informed medical opinion world-wide, was a decidedly eccentric approach to the AIDS/HIV debate having seemingly consulted a variety of Internet sites in developing his policy. As a result, many pregnant women were denied access to life-saving drugs. As Jerry Koovadia, the chairperson of the International AIDS conference in Durban in July 2000 lamented,[49] no one in the Cabinet and no one in the ANC had openly criticised the President.[50] Yet it can be done. For example, in 2001 in Zambia, senior government Ministers, MPs officials and members of the ruling party, MMD, openly opposed the plan of President Chiluba to seek a third term in office and thus ensured that the necessary constitutional amendment was not forthcoming. The stand of Ministers opposed to the third term was strengthened by overwhelming

[47] See s.101(2) Constitution of South Africa.

[48] See *Parliamentary Debates*, 27 October 1987.

[49] In a speech to the Society of Law Teachers of Southern Africa conference, July 2000, Durban, South Africa.

[50] It was eventually left to the Constitutional Court in *Minister of Health and Others v Treatment Action Campaign and Others* (2002) 5 LRC 216 to force government to provide the necessary drugs.

public support for their position.[51] This raises a key issue. For too long we have seen those who can make a difference, i.e. Ministers, political allies and government supporters, maintaining a 'deafening silence' towards controversial presidential decisions and policies. The challenge is to overcome the fear to criticise the President. S/he is, and must be perceived as, a servant of the people and subject always to the Constitution. Further s/he should be left in no doubt of this fact by her/his political allies.[52]

Presidential power of appointment

Another crucial aspect of the presidential power relates to control over the appointment, promotion, dismissal and discipline of senior public servants. Power over peoples' means of livelihood is likely to render them more amenable to the will of the person wielding that power. The Public Service is the bedrock of the government, providing not only the expert advice on the basis of which policy is determined but also the machinery for executing such policy. It is important, therefore, that the Public Service is representative of the various population groups in the country and that it functions efficiently and free from any political interference. The British policy at independence in handing over power to nationalist governments was to remove the Public Service from political control and vest it in an independent Public Service Commission established by the constitution. The object was to ensure that merit rather than political considerations would be the criterion for appointment and promotion; that dismissals and disciplinary control would not be used as an instrument of political victimisation; and that the political neutrality of the Public Service would not be jeopardised. The device was also part of the total scheme of institutional safeguards for political and ethnic minorities. Regrettably in most ESA states attempts to build and maintain an independent Public Service have largely failed as it has become almost universally politicised and turned into what might be termed the 'presidential' service.[53] The

[51] A coalition of NGOs and the churches organised public mass action to oppose the third-term bid. See 'OASIS Resolution on the Third Term', *ICENGELO* newspaper, Special English edition, no.1, March 2001.

[52] The acceptance by Nelson Mandela of the decision of the Constitutional Court in *President of the Republic of South Africa and Others v South African Rugby Football Union* 1999 (4) SA 147; 1999 (7) BCLR 725 (CC) is an excellent example of a head of state who was prepared to recognise both the supremacy of the Constitution and that, in a particular matter, he had acted wrongly.

[53] As noted in chapter 2, during discussions on the independence Constitution in Malawi, the politicisation of the Public Service in Malawi was one of the 'bees in the bonnet' of Dr Banda in Malawi. The whole ethos of the one-party-state systems was to turn the

same goes for other key commissions such as Election Commissions and Delimitation Commissions as well as Judicial Service Commissions that are entrusted with the appointment and removal of judges.[54]

Yet the principle still holds good that a constitution should provide for an independent transparent appointment and removal system for public servants that the President cannot dominate and some SEA states still seek to uphold it. Uganda, in particular, has made considerable efforts to achieve this position, especially in the case of the Judicial Service Commission[55] and the Public Service Commission (PSC). Presidential influence on the PSC is tempered by the requirement that members of the Commission are appointed with the approval of Parliament and that senior Public Service appointments are made by the President 'acting in accordance with the advice of the Public Service Commission'.[56] Further, the grounds for the removal from office of commissioners are similar to those for a senior judge.[57] A different approach adopted in Zambia is to require parliamentary approval for such appointments. The effectiveness of this attempt to make the legislature the principal organ for checking and supervising the executive branch will largely depend for its success on the existence of an effective and properly structured parliamentary committee system. If not there is a danger that the approval will be given as a formality.[58]

The President and the legislature

The executive has no independent legislative power for this vests solely in the legislature.[59] It follows that whatever power the executive possesses

Public Service, along with all other organs of state, into instruments for serving the party's interests.

[54] See, for example the *Report of the Advisory Panel of Eminent Commonwealth Judicial Experts* on the problems of the judiciary and Judicial Service Commission in Kenya, 2002, pp. 27–9. See chapter 8 for a full discussion on Judicial Service Commissions.

[55] Through reducing presidential influence over appointments.

[56] Arts. 165(2) and 172(1)(a). Unusually, the Constitution also provides for a separate Education Service Commission (ESC) and a Health Service Commission (HSC) which operate along the same lines as the PSC: arts. 167 and 169.

[57] PSC art. 165(8), ESC art. 167(9) and the HSC art. 169(9).

[58] Certainly the existence of the requirement for parliamentary approval in Zambia has not translated into a real check. This is largely because the committees established have not reflected the expertise required to discharge the functions of vetting. In the end the committees have regarded their work as one of checking security credentials.

[59] For example, article 79(2) of the Constitution of Uganda provides: 'Except as provided in this Constitution, no person or body other than Parliament shall have power to make provisions having the force of law in Uganda except under the authority conferred by an Act of Parliament.'

to make laws is a derivative or delegated one, and therefore subordinate to parliament's supreme legislative authority under the constitution.[60] The importance of legislation lies in the fact that it is the means by which Parliament regulates the life of the nation and from which the government derives its authority to govern. In the light of this, the power of a president who controls the legislature becomes apparent. It is not just that the executive can have tyrannical laws passed and executed and utilise excessive emergency powers[61] but also that it can act in flagrant disregard of the limits of its powers and then proceed to legalise its action by retrospective legislation. Political opposition under such circumstances becomes both futile and dangerous.

The following discussion therefore examines the relationship between the President and legislature and the adequacy of the safeguards that the latter can offer against the abuse of presidential power. In chapter 7 we consider other aspects of the role of the legislature.

Parliamentary vote of no confidence

Parliament has the time-honoured power to pass a vote of no confidence, which leads to the government's resignation and indeed that of an indirectly elected president. Thus in South Africa, if the National Assembly, by a vote supported by a majority of its members, passes a motion of no confidence in the President, the incumbent, Cabinet members and any Deputy Ministers must resign.[62] Yet this power is not applicable in the case of a president who is directly elected by the people for a fixed term. Of course a vote of no confidence could make it difficult for a president to run a country as it would be impossible to push through the government's legislative agenda and might force the removal of unpopular ministers (see below). In reality the matter is somewhat academic in that in most ESA states the President has the power to dissolve Parliament at

[60] This power may be subject to abuse. Under the Presidential Powers (Temporary Measures) Act 1986, the President of Zimbabwe is given sweeping regulatory powers to deal 'with . . . situations that require to be dealt with as a matter of urgency'. This was used in 2000 to make 'fundamental alterations' to the Land Acquisition Act, thus usurping the legislative power. See *Commercial Farmers' Union v Minister of Lands, Agriculture and Resettlement* [2001] 2 LRC 521. See chapter 12 for further discussion on the 1986 statute.

[61] See chapter 12.

[62] S.102(2) Constitution of South Africa. See also the presidential removal provision in section 34(1) of the Constitution of Botswana.

any time and thereby avoid a vote of no confidence.[63] Another difficulty is that anti-floor-crossing provisions are commonly in place. This means that parliamentary supporters of the government have the dilemma that if they vote against the President they face expulsion from the ruling party with the resultant loss of their parliamentary seat.[64]

Whatever the position of the president, this does not prevent the legislature taking action against Cabinet Ministers as they are accountable collectively and individually to Parliament for the exercise of their powers and the performance of their functions.[65] This is well illustrated in Uganda where article 118(1) of the Constitution provides that Parliament may by a resolution supported by more that half of all members of Parliament, pass a vote of censure against a Minister on any of the following grounds: (a) abuse of office or wilful violation of the oath of allegiance or oath of office; (b) misconduct or misbehaviour; (c) physical or mental incapacity; (d) mismanagement; or (e) incompetence.[66] Following a vote of censure the President must take 'appropriate action in the matter' unless the Minister resigns his or her office.[67] This procedure can target individual ministers who abuse their authority without involving the whole Cabinet. Just as significantly, the procedure might be used to embarrass the President. Equally, there is no reason why a vote of no confidence should not be targeted against the Cabinet. If successful, the vote should force the resignation of its entire membership.[68]

[63] An attempt to deal with this problem comes from Namibia. Here the National Assembly may be dissolved by the President on the advice of the Cabinet if the government is unable to govern effectively. In this case the President's term in office also expires: see arts. 29(1)(b) and 57(1) of the Constitution of Namibia. Such a 'suicide' provision will certainly cause a president to think carefully before dissolving the legislature.

[64] For a discussion on floor crossing, see chapter 7.

[65] See, for example, s.92(2), Constitution of South Africa.

[66] In Namibia the process is simplified in that the President is obliged to terminate the appointment of any Cabinet member if a majority of all the members of the National Assembly resolve that they have no confidence in that member: see art. 39 Constitution of Namibia.

[67] Ibid., art. 118(2). The proceedings for censure of a Minister are initiated by a petition to the President through the Speaker signed by not less than one third of all members of Parliament giving notice that they are dissatisfied with the conduct or performance of the Minister and intend to move a motion of censure and setting out particulars of the grounds in support of the motion: see art. 118(3).

[68] See, for example, s.102(1) of the Constitution of South Africa which provides that if the National Assembly, by a vote supported by a majority of its members, passes a motion of no confidence in the Cabinet excluding the President, the President must reconstitute the Cabinet.

Exercise of the legislative power

The legislative power of Parliament is exercised through Bills passed by Parliament to which the President assents. In practice the President largely controls the process by initiating, directly or indirectly, virtually all legislation as well as retaining the power to withhold assent to a Bill.[69] Typically when such consent is withheld the Bill can be returned to Parliament and re-enacted, provided that it has the support of two-thirds of the members of Parliament.[70] If the Bill is presented to the President again, the most common constitutional procedure is for the incumbent to choose either to sign the Bill or to dissolve Parliament. It is the threat of dissolution that is likely to persuade parliamentarians to comply with presidential wishes and thereby removes a potentially useful safeguard.[71]

Experience in the ESA states has shown that Parliaments generally have dutifully legislated in accordance with presidential wishes and examples of the rejection of Bills or their re-submission are rare indeed.[72] In view of this, some ESA constitutions seek to strengthen the position of parliamentarians. One useful approach is in Uganda where if Parliament reconsiders and then passes a Bill for a second time it automatically becomes law without the need for presidential assent.[73] The South African Constitution goes further. Section 79 provides that where the National Assembly passes a Bill, the President must assent to the Bill unless he/she has reservations about its constitutionality. In that case he/she must refer the Bill back to the National Assembly for reconsideration. If after reconsideration, the Bill fully accommodates the presidential concerns, the President must either (a) assent to and sign the Bill or (b) refer it to the Constitutional Court for a decision on its constitutionality.[74] If the court decides that the

[69] See, for example, art. 78(4) Constitution of Zambia 1996.

[70] See, for example, art. 78(5) Constitution of Zambia 1996.

[71] This again highlights the importance of the approach in Namibia where the President's term of office expires following the dissolution of the legislature: see note 64 above.

[72] One example comes from Kenya when three attempts were made to pass a Bill reforming the law of marriage and succession. All were unsuccessful on the principal ground that the Act was too 'Western' and gave too many rights to women. In the parliamentary debate in 1979, for example, the government was accused of 'throwing our customs to the dogs'. See E. Cotran, 'Kenyan marriage, divorce and succession law' (1996) 40 JAL 194 at p. 202. In Zimbabwe the Public Order and Security Bill was passed by Parliament in 1999 and sent to the President. He refused to assent to the Bill on the ground that it had 'inadequacies': a word that was never clarified but which plainly implied that the Bill failed to go far enough in criminalising certain conduct. Regrettably, thereafter, parliamentarians resolved to let the Bill lapse. For a short comment see John Hatchard, 'The Sad Tale of the POSB in Zimbabwe' (2000) 44 JAL 132–3. A more draconian statute was enacted in 2002. See further note 83 below.

[73] Art. 91(4) and (5). [74] S.79(4).

Bill is constitutional, the President must assent to and sign the Bill into law.[75] Crucially, the President does not have the alternative of dissolving Parliament. This approach gives the legislature some teeth in that it provides a check on the President's power to block the passage of legislation and at the same time emphasises Parliament's independence.

Determining sessions of Parliament

In most states the President is constitutionally bound to call a session of Parliament once every year at intervals of less than twelve months and to bring it to an end by prorogation.[76] This position, reflecting as it does the British tradition, is outdated and it is crucial instead to give the legislature itself the right to determine when and for how long it meets. This provides an opportunity for members to discharge their functions adequately and effectively and for Parliament to undertake its own business as well as that of the government.

Uganda, South Africa and Namibia lead the way in seeking to address this issue and other ESA states would do well to follow their example. In Uganda, article 95(5) of the Constitution provides that a minimum of one-third of all members may request a meeting of Parliament and the Speaker is then required to summon it within twenty-one days. Similarly, the South African Constitution provides that after an election, the first sitting of the National Assembly must take place at the time and on a date determined by the President of the Constitutional Court, but not more than fourteen days after the declaration of the election result. Once the first sitting has taken place the National Assembly determines the time and duration of its future sittings and recess periods.[77] Similarly in Namibia, the Assembly itself must sit for at least two sessions during each year to commence and terminate on such dates as the National Assembly determines.[78]

Limiting the number of ministers

In some states the proportion of members of Parliament enjoying a presidential appointment of one kind or another, especially to ministerial

[75] S.79(5).

[76] For instance, article 88 of the Constitution of Zambia 1996 provides: 'Each session of Parliament shall be held at such time as the President may appoint' and 'The President may at any time summon a meeting of Parliament and may at any time prorogue Parliament'.

[77] S.51(1). The President still retains the right to summon the National Assembly to an extraordinary session at any time to conduct 'special business': s.51(2).

[78] Art. 62(1)(b), Namibian Constitution.

office, is often significant. In Zambia, for example, those holding ministerial positions have sometimes been as high as 40 per cent of the parliamentary membership.[79] Needless to say, a minister bound by the obligations of collective responsibility (and the desire to remain in government) is unlikely, publicly at least, to oppose or criticise a government measure. It is therefore unfortunate that the useful check of imposing a constitutional limit on the number of Cabinet Ministers and Ministers of state has attracted little support.[80]

Overview

Overall, ESA Parliaments do not often exhibit much freedom to discuss, criticise and reject government legislation or presidential decisions. In reality the President has considerable control over the legislature with the result being a lack of presidential accountability to Parliament.[81] The South African Constitution is unique as it requires the National Assembly to provide mechanisms that ensure the accountability of all executive organs of state in the national sphere of government and maintains oversight of the exercise of national executive authority, including the implementation of legislation by any organ of state.[82] These measures are designed to strengthen further Parliament's role and to give people the added assurance that ultimately all-important matters are subject to public scrutiny through their elected representatives. The legal sovereignty of the National Assembly as well as the political sovereignty of the people are thereby underpinned and expressed through concrete institutional mechanisms. The importance of a legislature that can independently ensure the President's accountability needs no special emphasis. Unless Parliament is in fact independent of the President, its sovereignty means simply the sovereignty of the executive.

[79] Nwabueze, *Presidentialism*, at p. 276.

[80] The Constitution of Uganda refers to a 'number of Ministers as may appear to the President to be reasonably necessary for the efficient running of the State' (art. 111(1)), but adds: 'The total number of Cabinet Ministers shall not exceed twenty-one except with the approval of Parliament' (art. 113(2)). The Zambian Constitution of 1964 set a limit of nineteen ministers (see art. 44(1)). The proposed Constitution of Zimbabwe that was rejected in the 2000 referendum also provided for a limit on the number of ministers.

[81] As Nwabueze observes the right of government to determine the business of the assembly has translated into government monopoly of the legislative process (*Presidentialism*, p. 268).

[82] S.55(2) Constitution of South Africa 1996.

The final process by which policy is turned into law binding on the community must be separated from, and independent of, the executive. Securing and protecting liberties in an open, plural and democratic society requires an effective Parliament that is able to play a crucial role in checking and balancing other powers. No constitution, however, strongly entrenched, can guarantee liberty against excess of power on the part of the executive without an independent legislature to act as a counterpoise against such excesses and a strong national ethic against executive pretensions.

The President and the media

The development in many ESA states of a vibrant media, both print and electronic, has encouraged public debate and criticism of executive action that was unthinkable during the period of the one-party state. Yet in these states the social and legal relations of presidents with their fellow citizens are still not characterised by anything like the same degree of equality and respect as in developed democracies. For instance, it is commonly a criminal offence to 'insult' the President or bring his/her name into 'disrepute'. Part of the problem stems from combining the role of Head of State and Head of Government, for criticism of the President, of whatever nature, is often seen as being tantamount to criticism of the state. Yet it is an insecure and/or authoritarian president who resorts to the criminal law to protect him/herself and the government against legitimate media criticism.[83]

Providing and maintaining an effective constitutional right to freedom of expression and information is vital. Whilst the judiciary can play an important role in helping to shape and protect the right, this must go hand in hand with political reform. In particular those in political power must accept that theirs is a responsibility to develop conditions conducive to good governance and that criticism, even of a derogatory nature, is inseparable from competitive politics.[84] This, in turn, will

[83] This perhaps explains the introduction of a series of offences under section 16 of the Public Order and Security Act, (Cap. 11:17, Act 1/2002) in Zimbabwe under the heading of 'Undermining authority or insulting the President'. For example, the offence of making a false statement about or concerning the President 'whether in respect of his person or his office' carries a maximum of one year imprisonment (see s.16(2)(b)).

[84] In Zambia for instance in the run up to the 2001 elections several leading politicians were charged with insulting the President for calling him a 'thief'. See *The Post* (Lusaka) 14 August 2001: 'There is no Evidence of Theft Against Chiluba says Sata'. This was under section 69 of the Penal Code, a provision that has its roots in the pre-independence period.

encourage conditions that enable the media to disseminate freely and responsibly information and views about the president and government and party officials, whilst recognising that their work has justifiable limits. Here the *Guidelines on the Independence of the Commonwealth Media and those Working within it* provide an appropriate balance.[85] Amongst other things, the *Guidelines* state that (i) journalists must be free to operate without fear of their physical safety and liberty; (ii) proprietors and journalists should adhere to a professional code of practice; and (iii) the media should be safeguarded by a system of self-regulation including an effective complaints procedure. The *Guidelines* also condemn the continued use of criminal laws that often date back to the pre-colonial period and, in particular wide-ranging security legislation, sedition and criminal libel laws.[86] Rightly these are seen as one of the most insidious threats to freedom of expression and information and the *Guidelines* call on states to examine their laws 'with a view to removing those which unreasonably impede the freedom of the media'.[87]

Coupled with this is the need to develop an effective right to information. Increasingly such a right is seen as a necessary part of just and honest government. This is emphasised by the decision of Commonwealth Law Ministers in 1999 to formulate and adopt the *Commonwealth Freedom of Information Principles.* These state as follows (1) member countries should be encouraged to regard freedom of information as a legal and enforceable right; (2) there should be a presumption in favour of disclosure and Governments should promote a culture of openness; (3) the right of access to information may be subject to limited exemptions but these should be narrowly drawn; (4) governments should maintain and preserve records; (5) in principle, decisions to refuse access to records and information should be subject to independent review. The development of these rights remains in its infancy within the ESA region and this calls for states to follow the South African lead by introducing a specific constitutional provision on access to information backed up by appropriate freedom of information legislation.[88]

85 These are being developed by the Commonwealth Press Union and the Commonwealth Journalists Association. See Commonwealth Press Union, *The Independence of the Commonwealth Media and those Working within it,* 1999, CPU, London.

86 For a useful critique of pre-colonial laws in this area see J. Stevens, 'Colonial Relics I: the Requirement of a Permit to Hold a Peaceful Assembly' (1997) 41 JAL 118.

87 Paragraph 2, *Guidelines.*

88 Section 32(1) of the Constitution provides: 'Everyone has a right of access to (a) any information held by the state; and (b) any information that is held by another person and that is required for the exercise or protection of any rights.'

Presidential removal

There is no question of a president being personally amenable to the process of the court while in office for constitutions in the region typically provide that presidents enjoy immunity from both criminal and civil suit during their incumbency.[89] This is a procedural immunity only and is designed to enable the President to fulfil his or her constitutional obligations whilst personal liability becomes enforceable again at the end of the presidential term of office.[90] Such immunity makes having a mechanism for removing an incumbent president more important. In the case of a directly elected president, this is done through an impeachment process.

Whilst constitutional provisions providing for the impeachment of the President are commonplace,[91] in the abstract, it may be asked whether such a process is required at all. There is some merit in the argument, at least in the case of a directly elected president, that the possibility of impeachment unnecessarily inhibits presidential freedom of action as the incumbent is answerable to the electorate and it is for them to decide whether or not s/he retains their confidence at the next presidential election. Yet this is really an argument for *restricting* the circumstances in which to utilise the impeachment process rather than for rejecting it entirely. After all, there may be cases where the allegations against the President are too urgent or serious to leave until the next presidential election or they may involve some major scandal of which the electorate was previously unaware. The point merely emphasises the fact that the

89 Article 43 of the Constitution of Zambia 1996 provides: '(1) No civil proceedings shall be instituted or continued against the person holding the office of President or performing the functions of that office in respect of which relief is claimed against him in respect of anything done or omitted to be done in his private capacity. (2) No person holding the office of President or performing the functions of that office shall be charged with any criminal offence or be amenable to the criminal jurisdiction of any court in respect of any act done or omitted to be done during his tenure of that office or as the case may be, during his performance of the functions of that office.'

90 As demonstrated by the case of the former Zambian President, Frederick Chiluba, who was charged with a series of corruption-related offences following the expiry of his term of office.

91 Whilst impeachment proceedings originated in fourteenth-century England, they really came to prominence in the seventeenth century when used by Parliament to bring to heel corrupt and oppressive nobles, ministers, and Crown officials who could not be dealt with by the ordinary criminal process. In doing so it emphasised the fact of parliamentary supremacy over the absolutist pretensions of the Crown. Impeachment proceedings were later included by the founding fathers in the US Constitution. See generally John Hatchard, 'Presidential Removal: Unzipping the Constitutional Provisions' (2000) 44 *Journal of African Law* 1.

grounds for impeachment, and the relevant procedure therefor, must be carefully defined. Removal on grounds of ill-health gives rise to very different considerations and these are discussed later in the chapter.

Grounds for removal

The starting point for a discussion of the impeachment process is the presidential oath of office. This is broadly similar in the ESA states and requires the President-elect to solemnly swear to well and truly perform the functions of the office, to preserve, protect and defend the Constitution and to do 'right to all manner of people according to the law'. Specific grounds for removal are usually spelt out in the Constitution and cover a situation where the incumbent is guilty of a violation of the constitution (and/or oath of office) or of gross misconduct. On the face of it, these grounds are wide enough to encompass, for instance, the failure to perform some minor constitutional obligation. Yet it surely cannot have been the intention of the makers of the Constitution to thwart the will of the electorate by providing for the removal of the President for relatively minor acts alone. Arguably the true basis for impeachment is that the actions (or inaction) of the incumbent undertaken in his/her official capacity have rendered that person unfit to exercise the functions of the office of President. The test is not therefore one of 'gross misconduct' or constitutional violation *per se*, but whether the conduct has had a 'destructive impact upon confidence in public administration'.[92] In effect, this excludes presidential conduct undertaken in his/her private capacity. Thus a president's sexual antics with his/her lover in the privacy of State House may cause moral outrage but should not as such trigger the impeachment process. Further, the impeachment process is not designed to *punish* the President nor to facilitate a 'witch-hunt' by political opponents. Rather it seeks to secure the state and the constitution against the *personal* failings of the President in office that lead to his/her disqualification from office.

In Malawi and Namibia a further ground of removal involves a 'serious breach of the written laws of the land'.[93] This is presumably intended to cover the commission of a criminal offence[94] but the wording raises difficulties. In particular, is the provision applicable to offences committed in

[92] See R. Berger, *Impeachment: the Constitutional Problem* Harvard University Press Cambridge, MA, 1973, at p. 210.

[93] See art. 86(2), Constitution of Malawi and art. 29(2), Namibian Constitution.

[94] Although presumably this could be covered by the phrase 'gross misconduct' in other constitutions.

a personal capacity? In principle, as argued above, the removal provisions should relate solely to a breach of the presidential power.[95] A set of possible cases for removing a president will help clarify the position:

1. The President introduces an economic structural adjustment programme that results in severe economic hardship for millions of ordinary citizens and makes the incumbent extremely unpopular. This is not a case for impeachment. Government economic policies are political issues that are open to criticism and challenge through the normal parliamentary process or lead to the electorate rejecting the incumbent in the next presidential election.
2. The President uses his/her position to siphon off vast sums of government money into his/her private foreign bank accounts. This may constitute grounds for removal.[96]
3. Members of the security forces unlawfully detain and torture journalists whom they accuse of publishing an article critical of the military and refuse to comply with an order of habeas corpus. The President then publicly endorses the action of the security forces. This represents a personal violation of the oath of office and can trigger the removal procedure.
4. The President has proved inept in the handling of national affairs. This should not provide a ground for impeachment[97] for an incumbent doing his/her 'incompetent best' is answerable to the electorate.
5. The President smokes mbanje/cannabis/dagga in State House. The act does not, in itself, constitute a ground for removal as it was undertaken in a private capacity. Criminal proceedings can be brought at the end of the presidential term of office.
6. The President habitually rapes a member of his security staff.[98] This is a difficult case. The conduct itself is of a purely personal nature and on the face of it there is no impeachable conduct. Yet it constitutes an extremely serious violation of the law which makes it unlikely that the President can continue to govern the country. A constitution would

[95] Although see the discussion in example 6 below.

[96] This is specifically reflected in the Constitution of Uganda which provides for the removal of the President if 'he or she has *dishonestly* done any act . . . which is prejudicial or inimical to the economy . . . of Uganda' (art. 107(1)(b)(ii) (our emphasis)).

[97] Cf article 29(2) of the Namibian Constitution which provides for removal due to presidential ineptitude such as 'to render him or her unfit to [up]hold with dignity and honour the office of President'.

[98] This is not such an outrageous example as one might imagine. See below the bizarre case of Canaan Banana and his sexual activities during his term as President of Zimbabwe.

enjoy little public confidence if in such circumstances it both precluded removal proceedings and postponed any criminal proceedings against the incumbent until the expiry of his term in office. It may be necessary here to follow the approach of Malawi and Namibia and to provide for removal for a serious breach of a written law as an exception to the general proposition restricting removal to acts committed within the scope of office.[99]

The removal process

In respect of directly elected presidents[100] the most common removal procedure is the tribunal/Parliament approach. Here a specially constituted tribunal is mandated to investigate the allegations against the incumbent at the behest of the legislature which also retains the final decision on removal. This involves a three-phase process: the initiation stage, the investigation stage and the determination stage.

The initiation stage

Typically, the removal process is initiated by a notice of a motion given to the Speaker and signed by a specified number of the members of Parliament. This sets out the particulars of the allegations and proposes that they be investigated. The Speaker is then required to have the legislature consider the motion within a fixed period and the motion is passed if it receives the support of a specified majority of parliamentarians. There is no consensus as to the necessary parliamentary majority which ranges from one-third of all members of Parliament in Uganda to a two-thirds majority of all members of the National Assembly in Zambia.

A particular weakness here is that parliamentarians from the President's party who support the motion face expulsion from the party and the resultant loss of their parliamentary seats. For example, in Zambia in 2001, the MMD used its internal disciplinary procedures to expel twenty-two

[99] Sunstein (p. 314) also notes this type of problem in the American situation. His solution is to view it as an extremely unusual case and an 'exception to the general proposition' although he fails to demonstrate the basis for doing so. In fact such an argument undermines the basic principle of providing clarity in the removal process. It is surely better to deal with this type of situation head-on. See C. R. Sunstein, 'Impeaching the President' (1998) 147 *University of Pennsylvania Law Review* 279.

[100] Of the SEA states only the Namibia and Malawi Constitutions provide for the removal of a directly elected president by members of the legislature alone: see arts. 29(2) and 86 respectively.

of its MPs from the party and thence from Parliament.[101] An additional problem was that the Speaker of the National Assembly declined to call Parliament into session. This clearly contravened article 37 of the Constitution which provides that where notice of impeachment is given by the requisite number of members of Parliament, the Speaker must convene Parliament within twenty-one days. His refusal to do so not only highlighted a disregard for the Constitution but also starkly demonstrates the importance of an independent Speaker.[102]

The investigation stage

The establishment of a tribunal supposedly provides for an independent, transparent and non-partisan investigation into the allegations against the President. Members are appointed by the Chief Justice and almost invariably consist of senior members of the judiciary.[103] The procedure before the tribunal is nowhere well articulated although some principles can be suggested. Tribunals generally adopt an inquisitorial approach to fact finding and this is clearly the most appropriate in this instance.[104] In view of the nature of the proceedings, the need for a fair hearing is paramount. Thus the President is always entitled to appear before the tribunal and to enjoy legal representation.[105] It follows that the tribunal should be empowered to sub poena witnesses, a potentially useful power in the face of a recalcitrant president. In view of their importance, proceedings should be open to the public. Given the political uncertainty hanging over the nation at this time, it is in no one's interests to have an unduly protracted investigation: indeed an incumbent may be perfectly content to prolong the process for as long as possible in the hope of strengthening his/her position by raising parliamentary and public support. A time limit within which the tribunal must report is therefore appropriate.

[101] See *The Post*, 4 May 2001, 'MPs Petition Speaker to Impeach Chiluba', p. 1.

[102] But cf. *The Post*, 31 May 2001, 'Ndulo advises Mwanamwambwa', p. 1.

[103] A useful variant is found in Sierra Leone and The Gambia where the Chief Justice may appoint up to two non-judicial figures to the tribunal. This provides the flexibility to include appropriate additional expertise, for example the appointment of an accountant when the allegations against the President involve financial impropriety.

[104] As Lord Denning suggested in *R v National Insurance Commissioner, ex parte Viscusi* [1974] 1 WLR 646, p. 649, hearings before tribunals are 'more in the nature of an inquiry before an investigating body charged with the task of finding out what happened'.

[105] In the absence of a clear constitutional provision there is an absolute right to legal representation at common law where a person is charged with a serious disciplinary offence before a tribunal of enquiry. see Gubbay C. J., in *Nhari v Public Service Commission*, Supreme Court of Zimbabwe, unreported, SC 71/99, p. 8.

Two other potentially controversial issues concern 'presidential privilege' and pre-hearing publicity. As regards the former, the tribunal may require access to personal presidential papers, Cabinet minutes and other government documents but be met by a presidential refusal to divulge any material or information on grounds of privilege. The ESA Constitutions offer no guidance here and the matter will presumably be dealt with under the general law of privilege. Arguably, in view of the significance of the case, there should be a presumption in favour of disclosure, with the tribunal only entertaining a claim of privilege on grounds of national security. Even here, judges are well able to deal with such sensitive material and should have the right to hear the evidence in camera.

The issue of pre-hearing publicity stems from the fact that inevitably the whole affair will have generated considerable publicity, both nationally and internationally, with well-rehearsed allegations against the incumbent. This raises the issue of whether adverse publicity prevents the President from enjoying a fair hearing. Somewhat similar issues were aired in the case of the former President of Zimbabwe, Canaan Banana, who was indicted (and later convicted) on several charges involving sexual misconduct committed against his aide-de-camp whilst in office. There was widespread adverse and hostile pre-trial publicity. Banana applied for a permanent stay of proceedings on the grounds that there was a real risk that, as a consequence of such publicity, he would not receive a fair trial.[106] The case revolved around the tension between the right of the press to freedom of expression and the right of the applicant to a fair trial. After a review of Commonwealth authorities, the Supreme Court of Zimbabwe held that the applicant bore the burden of establishing the 'existence of a real or substantial risk of not being afforded a fair hearing before the trial court'.[107] Following this approach in the context of the tribunal, it will be extremely difficult for a president to satisfy this burden especially given the presence at the tribunal of senior judicial figures and the fact that the body itself is rarely the final arbiter on the removal issue.

Tribunals are normally tasked with determining facts and deciding the issue before it on its merits. Yet whilst an 'impeachment' tribunal is required to investigate the allegations against the President, its role thereafter is uncertain. In states such as Zambia, the tribunal is required to determine whether the allegations are 'substantiated'.[108] This must mean 'proved' for if the tribunal reports to Parliament that any allegation made

[106] *Banana v Attorney-General* [1999] 1 LRC 120.
[107] Per Gubbay C. J., p. 135. [108] Constitution of Zambia 1996 art. 37(4).

against the President has not been substantiated, 'no further proceedings shall be taken'.[109] If the allegation is substantiated, the tribunal is required to report the fact to Parliament which then decides whether or not to remove the incumbent from office. In others countries, the tribunal is to consider whether the evidence establishes a 'prima facie case' against the president and if this is the case, to report the matter to parliament. Curiously, the constitutional provisions do not deal with the position where the tribunal decides that there is no case to answer. Presumably, in this case the impeachment process comes to an end. However, if the role of the tribunal is purely *advisory* it might be argued that the legislature is still entitled to disregard such advice and continue with the removal process.[110] The confusion arises because the constitutional drafters have sought to provide for an independent investigation into the merits of the allegations whilst leaving the legislature with the ultimate decision as to removal. The result is that, except where the findings are that the allegations are not 'substantiated', the tribunal operates essentially as an evidence gathering forum on behalf of the legislature. This calls into question the value of an independent assessment of the facts untrammelled by any political and/or party considerations when these findings themselves can be overridden by those very same political and party considerations thereafter.

Overall, two main points are worth emphasising. Firstly, there is a need to develop appropriate rules and procedures for the operation of the tribunal based on the traditional principles of 'openness, fairness and impartiality'. These should detail the rules of evidence, burden and standard of proof, rules regarding privilege, appropriate time limits for determining the matter, the right of the public to attend proceedings as well as making provision for the report of the tribunal to be published prior to or at the time of the Parliamentary debate on removal. These principles should be enshrined in the constitution.[111] Secondly, the role of the tribunal itself must be re-assessed. This matter is considered below.

[109] Ibid.

[110] In cases where the tribunal is tasked with determining whether the allegations are sustained, the issue of who bears the burden of proof and to what standard becomes significant. This is nowhere addressed. In principle, the burden of proof should be placed on those seeking to support the accusations. In view of the gravity of the matter, the standard required is a heavy one. Not the criminal standard perhaps, but certainly more than the ordinary civil standard of the balance of probabilities. See further the English decision of *Hornal v Neuberger Products Ltd* [1957] 1 QB 247.

[111] A useful model here is article 69(8) of the Constitution of Ghana 1992 that states: 'The Rules of Court Committee shall, by constitutional instrument, make rules for the practice and procedure of the tribunal . . . for the removal of the President'.

The determination stage

In most ESA states the final decision regarding removal lies with the legislature. Invariably removal requires a two-thirds majority.[112] This is unsatisfactory for the decision is not a party political issue but a *constitutional* one. This suggests that a president should not be subject to impeachment proceedings unless there is all-party support for the action. This in turn suggests that a bipartisan approach is more suitable, i.e. removal requires the support of a specified majority of the members of the ruling party together with a specified majority of the members of the main minority party (or parties) in Parliament. This would ensure that impeachment proceedings are avoided:

> . . . unless and until people who disagree on political questions can be brought to agree that the President has committed deeds that justify his [or her] removal from office.[113]

Alternative approaches

The inadequacies and procedural uncertainties of the tribunal/Parliament approach raise the issue of whether a different approach to presidential removal is needed. Two devices are worth exploring. The first is to give the legislature sole responsibility for the removal process. Malawi and Namibia, both of which have directly elected presidents, have adopted this approach. In Malawi, the drafters of the Constitution opted for impeachment proceedings based on the United States model. Section 86 of the Constitution provides that the President is removed from office where the National Assembly indicts and convicts the President by impeachment. The procedure is laid down by the Standing Orders of Parliament 'provided that they are in full accord with the principles of natural justice'. Indictment on impeachment requires the affirmative vote of two-thirds of the members of the National Assembly in a committee of the whole house. Conviction on impeachment requires the affirmative vote of two-thirds of the members of both chambers.[114] The Speaker presides over proceedings of indictment by impeachment and the Chief Justice over the trial on impeachment. In Namibia, there is no formal procedure laid down in the

[112] Although there is no consensus as to whether this requires two-thirds of all members voting at the same time. See chapter 3 for problems associated with special parliamentary majorities.

[113] Sunstein, 'Impeaching the President', at p. 314.

[114] This must refer to *all* members rather than merely to those actually present.

Constitution, but removal is by a two-thirds majority of all the members of the National Assembly, confirmed by a two-thirds majority of all the members of the National Council.[115]

The Malawian approach at least has the benefit of providing a detailed procedure but, even so, it is questionable whether the legislature is the appropriate body to take sole responsibility for determining the removal issue. In the case of the United States the Founding Fathers' recognition that 'the Assemblies were their own, whereas Governors and Judges had been saddled on the Colonists by the King or his minions' resulted in requiring the legislature to perform this function. One can hardly describe the majority of Parliaments in the ESA states in these terms and therefore the United States model is not the way forward.

Another possibility is to leave the final decision on removal with the judiciary. Here the legislature might instigate the removal process, using the bi-partisan approach discussed earlier. Thus the matter would only proceed if parliamentarians had voted to support an investigation into presidential conduct. Crucially, it would then be up to a tribunal to determine whether the grounds for removal are substantiated. If so, the President is automatically removed from office.

Implications following the decision to remove

Most states now specifically provide terminal and other benefits and a pension for former presidents. This is welcome as it provides an incentive for leaders to withdraw gracefully from the political scene secure in the knowledge that they and their immediate family have lifelong financial security.[116] What is often not clear is the effect impeachment has on these benefits and upon any future political aspirations of the now ex-President. The South African Constitution provides that a president removed from office for cause 'may not receive any benefits of that office and may not

[115] Art. 29(2). In South Africa as the President is elected to office by members of the legislature he/she essentially holds office at 'their pleasure'. Here a resolution for removal requires the support of at least two-thirds of the members of the National Assembly. See Constitution of South Africa, s.89(1).

[116] For example, the first President of Zimbabwe, Canaan Banana, stood down from office in 1987 to enable the executive presidency to come into effect. In addition to his pension, he became entitled to (at the state's expense) (a) the services of one domestic worker, one cook, one gardener, two drivers and one private secretary; (b) one Mercedes-Benz motor car, two colour television sets and a Government office and telephone. See statement of the Vice-President in *Parliamentary Debates*, 24 March 1988.

serve in any public office',[117] whilst in Malawi, conviction leads to disqualification from future office.[118] The other ESA constitutions are silent on the two points, although in some cases this is no doubt because the legislation providing for presidential benefits only covers incumbents who have actually completed their term in office leaving the implication that impeached presidents are not eligible to enjoy the retirement benefits.

The South African approach has two advantages. Firstly, it opens the possibility of a bargain being negotiated in which the President resigns (and in doing so saves the nation from the potentially divisive removal procedure) but retains his/her benefits. Secondly it prevents the former incumbent from causing any future political uncertainty by seeking (or even by merely threatening) to return to the political stage.

Removal on grounds of ill health

Very different constitutional procedures are required for removing a President on grounds of ill health.[119] This process invariably comes into play where the ability of the President 'to perform the functions of office by reason of infirmity of body or mind' is in question. Several constitutions place responsibility for instigating the process on Parliament although, as in the impeachment process, there is no agreement as to the appropriate majority necessary to initiate action.[120] In Kenya and Zambia the Cabinet is given the instigation role.[121] Presumably this is based on the view that Cabinet members will have a better idea of the mental or physical health of the President than parliamentarians: although reality suggests that Cabinet Ministers may have their decision influenced, largely or wholly, by political expediency. Perhaps the most satisfactory approach is to allow either Parliament or the Cabinet to instigate the removal process.

As regards the investigation stage, the Chief Justice is responsible for setting up a tribunal to investigate the health of the President. The procedure in Uganda provides a useful model. Here the Speaker is required, within twenty-four hours of the parliamentary resolution to commence removal proceedings, to send a copy of the notice of the motion to the President and the Chief Justice. Thereafter the Chief Justice, in consultation with

[117] S.89(2). [118] Art. 86(2)(e).

[119] The sole exception being the Namibian Constitution which is silent on the matter.

[120] This varies from one-third of all the members of Parliament in Ghana and Uganda to a majority of members in The Gambia.

[121] There is no special majority required and, perhaps through an oversight, only in Zambia is there a requirement for the resolution to be by a majority of *all* members of the Cabinet.

the professional head of the medical services, constitutes a medical board of five eminent medical specialists[122] to examine the President. The President must submit him/herself to the Board for examination within seven days and is entitled to appear in person and be heard and to be assisted or represented by a lawyer or other expert of his or her choice during the proceedings. In the event of a refusal by the incumbent to co-operate with it, the medical board must report this to Parliament which can, with a two-thirds majority of all members, immediately remove the President from office.[123]

The role of the medical board/tribunal is unclear. In the abstract, the issue of the health of the president is a purely medical one and it is appropriate for the board/tribunal to make the actual determination. This is reflected in Kenya where a finding by the board/tribunal that the President is unfit to discharge the functions of office must be reported to the Speaker of the National Assembly by the Chief Justice whereupon the President ceases to hold office.[124] However the most common constitutional formulation requires the board/tribunal, if it determines that the President is incapable of discharging the functions of office, to report that fact to Parliament which then decides by a special majority whether or not to remove the President. This is extraordinary for it means that parliamentarians, for whatever motive, can decline to follow the findings of the tribunal/board and refuse to vote a comatose or insane president out in office.[125] The Kenyan approach is undoubtedly preferable.

All the ESA constitutions are silent as to the publication of the medical report. In view of its significance and the need for transparency at every stage of the process, it is surely in the public interest to require its publication. In practice this could occur by requiring the board/tribunal to lay a copy of the report before Parliament within a specified period (perhaps seven days) and before any parliamentary vote on removal. The highly publicised tribunal findings that the President is medically unfit for office might at least make its rejection by parliamentarians more difficult.

[122] Presumably some of whom are skilled in the field relevant to the nature of the examination to be conducted.

[123] Art. 107(7)–(14). Another potentially useful approach to encourage presidential co-operation is found in Sierra Leone where the President must hand over power to the Vice-President pending the submission of the report of the medical tribunal.

[124] Constitution of Kenya, s.12(4).

[125] An old example is the United States case of the insane Judge John Pickering in 1804 where 'members of the Judge's own party strongly opposed his resignation for purely political reasons'. See Berger, *Impeachment*, p. 101.

The position changes where a tribunal/board finds that the President is *temporarily* incapacitated, i.e. is *currently* unable to perform the functions of office through ill health but may be able to do so in the future. In Kenya, the formal removal of the President is delayed by three months pending his/her possible recovery. During that time the Vice-President exercises the presidential functions. In Malawi, the Vice-President acts as president until the incumbent is able to resume his/her functions. Here it is open to the President at any time within a year to submit to the National Assembly a declaration, certified by a board of independent medical practitioners stating his/her fitness to resume presidential duties.[126] If a two-thirds majority of the National Assembly determines the President is fit to resume office, he/she must resume the reins of power within thirty days. With the temporary incapacity of the incumbent likely to lead to acute political instability and uncertainty, it is in no one's interest to prolong the removal process. Hence the Kenyan approach to temporary incapacity is preferable.

In principle, the removal of a president from office through ill health carries with it no stigma and thus there is no question of any loss of terminal benefits and/or pension rights. Surprisingly only the South African Constitution specifically provides for this and others would do well to follow this example.

Removing a president from office is a serious matter and is inevitably accompanied by acute political and constitutional tensions.[127] It must therefore be recognised and accepted that the removal procedure is not just another tactic in the armoury of the President's political opponents but is a last resort mechanism to be used only in very carefully defined circumstances. As Sunstein puts it:

> . . . the impeachment device stands not as a political tool, but as remedy of last resort, designed to make possible the removal from office of those presidents whose egregious official misconduct has produced a social consensus that continuation in office is no longer acceptable.[128]

[126] See art. 87. The Malawi Constitution is silent as to who appoints the medical board. Thus it seems possible for the President to arrange for an entirely different board of (perhaps) more sympathetic medical practitioners to certify his/her fitness to resume office.

[127] For example, in 1999 an effort to impeach the President of Venezuela was accompanied by wide-spread public demonstrations calling for his removal. The President forestalled the process by resigning.

[128] 'Impeaching the President', p. 315.

The monarchies

Any study of the executive in the ESA states inevitably concentrates, as this chapter does, on the exercise of presidential power in the republics. However, by way of contrast, the role of the executive in the two indigenous monarchies of Lesotho and Swaziland repays a short separate study.

We have observed above that the development of the authoritarian executive presidency may in part be traced back to the tradition of colonial governance under which the governor exercised locally the prerogatives of the British Crown.[129] The concentration of executive power is thus seen as a foreign import and alien to the African tradition of consensus. One might therefore suppose that the 'restored' indigenous constitutional monarchies would provide an autochthonous model of sustainable restraint in the exercise of executive power. Unfortunately, since independence, the governance history of both Lesotho and Swaziland hardly supports this optimistic prognosis being characterised by turbulence and authoritarianism. Both states were endowed at independence with Westminster-model constitutions in the expectation that the indigenous rulers would play the role assigned to the British monarch.[130] However, constitutional monarchy has not proved a formula for good governance.

In Lesotho, the independence constitution of 1966, which provided for a constitutional monarchy, was suspended in 1970 in a 'prime ministerial coup' by Chief Lebua Jonathan, who justified his seizure of power by the familiar argument that the 'western concept of democracy differed from African democracy'. Accordingly King Moshoeshoe II was reduced to a cipher in the hands of the Prime Minister.[131] Chief Jonathan was overthrown in 1986 by a military coup. The Order establishing the military government was made in the name of the King, who was obliged to act in the exercise of his functions under the Order on the advice of the Military Council.[132] The existence of a traditional monarchy therefore proved to be no bulwark against civilian and military dictatorships. Indeed, in holding

[129] Above, p. 14.

[130] '[T]he sovereign has, under a constitutional monarchy . . . three rights – the right to be consulted, the right to encourage and the right to warn', W. Bagehot, *The English Constitution*, Collins, Fontana edn, London 1963, p. 111. The monarch's rights to information and to be consulted are enshrined in section 92 of the present Constitution of Lesotho.

[131] The complex constitutional devices adopted by Chief Jonathan are expertly dissected by Cullinan C. J. in *Mokotso v HM King Mosheshoe II* [1989] LRC (Const) 24, p. 49.

[132] Ibid., p. 55.

that the military government was the lawful government of Lesotho, the Chief Justice later cited popular acceptance of the coup derived from the loyalty of the revolutionary regime to the King, who, in turn, 'was pleased to accept the new order and to exercise his function as Head of State'.[133] However, in 1990, the King was himself deposed and replaced by his son, Letsie III. Local and external (mainly donor) pressure eventually forced the military to retire to barracks and permit free elections in 1993.

Under the new dispensation, the King, as a constitutional monarch, was bound to act on advice of the Cabinet or other person or authority when required by the Constitution and had the right to be consulted and informed concerning matters of government.[134] Yet the path to constitutional government still did not run smoothly. The 1993 election resulted in a de facto one-party regime as the former opposition Basotho Congress Party (BCP) won all the seats in the legislature. A period of acute political instability and increasing violence followed, fuelled by faction fighting within the ruling party. Moshoeshoe II was restored in 1994 and ruled until his death 1996, when Letsie III once more ascended the throne.

However, in 1998 a general election in which a faction of the BCP swept to power as the Lesotho Congress for Democracy[135] led to political chaos and a breakdown of law and order with opposition parties petitioning the King to nullify the elections. With the government paralysed the Prime Minister summoned outside military assistance. This came in the form of troops from Botswana and South Africa, under the auspices of the Southern African Development Community. That intervention sparked off riots which led to the burning down of business premises and government offices in the capital Maseru and other towns.[136] Although law and order was eventually restored and fresh elections held in June 2002, Lesotho has yet to establish a stable constitutional order which will provide a secure basis for sustainable development.[137]

Swaziland fared no better under King Sobhuza II who was instrumental in the overthrow of the democratic constitution in 1973. Assuming supreme powers by royal proclamation, the King abolished Parliament

[133] Ibid., pp. 167–8. [134] Constitution of Lesotho 1993 ss.91 and 92.

[135] Taking seventy-nine of the eighty seats contested.

[136] K. Matlosa, 'Democracy and Conflict in Post-Apartheid Southern Africa' (1998) 74 *International Affairs* 319, at p. 333.

[137] In the 2002 general election a modified system of proportional representation was introduced in an effort to ensure a voice in the National Assembly for minority parties ('Battered Lesotho tries a proportion of democracy', *The Times*, 25 May 2002).

and banned political parties on the pretext that parliamentary democracy was alien to the Swazi way of life. Since then, under Sobhuza II and his successor, King Mswati III, Swaziland has functioned as an absolute monarchy with supreme executive and legislative power vested in the King. The National Assembly has a purely advisory role, although members are directly elected from non-party candidates chosen by traditional local councils known as *tinkhundlas*. While neighbouring countries sought in the 1990s to liberalise their political systems and introduce multi-party constitutions, Swaziland remained 'an island of aristocratic autocracy in a sea of democratic transition'.[138] With the King's rule facing increasing opposition from civil society groups, he appointed, in 1996, a Constitutional Review Commission. This had minimal effect as it did not complete its report until the end of 2000 and this was never published.[139]

Overall the experiences of Lesotho and Swaziland indicate that a traditional monarchy is a threat to rather than a support of constitutional government. In Lesotho the monarchy has condoned the overthrow of constitutional rule and its own ambitions have proved a source of political instability.[140] In Swaziland, the King was himself responsible for the overthrow of the constitution and the maintenance of an autocracy. Further, the histories of the two countries suggest that the absence of ethnic or religious divisions does not, of itself, prevent the domination of the political order by factional or clan conflicts. Indeed, since 1973, the Swazi dispensation provides a glimpse of what post-independence constitutions in other parts of the ESA region might have looked like had they been based on the development of the notions of indirect rule, propounded by the school of Lugard and Cameron, so as to produce independent monarchies in Barotseland, Buganda and elsewhere.[141]

Overview

The first generation of post-colonial leaders have largely vanished from the political scene. Enjoying what Weber called 'charismatic authority' by

[138] Matlosa, 'Democracy and Conflict', p. 333. See also J. Baloro, 'The Devolution of Swaziland's Constitution: Monarchical Responses to Modern Challenges' (1994) 38 JAL 119.

[139] *Africa Confidential* (2000) 41: 24.

[140] Those in favour of traditional rulership might point to Lesotho where democratic elections on a number of occasions have been the cause rather than the cure of disorder and constitutional upheaval. However, the 2002 election suggests that the electoral system rather than the democratic principle itself may be at fault.

[141] See further the discussion in chapter 2.

virtue of being the leaders who had successfully challenged the colonial power, they created executive dictatorships through the centralisation of state power in their own hands and in so doing strangled the development of democratic institutions. As Wanjala notes, the result was that:

> The African leadership has presided over the plunder and mismanagement of the continent's institutions to such an extent that despair and apathy have replaced hope.[142]

In any discussion on the failure to restrain executive power, it should be appreciated that the Constitution is only one of the sources of that power, though no doubt a supremely important one. The reality of power depends on other factors besides its formal structures as defined in the constitution. Two such factors of overwhelming importance are the character of the individual president and the country's circumstances that include social and political forces, conditions and events. Conditions in Africa may encourage the development of an authoritarian presidency. To begin with, little importance is attached to constitutional sanctions against the abuse of power and there is often a lack of a democratic ethic amongst politicians in the country. The social values of the advanced democracies are enshrined in a national ethic which defines the limits of permissive action by the wielders of power.[143] This national ethic is sanctified in deeply entrenched conventions operating as part of the rules of the game of politics. Thus, although an action may be well within the President's constitutional powers, he or she will not act in this way if it violates the moral sense of the nation, for he or she would then risk attracting the wrath of public censure. When the force of public opinion is sufficiently developed to act as a watchdog, no action that seriously violates the national ethic can hope to escape public condemnation. More than any constitutional restraints, perhaps, it is the ethic of the nation, its sense of right and wrong, and the capacity of the people to defend its ethics, which provides the ultimate bulwark against tyranny.

The traditional African attitude towards power has limited assistance in this regard. Nwabueze argues that in African traditional society, authority is conceived as being personal, permanent, mystical and pervasive. The chief is a personal ruler, and the office is held for life. This pervades

[142] Smokin Wanjala, 'Presidentialism, Ethnicity, Militarism and Democracy in Africa: the Kenyan Example', in J. Oloka-Onyango, Kivutha Kibwana and Chris Maina Peter (eds.), *Law and the Struggle for Democracy in East Africa*. Nairobi: Clari Press, 1996, p. 86.

[143] Nwabueze, *Presidentialism*, p. 397.

all other community relations for he or she is legislator, executive, judge, priest, medium and father of the community.[144] He asserts that these characteristics are reflected in the modern African presidency.[145] Tradition has inculcated in the people a certain amount of deference towards authority.[146] Since the chief's authority is sanctioned in religion, it is a sacrilege to flout it except in cases of blatant and systematic oppression when the whole community might rise in revolt to de-stool, banish or even kill a tyrannical chief. Thus, while customary sanctions against extreme cases of abuse of power exist, there is also considerable public toleration of abuses by the chief. This attitude towards authority tends to be transferred to the modern political leader. The vast majority of the population, many of whom remain illiterate, are not disposed to question the leader's authority and indeed disapprove of those who are inclined to do so.

There is yet another respect in which the conditions in African societies are not conducive to the control of presidential power. In a developing country where there is grinding poverty, mass unemployment, where the state is the principal employer of labour and almost the sole provider of social amenities and where personal ambition for power and wealth and influence rather than principle determines political affiliations and alliances, the president's power to dispense jobs and patronage is a very potent weapon enabling him or her to gain considerable political advantage. Moreover, loyalty secured by patronage can often border on subservience and produces an attitude of dependence and a willingness to accept without question the wishes and dictates of the person dispensing the patronage.[147] Patronage has, therefore, been one of the crucial means by which African leaders have secured the subordination of the legislature, the bureaucracy, the police and the military. This means, therefore, that in order to keep excessive presidential power in check, special attention must be paid to the electoral process and its ability to ensure that qualified candidates are elected to the office of president and the reins of power are held for a strictly limited period. Further, meaningful accountability processes must be maintained. An indirectly elected president provides clear advantages in this area.

Some constitutions have incorporated mechanisms that are designed specifically to provide adequate safeguards on the exercise of presidential power. There is room for some optimism about their effectiveness.

[144] Ibid., p. 107.

[145] Ibid. And of course, in the surviving 'traditional' monarchies discussed above.

[146] Ibid., p. 65. [147] See also the discussion in chapter 13.

The development of a vibrant, more independent media, both print and electronic, has encouraged public debate and criticism that was unthinkable during the period of the one-party state. Criticism of undemocratic practices has become more persistent from a range of civil-society bodies, including a diversity of pressure groups, trades unions and civil associations both formal and informal.[148] Indeed the voice of dissent has even been heard occasionally from presidential supporters. The voice of dissent has also found an ally in the form of the economic recession. The deepening economic crisis has forced governments to become more dependent on western aid and, consequentially, to accept the role of good governance in the development process since this is increasingly insisted upon by donors as a condition for aid. As a result, apart from other factors involved in providing foreign aid, the democratic practices of various regimes and their human rights record have become key factors.[149] As the New Partnership for Africa's Development (NEPAD) initiative progresses, the democratic standing of a nation may well become increasingly significant. With this trend, many states are beginning to respond more positively to criticism of the constitutional and legal arrangements that constrain the democratic participation of the people in the governing of their country and jeopardise effective government accountability. In this situation we may well see a more accountable exercise of presidential power in the ESA states so that the pessimistic view of Nwabueze recorded at the beginning of this chapter may yet become a thing of the past.

[148] See generally Phiroshaw Camary and Anne Gordon (eds.), *Advocacy in Southern Africa: Lessons for the Future*, Johannesburg: Core, 1998.

[149] Patricia Armstrong, 'Human Rights and Multilateral Development Banks: Governance Concerns in Decision Making' (1994) 88 *American Society for International Law Proceedings* 271.

6

Enhancing access to the political system

Introduction

Access to the political system is an integral part of good governance and is fast becoming a normative rule of the international system. Increasingly, governments now have to recognise that their legitimacy depends on meeting the international community's expectations and that those seeking validation of the empowerment process must patently govern with the consent of the governed.[1] 'Access' in this context raises several constitutional issues. These include, firstly, freedom to organise political parties and generally to participate in the political process, including ensuring fair access for women and minorities; secondly, freedom of political expression and the right to campaign free from intimidation or other undue influences; and thirdly, the right of the adult population to vote and to elect or re-elect governments at regular intervals in free and fair elections.[2] It is on such issues that this chapter and the next focus attention.

Political parties and democratic governance

Political parties, defined as distinctive organisations whose principal aim is to acquire and exercise political power,[3] are the dominant feature of

[1] See generally T. Franck, 'The Emerging Right to Democratic Governance' (1992) 86 *American Journal of International Law* 46.

[2] Article 25 of the International Covenant on Civil and Political Rights (ICCPR) provides that every citizen has the right and the opportunity, without unreasonable restrictions to take part in the conduct of public affairs, directly or through freely chosen representatives, and to vote and to be elected at genuine periodic elections which shall be by universal and equal suffrage and shall be held by secret ballot, guaranteeing the free expression of the will of the electors. This right is also recognised in article 21 of the Universal Declaration of Human Rights. The African Charter is somewhat less specific providing that 'Every citizen shall have the right to participate freely in the government of his country, either directly or through freely chosen representatives in accordance with the provisions of the law' (art. 13).

[3] In addition, a political party must enjoy certain minimum characteristics. These normally include a party constitution; a defined party structure including identifiable officers and

contemporary organised political systems. The freedom to organise such bodies is widely viewed as a linchpin to the functioning of democracy because, at least in theory, they perform several essential functions: firstly, by acting as agencies for the articulation and aggregation of different views and interests; secondly, by serving as vehicles for the selection of leaders for government positions; thirdly, by organising personnel around the formulation and implementation of public policy; and fourthly, by serving in a mediating role between individuals and their government.

Political parties in the ESA states have had a chequered history. In the colonial period, they tended to reflect racial identities with 'white' parties such as the United Federal Party in the Rhodesias and Nyasaland facing the growing nationalist movements represented by UNIP/ANC in Northern Rhodesia and the MCP in Nyasaland. In the Rhodesias and Kenya where there were substantial European settler communities, notions of 'multi-racialism' or 'partnership' came into vogue in the last years of colonial rule.[4] After independence, it was the former nationalist parties that seized power and in many cases sought to retain it through the introduction of a one party state. Today, the return to multi-party politics means that there are a plethora of new political parties. In the case of Malawi and Zambia, for instance, these have seized power from the nationalist parties. However, some nationalist parties such as the BDP in Botswana and ZANU(PF) in Zimbabwe still remain in power.[5]

Yet multi-party politics alone does not necessarily ensure just and honest government for political competition presupposes the existence of more than one *effective* political party (or organisation) in a

other party officials; active members; procedures for electing party leaders and other officials; and a published manifesto. A formal registration requirement is also commonplace, for example, to establish its legal personality and for banking and tax purposes.

[4] As to the former, Ghai and McAuslan observe that 'in its concern with groups, regardless of numerical strengths rather than individuals, it was in conflict with the basic premise of a true democratic society' (Y. Ghai and P. McAuslan, *Public Law and Political Change in Kenya*, Oxford University Press, Oxford, 1970, p. 66). On developing a racial partnership between Europeans and Africans in Central Africa, Sir Geoffrey Huggins, the first Prime Minister of the Federation of Rhodesia and Nyasaland succinctly described the relationship as that of a 'rider and the horse'.

[5] Sometimes this is due more to disunity within the opposition than anything else. This was starkly illustrated in the 1992 elections in Kenya where the ruling party KANU received just 24.5 per cent of the vote whilst the eight main opposition parties between them mustered 59.3 per cent. However the disunity of the opposition groups meant that KANU remained the party of government. It took until 2002 for KANU's grip on power since independence to be ended by the victory of the National Rainbow Coalition in the presidential and parliamentary elections.

country.[6] Addressing the underlying problems that inhibit effectiveness is no easy matter. In particular we must acknowledge the often limited focus and outreach of political parties. Thus many parties, especially during the recent era of political pluralism, have emerged in order either to advance the presidential ambition of a particular individual, or to coalesce for short-term political advantage. As a result, viable alternative policies are rarely propounded. Further, the inherent defect of the majority of political parties is their disproportionate concentration on the interests of the most politically conscious in the urban areas. Indeed despite the fact that most people live in rural areas, many political parties scarcely exist beyond the capital city and other major urban centres. Thus such parties do not insert themselves into the conditions, experiences and aspirations of the rural majority. To some extent this is a result of poor communications and their inability to raise funds to enable them to finance their operations countrywide but to a large extent it is a matter of focus.

Problems of factionalism and party funding require special attention.

Factionalism and political parties

Given the longstanding concerns over the need for national unity, some states have placed curbs on political parties that have a regional, religious or ethnic base.[7] One method is to impose strict registration requirements. For example, in Tanzania all political parties must support the union with Zanzibar with parties based on ethnic, religious or regional affiliations forbidden. Parties granted provisional registration may hold public meetings and recruit members but within six months they must submit lists of at least 200 members in ten of the twenty-five regions, including two in Zanzibar, in order to secure full registration and thus be eligible to contest elections. Non-registered political parties are prohibited from holding meetings, recruiting members or fielding candidates.[8]

[6] J. T. Mwaikusa, 'Party Systems and Control of Government Powers: Past Experiences, Future Prospects', in J. Oloka-Onyango, Kivutha Kibwana and Chris Maina Peter (eds.). *Law and the Struggle for Democracy in East Africa*, Claripress, Nairobi, 1996, pp. 79–82.

[7] See, for example, the views of S. Mubako, 'Zambia's Single Party Constitution – a Search for Unity and Development' (1973) 5 *Zambia Law Journal* 67.

[8] See further J. T. Mwaikusa, 'The Limits of Judicial Enterprise in the Process of Political Change in Tanzania' (1996) 40 JAL 242 at pp. 247–50. In Uganda the Constitution prohibits political parties that base their membership on sex, ethnicity, religion or 'other sectional division' (art. 71(a) and (b)). Of course this only comes into effect if and when the country moves away from its 'no party' approach.

Yet a requirement for a 'national character' hampers the formation and operation of political parties and inevitably invites criticism that it is merely a ploy to inhibit political competition.[9] There is also a constitutional dimension in that over-wide restrictions arguably breach the constitutional right to freedom of association and assembly. Such a restriction also overlooks the value of smaller 'single issue' parties or those concerned with purely regional or local issues. As Conrad J. A. in *Reform Party of Canada v A-G of Canada*[10] noted:

> It is the discourse of political views that is important. 'Single issue' or 'fringe' parties may raise for discussion the most critical issues of a particular election. It matters not that they cannot form a government. What is important is the content of the message being communicated.[11]

Basic registration requirements for establishing the legal status of political parties and the like are always necessary. Imposing other restrictions need careful consideration and perhaps the only area where it is appropriate to prohibit political parties is where they advocate the superiority or a dominant status of some ethnic groups over others.[12]

The funding of political parties

Southall and Wood[13] note that party funding has, broadly speaking, proceeded through three phases. First, during the post World War II nationalist phase, mass-based political parties, such as UNIP and ANC in Zambia, were largely funded through party membership subscriptions. External agencies and/or governments interested in influencing the outcome of de-colonization also provided substantial financial support to nationalist

[9] Restrictions on the formation of political parties have led to the development of so-called 'pressure groups'. For example, in Malawi in 1992 the task of organising support for a return to multi-partyism fell on the Public Affairs Committee and the Alliance for Democracy (AFORD) which was formed in September 1992 as a 'pressure group' to avoid being labelled a political party and thus being proscribed. A similar process took place in Zambia with the development of the Movement for Multi-Party Democracy (MMD).

[10] (1995) 117 DLR (4th) 366. [11] Pp. 418–19.

[12] Commonwealth Human Rights Initiative, *The Right to a Culture of Tolerance*, London, 1997, 82. Arguably the outlawing of ethnically based parties is in line with the prohibition on the advocacy of national, racial or religious hatred that constitutes incitement to discrimination, hostility or violence enshrined in article 20 of the ICCPR.

[13] A. Southall and T. Wood, 'Political Party Funding in Southern Africa' in P. Brunell and A. Ware (eds.), *Funding Democratisation*, Manchester University Press, Manchester and St Martin's, New York, 1998, p. 203.

movements. In the second phase, 'the effective merging of the ruling party with state structures which took place during the post-colonial phase was accompanied by ruling parties moving away from reliance upon membership subscriptions to the utilization of state resources'.[14] In the third phase, 'when confronted by the need to embrace a return to multi-partyism in the early 1990s, ruling parties continued to rely principally upon their control of state resources'.[15] In contrast, the new political organisations sought grass-root financing as well as material provision directly or via local non-governmental organisations (NGOs) from foreign donors, both government and private.

Today we have entered a fourth phase where state funding for political parties is recognised as being necessary in order to strengthen democracy and to help create a level political playing field. Firstly, without it, the feasibility of maintaining an effective multi-party system comes into question[16] for such funding can help overcome the lack of financial support that contributes to the high rate of attrition and defection experienced by many newly formed political parties.[17] Secondly, political parties need financial support not only for election campaigns but also to maintain their party organisation between elections. Thirdly, the private sector may be pressurised into refusing funding for minority parties.[18] Fourthly, the constitutional right to impart ideas and information is arguably infringed when a political party is precluded from putting its message across to the electorate by virtue of its impecuniosity.[19]

Regulating the system is essential because the nature and modality of party funding has proved one of the most pernicious aspects of political life. Thus concern about corruption in relation to party funding has led to some states imposing a legal obligation on political parties to declare

[14] Ibid., at p. 203. [15] Ibid., at p. 204.

[16] For example, the majority of respondents to the Mwanakatwe Constitutional Review Commission in Zambia viewed the lack of financial support for political parties as the major reason for the lack of effective opposition parties in the country.

[17] These factors provide an adequate response to those who argue that the state is not obligated to help meet the financial needs of parties and that it should not relieve parties of the risk of failure and the responsibility that goes with it. See Herbert C. Alexander, 'Money and Politics: Rethinking a Conceptual Framework', *Comparative Political Finance in the 1980s* Cambridge University Press, New York, 1989 pp. 9–20.

[18] For example, an intimation to an enterprise by a government minister or officials of the ruling party that lucrative government contracts may be cancelled or not renewed if funding is provided to rival political organisations.

[19] See the decision in the *United Parties* case below. Arguably, such a restriction also represents a potential breach on the constitutional right to freedom from discrimination.

donations exceeding a specified amount as well as the imposition of statutory bars on non-citizens funding such parties.[20]

Controversy also extends to how political parties share the funds, for the principle of public funding does not necessarily mean equality of funding. Commonly a formula is devised determining the amount payable to individual parties and this is a good indication of government's willingness to provide a level playing field. The issue arose in an acute form in Zimbabwe with the Political Parties (Finance) Act 1992 that introduced, for the first time, state funding for political parties. Its provisions were seemingly even-handed. In particular section 3(3) entitled any political party with more than fifteen elected members of Parliament (12 per cent of the total membership) to receive annual state financial assistance. On closer inspection, the Act's major flaw was that ZANU(PF) enjoyed overwhelming parliamentary support (at that time 117 out of the 120 elected members of parliament) and therefore it alone qualified for state funding.

A formula that makes the ruling party the sole beneficiary of state largesse requires a convincing explanation. During the Bill's Second Reading, the Attorney-General informed Parliament that it was intended to:

> Facilitate those political parties who will have demonstrated to the electorate that they are a *serious party* by winning at least 12 per cent [of the parliamentary] seats . . .[21]

He added that state funding would enable such parties to 'service the nation' and to 'execute these duties with facilitation'. Conversely, parties with no parliamentary seats had no such obligations and it was 'improper to burden the taxpayer with the financing of such parties'.

This provokes two comments. Firstly, asserting that only a political party winning a significant number of parliamentary seats is entitled to receive state funding is questionable, particularly when a first-past-the-post electoral system operates. Whilst support for new parties or those representing minority interests, for example, may not have been translated into significant parliamentary representation this does not mean they are not 'serious parties'.[22] For example, in the 1990 Zimbabwe general election the Zimbabwe Unity Movement (ZUM) polled 17 per cent of

[20] Although this may be a pretext for government to ban external funding to minority parties in the hope of preventing them mounting a serious electoral challenge.

[21] Emphasis added. See *Parliamentary Debates*, 27 August 1992.

[22] See again the view of Conrad J.A. in *Reform Party of Canada v A-G of Canada* above.

the popular vote. Under a system of proportional representation, ZUM would have obtained at least twenty-one parliamentary seats and been entitled to receive 17.5 per cent of the state funding. In fact, the first past the post electoral system meant it won just three seats and received no state funding.[23] As a relatively new organisation, ZUM had no national presence but it clearly enjoyed support from a significant proportion of the electorate and was thus a 'serious party'. Secondly, arguing that the qualifying party required state funding to 'service the nation' suggests a continuing inability and/or refusal to separate party activities from those of the state.[24]

The constitutionality of section 3(3) was challenged in *United Parties v Minister of Justice, Legal and Parliamentary Affairs and Others.*[25] Here the plaintiffs argued that the sub-section breached their freedom to receive and impart information without interference. Gubbay C. J., giving the judgment of the Supreme Court, recognised that placing reasonable limitations on the payment of state funds was understandable and that it was determining the appropriate basis that was crucial. The key issue was the effect of the funding system in practice. Here it benefited only one political party despite the fact that another party had obtained 17 per cent of the votes cast. As the Chief Justice pointed out, a 'public funding regime that systematically excludes all but one or two political parties strongly suggests that the threshold is set too high'.[26] The court therefore declared section 3(3) inconsistent with the constitutional right to freedom of expression.[27]

In view of its significance, it is surprising that the party funding is rarely a constitutional issue. The Malawian Constitution requires the state 'where necessary' to provide funds to any political party that secured more than one-tenth of the national votes in parliamentary elections to help it

[23] See J. Moyo, *Voting for Democracy*, Harare University of Zimbabwe Press, 1992, p. 160.

[24] The Attorney-General also informed Parliament that the approach was based on that practiced in Scandinavia, Germany and Poland. He seemingly overlooked the fact that in these countries the receipt of funding by political parties is dependent *either* on the number of parliamentary seats secured *or* on obtaining a certain percentage of the votes cast. This changes the position significantly, the more so in that elections in those countries are based on various forms of proportional representation so that even relatively small parties can obtain a share of the seats.

[25] [1998] 1 LRC 614. [26] Ibid., at p. 626.

[27] The Zimbabwean government was forced to act swiftly to maintain funding for the ruling party with an amendment Bill fixing the threshold for state funding of a political party at 5 per cent of the total vote at the previous general election. See Political Parties (Finance) (Amendment) Act 1998.

'represent its constituency'.[28] Arguably this vague provision still carries an unduly high threshold for access to funding. The South African approach is more promising for in order to 'enhance multi-party democracy' the funding of political parties participating in national and provincial legislatures must be made on an 'equal and proportional basis'.[29] Who makes the relevant assessment based on this uncomfortably vague criteria is not clear and it is surely preferable to provide a specific formula for determining the distribution of the funds.[30] Obtaining 5 per cent of the popular vote in the last general (or local) elections, as suggested in the *United Parties* case, is arguably an appropriate threshold.

Given the threat of corrupt practices, it is curious that no SEA constitution specifically addresses the issue of the control of political funding. Article 118 of the Constitution of the Seychelles is worth considering here. This places the control of funding, including financial support from public funds to political parties, in the hands of an independent Electoral Commissioner.[31]

Overview

The Westminster system is based on the notion of two major political parties dominating parliament. The system is essentially adversarial and confrontational with the 'opposition' party's major preoccupation being to criticise and scrutinise governmental actions and to mobilise popular support for alternative policies in the hope of eventually defeating the government and taking over the reins of power.

Whilst most ESA states have opted to retain a Westminster-style approach, maintaining a traditional competitive political party system is problematic. In particular there is no tradition of a 'loyal opposition' nor of major party differences based on policy or ideology[32] but rather a curious mixture of attempts to weaken possible rival political parties and/or the establishment of a host of small and largely ineffective political parties. Indeed disillusionment with the multi-party system in Uganda

[28] Art. 40(2). [29] S.236.

[30] A mechanism is also needed to ensure that the monies are paid expeditiously, and at the same time, to all qualifying political parties.

[31] The presidential appointment of the office-holder from candidates proposed by the Constitutional Appointments Committee enhances the prospect of an objective distribution exercise.

[32] The term 'opposition parties' is therefore not appropriate. Perhaps the approach in Ghana where the protagonists are referred to as the 'majority' and 'minority' parties is more appropriate.

led to the creation of the Movement system. Whether this is best described as a 'no-party' state or a disguised 'one-party state', its potential advantage is based on the view that it is an inclusive, decentralised system that means all citizens can participate in the country's political life. Certainly the efforts to provide real participatory democracy from the grassroots level upwards through the system of local councils has seemingly proved quite successful. Since its introduction with the coming to power of Yoweri Museveni, Uganda has experienced political stability that is in stark contrast to the previous catastrophic era of bloodshed and the collapse of the rule of law. Whether such a system can survive without Museveni remains to be seen. Similarly, whether it is a system that other ESA states might wish to explore is questionable.[33] But the Ugandan experience demonstrates the need for states to explore anew their approach to party politics and to move from the Westminster confrontation model towards a 'consensus' model.

Holding free and fair elections

While regular periodic elections, by themselves, do not guarantee good governance, they are the obvious and traditional way of ensuring accountability and for providing an institutional framework for the peaceful resolution of conflicts between competing political organisations.[34] However, when the rules are not universally accepted and respected the process becomes controversial and a source of conflict rather than a mechanism for resolving strife.[35] An election must be organised in a manner that is transparent and which ensures the maximum participation of all stakeholders in the political system. Yet some elections are still manipulated or controlled by the ruling party and this can lead to conflict rather than clarifying who has the people's mandate to govern the country. For instance, disputes over the May 1998 elections in Lesotho led to a total breakdown of law and order and the intervention of Southern African Development Community military forces to restore peace in the country. Similarly, the

[33] See art. 70 Constitution of Uganda. Rwanda and the then Zaire have also, at least in theory, dabbled with the Movement system, albeit unsuccessfully.

[34] A point emphasised by the attention paid to it by international and regional human rights instruments: for example article 21 of the Universal Declaration of Human Rights, article 25 of the International Covenant on Civil and Political Rights and article 13 of the African Charter on Human and Peoples' Rights.

[35] D. Anglin, *Conflict in Sub-Saharan Africa*, Bellville: Centre for Southern African Studies, 1997, p. 4.

controversial 1996 Zambian elections led to unprecedented tensions in the country and to an attempted coup.[36] We must also recognise that sometimes electoral irregularities are not necessarily calculated to defraud, but are instead caused by the state's inability to conduct effectively such a formidable managerial and logistical undertaking.[37]

It follows that the development of an appropriate electoral system is a key lever towards the promotion of political accommodation and stability in ethnically divided societies.[38]

Developing an appropriate electoral system

The Westminster export model provides for the first-past-the-post system in single member constituencies. In each constituency the candidate with the most votes is the winner and it is not necessary to obtain an absolute majority. The system's perceived advantage is that it almost invariably leads to one party winning an absolute parliamentary majority and forming a new government, albeit without necessarily obtaining the majority of overall votes cast in the election.

The system is based on the principle of territorial representation, emphasising the relationship between the voters and their representatives.[39] Its potential weakness is that a party's parliamentary representation is determined not only by the number of votes received, but also by their geographical concentration. Should a party's votes be too widely scattered or too highly concentrated it is liable to be under-represented (or not represented at all) in parliament. In such a situation, groups that are numerically small can never win an election and remain permanently

[36] See generally Zambia Human Rights Commission, 'Report, Findings and Recommendations of the Human Rights Commission's Visits to Prisons and Places of Detention Made Between November 1997 and February 1998', Lusaka, Zambia, 1998.

[37] The Report of the Commonwealth Observer Group to the South African Elections, 'End of Apartheid', 26–29 April, 1994 and Final Report of the United Nations Observer Mission in South Africa (UNOMSA) to the United Nations Secretary-General, 26 May 1994 both cite difficulties encountered during the elections which were due to the gigantic nature of the task of organising the first ever democratic election in such a large country.

[38] See Andrew Reynolds, 'Constitutional Engineering in Southern Africa' (1995) 6 *Journal of African Democracy* 86, at p. 100.

[39] B. de Villiers, 'An Electoral System for the New South Africa', in A. Johnson, S. Shezi and G. Brandshaw (eds.), *Constitution-Making in the New South Africa*, Leicester University Press, Leicester, 1993, p. 29. Cf. the *tinkhundla* system in Swaziland where there are fifty-five 'constituencies' or community committees. Candidates are nominated by a show of hands and then reduced in secret ballots to three candidates per *tinkhundla*. Fifty-five Assembly members are then elected in the general election.

aggrieved. It creates permanent losers and permanent winners and hinders the implementation of democratic principles in deeply divided societies that are non-homogeneous.[40]

In this respect, there is much to commend the adoption of a proportional representation system for elections in ethnically and racially divided societies.[41] In this system, political parties compete for support in multi-member constituencies and the division of seats is determined by the actual support a party receives. The main objective of proportional representation, in contrast to the first-past-the-post system, is to ensure that there is a proportional ratio between the votes received and the seats allocated to a particular party. The net effect of proportional representation is that all political parties, and not only the majority or larger ones, are represented in accordance with their support base.[42] The experiences of South Africa and Namibia[43] suggest that proportional representation in one form or another is a more inclusive system than that of the winner-take-all system. If minorities are to accept their legislature, they must be adequately represented in it.[44]

The South African experience highlights the point. Adopting the first-past-the-post system in the 1994 elections would have had serious negative consequences in that it would have denied parliamentary representation to critical minority parties such as the Freedom Front, Democratic

[40] Bogdanor argues that it seems that a national culture unified both ideologically and ethnically may be a precondition for the successful working of the plurality and majority methods. See V. Bogdanor, *The Blackwell Encyclopedia of Political Institutions*, Blackwell, Oxford, 1987.

[41] See, for example, the views of Antonia Nadais, *Choice of Electoral Systems in New Democratic Frontiers*, National Democratic Institute, Washington DC, 1992, 190–203. Further, Guinier points out how proportional representation can be less polarising than conventional race-conscious districting. See Lani Guinier, *Lift Every Voice: Turning a Civil Rights Setback into a New Vision of Social Justice*, Free Press, New York, 1994, p. 117.

[42] There are many variations of both winner take all and proportional-representation systems. See de Villiers, 'Electoral System', at p. 33.

[43] Andre du Pisani, 'Namibia: the Making of a New State in the Region', in Johnson *et al.*, above at p. 234. For opposing views, see Lardeyret who argues that proportional representation tends to reproduce ethnic cleavarages in the legislature (G. Lardeyret, (1991) 2 *Journal of Democracy* 30).

[44] As long ago as 1965, Lewis observed that 'the surest way to kill the idea of democracy in a plural society is to adopt the Anglo-American system of first-past-the post'. He added: 'The vagaries of plurality elections would produce racially exclusive and geographically parochial governments that would exploit a "mandate" from a plurality of the electorate in order to discriminate systematically against minorities.' (A. Lewis, *Politics in West Africa*, Allen and Unwin, London, 1965, p. 71). For other mechanisms to enhance minority participation in the political process see the discussion in chapters 7 and 9 below.

Party and Pan Africanist Congress. In fact proportional representation allowed the South African parliament to be fairly reflective of society as a whole.[45] Of course a system of proportional representation has its own shortcomings for it enables extremist parties to gain parliamentary representation and some consequent legitimacy.[46] There is also the perception that the system leads to weak coalition governments. These objections are far outweighed by the benefits the system contributes to stability and political representation for all population groups in a country. No government, not even one with a large majority, can work effectively if society is perpetually on the verge of permanent breakdown, aggravated by the threats of extra-constitutional action by under-represented minorities. Moreover, proportional representation is arguably more in line with traditional African political organisation which insisted that major decisions affecting the whole community should not be made by a bare majority of the society. As Bentsi-Enchill has observed: 'Our ancestors insisted that everything should be done on achieving the consensus of all key sectors of the community before a decision was made.'[47]

The type of electoral system also seemingly affects the election of women, for the highest proportion of women MPs are found in countries that have proportional or mixed systems. Certainly a proportional system makes it easier for women (and ethnic minorities) to be nominated, although it should be emphasised that it is the whole electoral system that needs examination in order to encourage equal access to political opportunities.

Overall, the benefits of a proportional representation system means that retaining the first-past-the-post system, as is the case in most ESA states, is now inappropriate. Electoral reform is essential.

Maintaining effective electoral commissions

During one-party rule, little turned on the impartiality and independence of electoral commissions as their role was essentially an organisational one on behalf of the ruling party. The era of multi-party politics has now

[45] The results were as follows with number of seats in brackets: African National Congress (252); National Party (82); Inkatha Freedom Party (43); Freedom Front (9); Democratic Party (7); Pan African Congress (5) and African Christian Democratic Party(2). See Final Report of the United Nations Observer Mission in South Africa (UNOMSA) to the United Nations Secretary-General, 26 May 1994.

[46] See, for example, Nadais, *Choice of Electoral Systems*, p. 193.

[47] K, Bentsi-Enchill, 'Civitas Africana: Realizing the African Political Dream' (1965), 2 *Zambia Law Journal* 65, at p. 72.

placed them firmly in the spotlight. Any failure to perform their duties satisfactorily can affect not only the election results themselves, but also the public and international perception of those results and the acceptance or otherwise of the new government.

Electoral commissions are constitutional, multi-member bodies tasked with directing, supervising and controlling the conduct of elections, normally at the national, regional and local levels. They are also required to oversee and control areas in which electoral malpractice is a constant threat. These include the registration of voters, the preparation and publication of voters' registers and the registration of political parties.[48] It follows that electoral commissions must demonstrate independence and impartiality and develop operational effectiveness.

International election observer missions have highlighted perceived failures by electoral commissions and emphasised the need to develop basic operational principles. Devising a suitable appointment process for commission members is one such area. In most ESA states, commissioners are presently appointed by the President (often in consultation with parliament and/or the Judicial Service Commission). Yet any presidential (or executive) involvement in the appointment process is troubling, especially because of his or her direct interest in the outcome of the election. Thus during the 1992 General Election campaign in Kenya the Commonwealth Observer Group received several complaints from opposition parties and other interested groups about the performance of the Electoral Commission and its perceived lack of independence and impartiality. Of particular concern was the refusal of government to allow others to propose nominees to serve on the Commission and, as the Observer Group put it, this would have 'gone some way to increasing confidence in the process'.[49] Placing the electoral commission under the auspices of an independent Human Rights Commission or providing for a fixed membership that includes nominees of major political parties and relevant organs of civil

48 Some are also responsible for determining the boundaries of constituencies, although ideally this is the responsibility of a separate and independent Delimitation Commission. Much of the discussion in this section also applies to the appointment and functioning of such commissions.

49 The Commonwealth Observer Group also received complaints from opposition parties concerning the alleged partiality of the Chairman of the Electoral Commission, Mr Justice Chesoni, who was a presidential appointee. The Group noted that public and judicial records revealed that there were reasonable grounds for challenging his fitness for office. It was public knowledge that he was financially embarrassed and had been removed from office as an Acting Judge of Appeal shortly before his appointment as EC Chairman: for details see Annex IX to the Report. His later appointment by the President as the Chief Justice did little to allay these concerns.

society is perhaps the way forward here. Security of tenure for commissioners is also a prerequisite[50] as is providing them with a fixed term of office that spans two general elections.[51]

The Directorate of Elections (or equivalent) organises and runs the electoral process and normally operates as a separate unit within the relevant government ministry. The Directorate inevitably functions through public servants who supposedly uphold the convention that no action or statement by any public servant should benefit (or be perceived as benefiting) any political party. Given the politicisation of public servants in some states, this is a considerable challenge and not surprisingly it is often breached.[52] The only effective long-term solution is the de-politicisation of all public servants. In the meantime, providing on-going training for all election officials[53] coupled with constant scrutiny of the election commission by political parties, civil society organisations and the media is essential.[54]

An independent and effective commission can also help reduce tensions between political parties. This is well illustrated by the *Political Parties' Code of Conduct* that was developed during the 1994 Namibian Presidential and National Assembly elections. This was a joint project by the electoral commission and political parties and addressed many sensitive areas that might have inflamed political tension including the holding of political rallies[55] and dealing with allegations of voter intimidation.[56] Such a code should be a standard feature of every national and local election throughout the ESA states.[57]

[50] For example, in its 'Report on the 1991 Presidential and National Assembly elections in Zambia', the Commonwealth Observer Group raised concerns over the fact that the President was empowered to remove electoral commissioners at will. This was criticised 'as lacking that degree of independence which would create a feeling of trust among the opposition parties', at p. 14.

[51] This is designed to ensure that experience is retained within the commission.

[52] See, for example the 'Commonwealth Observer Report on the 1996 General Elections in Zambia', Commonwealth Secretariat, 1996, at p. 15.

[53] This is seemingly quite effective; see 'Commonwealth Observer Report on the General Election in Lesotho', Commonwealth Secretariat, 1993 at p. 13.

[54] It is now widely recognised that electoral fraud can also occur well before the election itself through, for example, manipulation of the voters' roll.

[55] 'Parties shall avoid holding rallies close to each other at the same time' (rule 3).

[56] 'All allegations of intimidation and other unlawful conduct in the election campaign shall be brought to the attention of the Police or the Directorate of Elections for action' (rule 9).

[57] Compare the comments of the Commonwealth Observer Group to the Parliamentary Elections in Zimbabwe in 2000: 'We found that the Elections Directorate and the Registrar-General could have been more helpful to Zimbabwe's civil society in its legitimate desire

Elections and the role of the media

Multi-party elections are all about people making choices. To assist them, the electorate must have access to an effective, critical and independent print and electronic media. The emergence of new and vibrant independent newspapers in recent years, many with Internet editions, is a particularly encouraging development. Even so, with newspapers being generally confined to urban areas and given the significant levels of illiteracy, it is radio that is of special importance. Particularly where the electronic media is state-owned, ensuring broadcasters' independence and an even-handed approach to election coverage is paramount. Thus adopting the common practice of reporting favoured candidates' speeches word for word and/or ignoring the views of other political parties is quite unacceptable. The South African Independent Media Commission Act provides a suitable model here. The Act lays down three specific requirements for the treatment of political parties during an election period by broadcasters in their editorial programming. These are (i) that the broadcaster 'shall afford reasonable opportunities for the discussion of conflicting views'; (ii) that each broadcaster shall 'afford [political parties] reasonable opportunity to respond to . . . criticism'; and (iii) that broadcasters must treat all political parties equitably.[58] Providing political parties with the right during election campaigns to broadcast, free of charge, an agreed number of party political programmes can also strengthen the perception of a country committed to holding free and fair elections.

The media's role often extends to assisting in voter education. How to register and how to vote are two essential elements and broadcasting public education programmes on such matters has proved valuable.[59] Sensitising the public to possible electoral malpractice, vote-buying, vote-rigging or the like is also important. Thus people need to know that the

to play a role in monitoring the conduct of the elections . . . For the future we hope that the election authorities will promote a culture of co-operation so far as civil society is concerned. We would have likewise hoped to see the Registrar-General play a mediating role in defusing political tensions and bringing the contesting parties and candidates together to resolve misunderstandings and create a more positive atmosphere for the conduct of the elections' ('The Parliamentary Elections in Zimbabwe', Report of the Commonwealth Observer Group, Commonwealth Secretariat, 2000, p. 34).

58 S.3.

59 See, for example, the Report of the Commonwealth Observer Group to the 1998 National Assembly Elections in Lesotho which noted approvingly that the Independent Electoral Commission used the electronic media to broadcast on election matters for about two hours a week in the run-up to the election and nearly six hours over the two days before the election. It also used dramas and phone-ins to help provide further civic education.

food ostensibly (and very publicly) being distributed by the President to drought-ridden rural areas is not a personal gift from him or her (or the government or ruling party) but an attempt to buy votes using public money.

Yet attempts continue to silence a critical media through physical assaults on, or threats against, journalists and their families and/or the use of draconian criminal laws.[60] Ensuring fair media coverage and protecting journalists from harassment is a multi-faceted issue. A major step forward is the establishing of an independent Media Commission with clearly defined responsibilities. In the context of elections, these should include (i) developing rules on election broadcasting and reporting with all interested parties and reviewing such rules on a regular basis (this could be done through a Code of Practice agreed between all political parties and the media), and (ii) overseeing election broadcasting and hearing and determining complaints of alleged breaches of the Code from aggrieved parties.[61] Such a body might also develop training programmes on election reporting utilising, in particular, experiences from other Commonwealth jurisdictions.

Election monitoring

Disputes over whether or not elections were 'free and fair' raise considerable tensions and can result in violence and political instability.[62] To encourage acceptance of the electoral process, election monitoring has gained considerable popularity in recent years, particularly through the work of the Commonwealth and United Nations. For example, since 1990, Commonwealth Observer Groups have monitored elections in Namibia, South Africa, Malawi, Zambia, Tanzania (including Zanzibar), Kenya, Zimbabwe and Lesotho. Whilst monitoring is only undertaken at the request of the country holding the election, it is attractive in that having an election declared 'free and fair' by experienced international observers carries with it the hope that all political rivals will accept the election results. At the same time, international election observers can also benefit minority political groups by investigating incidents of alleged electoral

[60] Especially through the use of criminal libel laws and the vague security laws often inherited from the former colonial regime. See chapter 7 for further discussion.

[61] This might be in the form of an Independent Media Commission (as in the case of South Africa) or a function of an independent Electoral Commission.

[62] See Anglin, *Conflict*. See also Boutros Boutros-Ghali, *An Agenda for Peace*, United Nations, New York, 1992.

malpractice. Monitors can also offer logistical support to a country that may have little or no experience in registering voters or running an election that emphasises free choice and secret ballots.[63]

Requesting monitoring

Any state can request monitoring but seemingly it cannot be imposed whatever the concerns about the electoral system. This follows from UN General Assembly resolution 46/137[64] which emphasises that all states enjoy sovereign equality; that each state, in accordance with the will of its people, has the right freely to choose and develop its political, social and cultural systems; and that no single political system or electoral method is equally suited to all nations and their peoples. It recognises further that the efforts of the international community to enhance the effectiveness of the principles of periodic and genuine elections should not call into question each state's sovereign right, in accordance with the will of its people, freely to choose and develop its political, social, economic and cultural systems, whether or not they conform to the preferences of other states.

The UN Secretary-General has suggested that four criteria need satisfying before a UN mission is considered. Firstly, requests should pertain primarily to situations that have a clear international dimension and that may relate to the maintenance of international peace and security. Secondly, monitoring should cover, both geographically and chronologically, the entire electoral process, from the initial stages of voter registration to the elections themselves. Thirdly, there should be a specific request from the government concerned as well as broad public and political support within the country for a UN role, and fourthly the competent UN organ should give its approval.[65] The need to avoid legitimising a flawed election explains the insistence that the monitoring involve the entire electoral process. Further, the requirement that a government must request monitoring and that there is broad support within the country for UN and/or Commonwealth involvement also reflects the fact that, without such support, election monitoring is impossible. For the Commonwealth

[63] See United Nations, 'Report of the Secretary-General on ONUMOZ' (S/125518)(1993); 'The End of Apartheid: Report of the Commonwealth Observer Group to the South African Elections', 1994, Commonwealth Secretariat, pp. 22–9.

[64] Resolution 46/137 of 17 December 1991.

[65] See United Nations, 'Report of the Secretary-General to the General Assembly at its Forty-sixth Session' (A/46/609/Corr/1 and Add. 1–2).

this means that before any decision is taken, a small team is sent to gauge the views of the major political parties and without their clear support the Commonwealth will decline to send a monitoring team.

The controversy over the presence of observers from the European Union to the March 2002 presidential elections in Zimbabwe introduced a potentially significant new dimension concerning election monitoring. Here the Zimbabwean government refused to accept certain nationals as members of the EU election monitoring team and as a result, the EU withdrew its entire team and then imposed so-called 'smart sanctions' on President Mugabe and his allies. Based on the sovereignty argument, the Zimbabwean government was within its rights to act as it did. Yet the widespread international concern over state-sponsored intimidation of political rivals cannot be ignored. It is precisely in such situations of political uncertainty and controversy that international election monitors can make a difference. It follows that rather than hiding behind the sovereignty issue, states may have to recognise that an 'emerging right to democratic governance' is the right of any political party to invite international monitoring of elections.[66]

Approaches to monitoring elections

The main focus of international involvement in elections is to ensure that they are free and fair and run in accordance with internationally accepted election norms.[67] In Namibia in 1989, for example, the United Nations developed and applied standards that moved beyond a limited formula and sought to ensure that the election occurred in a free environment and in the context of administratively fair rules. A consensus was developed as to what constituted free and fair elections, the most important standards being: (1) the right of all voters to participate in the electoral process without hindrance; (2) free campaigning for all political parties; (3) a secret ballot; (4) reasonable speed in counting the ballots; (5) accountability and openness of the electoral process to the competing parties; and (6) an acceptable electoral law.[68]

[66] Indeed the Zimbabwean Government's frantic attempt to pass legislation outlawing external election monitoring just weeks before the 2002 presidential election perhaps illustrates its concern at the impact of such exercises.

[67] See in particular article 21 of the Universal Declaration of Human Rights.

[68] See National Democratic Institute for International Affairs, *Nation Building: the United Nations and Namibia*, 1990, NDIIA, Washington, DC, p. 26.

The typical UN observer mandate highlights the key factors that determine whether an election is free and fair. These are to observe:

(a) the actions of the electoral commission and its organs in all aspects and stages of the electoral process and verify their compatibility with the legislation governing free and fair elections in the country; and
(b) the extent of freedom of organisation, movement, assembly and expression during the electoral campaign and ascertain whether adequate measures are taken to ensure that political parties and alliances enjoy those freedoms without hindrance or intimidation.

Further, to verify:

(a) access to the media by all political parties contesting the elections;
(b) whether voter education efforts of the electoral authorities and other interested parties are sufficient and result in voters being adequately informed on both the meaning of the vote and its procedural aspects;
(c) the registration of voters so that qualified voters are not denied the identification documents or cards that would allow them to exercise their right to vote;
(d) that voting occurs on election day in an environment free of intimidation and under conditions that ensure free access to voting stations and the secrecy of the vote;
(e) that adequate measures are taken to ensure the proper transport and custody of ballots and security of the vote count and that a timely announcement of election results is made.

Election monitors themselves are largely drawn from persons experienced in running or participating in elections and, in the case of the Commonwealth, they serve in their personal capacity. During the campaign period they report on voter education and registration, interact with political parties, attend rallies and other public events, investigate complaints, ascertain the adequacy of the electoral infrastructure, determine whether the media coverage is balanced and offer their observations and concerns to the electoral commission. This is a key period, for, as noted earlier, irregularities in the work of an election commission can seriously impact on the poll.

As regards the casting of votes, it is usually impractical to have a 'total observation' system in which an international observer remains at each polling station at all times during the election. Such observers are better employed undertaking 'sample observations', i.e. visiting a selection of polling stations during the actual election. However, local observers can usefully supplement their work (as was the case in South Africa in 1994) and, given appropriate co-ordination, 'total observation' can be achieved.[69]

At the end of the electoral process the international observers certify whether or not the elections were free and fair, i.e. whether any irregularities were of such a magnitude that they undermined the integrity of the process. If this is undertaken as a holistic exercise difficult issues arise. For example, organising an election is a major undertaking for which some ESA countries still have a limited capacity. Thus should irregularities caused by the incompetence or inexperience of election officials be viewed in the same way as those caused by deliberate electoral malpractice? Arguably, the best approach is to deal with the electoral process in phases. Observers must publicly pronounce on the fairness of each and every stage as soon as it is completed, and if necessary, ask for steps to be taken to remedy any defects in that particular process. This should certainly cover the four main stages: voter registration, the election campaign, voting and the counting of votes. In this manner, they are likely to be able to exert greater influence on the electoral process and prevent later controversy. This emphasises that election monitoring is an on-going process and must not be confined solely to the immediate election period.

Overview

International observer missions can make a significant contribution to the electoral process. Even if their findings are not always accurate,[70] declaring an election 'free and fair' lends credibility to the results. Further providing advice on organising and running elections can make an enormous difference to the success of the process, a point exemplified by the work of the Commonwealth's election monitoring team leading up to the 1994 South African elections. Even so, the true value of such missions can only be assessed in respect of 'difficult' cases. Unless observers are prepared to declare that an election was not free and fair, then monitoring is a cruel farce. This is epitomised by the Commonwealth Observer

[69] It is important not to confuse party agents and election observers here. Party agents are the representatives of the interests of their party and are not required to be neutral. In contrast, observers must be neutral.

[70] For example, the May 1998 elections in Lesotho in which the opposition won only one seat were pronounced as 'free and fair' by international observers. The Langa Commission of Inquiry later found them riddled with irregularities. See *Mail and Guardian*, 12 October 1998.

Group's conclusions on the 1992 Kenyan presidential and parliamentary elections. In their report[71] they identified many aspects of the elections that 'were not fair' including the Electoral Commission's lack of transparency, intimidation of voters, partisanship of the state-owned media and the reluctance of government to de-link itself from the ruling KANU party. There was also the 'late delivery of materials, polls with too many voters, lack of adequate training of officials and an ineffective public education programme'.[72] These all fell within the United Nation's checklist noted above but even so the Observer Group concluded that:

> Despite the fact that the whole electoral process cannot be given an unqualified rating as free and fair, the evolution of the process to polling day and the subsequent count was increasingly positive to a degree that we believe that the results in many instances directly reflect, however imperfectly, the expression of the will of the people.[73]

Concern was expressed in many quarters over the Observer Group's perceived failure to pronounce the poll invalid and this undoubtedly significantly reduced the credibility of the whole process.[74]

Those anxious to see international observer groups denounce fraudulent elections can gain some comfort from the Commonwealth response to the 2002 presidential election in Zimbabwe. Here the Commonwealth Observer Group concluded: 'The Presidential Election was marred by a high level of politically motivated violence and that the conditions in Zimbabwe did not adequately allow for a free expression of will by the electors'.[75] As a result, the Commonwealth Chairpersons' Committee on Zimbabwe decided to suspend Zimbabwe from the Councils of the Commonwealth for one year but mandated the Commonwealth Secretary-General to engage with the Government of Zimbabwe 'to ensure that the specific recommendations from the Commonwealth Observer Group Report, notably on the management of future elections, in Zimbabwe are

[71] Report of the Commonwealth Observer Group, *The Presidential, Parliamentary and Civic Elections in Kenya*, Commonwealth Secretariat, 1993.

[72] Ibid., at p. 39. [73] Ibid., at p. 40.

[74] Including some in the Commonwealth Secretariat itself. *The Independent* (UK) of 25 January 1993 charged that the 'Commonwealth failed Kenya', that the observers had 'ducked the crucial issue' by failing to pronounce the poll invalid and, as a group, were prepared 'to tolerate fraud and clumsily avoid a damning verdict'. An unconvincing attempt was made by the Commonwealth Secretary-General to defend the group: see *The Independent*, 1 February 1993.

[75] Quoted from the 'Marlborough House Statement on Zimbabwe' 19 March 2002, para 3.

implemented'.[76] This is a sensible approach as it leaves open the possibility of maintaining a 'constructive dialogue' that may provide an opportunity for positive change.

Challenging election results

When pre-election violence, corrupt practices and/or intimidation has allegedly occurred or defeated candidates and parties dispute the veracity of election results, it is the duty of the courts to hear election petitions and, in appropriate cases, to set aside election results. It follows that any attempt to oust the jurisdiction of the courts to hear election petitions is a matter of grave concern. This is epitomised by another example from Zimbabwe.

In 2000 President Mugabe promulgated the Election Act (Modification) (No. 3) Notice.[77] Through it he purported to use statutory powers under the Election Act to 'validate' any corrupt and illegal practices in the June 2000 general election. This was in response to a series of electoral petitions from a minority party, the Movement for Democratic Change, which alleged electoral malpractice in thirty-eight constituencies in the June 2000 election. In a quite extraordinary and bizarre preamble, the Notice sought to validate the election results by a series of assertions, as follows:

> RECOGNISING that the general elections held following the dissolution of Parliament on the 11th April, 2000, were held under peaceful conditions and that the people who voted did so freely and that the outcome thereof represents a genuine and free expression of the people's will;
>
> NOTING that the candidates who lost in that general election have instituted civil suits challenging the results and that these suits are frivolous and vexatious as evidenced by the results of the recount of the ballot papers relating to some constituencies;
>
> REGRETTING that the litigation referred to above is sponsored by external interests whose motives and intentions are inimical to the political stability of Zimbabwe;

[76] Ibid., paras 8 and 9. The Committee consisted of the Prime Minister of Australia and the Presidents of Nigeria and South Africa. Their mandate from the Commonwealth Heads of Government was to 'determine appropriate Commonwealth action on Zimbabwe in the event of an adverse report from the Commonwealth Observer Group' ibid., para 2. The suspension was later extended to December 2003. See further p. 11 above.

[77] SI 318 of 2000.

> CONCERNED that the institution of such litigation has placed intolerable burdens on duly elected Members of Parliament and is compromising their duties as Members of Parliament;
>
> CONCERNED further that the multiplicity of such suits has already over-stretched the limited resources of the Registrar-General of Elections and the judicial system and other national resources and that the involvement of external interests is undermining the political stability of Zimbabwe and the democratisation process;
>
> NOW, THEREFORE, in the interests of democracy and the peace, security and stability of Zimbabwe it is hereby notified that His Excellency the President, in terms of section 158 of the Election Act has made the following Notice.

The Notice itself purported to validate the election of candidates in the following terms:

> The election of a [member of Parliament] shall not be rendered void . . . nor shall he or his election agent be made subject to any incapacity . . . upon a finding that any contravention of the [Electoral] Act was committed with reference to the election, and the doing of anything in connection with, arising out of or resulting from the general election . . . which is or may be such a contravention is to that extent hereby validated and shall be deemed not to be such a contravention.

In *The Movement for Democratic Change and Mushonga v Chinamasa NO*[78] the applicants (who included one of the unsuccessful candidates in the June 2000 election) sought a Supreme Court order setting aside the Notice. They argued that it infringed their constitutional right to protection of the law and, in particular section 18(9) of the Constitution that provides:

> . . . every person is entitled to be afforded a fair hearing within a reasonable time by an independent and impartial court or other adjudicating authority established by law in the determination of the existence or extent of his civil rights and obligations.

The Supreme Court noted[79] that the right of full and unimpeded access to courts is of cardinal importance for the adjudication of justiciable

[78] [2001] 3 LRC 673.

[79] It is worth recording that this highly sensitive case came before the Supreme Court in January 2001 at a time when there was considerable tension between the judiciary and the government. Prior to this, the lead judgment in constitutional cases was almost invariably delivered by the Chief Justice. On this occasion, the judgment was delivered by 'The Full

disputes for it ensures 'a mechanism by which such disputes are resolved in a peaceful, regulated and institutionalised manner'.[80] The court held that the existing civil right of the applicants was to participate in a free and fair election and that they were legitimately entitled to expect that the result in every constituency would be free and fair and properly representative of the will of the voters. Therefore they had a civil right to challenge in the High Court the result of an election which was claimed to have been tainted by corrupt and illegal practices. The Notice had effectively denied them such access. Accordingly, it was declared null and void as being contrary to section 18(9).[81] More generally, the President's blatant attempt to undermine the electoral and judicial system merely emphasises the enormous (and sometimes seemingly impossible) task of curbing presidential excesses.

Court'. This is only explicable as a ploy to emphasise the unity of the Court and is a sad reflection on the political pressures being faced by the judges.

80 Ibid., at p. 683.

81 In contesting election results, one issue is whether witnesses are entitled to keep their identity secret in the face of well-grounded fears of intimidation and harassment. This is essentially a matter of discretion for the court but should generally be exercised in favour of the complainants.

7

Making legislatures effective

The return of multi-party democracy to ESA states has renewed interest in the role of parliaments and parliamentarians. As discussed in chapter 5, the executive's right to govern derives from the legislature and, as Fall puts it, legislatures are:

> One of the crucial elements in a democratic society and essential in ensuring the rule of law and protection of human rights. In fact, in their daily work of transforming the will of the people into law and in controlling the executive and public administration, parliaments and parliamentarians are often the unsung heroes of human rights.[1]

Executive dominance of the legislature means that others are less sanguine and regard them as largely 'rubber-stamp' bodies. Some have even questioned the competency of members themselves. As a former Speaker of the House of Assembly in Zimbabwe once reportedly put it:

> I do no think the calibre of members is very good; that is why parliament is meaningless . . . I wonder if some MPs read newspapers and books or even discuss with friends before coming to parliament.[2]

Such critical views probably represent the majority of opinion. Yet good governance requires that legislatures function effectively and this chapter explores some ways in which Fall's view might yet be achieved.

Membership of the legislature

The calibre and make-up of parliament is key to developing an effective legislature. There are some standard, and largely uncontroversial, grounds relating to disqualification from membership. These commonly include allegiance to a foreign state, mental incapacity, being an undischarged

[1] See *Parliament: Guardian of Human Rights*, International Parliamentary Union, Geneva, 1993, p. 5.

[2] For his pains he was found guilty of contempt of Parliament and severely reprimanded by the Speaker. See *Mutasa v Makombe* [1997] 2 LRC 314.

bankrupt or being under sentence of death or serving a prison sentence of a specified length.[3] Of more concern are the age, literacy and language qualifications that feature in some states. As the right to vote is almost universally exercisable from the age of eighteen years, it is curious that some constitutions still require a minimum age of twenty-one years for election to parliament. This is unnecessary particularly because young voters form a significant proportion of the electorate and have their own specific needs, concerns and interests. It follows that, far from limiting their participation, states should encourage young persons to enter parliament. Some constitutions impose specific educational qualifications on parliamentary candidates whilst others require proficiency in English.[4] The language requirement is a sensitive one. It is important to consider giving local languages the same status as English which, in any event, may be the second or third language of many members. Certainly the use of a local language may improve the quality and intensity of debates. However, problems emerge when a choice of language is available. As South Africa is finding, it is very expensive to produce legislative texts and other documents in numerous languages as well as providing suitable translators and interpreters. One further restriction concerns the position of public servants who are, in some states, barred from standing for election. This is quite unreasonable and the appropriate formulation is to require such persons to resign from office immediately after election.[5]

The fact that elected members of parliament are *representatives* of the people does not mean that they are necessarily *representative* of the people. Factors such as the selection process for party candidates and the electoral system itself mean that it is probably unrealistic to seek, through the normal electoral process, a legislature that accurately reflects society. As the state has an interest in encouraging a representative legislature, rewarding financially those political parties that take adequate steps to ensure their candidates reflect as far as possible the nation's gender and ethnic balance is a potentially helpful approach. Even so, maintaining a representative legislature may require other strategies.

[3] This is on the basis that prisoners cannot take up their seats in the legislature. This is unconvincing, for a government may seek the imprisonment of political opponents by the laying of false charges in order to remove them from the political scene.

[4] Has completed a minimum formal education of advanced level standard or equivalent (Uganda, art. 80(1)(c)); has attained a satisfactory standard of English (Malawi, s.51(1)(b)); is literate and conversant with the official language (Zambia art. 64(c)).

[5] As is the case in Uganda. See art. 80(3) Constitution of Uganda. This principle should not apply to the police or members of the security forces: see the discussion below.

Nominating a fixed number of additional members is one approach. In theory, this not only makes the legislature more representative but also helps strengthen its membership. In particular it supposedly allows entry for those who do not wish to be involved in the rough and tumble of party politics but who bring with them special expertise, status, skill or experience. The nomination system remains popular. Indeed it was introduced in Tanzania as recently as 2000.[6] Yet as a system it has serious shortcomings. In particular, the President often has the sole power to nominate members. This has led to appointments being made on the grounds of loyalty to the incumbent and further enhances the presidential grip over the legislature.[7] A further concern is that although unelected, nominated members may hold the balance of power or provide the government with the necessary majority to undertake constitutional amendments. In reality, even if experts are needed, the President can hire them as 'special advisers' whilst parliamentarians can invite them to give evidence before parliamentary committees. It follows that, in principle, the system of nominated members is detrimental to Parliament. However, where they are retained, a more appropriate nomination and appointment procedure is needed. This might be overseen by an independent and fully representative Electoral Commission. Further, to eliminate their potential political influence, the Namibian approach of denying them parliamentary voting rights could be adopted.[8]

Holding separate elections for members representing 'special interest' groups is another approach. This system is now well established in Uganda where the legislature consists not only of directly elected members and women members (see below), but also elected representatives of the army, youth, workers and persons with disabilities.[9] The 'special interests' system provides parliamentary seats to members from groups that are likely to be otherwise under-represented and whom their peers have elected. Of course it begs the question as to which special groups to include although this is arguably a matter for individual states. The one caveat concerns the security forces. The right of the Ugandan armed forces to elect ten representatives to parliament is a concern. It suggests

[6] By a constitutional amendment: see Act 3 of 2000, s.11.

[7] Particularly objectionable is the practice of nominating former government ministers and presidential supporters who have been rejected by the electorate in the general election.

[8] Art. 46(1)(b) Constitution of Namibia.

[9] Art. 78 Constitution of Uganda. Youth is represented, for example, by four persons elected by their respective regions and a fifth, who must be female, elected by the national youth conference.

that the military is entitled to share in the legislative process on the same terms as civilians. Some may argue that this strengthens the military's commitment to and involvement in the democratic process and ensures that their voice is heard in national debates. Whilst superficially attractive, there are theoretical and practical problems here. In particular, the military's role must always remain limited to operational matters with policy issues being strictly a civilian matter. Any alteration of this position can adversely affect the delicate civilian–military relationship,[10] the more so in that such representatives are likely to support the views of the Armed Forces Commander in Chief, i.e. the President. Uganda's chaotic constitutional history probably accounts for the position there but it is not a model for other countries and this is widely recognised.[11]

A second chamber can also contribute towards a more representative legislature. In particular it can either reflect the state's federal or quasi-federal nature with the second chamber comprising a popularly elected body of regional representatives, as in South Africa, or provide access for special groups.[12] Even so, with such chambers normally enjoying only limited powers, members of these groups will probably have less impact than if they formed part of the lower chamber.

Including chiefs and other traditional leaders, elected by a Council of Chiefs or the like, can make the legislature more representative. However, ambivalence towards their role in national affairs may restrict them to providing an authoritative voice on customary law issues. Thus in Botswana there is a separate House of Chiefs, now known as the *Ntlo*

[10] See chapter 11. It might be noted that in 1979 in Ghana, proposals for a 'Union Government' in which political power would be shared amongst all sections of society including the military provoked massive dissent and brought about the downfall of the then military leader General Acheampong.

[11] For example, the Constitutions of Malawi, s.51; Namibia, art. 47; South Africa, s.47; and Zambia, art. 65 all disqualify serving members of the military and police from standing for election.

[12] For example the proposed composition of the Senate in Malawi provided for thirty-two of the eighty senators to come from 'interest groups' including women's organisations, the disabled, the health, education, farming and business sectors and from trades unions: see s.68(1), Constitution of Malawi. Also to be included were individuals 'who are generally recognized for their outstanding service to the public or contribution to the social, cultural or technological development of the nation' and representatives of the major faiths in Malawi. The Senate was never established and was formally abolished by a 2001 constitutional amendment. An unsatisfactory approach was that in Zimbabwe between 1980 and 1986 where the Senate was an indirectly elected upper chamber that merely reflected the make-up of the lower house – thus giving the ruling party an overwhelming majority and rendering nugatory any effective oversight role. The Senate played no useful part in the political life of the country and was abolished in 1986.

ya Dikgosi. Concerns over the inherent conservatism of traditional leaders ensured that the House does not form part of the legislature and its functions are accordingly restricted. This said, it must be consulted on all issues relating to customary matters and on Bills concerning tribal land and chieftainship.[13]

Seeking gender equality

ESA constitutions enshrine the formal equality of participation between women and men in the political process. In practical terms, a critical mass figure of some 30 per cent is generally regarded as the minimum number of women parliamentarians necessary to sustain and advance gender equality[14] but as the table on p. 128 indicates, only South Africa comes close to achieving even this target.

Women in parliament in the ESA states

Explanations for the low number of women parliamentarians largely fall into two categories. The first deals with the so-called 'electability' question. The main thrust is that women candidates are not popular with voters and so political parties are reluctant to adopt them as candidates. A variation is that there are just not enough women of suitable calibre and experience available to put up as candidates. These are spurious arguments. Yet it requires positive action, particularly through the democratisation of political parties, to lay them to rest. In 1997 the African Symposium on Gender, Politics, Peace, Conflict Prevention and Resolution made a number of helpful recommendations in this regard. Firstly, governments should ensure that where public funds are allocated to political parties, these are made equally available to female and male candidates. Secondly, NGOs, the private sector and others should establish funds and support mechanisms for women candidates and parliamentarians. Thirdly, political parties should ensure that women candidates are assigned to seats

13 S.85 Constitution of Botswana. Proctor has pointed out that when the House of Chiefs was originally proposed, the chiefs favoured a British House of Lords model. This was rejected by politicians who feared that such a chamber in a bi-cameral parliament would seriously erode efforts to modernise the country. See J. H. Proctor, 'The House of Chiefs and the Political Development of Botswana' (1968) 6 *Journal of Modern African Studies* 59. See further the discussion in chapter 8.

14 In November 1996 the Fifth Meeting of the Commonwealth Ministers Responsible for Women's Affairs recommended that member countries be encouraged to achieve a target of not less than 30 per cent of women in decision-making in the political, public and private sectors by the year 2005. This is also the goal of the Southern Africa Development Community (SADC).

COUNTRY	NAME OF ASSEMBLY	NUMBER OF WOMEN REPRESENTATIVES	TOTAL NUMBER OF REPRESENTATIVES	WOMEN REPRESENTATIVES AS A PERCENTAGE OF THE TOTAL NUMBER
BOTSWANA	NATIONAL ASSEMBLY	8	49	16.3
BOTSWANA	HOUSE OF CHIEFS	0	15	0
KENYA	NATIONAL ASSEMBLY	9	224	4.0
LESOTHO	NATIONAL ASSEMBLY	3	80	3.8
LESOTHO	SENATE	10	33	30.3
MALAWI	NATIONAL ASSEMBLY	18	193	9.3
NAMIBIA	NATIONAL ASSEMBLY	18	78	23.1
NAMIBIA	NATIONAL COUNCIL	2	26	7.7
SOUTH AFRICA	NATIONAL ASSEMBLY	121	400	30.3
SOUTH AFRICA	NATIONAL COUNCIL OF PROVINCES	8	54	14.8
SOUTH AFRICA	PROVINCIAL LEGISLATURES	119	433	27.4
SWAZILAND	HOUSE OF ASSEMBLY	4	65	6.2
SWAZILAND	SENATE	6	30	20.0
TANZANIA	NATIONAL ASSEMBLY	46	275	16.7
UGANDA	NATIONAL ASSEMBLY	51	279	18.3
ZAMBIA	NATIONAL ASSEMBLY	15	158	9.45
ZIMBABWE	PARLIAMENT	22	150	14.7
TOTALS		460	2542	18.1

Source: Commonwealth Parliamentary Association, 2001

where they stand a good chance of winning (where a constituency-based system exists) or are strategically placed on the list (in a proportional representation system). This is reflected in South Africa where the relatively high number of women members is attributable largely to aggressive demands by the ANC Women's League for women's participation in the political process both during and after the negotiations for the new constitution.[15] Appointing more women to executive roles within political parties themselves (and not relegating them to the Womens' Affairs departments, womens' brigades or the like) can also help encourage the advancement of women.[16] Using quotas or reserving seats for women is another possible approach. Thus in Uganda women are entitled to elect one woman from each district to parliament[17] whilst in Tanzania up to 20 per cent of parliamentary seats are reserved for women.[18] Although useful, quotas and the like are, at best, a strictly temporary measure and securing adequate and long term representation for women lies in working to make the conditions conducive for their entry into parliament through the normal electoral process.

The second set of 'explanations' are based on practical considerations concerning the nature of the legislature itself. It is said that legislatures are masculine institutions and the adversarial, aggressive and confrontational system makes it an inhospitable place for women. In addition, parliament's long hours and physical demands make it difficult for women to combine a parliamentary career with a family life. Such arguments are merely an excuse used to seek to maintain the status quo. The real problem is cultural bias on the part of men. The challenge then is to provide facilities enabling women to participate effectively. These might include moving towards a consensus rather then a confrontational parliamentary model, adjusting meeting times and dress codes, and making available adequate crèche and child-minding facilities.

Overall, the issue is not about percentages, quotas or reserved seats, useful as they are in the short-term. The need is to democratise political parties and to overcome the cultural biases that prevent the full participation of women in the political process.[19]

[15] In comparison, the figure for women parliamentarians in the last apartheid government was 2.3 per cent.

[16] See the *Latimer House Guidelines*, para IV. 1.

[17] Art. 78(1)(b) Constitution of Uganda.

[18] S.11 of Act 3 of 2000.

[19] For useful details about the use of organisational strategies to overcome barriers to the participation of women in both Uganda and South Africa see WEDO, *Getting the Balance* Women's Environment and Development Organization New York, 2001 and UNDP,

Maintaining executive accountability

> Parliamentary procedures should provide adequate mechanisms to enforce the accountability of the Executive to Parliament.
>
> (*Latimer House Guidelines*)

Some aspects of presidential and ministerial accountability to the legislature were discussed in chapter 5. This section examines other accountability mechanisms available to the legislature in a functioning multi-party parliamentary democracy.[20] These fall into three general categories: oversight of executive action; oversight of public spending; and oversight of legislation.[21] In carrying out their work, parliamentary privilege provides a vital protection for members.[22] The ancient right of freedom of speech is perhaps its most important aspect and is encapsulated in the provision: 'That the freedom of speech, and debates or proceedings in Parliament, ought not be impeached or questioned in any court or place out of Parliament'.[23] The principle is firmly established in ESA legislatures and remains the basis for prohibiting outside action of any kind against parliamentarians for what they may say in the legislature, including any of its committees.

The Speaker

The Speaker enjoys numerous constitutional powers, many involving personal discretion over the control and conduct of parliamentary proceedings and the protection of parliamentary privilege. The Speaker is always a member of the legislature and is elected by members themselves. Ideally the appointment should attract cross-party support thus emphasising the Speaker's neutral role and lending support to the view that he/she represents the legislature's interests in its dealings with the executive (and the judiciary). This is further emphasised by prohibiting

Women's Political Participation and Good Governance: Twenty-First Century Challenges United Nations, New York, 2000.

20 These largely derive from those adopted in the British Parliament with *Erskine May's Parliamentary Procedure* remaining the parliamentary 'bible'.

21 Another key oversight function, the approval of a state of emergency, is considered in chapter 12.

22 These relate to the privileges, powers and immunities that are often enshrined by statute or Standing Orders and are almost invariably based on those existing in the United Kingdom Parliament. In some countries, the 'law and custom of the Parliament of England' is specifically said to apply (as modified by any local statutory provisions). See, e.g., art. 87, Constitution of Zambia.

23 Article 9 of the Bill of Rights (UK) (translated into modern English by the authors).

the appointment to the office of any serving member of the executive. Yet the politicising of the Speaker's role has occurred all too frequently with former senior Cabinet Ministers being elected or former Speakers being 'rewarded' with senior Cabinet positions. Accordingly greater scrutiny as to the appointment process and qualifications for the post of Speaker is required.[24]

It follows that a weak Speaker can seriously affect the legislature's work and effectiveness. For instance, in some ESA states it is the Speaker who determines the date for the commencement of a new parliamentary session.[25] So it is quite possible for an executive-minded Speaker to delay calling parliament into session when there is a fear that members may seek to impeach the President.[26] This highlights again the desirability of members themselves having the right to choose the time and place of parliamentary sessions and sittings.[27]

Oversight of executive action

Parliamentary questions

Parliamentary questions (PQs) provide members from all political parties with an opportunity to interrogate Ministers on current issues and events that fall within the mandate of their ministry. PQs are especially useful for they are one of the few ways in which back benchers can raise their concerns publicly and expect a public ministerial reply.

The value of the exercise varies from parliament to parliament but common problems persist. One is that Ministers do not always turn up on time, or at all, to answer questions (often pleading 'affairs of state'). This requires a strong, independent Speaker who is prepared to intervene and ensure Ministers comply timeously with their parliamentary responsibilities. Keeping a register of recalcitrant Ministers and publishing it

[24] For instance, a prohibition on Ministers in the previous administration standing for election or on the appointment of an outgoing Speaker to any political post for a specific period.

[25] Article 95(2) of the Constitution of Uganda provides: 'A session of Parliament shall be held at such place within Uganda and shall commence at such time as the Speaker may, by Proclamation, appoint.'

[26] A situation that occurred in Zambia in 2001.

[27] Article 95(5) of the Constitution of Uganda provides: '. . . at least one-third of all members of Parliament may, in writing signed by them, request a meeting of Parliament; and the Speaker shall summon Parliament to meet within twenty-one days after receipt of the request'. An alternative approach in the Namibian Constitution states: 'The National Assembly [Parliament] shall sit . . . (b) for at least two sessions during each year to commence and terminate on such dates as the National Assembly might from time to time determine' (art. 62(1)(b)).

periodically in a 'name and shame' exercise might help here. A further weakness is that members often have little or no assistance with researching questions and ministerial answers and are thus unable to respond to or challenge effectively Ministers who are reluctant to provide full or reasoned answers.[28]

Even the most effective PQ system suffers from the fact that it operates only when parliament is in session and inevitably there are often significant periods when it is not sitting. Events do not wait for its reconvening and whilst there is normally provision for the recall of parliament in the event of an emergency situation, this is only at the President's behest. It follows that a useful practical alternative step is to provide the Speaker with the same authority to reconvene parliament. More generally, there is also much to support a system of written parliamentary questions and answers even when parliament is not in session. These might be limited to 'urgent' matters (perhaps as defined by the Speaker) but would require a public ministerial response within a fixed period of time and would retain an on-going scrutinising role for back benchers.

Parliamentary debates

Standing orders determine the opportunities for debate in the legislature. Inevitably, government business takes priority and this leaves limited time for back benchers to debate matters of their choice.[29] One potentially significant right of members is seeking leave from the Speaker to hold a debate on a matter of urgent public importance. This provides an opportunity for highlighting key issues of public concern although its usefulness depends largely upon members' access to information, their willingness to question executive action (or inaction) and the Speaker's independence.

Parliamentary committees

Some of parliament's most effective work is done in committees.[30] Normally these comprise an all-party group of members who oversee

[28] The need to improve members' access to information is discussed below.

[29] This is another good reason for leaving members to decide the length of parliamentary sessions.

[30] Entrenching at least the major parliamentary committees in the constitution provides added protection for their work. For example, article 96(1) of the Tanzanian Constitution provides for the establishment of eight parliamentary standing committees: the Steering Committee; Finance and Economic Committee; Constitutional and Legal Affairs Committee; Political Affairs Committee; Public Accounts Committee; Parastatal Organisations Committee; Foreign Affairs Committee; and General Purposes Committee. The National Assembly may also establish other committees as appropriate.

key areas of public life, such as defence, foreign affairs, public spending, and who can call ministers and public servants to formal (normally public) hearings to account for their actions. Their particular value lies in the fact that the development of expertise by committee members should ensure that they are better able to oversee the work of specific areas of government and publicly raise concerns when all is not well.[31]

Developing an oversight role

The 'we did not know what was going on' defence has often been used in the face of accusations that parliamentarians have failed to speak out or take action to prevent executive lawlessness. For example, the gross human rights violations that occurred in Matabeleland, Zimbabwe, during the 1980s took place whilst Parliament remained in session. Yet there was little or no effort made by members to penetrate, or even question, the veil of secrecy that was drawn over security forces' activities. Members palpably failed to question Ministers about these activities and meekly assented to every government request to renew the state of emergency under whose guise many of the atrocities were perpetrated.[32] As a later report on the atrocities pertinently asks:

> Why was it that these human rights violations could occur on our very doorstep without most of us knowing about it? Why is it that it has taken so long for victims to be heard?[33]

If parliaments and parliamentarians wish to be taken seriously, they must be prepared to debate and investigate such issues. The tools with which to do so are already to hand. What is often needed is access to relevant information and a willingness to use it. A good way of alleviating an information vacuum comes from South Africa where the Human Rights Commission is required to submit an annual report to Parliament on the state of human rights in the country. Aimed at ensuring that parliamentarians have an objective and reliable assessment of the human

[31] In Botswana, for example, the Parliamentary Law Reform Committee is tasked with reviewing the operation of legislation and making recommendations for law reform. Whilst this task is probably best undertaken by a separate law reform commission, it emphasises another way in which a parliamentary committee can oversee executive action (or inaction).

[32] See further the discussion in chapter 12.

[33] *Breaking the Silence: Building True Peace – A Report on the Disturbances in Matabeleland and the Midlands 1980–1988*, Catholic Commission for Justice and Peace in Zimbabwe/Legal Resources Foundation, CCJP, Harare, Zimbabwe, 1997, p. 213.

rights situation, this procedure can help prevent the 'we did not know' syndrome.[34]

Moving further afield, the 'partnership' approach adopted by the New Zealand Human Rights Commission also provides an excellent model for developing a meaningful relationship between parliamentarians and human rights commissions. In the Foreword to its publication *Information on Human Rights for Members of Parliament* that is given to every MP, the Chief Commissioner sets out an appropriate approach:

> Yours is the responsibility to provide a legislative environment, both domestically and internationally, in which all people present in New Zealand, both the privileged and marginalised, can reach their full potential to the benefit of us all.
>
> Commissioners and staff of the Human Rights Commission are your partners in this task. *Information and assistance is freely available to you.* Together we have a responsibility to protect and promote the human rights of the people of Aotearoa/New Zealand.
>
> The Commission is committed to keeping MPs as well briefed as possible on human rights issues. To this end we will provide you with topical updates to this folder, occasional papers based on work done by and for the Commission and bring you up to date with other news as appropriate.

The development of this type of 'partnership' is still in its infancy and operates at a formal level in only a handful of countries worldwide. Even so, it is an approach that is worth developing in the ESA states. In the interim, introducing a standing order in all ESA states requiring parliamentary debate on the annual reports of, in particular, the ombudsman, human rights commission, anti-corruption commission (if any) and auditor-general, together with a requirement for the executive to respond formally to the issues raised would be a useful step forward.[35]

Oversight of public spending[36]

Although Ministers may seek to circumvent the legislature in other respects, annual parliamentary approval for the financing of government

[34] The South African Parliament seemingly has no statutory duty to debate such reports and this is an unfortunate oversight.

[35] Rather than merely requiring the reports to be laid before parliament.

[36] For a useful comparative overview of this complex area see generally J. Wehner, 'Parliament and the Power of the Purse: the Nigerian Constitution of 1999 in Comparative Perspective' (2002) 46 JAL 216.

remains a constitutional necessity. It follows that a rigorous and well-informed scrutinising exercise of government financial management systems is a most effective method for parliament to exercise its oversight role and ensure that the public obtains as clear and detailed information as possible about government spending.

Most constitutions explicitly assign budget preparation to the executive in one form or another. In Kenya, Zambia and Zimbabwe, the function is assigned to the Finance Minister, in Uganda the President has the duty, whilst in Malawi and Namibia it is a Cabinet responsibility. Given the perennial shortage of financial resources, choices are inevitable. These may have a clearly defined basis such as the fulfilment of an election pledge, compliance with a constitutional or statutory requirement, or in accordance with the terms demanded by an externally imposed economic structural adjustment programme. Yet choices may also involve other, more troubling, aspects raising concerns about possible corrupt or improper motives on the part of policy-makers or the failure to prioritise expenditure appropriately.

Effective parliamentary scrutiny compels the executive to justify publicly the reasons for its choices and is a major contribution towards fiscal transparency. The government is forced to take the greatest care both with its budget preparation and presentation and with its public spending proposals. It must seek to demonstrate to the legislature that it has made rational choices and to defend itself against concerns over, for example, continued high defence spending or other allegedly wasteful financial practices. Transparency in financial management also requires abandoning the practice of prohibiting parliamentary debate on, or scrutiny of, the presidential vote. This vote often constitutes a huge financial 'black hole' that potentially hides all manner of nefarious activities. Further, it encourages the perception that somehow the President is above the law and Parliament. Once again we must not forget that s/he is merely an elected servant of the people who remains answerable to the people. To deny parliamentary scrutiny of the budget allocation is to deny the people their right to open government and can fuel corruption on a grand scale.[37]

A related issue concerns executive attempts to seek additional funding through the system of supplementary estimates. Here the use and extent of these is an excellent indicator as to the budget's comprehensiveness and accuracy. Whilst exceptional circumstances, such as a natural disaster,

[37] See the IMF Code of Good Practice on Financial Transparency, March 2001. It follows that parliament is commonly limited to 'reduction only' powers. See, for example, s.48 Constitution of Kenya.

may warrant additional expenditure, excessive use of supplementary estimates indicates fiscal-policy deficiencies and/or irregularities. It follows that empowering a Minister to seek 'condonation' of unauthorised or excess spending by means of a parliamentary Bill,[38] or the retrospective authorisation of otherwise unauthorised expenditure, is fraught with danger and that parliamentarians must be extremely wary of any such proposed legislation.[39]

Approving the budget, Finance Bill(s) and spending proposals is merely the first step. Parliamentarians must remain fully involved in monitoring public spending. They must insist upon proper and adequate accounting procedures, regular reporting within a fixed period on expenditure (including the appropriate guiding administrative rules) and the full disclosure and examination of government finances. It is the perceived failure of parliamentarians to do this effectively that has contributed much to the negative view of their work. The sheer complexity and scale of the task means that unless they receive adequate information and advice on such matters, they may not be in a position to appreciate fully the repercussions. Such information is already available through the reports and recommendations of oversight bodies such as the Auditor-General and anti-corruption commissions.[40] It is incumbent upon Parliament to act upon them if they disclose malpractice. Here the Public Accounts Committee can play a key oversight role by calling before it relevant Ministers and senior public servants to account for their actions/inactions. Ideally its membership must include those with financial expertise, its meetings must be open to the public and the media and it must enjoy adequate publicity for its reports and recommendations.

Developing transparency in government procurement practices also presents a difficult but rewarding challenge. Corruption is often widespread, both in the award of contracts and during their implementation. Again, the legislature has the duty to oversee the entire process, particularly through the work of its parliamentary committees. Developing a 'partnership' approach with anti-corruption agencies could prove useful here. In addition, a constitutional requirement to obtain parliamentary approval before entering into international loan agreements, including arms sales and purchases, again potentially provides for transparency and an opportunity for effective public debate and scrutiny.

[38] Such as in Zimbabwe: see s.103(5), Constitution of Zimbabwe.

[39] See, for example, art.117(5), Constitution of Zambia.

[40] It is also beholden upon such bodies to lay their Annual Reports timeously before Parliament and, where necessary, any special reports.

Oversight of legislation

The legislature is required to examine and pass Bills, the vast majority of which are government inspired.[41] Some, such as the Finance Act, must be passed annually. Others, such as a constitutional amendment Bill, require a special parliamentary procedure. Yet all Bills require effective parliamentary scrutiny. The sheer volume and complexity of proposed legislation, both primary and secondary, and the speed with which it is sometimes introduced,[42] makes the task of meaningful scrutiny by individual members extremely difficult. The implications of a Bill, particularly concerning fundamental rights, may not always be readily understood or apparent.[43] To carry out their functions, parliamentarians must have access to objective and independent information and advice. Here several mechanisms already exist. In Zimbabwe the Parliamentary Legal Committee, which comprises members with legal qualifications, is tasked with examining Bills and delegated legislation and giving an opinion as to whether they 'would be or are in contravention of the Declaration of Rights'.[44] If necessary, an adverse report is then laid before Parliament.[45] A different approach is taken in South Africa where at least one-third of the National Assembly membership, within thirty days of a Bill receiving presidential assent, may apply to the Constitutional Court for an order declaring all or part of an Act unconstitutional.[46] The 'partnership' approach with human rights commissions noted earlier is another possible assistance mechanism. Indeed in South Africa the Human Rights Commission is required to examine all Bills to assess whether they are in accordance with the Bill of Rights and, if not, to lobby and submit proposals to Parliament.[47]

In theory, individual members may introduce Private Members' Bills. In practice there is little or no hope of these succeeding without government

[41] Private members Bills remain a rare phenomenon in all the ESA states.

[42] For example, through the use of the 'guillotine' procedure inherited from the parliament at Westminster.

[43] Ministers may not be particularly helpful in their contributions on the Bill: for an example see chapter 4.

[44] S.40B(1) Constitution of Zimbabwe.

[45] In practice this procedure has almost invariably led to offending provisions being amended. See further J. Hatchard, *Individual Freedoms and State Security in the African Context: the Case of Zimbabwe*, Ohio State University Press, Athens, Ohio, 1993, p. 127.

[46] S.80 Constitution of South Africa.

[47] The Commission is also required to monitor the implementation of socio-economic rights by requiring organs of state to submit information on measures taken to realise those rights. It is thus in an excellent position to provide appropriate information to parliamentarians.

support and they remain a very rare commodity. Even so, they have the potential to publicise an area of public concern and provide an opportunity for members to debate the issue.

Enhancing the effectiveness of parliamentarians

As the discussion in the previous section has indicated, the means for the legislature to play a useful oversight role largely already exists. Arguably, these can be can made more effective and indeed improved in several ways. Firstly, by providing appropriate training to parliamentarians. It is unrealistic to assume that, upon election, new members somehow automatically acquire the necessary range and depth of expertise in legal, financial, human rights and political matters together with the necessary parliamentary skills to enable then to carry out their duties effectively. That such members require training on the complexities of parliamentary procedure and the like is now widely accepted and, in recent years, the Commonwealth Parliamentary Association (CPA), amongst others, has provided appropriate courses to new parliamentarians throughout the region. Human rights commissions might also provide useful expertise and assistance in developing training programmes for all parliamentarians. There is often a need to provide on-going training to all members in an effort to improve parliamentary skills. These might include holding gender sensitising sessions and improving research and IT skills. Parliamentarians should also be provided with appropriate training materials and handbooks that draw particularly on African experiences and best practice elsewhere.

Secondly, and directly related to the previous point, by providing all members with adequate research facilities and access to information, including the Internet. Amongst other things, this will enhance access to comparative materials especially because many legislatures have now established their own web sites whilst more invaluable material appears on those of international parliamentary organisations such as the CPA and the Inter-Parliamentary Union. Further, the provision of a well-stocked parliamentary library should be the goal of every parliament.

Thirdly, and where these do not already exist, by encouraging women parliamentarians to form caucuses across party lines which should be recognised and resourced by parliaments themselves.[48] These could be

[48] See further J. Hatchard, 'Engendering Political Decision-Making' (1998) 42 JAL, at pp. 141–3.

used to lobby for improvements in parliamentary accommodation and its timetable in order to assist women members to better fulfil their obligations. Fourthly, by providing technical assistance for the drafting of Private Members' Bills, in scrutinising proposed legislation and in drafting appropriate amendments.[49] Further, the provision of independent advice to members on the implications of proposed legislation, especially in relation to human rights, is needed. Here use should be made of the local human rights commission or office of the ombudsman.

Fifthly, by encouraging members to oversee the implementing of the country's international human rights obligations. The ESA states are now parties to many international human rights instruments and all are parties to the African Charter on Human and Peoples' Rights. Such oversight might involve ensuring that the state complies with its treaty obligations and submits regular periodic (and accurate) reports on the measures taken by it to give effect to the rights contained in the instruments and on the progress made in the enjoyment of those rights. This is essential as the position in many ESA states is woeful.[50] Often reports are not submitted or are submitted very late. A good example of how to facilitate this responsibility is provided by the Uganda Human Rights Commission which is tasked by the Constitution with 'monitoring Government's compliance with international human rights treaty and convention obligations'.[51] It remains to be seen how the Commission views this function but a broad interpretation of 'monitoring' will require government to report to the Commission on compliance with its international human rights obligations. Presumably, the Commission will then recommend remedial action and inform Parliament accordingly. Parliamentarians will then be able to further pressurise the government to comply with relevant treaty obligations, through, for example, holding a full parliamentary debate on the matter or even seeking to bring in a Private Member's Bill.[52]

[49] Article 94(4)(c)(d) of the Constitution of Uganda requires the relevant government department to give the mover of a private member's Bill 'reasonable assistance' whilst the office of the Attorney-General must give 'professional assistance' in the drafting of the Bill.

[50] See, for example, John Hatchard, 'Reporting under International Human Rights Instruments by African Countries' (1994) 38 *Journal of African Law* 61.

[51] Article 52(1)(h) Constitution of Uganda.

[52] For example in 2000 the Parliament of Zimbabwe passed a motion calling on the government to sign up to the United Nations Convention Against Torture and Other Cruel, Inhuman or Degrading Treatment or Punishment (CAT). Given the record of the Mugabe regime, this is most unlikely to occur, but the debate at least raised public awareness of CAT and its importance.

Sixthly, by monitoring the performance of individual members. Parliaments and electors cannot afford to countenance lazy, ineffective and incompetent members. In some countries, this has resulted in the introduction of a procedure for the recall of members. On the face of it, the power of constituents to recall and replace their member of parliament is a legitimate exercise of their right to oversee the performance of elected representatives.[53] This power exists in Uganda where the electorate of any constituency or any interest group have the right to recall their MP on grounds of physical or mental incapacity, misconduct or misbehaviour or persistently deserting the electorate without reasonable cause.[54] The problem with the recall mechanism is that it is open to abuse and poses a threat to members' independence.[55] Thus some may prefer the matter to be dealt with through an integrity mechanism (as discussed below) or at the party/grassroots level. Finally, by ensuring that the legislature meets regularly and frequently and that members are able to continue their oversight role even when parliament itself is not in session.

Parliament and the media

An ineffective, compliant legislative body does not deserve anything better than media criticism or disinterest. But a vibrant, effective legislature requires and must receive appropriate media support. Here the building of an effective working relationship between parliamentarians and an independent media is essential. Parliamentarians must recognise that an independent media serves as a 'watchdog' on public affairs and that it must receive appropriate support and assistance. This should include ensuring

[53] Stories of the poor performance of members as regards carrying out their constituency duties are legion. For example, in July 1998 the *Times of Zambia* commented on the 'disgrace and shame' following the revelation of the Central Province Minister, Abel Chambeshi, that he was the first minister or MP to visit his constituency since independence in 1964. See *Times of Zambia*, 17 July 1998.

[54] The recall process is instigated by a petition in writing signed by at least two-thirds of the registered voters of the constituency or interest group delivered to the Speaker who must then require the Electoral Commission to conduct a public inquiry and the Speaker declares the seat vacant 'if the Electoral Commission reports that it is satisfied from the inquiry with the genuineness of the petition' Constitution of Uganda, art. 84(3)–(5). In this context, the 'interest groups' are those of the army, women, youth, workers and persons with disabilities.

[55] See, for example, the views of the Working Group on Accountability Mechanisms in J. Hatchard and P. Slinn (eds.), *Parliamentary Supremacy and Judicial Independence: a Commonwealth Approach*, Cavendish Publishing, London, 1999 p. 134.

full access to documentation and other materials relating to parliamentary proceedings and facilitating coverage of parliament, including opening up select and other committees to the media. On the media's part, there is a responsibility to report parliamentary proceedings fairly and accurately and to take steps to develop imaginative ways of raising public interest in the legislature's work. In addition, there is much to be said for providing training both for journalists so that they can better understand and report on the complex procedures and issues in parliament, and parliamentarians themselves so that they can better appreciate and respond to the media's needs.[56]

A related issue is the need to revisit the anachronistic practice of only publishing government documents, Bills, statutes and the like in the *Government Gazette* (and generally only in English). It is crucial to encourage the widespread dissemination of such information to all people, especially targeting those in the rural areas who currently have little access to such information. Governments and the media should work together to disseminate the materials as widely as possible, particularly by using radio and local language newspapers.

Maintaining the independence and integrity of parliament and parliamentarians

Parliamentary control of budget, staffing and facilities

Most legislative bodies have a committee that is responsible for internal administrative matters. However, in an effort to strengthen parliamentary independence, Kenya, Tanzania and Uganda have gone further and formally empowered Parliament to control its own budget, staff and facilities through the establishment of a Parliamentary Service Commission.

There are two main reasons for establishing an independent parliamentary service. Firstly, it is essential that staff are responsible to parliament rather than to the executive. If they remain members of the public service they may be more readily susceptible to political pressure and, indeed, may be appointed to it with a view to furthering the executive's interests. For example, security officers provided for parliament and parliamentarians may, in reality, be members of the state security apparatus whose

[56] For a discussion on the relationship see Commonwealth Parliamentary Association, *Parliament and the Media: Building an Effective Relationship*, CPA, London, 2000 http://www.comparlhq.org.uk/parlam/parlam3.htm.

main task is to report to their political masters.[57] The point was well put by a former Indian Speaker who observed:

> Every officer, subordinate or otherwise, serving in the Secretariat of the Legislature must be in a position to carry out his [or her] duties without fear or favour of the Executive Government, and obviously this cannot be done if persons in the employ of the Secretariat have to look upon such bodies as the Selection Board, consisting of the officers and nominees of the Executive Government, for their chances and career in the Secretariat of the Legislature.

The effect of establishing such a commission is that during their tenure in the service of parliament, officials are not answerable to any other person, authority or body outside of parliament in respect of their employment, unless parliament so provides. Any such interference may itself amount to contempt of parliament.

Secondly, the specialised nature of parliamentary work differs markedly from that of the general public service. Thus, experience and training are essential for the development of an effective specialist parliamentary support staff. For example, the type of legal problems faced by parliamentary counsel are often of a highly specialised nature involving perhaps complex areas of parliamentary privilege or contempt.

Floor-crossing

Floor-crossing occurs when a sitting member of parliament leaves the party under the colours that he or she was elected either to join another party or to sit as an independent. Such behaviour is a hallowed tradition in the House of Commons at Westminster and the right of sitting members to follow their consciences and switch their allegiance to another party (or to sit as independents) is seen as an integral part of a competitive party system. Not surprisingly, the Westminster-export constitution did not seek to regulate the matter.

A typical anti-floor-crossing provision provides that members automatically vacate their seats if the party to which they have ceased to be members notifies the Speaker that they no longer represent its interest in parliament. Arguments to support this approach largely centre on the fact that floor-crossing defeats the electorate's wishes since they have

[57] Compare Uganda where the Parliamentary Commission is to 'provide security staff' for Parliament and parliamentarians.

demonstrated by their votes that they wish to be represented in parliament by a particular political party. Thus under a constituency electoral system, if a sitting member wishes to leave that party, he/she must seek a fresh mandate from the electorate by means of a by-election. The matter is more acute under a system of proportional representation, as this seeks to provide a quorum of representatives of individual parties as determined by the entire electorate: thus there is no room for floor-crossing.[58]

Against this view is the fact that members will lose their parliamentary seats when the party to which they belong unilaterally decides to terminate their membership for whatever reason (or for no reason at all). This arguably contravenes their constitutional right to freedom of association.[59] From a practical standpoint, floor-crossing enables independent-minded members to escape the sometimes constricting party hegemony forced upon them by party managers, and enhances freedom of debate by removing the concern that, despite parliamentary privilege,[60] criticism of the President or Ministers may lead to expulsion.[61]

Perhaps a suitable compromise is to recognise that whilst floor-crossing is constitutionally permissible in principle, there is one situation where anti-defection measures are defensible. This is to combat corrupt practices or the buying of opposition votes. For example, shortly after independence, the Kenyan Government reportedly made determined efforts

[58] See van Reenan J. in *De Vilheis v Municipalieit, Beaufort-Wes en Andere* 1998(9) BCLR 1060 (C). For example, the Namibian Constitution provides that members lose their seats if the political party which nominated them to sit in the National Assembly informs the Speaker that such members are no longer members of that political party. The party can then nominate replacements from the its election list from the previous general election or, by nominating any party members (art. 48(1) and (2)). See *Federal Convention of Namibia v Speaker, National Assembly* 1994 (1) S.A. 177.

[59] Malaysia provides a particularly helpful example. See generally A. J. Harding, 'When is a resignation not a resignation? The Sabah Constitutional Crisis of 1994' (1995) 335 *The Round Table* 353.

[60] The limits of the privilege is well illustrated by the case of a Zimbabwean MP, Dzikamai Mavaire, who was a member of the ruling party ZANU(PF). Whilst moving a motion in the legislature he used the phrase 'the President must go'. This led to the disciplinary committee of ZANU(PF) ordering him to appear before it. Relying on the Constitution and the Privileges, Immunities and Powers of Parliament Act, the Speaker then issued a certificate under section 6(1) of the Act stating that the matter concerned the privilege of Parliament and accordingly the matter could only be raised and adjudicated upon in Parliament. Pressure from his party then led to Mavaire waiving his privileges and immunity, whereupon he was suspended from the party for two years.

[61] See further J. Hatchard, 'The Constitution of Zimbabwe: a New Model for Africa?' (1991) 35 JAL 79, at p. 82.

to undermine the main opposition party, KADU, by allegedly luring members of that party to cross the floor and join the ruling party, KANU, by offers of ministerial posts and other benefits.[62] Such practices can only further weaken opposition parties that have traditionally suffered from both a high rate of defection and attrition.

The dangers to the party-political system associated with floor-crossing do not extend to a situation where a member decides to renounce party membership and to sit in parliament as an independent. This point was seemingly recognised in article 71(2) of the 1991 Constitution of Zambia which provides as follows:

> A member of the National Assembly shall vacate his seat in the Assembly . . . (c) in the case of an elected member, if he becomes a member of a political party other than the party of which he was an authorised candidate when he was elected to the National Assembly or, if having been an independent candidate, he joins a political party . . .

The matter was examined in *Attorney-General v Kasonde and Others.*[63] Here four members of Parliament from the Movement for Multi-Party Democracy (MMD) publicly announced their resignations from the MMD. They were then notified by the Clerk of the National Assembly that, in accordance with article 71(2)(c) they had ceased to be members of Parliament. They petitioned the High Court, challenging their exclusion from Parliament. They were successful at first instance, the trial judge pointing out that it was a reasonable inference that, in omitting any reference to the position of a former party member who became an independent, the drafters of the Constitution had chosen deliberately to allow such persons to sit as independents.[64] On appeal by the Attorney-General, the Supreme Court unanimously held the respondents had vacated their seats on resignation from the MMD. It was not deterred by the apparent lacuna in the article, holding that it should be interpreted purposively in order to promote the general legislative purpose underlying the provision which was to prohibit floor-crossing generally. The Supreme Court accepted that the literal interpretation had been correctly applied by the

[62] Amongst those who crossed-over was Daniel Arap-Moi who later became President of Kenya. For details see P. H. Okondo, *A Commentary on the Constitution of Kenya*, Phoenix, Nairobi, 1995, pp. 21–22.

[63] [1994] 3 LRC. 144.

[64] Ibid., On the facts, the judge found that the petitioners had intended to form and join a new party, the National Party, and that in accordance with the express terms of article 71(2)(c) they had vacated their seats.

court below but found that this led to 'manifest absurdity or repugnance'. This somewhat surprising conclusion was based on reference to article 23 of the Constitution which afforded protection from discrimination on political grounds. The court held that to permit former members of a political party to remain as independent members would unreasonably and unfairly discriminate against independent members who would lose their seats on joining a political party or indeed against a member who resigned from one party in order to join another party. The remedy was to read into the article words necessary so as to make the constitutional provision 'fair and undiscriminatory'. Accordingly, the words 'or vice versa' should be added to the end of paragraph 71(2)(c) so as require former party members to vacate their seats on becoming independents. This decision is open to some criticism. We have some sympathy with the trial judge who was not prepared to find that the legislature's intention was to include a situation where a member merely resigned from a political party without joining another: 'asking the court to read these words into article 71(2)(c) is asking the court to directly legislate by including that which was omitted'.[65] The Supreme Court relied on the modern English approach to statutory interpretation to justify a purposive approach. It could have, of course, invoked the much quoted principle that constitutions, particularly when dealing with human rights issues such as alleged discrimination, should be given a generous, liberal and non-literal interpretation. However, it would still be curious for such an interpretation to produce a result which expands the class of those deprived of their parliamentary seats to include those not covered by the express words of the Constitution. Moreover, it is at least arguable that the framers of the Constitution may have intended that party managers should *not* be given the weapon placed in their hands by the *Kasonde* decision: i.e. the threat against independent-minded MPs of expulsion from the party and consequent loss of their parliamentary seats. Rather, the constitutional provision was designed to ensure the accountability of members to their electorates and to prevent floor-crossing in circumstances where, for example, members of one party are induced by bribery into a direct transfer of allegiance.

Overall, a healthy and stable party system is an essential element in the search for accountability and just and honest governance in societies with all too fragile democratic political cultures. In theory, anti-defection measures can help create such stability and this may explain why most

[65] Ibid., at p. 159.

ESA states have opted to retain them.[66] However, their use must be limited and here certain propositions are suggested. Firstly, the security of parliamentarians is fundamental to parliamentary independence. This means that anti-defection measures should only apply in clearly defined circumstances. In practice this should only cover situations where there is evidence of bribery or other corrupt practices. Secondly, it is never appropriate for a party to remove any of its sitting members through rescinding their party membership. Thirdly, there is no justification for any legal or constitutional bar on sitting members leaving their parties to sit as independent members.

Maintaining integrity

All members of parliament, including Ministers, are required to maintain certain standards of integrity in their public and private lives. Conduct that falls below acceptable standards ranges from the most serious, such as the acceptance of bribes, to more minor breaches, such as the failure to disclose a possible conflict of interest when participating in a debate.

Establishing a register of interests for ministers, parliamentarians and their families has some potential as a probity mechanism. If effective, it offers the chance to strengthen public confidence in the political system by the public affirmation that there is a commitment to just and honest government. In doing so, a register can both deter potentially dishonest members as well as protect honest members against accusations of financial impropriety. A major objection to such a register is that it constitutes an unjustified invasion of privacy. The further the range of interests covered, the stronger this argument becomes, for such a register is undoubtedly such an invasion. However, by clearly demarcating the interests and persons affected, such a register is surely justified.

Codes of Conduct or Ethics set out the criteria relating to the conduct that people can expect of Ministers and parliamentarians. In the case of South Africa, for example, the code imposes positive obligations on Ministers such as the duty 'to act in good faith and in the best interests of governance' as well as prohibiting conduct such as 'using their position or any information entrusted to them, to enrich themselves or improperly benefit any other person'.[67] Some have argued that a code cannot cover

[66] See, for example, the Constitutions of Malawi, s.65(1); Uganda, art. 83(1)(g)(h) and Zambia, art. 71(2).

[67] See s.2(1) Executive Members' Ethics Act 1998.

every type of unacceptable behaviour and that it is up to the legislature itself to rule whether a person's conduct is or is not acceptable in the light of prevailing circumstances.[68] This is a valid point but such a code is not intended to provide some absolute exclusive standard and there is nothing to prevent parliament itself investigating actions of members that seemingly fall outside the code's purview.

Why such registers and codes have not proved popular in the ESA states is unclear. Certainly it is unrealistic to think that such mechanisms will necessarily deter those intent upon abusing their office. Yet they are potentially important in that they proclaim the state's commitment to good governance and provide the public and the media with a standard by which to assess the conduct of the country's elected representatives.

Judicial overview of the exercise of parliamentary powers

The right of parliament to regulate its own practices and procedures is a cornerstone to maintaining its independence. Thus parliamentarians claim that what was said and done in the legislature is its exclusive domain and no outside body or agency has the power to interject. As Rao notes, the basis for this contention is that:

> Members are exercising the sovereign and constitutional power of the public whom they represent, and therefore their activities in parliament are not justiciable by institutions created by the Constitution.[69]

Thus courts on several occasions have held that matters involving the internal proceedings of parliament are not susceptible to judicial review.[70] Even this does not prevent the courts from inquiring into whether, in relation to action against 'strangers', the appropriate procedure was followed.[71] There remains the question as to whether privilege extends to cover criminal activities that are perpetrated wholly within parliament.

[68] A point put forward in the Culliton Report (*White Paper on the Proposed Code of Ethical Conduct for Public Office Holders*), Ontario, 1986, at p. 43.

[69] K. M. Nagabhushan Rao, 'Parliamentary privilege versus the courts', in Hatchard and Slinn, *Parliamentary Supremacy*, at p. 65.

[70] See the views of the Zambian Supreme Court in *M'membe and Mwape v Speaker of the National Assembly* [1996] 1 LRC 584 and the Zimbabwe Supreme Court in *Mutasa v Makombe* [1997] 2 LRC 314.

[71] For example, whether the rules of natural justice were followed in relation to contempt proceedings against journalists. If such a breach is found, the courts can overturn the legislature's decision. For a good example see *M'membe and Mwape v Speaker of the National Assembly* above.

For example, the taking of bribes by members of parliament from minority parties offered by a government minister in order to induce them to vote for the government.[72] Arguably, in such a situation public policy demands that allegations of criminal conduct within parliament is a matter for the courts. This is based on the view that parliamentary privilege only covers activities that are being carried out within the scope of legislative and parliamentary functions. Thus any crossing of the line into criminal activity takes the perpetrators outside the protection of parliamentary privilege. The issue continues to provoke discussion throughout the Commonwealth and beyond and there is no consistent judicial authority on the matter.[73] However, the paramount objective must always be to maintain the integrity of parliament and parliamentarians and public confidence in the institution itself. It follows that the courts must have jurisdiction to hear and determine cases involving the alleged bribery of, or receipt of a bribe from, a member/s of parliament.

Overview

The executive has enormous advantages over the legislature and for members, whether individually or collectively, to play an effective oversight role is a considerable challenge. However, if parliaments and parliamentarians wish to be taken seriously, they must seek to fulfil the role envisaged by Fall. Of course, the executive's constitutional role is to run the affairs of state and it is not for parliament to 'control' its actions. However, a legislature that is and remains an independent, competent, well-informed, representative and confident body can maintain an effective oversight role.

In the first place, the issue of membership needs addressing: Are the right people coming into parliament? Are they adequately representative of the people? Are women adequately represented? Further, attention must be paid to providing members with adequate training, access to research assistance and information. Parliamentarians must also be prepared to

[72] Facts similar to the Indian case of *P V Narasimha Rao v State* 1998 SC 626 where the Prime Minister and other senior government ministers had allegedly bribed members of smaller parliamentary parties to get their votes in order to defeat a no-confidence motion.

[73] Courts in Australia (*R v Boston* (1923) 33 CLR 386 (High Court of Australia)) and the USA (*US v Brewster* 33 L.Ed 2d 507 (US Supreme Court)) have both held that privilege did not protect persons accused of involvement in bribery undertaken within the legislature. The Indian Supreme Court in the *Narasimha Rao* case thought otherwise. See further the discussion by Rao, above at pp. 66–9.

tackle sensitive issues, especially those involving corruption, arms sales and purchases, the operation of the military and presidential spending. The work of parliamentary committees is of great importance here, backed up by the development of effective partnerships, especially with the media and human rights commissions. There is also the need to protect members in the performance of their duties. Members must be able to exercise fully their parliamentary privileges and to stand up and say 'No Mr (or Ms) President' without fear of facing unacceptable consequences. These are all constructive strategies and can make a significant contribution towards a country fulfilling its obligations under the Harare Declaration. Finally, as this and the previous chapter have demonstrated, we must take a holistic or 'sectoral' approach to the development of a strong, effective and open political process.

8

The judiciary and the protection of constitutional rights

> Ordinary men and women need support in their fight to claim and protect their liberties. And their natural protectors are the courts.

The emergence of constitutions with wide-ranging and justiciable Bills of Rights has rekindled public awareness and interest in the role of courts through which to seek individual and collective justice and the sustenance of a democratic culture. The maintenance of an independent and accountable judiciary is fundamental to achieving such goals and these issues are discussed in the first part of the chapter. The second part considers the role of judges in undertaking their task as 'guardians of the constitution'.

Judicial independence

Judicial independence is recognised in many international and regional human rights instruments[1] and constitutes one of the Commonwealth's fundamental political values.[2] The principle is also enshrined in all the ESA constitutions with the Ugandan Constitution encapsulating the point:

> In the exercise of judicial power, the courts shall be independent and shall not be subject to the control or direction of any person or authority.[3]

Whilst discussion often centres on protecting and promoting the rights of judges in the higher courts, we must also recognise that magistrates require comparable protection, not least because it is they who deal with

[1] 'Everyone is entitled to a fair and public hearing by an independent tribunal . . .' (art. 10 Universal Declaration of Human Rights); '. . . everyone shall be entitled to a fair and public hearing by a competent, independent and impartial tribunal established by law' (art. 14.1 International Covenant on Civil and Political Rights). See also art. 7(1) African Charter on Human and Peoples' Rights.

[2] Its significance has also led to the development of the *United Nations Basic Principles on the Independence of the Judiciary* that are designed to 'secure and promote' judicial independence (para 1). See also the similar views of the International Commission of Jurists, *States of Emergency: their Impact on Human Rights* ICJ, Geneva, 1983, pp. 434–7 and J. Nyerere, *Freedom and Socialism*, Oxford, 1968, pp. 109–14.

[3] Art. 128(1). See also s.103(1) Constitution of Malawi.

the vast majority of cases, both criminal and civil, and it is upon them that much of the public confidence in the legal system resides.

The main pillars of judicial independence are institutional and financial autonomy. These encompass the need for an appropriate appointment procedure, security of tenure, satisfactory conditions of service which the executive cannot adversely affect, the provision of adequate financial resources and appropriate terms and conditions for all those involved in the administration of justice. These in turn are founded on the principle that the exercise of judicial functions is vested solely in the judiciary. As is made plain in the Constitution of Malawi: 'The judiciary shall have jurisdiction over all issues of a judicial nature and shall have exclusive authority to decide whether an issue is within its competence.'[4] Yet independence comes at a price. Judges and magistrates must recognise that they are duty bound to provide society with the highest possible standards of service and commitment and that a failure to maintain this is rightly a matter of public concern. As Stephens has observed: 'What ultimately protects the independence of the judiciary is a community consensus that such independence is a quality worth protecting.'[5]

The appointment process

Judicial Service Commissions

During the colonial period the judiciary formed part of the colonial legal service. Advancement to the Bench was a matter of promotion from the magistracy or from some other position in the judicial or legal departments such as the office of the Attorney-General. The appointment of judges was a matter for the Governor acting on the instructions of the Secretary of State for the Colonies. Judges technically held office during Her Majesty's pleasure and were removable at will, although it was well known that they would never be dismissed without reference to the Judicial Committee of the Privy Council.[6] Puisne judges were reported

[4] S.103(2). See also s.165(1) Constitution of South Africa. On the other hand, Zimbabwe's already beleaguered judicial system is also threatened by the power of Parliament to vest adjudicating functions in a person or authority other than court. See also the discussion in chapter 10 on the power of the Uganda Human Rights Commission to hear and determine complaints regarding alleged human rights violations.

[5] Noted by S. Cartwright, 'The Judiciary: Qualifications, Training and Gender Balance', in J. Hatchard and P. Slinn (eds.), *Parliamentary Supremacy and Judicial Independence: a Commonwealth Approach*, Cavendish, London, 1998, at p. 39. The issue of judicial accountability is discussed below.

[6] See *Terrell v Secretary of State for the Colonies* [1953] 1 WLR 331 but note the views of K. Roberts-Wray, *Commonwealth and the Colonial Law*, Stevens London, 1966, pp. 495–6.

on by the Chief Justice to the Governor, a procedure apparently justified on the basis that the Secretary of State needed the information when considering the question of promotions.

Such a system was not considered suitable for the newly independent states. A constitutional guarantee of judicial independence was viewed as a necessity, particularly given the political uncertainties and the newness of the states,[7] and the fact that judges would have the challenging task of ruling on constitutional provisions. The mechanism adopted was to establish a judicial service commission.[8]

Judicial Service Commissions (JSCs) remain responsible for overseeing judicial appointments in the ESA states although there remain significant divergences of opinion as to their composition. With one exception, all are chaired by the Chief Justice. As head of the judiciary, this is entirely appropriate. The one issue is over possible excessive presidential influence in the appointment of the Chief Justice and thence over the entire commission. This was the situation in Uganda where worries that previous incumbents had apparently improperly influenced judicial appointments led to the Constitution specifically excluding the Chief Justice from membership of the JSC.[9] The concern is a real one although, arguably, the matter is best dealt with by providing for a suitably independent and transparent appointment system for the Chief Justice. The involvement of other senior judicial figures in the appointment process is also commonplace and necessary, for their own experience together with their personal knowledge of potential candidates makes them well qualified to identify suitable individuals for appointment or advancement. Even so, the presidential influence as to the choice of the commission's judicial members is a cause of concern[10] and it is preferable to leave the selection to the judges themselves or to specify particular office-holders *ex officio* to serve as members.

Limiting membership of a JSC to the senior judiciary is now outdated. Fears that 'outsiders' may seek to unduly influence judicial appointments (or removal) for political or other improper motives are understandable

[7] See B. O. Nwabueze, *Judicialism in Commonwealth Africa*, Hurst, London, p. 266.

[8] This did not apply to magistrates who were public servants and whose appointment and promotions fell under the auspices of the Public Service Commission.

[9] The Deputy Chief Justice and the Principal Judge who were both formerly *ex officio* members of the JSC are also expressly excluded.

[10] For instance, the Namibian JSC includes a judge appointed by the President (art. 85 Namibian Constitution) whilst in Malawi, the judge is designated by the President acting in consultation with the Chief Justice (s.117 Constitution of Malawi). See also the similar position in Kenya and Lesotho.

and must be addressed. Yet without a more representative membership, appointments may be (or perceived as being) made as part of an 'old boys' network' designed to maintain the status quo and which imports potential bias (unconscious or otherwise) towards particular individuals, political parties or ethnic groups. In addition, there are sometimes fears that members of the senior judiciary are elitist and do not necessarily represent or understand the views of the wider community.[11] These are real concerns and provide strong support for opening up the membership of a JSC to others who have a legitimate interest in, and expectation of, involvement in judicial appointments and removals.

It is certainly desirable to include members from the wider legal community for they can offer peer assessment on fitness for office and can also identify candidates who might otherwise be overlooked through the official channels because of, for example, their anti-government attitudes. This category should include at least one senior legal practitioner. To maintain independence, ideally such person(s) should be designated by their local law society and/or bar association.[12] This raises an issue as to whether the person sits in his/her individual capacity, as a representative of all legal practitioners, or as a representative of the executive committee of the law society or bar association. The ESA constitutions offer no guidance but arguably, as other JSC members act in their individual capacity, this should also apply to legal practitioners. Representation by one or more law teachers designated by their peers is also desirable,[13] particularly as they are often in an excellent position to evaluate the academic capabilities of prospective appointees.[14] In addition, this provides an important link between the profession and law teachers. Government representation in the appointment process is also legitimate and is often provided for by the Attorney-General's inclusion *ex officio*.[15]

Opening the commission to lay members is a feature in both South Africa and Uganda. In South Africa the JSC includes six parliamentarians

[11] This was a particular problem in the South African context and helps explain the determined efforts to ensure that membership of the Constitutional Court reflected a broad spectrum of society.

[12] It follows that the Malawian approach of having the individual designated by the President after consultation with the Chief Justice is inappropriate.

[13] This is the position in South Africa.

[14] One advantage here is that it is not uncommon for senior legal academics to have taught the prospective appointees during their legal studies. This is certainly the experience of the current authors.

[15] As is the case in, for example, Lesotho, Zimbabwe, Kenya and Namibia. The steady politicisation of the office emphasises the need to ensure the independence of other JSC members.

designated by the National Assembly from among its members, with at least three being members of opposition parties represented in the Assembly, plus four permanent delegates to the National Council of Provinces.[16] Four members of the public are also included whom the President designates after consulting with the leaders of all the parties in the National Assembly.[17] In Uganda the JSC includes two lay members nominated by the President. A lay presence is supposedly justified on the grounds that the public and their elected representatives have a legitimate interest in the matter and can make it more difficult for political influence to sway appointments. Whilst these are valid considerations, it is still hard to justify the presence of such persons unless they also bring to the commission some specific expertise or experience that is otherwise lacking. This could be done through the appointment of commissioners designated by the trade union movement, religious/minority groups, civil society organisations, and the like.

A related issue is whether serving judges should form a majority of the membership of a JSC. This is proposed in the *Latimer House Guidelines*[18] but it does not reflect the practice in any ESA state. Indeed in Uganda only one of the nine JSC members must be a serving judge. It is certainly vital that judges enjoy a significant input in the selection and removal process, but the objective must be to provide for a demonstrably independent body whose membership comprises the necessary range of expertise and experience with which to assess the quality and competence of candidates.

Judicial appointment and tenure

Although some have argued that judicial independence requires the removal of political considerations from the appointment process,[19] this is not necessarily appropriate. In times of political and economic transformation, in particular, the judiciary must be sympathetic to the country's needs and its membership should reflect broadly the country's

[16] Their role is limited to dealing with the question of the appointment of judges: see s.178(5) Constitution of South Africa.

[17] S.178 Constitution of South Africa.

[18] Para II(1) of the *Latimer House Guidelines*, whose drafters included senior Commonwealth judicial figures, state that a JSC should comprise a majority of senior judges. This view has met with considerable disagreement throughout the Commonwealth, including at 1999 Commonwealth Law Ministers' Meeting and 2001 Meeting of Commonwealth Senior Law Officers. As a result, the provision has now been dropped.

[19] See e.g. Roberts-Wray *Commonwealth and Colonial Law*, 1966, at p. 478.

gender and racial composition. As a former Chief Justice of Zimbabwe has emphasised:

> What is important . . . is not necessarily the complete absence of any 'political' consideration, but a positive commitment to the choice of professionally competent persons of proven integrity. *No one should be appointed a judge for purely political reasons when he [or she] is not otherwise fitted for office.*[20]

The appointment of 'professionally competent persons of proven integrity' depends upon the development of a suitable procedure for doing so. In the first place, candidates must be drawn from as wide a pool as possible. This means a JSC must have the right to nominate candidates itself as well as advertising for them nationally. The practical importance of these measures is perhaps doubtful given that it is unlikely that a previously unknown candidate who satisfies the rigorous appointment criteria will suddenly materialise. But it does enable the JSC to consider candidates who may not enjoy the government's support, perhaps due to their anti-government sentiments. It follows that it is unacceptable to restrict the nomination process to the President, relevant Minister or other executive body.[21]

Even with a suitably constituted JSC, there remains the question of its role in the appointment process itself.[22] Some constitutions provide that the President must appoint 'after consultation with the Judicial Service Commission'. This is the weakest formulation, for the President is not bound by the Commission's views.[23] A stronger approach is one that requires the President to act 'on the advice of' or on the 'recommendation of' the JSC. This implies that the making of the appointment is a purely formal function. It may be argued, however, that the head of government does have a legitimate right to more than just a formal role in appointments. A

[20] P. T. Georges, 'The Court in the Tanzania One-Party System' in A. Sawyerr (ed.), *East African Law and Social Change*, East Africa Publishing House, Nairobi, 1967, p. 38.

[21] In Zimbabwe, for example, the JSC is limited to considering the suitability of those nominated by the Minister. Paradoxically, this has strengthened the position of senior judges against accusations that they favoured the appointment of those with anti-government sentiments.

[22] In view of the importance of the office-holder, the position of the Chief Justice is considered separately below.

[23] A futile attempt to provide presidential accountability appears in the Zimbabwean Constitution. Here if an appointment is inconsistent with the JSC's recommendation, the President must inform Parliament as soon as practicable (s.84(2)). However, the legislature has no power to overturn the decision and has no duty to even debate the matter. In practice, the task of the JSC is reduced to raising concerns about the suitability of individuals the President wishes to appoint to the Bench.

possible solution here is for the JSC to provide a shortlist of appointable candidates from which the head of government can select his/her preferred candidate(s).[24] Whichever approach is adopted, it is essential that candidates for judicial appointment are professionally competent persons of proven integrity who enjoy the confidence of both the governors and governed alike.

A further possible safeguard is a requirement that the appointments of High Court and apex court judges are subject to ratification by the legislature.[25] To be a meaningful process, however, requires that it is properly structured, preferably with the matter being considered by a fully representative and suitably qualified parliamentary committee. Given the ongoing weakness of many legislatures, this attempt to incorporate elements of the presidential system is more likely to have the effect of politicising appointments rather than providing for an independent assessment as to the suitability of nominees.[26]

Chief Justice

As head of the legal system, the Chief Justice has overall responsibility for the administration of justice. S/he must guard the judiciary against improper pressures and influences and respond to any matters touching on judicial independence including the unenviable task of dealing with a sometimes hostile President, government and parliament. It follows that an executive-minded appointee can detrimentally affect the judiciary's performance, cause unnecessary friction with other judges and the legal profession and adversely affect public perception of the judiciary. For example, a Report of the International Bar Association on Kenya refers to a Circular from the then Chief Justice which required judges to report to him well in advance giving full details of invitations to preside over or present a paper on any topic as well as requiring the Kenya Magistrates'

[24] A model here is the appointment of judges to the South African Constitutional Court, Here the President is required to make appointments from a list prepared by the JSC, which contains three names more than the number of appointments to be made. S/he can reject the nominees in which case a supplementary list must be prepared but it appears that the President cannot again ask for such a list. The procedure is necessary because of the multiple appointments to the Constitutional Court, see s.174(4) Constitution of South Africa 1996. The acute shortage of suitable candidates in several SEA states makes such a system more difficult to operate, but it does provide a mechanism for compromise between the JSC and President over judicial appointments.

[25] See, for example, Constitution of Zambia 1991, art. 93(2). The system was intended to reflect the approach in the United States.

[26] In the case of Zambia, the relevant parliamentary committee considered that security clearance of candidates was its prime task.

and Judges' Association (KMJA) to obtain permission from the Chief Justice for the holding of seminars on any topic. The report concludes that these demands:

> . . . do in fact interfere with the individual members of the judiciary. Such measures in effect declare a lack of confidence in the independent minds of individual members of the judiciary and more seriously in the integrity of the KMJA.[27]

In several states the President effectively has complete control over the appointment of the Chief Justice with the JSC either having no part to play or a merely consultative role.[28] This is the traditional approach[29] but in view of the high profile and key constitutional role played by the Chief Justice, this is quite unsatisfactory and calls for an appointment process in which the JSC is closely involved.[30] For similar reasons discussed earlier, the usefulness of the appointee's ratification by the legislature is debatable.[31]

It is also advisable to make specific provision for the appointment of a Deputy Chief Justice who will act in the Chief Justice's absence. Whilst, in itself, a convenient administrative arrangement, it can also avoid a situation where improper pressure is brought on the Chief Justice to resign in order to enable the President to appoint an Acting Chief Justice (particularly one from outside the apex court and perhaps for a lengthy period) who is seen as being more amendable to presidential wishes.

27 Circular C. J. 69 of 10 September 1996 referred to in the International Bar Association, 'Report on the Legal System and Independence of the Judiciary in Kenya' London, 1997, p. 19.

28 For example, section 61(1) of the Constitution of Kenya simply provides: 'The Chief Justice shall be appointed by the President.' Concern about the appointment of Chief Justice Chesoni by the President surfaced in December 1999 where the chairman of the Law Society of Kenya reportedly stated that this had generated 'unalloyed alarm, even outrage' among lawyers (*Daily Nation*, 22 December 1999). Even where there is no specific constitutional requirement, there is arguably a convention that calls for presidential consultation on the matter with senior judges: see for example the views of the Indian Supreme Court in *Supreme Court Advocates-On-Record v India* AIR 1994 SC 268.

29 Based on the view that the Chief Justice is appointed by the executive and not the JSC since 'a body which makes recommendations for the appointment of persons to any public office cannot properly include persons who may be candidates'. See Roberts-Wray, *Commonwealth and Colonial Law*, p. 482.

30 The setting of rigorous qualifications for candidature also provides a safeguard against inappropriate appointments.

31 This procedure is provided in Malawi where the appointment must be confirmed by the National Assembly by a majority of two thirds of the members present and voting (s.111(1) Constitution of Malawi). See also article 142(1) Constitution of Uganda, although here there is no provision for an enhanced parliamentary majority.

Judges

There are generally three types of judicial appointment: (a) permanent appointment; (b) appointment on a fixed-term contract; and (c) an acting appointment for a limited duration or for a specific purpose.

Permanent appointments Recruiting judges from the ranks of the most experienced and able private legal practitioners remains problematic. Their reluctance to accept judicial appointment (thus foregoing the considerable rewards of practice for the lesser rewards on the Bench) means that the appointment of experienced magistrates and senior government law officers to the Bench remains commonplace. Given the continuing unattractive conditions of service for many judges, this situation is likely to continue. Whilst this may not necessarily affect their competence and independence, it can result in judges having potentially less overall experience and expertise, especially concerning social or customary law issues or with international or Commonwealth human rights jurisprudence.[32]

Security of tenure is a key to judicial independence and explains the importance of maintaining judges on permanent appointment by prohibiting the abolition of their tenure of office without their consent.[33] A retirement age for judges is invariably provided, although it is curious that there is normally no comparable mandatory retirement age for members of the executive and legislature. A judicial term of office can be extended, but often only at the President's behest. Whilst this provides an opportunity for the most able judges to remain in office, the decision whether or not to retire is surely a matter for the individual judge (perhaps in consultation with the Chief Justice or the JSC).[34]

32 This emphasises the need for the development of judicial training programmes: see further the discussion below.

33 Cf. Kenya where the Constitution of Kenya (Amendment) Act 1988 repealed the security of tenure provisions in the 1962 Constitution. This blatant attempt to make judges serve at the whim of the President provoked considerable internal and external criticism and led to a 1990 constitutional amendment that substantially restored the pre-1988 position: see Constitution of Kenya (Amendment) Act 1990. See also G. K. Kuria and A. M. Vaquez, 'Judges and Human Rights: the Kenyan Experience' (1991) 35 *Journal of African Law* 142, at pp. 145–6.

34 And subject to a satisfactory medical report. In Namibia judges retire at the age of sixty-five but the President is entitled to extend the retiring age to seventy (s.82(4) Namibian Constitution). A curiously open-ended approach is found in Tanzania. Here if the President considers it in the public interest, s/he may direct that a judge who has attained the age of sixty (and with his/her written consent) to continue in office 'for any period which may be specified by the President' (art. 110(3) Constitution of Tanzania).

Contract and fixed term appointments Difficulties in recruiting adequate numbers of suitably qualified local candidates to the Bench has led to the appointment of expatriate judges on fixed-term contracts in several ESA states.[35] Given that such a position may also appeal to prospective appointees who may not wish to commit themselves to a new jurisdiction until retirement age, the contract system has some mutual benefits. For jurisdictions with smaller work loads, part-time appointments to the apex court have also proved useful. This is the case in both Botswana and Namibia where some highly distinguished expatriate judges have contributed significantly to the development of constitutional rights.[36]

The major difficulty with a system of fixed term appointments is reconciling it with security of tenure. There is a danger that concern over a future renewal of contract might influence a judge's decision in a case whilst disgruntled litigants might seek to use political pressure to block the contract renewal of a particular judge. Certainly appointees will never know whether unpopular decisions, particularly those on judicial review, will rebound upon them when their contracts come up for renewal.[37] The pressures that can be brought to bear on such judges are well illustrated by the case of Justice Derek Schofield in Kenya. In 1987 the expatriate contract judge was told by the then Chief Justice (also an expatriate contract judge) that if he persisted in dealing with a sensitive case involving the police in a particular way, the Chief Justice would have difficulty in recommending a renewal of contract. As Schofield himself has noted, '. . . if that was the price I had to pay for a renewal of contract I was not prepared to pay it'[38] and he subsequently left the country at the expiration of his contract.

[35] Kenya, Lesotho, Zambia, Zimbabwe and Uganda have all at one time or another appointed expatriates as full-time contract judges. In the case of Zimbabwe, four expatriate judges from Ghana and Tanzania were recruited on contract by the Zimbabwean government in the mid-1980s owing to an acute shortage of local judges.

[36] See cases such as *Unity Dow v Attorney-General* [1992] LRC (Const) 623 (Botswana) and *Ex parte Attorney-General, Namibia in re Corporal Punishment by Organs of State* 1991 (3) SA 76. Even here, there is some concern over the retention of such judges due to their (understandable) lack of knowledge of local conditions and the brevity of their visits.

[37] As a former contract judge in Kenya has put it: 'I suspect that if judges on contract were asked whether, when renewal time come around, they ask themselves if they have made any unpopular decisions, many would reply in the affirmative' (D. Schofield, 'Maintaining Judicial Independence in a Small Jurisdiction', in Hatchard and Slinn, *Parliamentary Supremacy*, at p. 76.

[38] Ibid.

To help address such problems, contract judges must enjoy at least the same terms and conditions of service as permanent appointees.[39] In addition, a contract judge must have the right to an automatic renewal of contract except where grounds for the removal of a permanent judge exist or where a suitably qualified local candidate is available. The appointment of expatriate contract judges has declined markedly in recent years and may well cease in due course. Even so, it is important to ensure that those who remain continue to enjoy, as far as possible, the same terms and conditions as permanent appointees.[40]

Acting/ad hoc judges A system of acting judges fulfils a number of useful functions. A senior High Court judge may be invited to sit as an acting Justice of Appeal to fill a temporary vacancy or to gain experience in the apex court. Further, it permits retired judges to return to the bench to help ease a backlog of cases as well as enabling senior legal practitioners to sit as judges for a certain period annually for similar reasons. Acting appointments are also a useful means of assessing the suitability of individuals for possible elevation to the Bench.

In general, such appointments are non-controversial and, indeed, perform a useful function. However, two safeguards are appropriate. Firstly, that they are made for a strictly limited period and only on the JSC's recommendation. Secondly, as far as possible, acting judges should not sit on constitutional cases.[41]

Undertaking non-judicial functions The use of senior judges to head presidential or governmental commissions of inquiry and the like is

[39] Until relatively recently, the British Government paid handsome supplements to British expatriate contract judges. This was justified as being necessary to 'compensate' them for the potential loss of career opportunities elsewhere. The system was fatally flawed in that (subject to the willingness of the British to continue the scheme) whether or not such supplements were continued and to whom they were payable was essentially a matter for the host government.

[40] The position of Constitutional Court judges in South Africa is unusual. The eleven judges are appointed for a non-renewable term of twelve years (or up to the age of seventy) (Constitution of South Africa, s.176(1)). Whilst perhaps a necessary provision given the constitutional position at the time, it is a far from satisfactory situation. In particular the mass exodus of the judges at the termination of their contracts would deprive the court of the expertise, experience and standing currently enjoyed by the judges. A review of the appointment process is certainly needed.

[41] This is to meet the concern of the possible 'packing' of the apex court with acting judges in order to encourage an interpretation of constitutional provisions that meets the wishes of the executive.

relatively common. This follows the British tradition and is seen as facilitating the organisation and running of the proceedings and helping to reassure public opinion as to the commission's objectivity. Few hard and fast rules are necessary for, as Goldstone has suggested, if judges act in a non-partisan manner 'they can hardly be accused with any justification of displaying bias or interfering with their independence or that of their colleagues'.[42] However one essential rule is that a judge should not agree to head (nor be a member of) a commission in circumstances that affect, or may be seen to affect, the independence of the judiciary or which could undermine the separation of powers.[43] For example, a judge should decline to chair a presidential constitution-making body to which there is significant public opposition.[44]

The involvement of judges with political parties and causes, non-governmental organisations and charitable activities also requires extreme care.[45] The principle that this should not 'reflect adversely upon [their] impartiality or interfere with the performance of [their] work'[46] is difficult to maintain in practice and it is advisable for judges, however well-intentioned, to avoid involvement in such activities. This is particularly the case in smaller jurisdictions, although the result may be that judges and their families are effectively cut off from society.

[42] R. Goldstone, 'Do Judges Speak Out?' (1994) 111 *South African Law Journal* 268.

[43] See paragraph 24 of *Judicial Ethics in South Africa.* The 'code' was issued in March 2000 by the Chief Justice and other senior judges. See also E. Kahn, 'Extra-judicial Activities of Judges' (1980) *De Jure* 188. Widner notes that Chief Justice Nyalali 'agonized' as to whether to accept President Mwinyi's request to chair the commission on the future of the one-party state in Tanzania precisely because he feared it might adversely affect the independence of the judiciary: J. Widner, *Building the Rule of Law: Francis Nyalali and the Road to Judicial Independence in Africa*, Norton and Company, New York, 2001, pp. 293–4.

[44] Cf. the case of Justice Godfrey Chidyausiku in Zimbabwe discussed in chapter 3.

[45] Especially following the problems caused for the House of Lords in the Pinochet affair: see in particular *R v Bow Street Metropolitan Stipendiary Magistrate, ex parte Pinochet Ugarte (Amnesty International and others intervening) (No. 2)* [1999] 1 All ER 577. In *President of the Republic of South Africa and Others v South African Rugby Union Football Union* 1999 (4) SA 147 the Constitutional Court was faced with allegations of perceived bias on the basis that some of the judges had had close links with the President and the African National Congress. The court applied the test of 'perceived bias', i.e. whether a reasonable and informed litigant would reasonably apprehend that the judges concerned would not decide the case impartially. The Court stated, somewhat impractically, that judicial officers are under a duty to withdraw from cases if there is a reasonable apprehension that they would not decide the case impartially. However, if there are no good grounds for such apprehension, judicial officers were under a duty to adjudicate cases before them.

[46] Rule 12 Code of Conduct for Judges, Magistrates and Other Judicial Officers 1989, Uganda.

Magistrates

Magistrates are often the 'forgotten' persons in discussions on judicial independence. This is most unfortunate for they play a crucial role in the entire judicial system given that they hear the vast majority of criminal cases and make other key decisions such as the granting of bail. Magistrates' courts are also the places where the most impoverished, powerless and defenceless in society often come. If they have no confidence in magistrates and their court officials, perceiving them to be pro-executive and pro-police, this has a significant detrimental effect on society. Not only does it impact adversely on the administration of justice but also it carries with it significant social and economic consequences including potential resort to instant justice.[47]

Yet in some countries the magistracy faces serious difficulties. Firstly, continuing the colonial practice of retaining magistrates as public servants can lead to their politicisation. To counter this, the trend towards bringing magistrates under the auspices of the JSC should become the norm.[48] Secondly, magistrates often face considerable operational problems including serious structural limitations.[49] These combined with isolation from a supportive legal community can lead to poor morale and performance. Here the only real solution is for states to provide magistrates with facilities and support comparable to that given to other judges. Thirdly, magistrates often experience poor conditions of service and a general lack of human rights training. Addressing such issues will inevitably take time but the goal must be to ensure that magistrates enjoy, as far as possible, comparable training and conditions of service as judges in the higher courts.[50] Finally, there remain serious problems relating to court staff. Corruption, inefficiency and lack of a 'service' ethos for court users must be addressed. As with magistrates themselves, the first challenge is to provide appropriate training and conditions of service for such staff.

[47] See further J. Hatchard and M. Ndulo, *Readings in Criminal Law and Criminology*, Multimedia, Lusaka, 1994, p. 94.

[48] A good approach is that in Malawi where magistrates are appointed by the Chief Justice on the recommendation of the JSC and hold office until the age of seventy. See s.111(3) Constitution of Malawi.

[49] These extend to such basic items as run down buildings, no lockable cupboards to store records and evidence securely, lack of reference materials and inadequate security for personnel and buildings.

[50] Local courts also function in all the SEA states. Given their wide-ranging jurisdiction over family law, succession and the like, their work impacts directly on the majority of the people and particularly those in the rural areas. In practice their structure and operation varies considerably and a discussion on the courts is therefore beyond the scope of this book.

Towards a fully representative judiciary

Upholding the judicial oath of office to administer justice *to all persons* represents a considerable challenge for judges who are inevitably the product of their social conditioning, education, gender and ethnicity. If they are to discharge fully their judicial oaths and to enjoy the broad confidence of the people, they must be drawn from a wide array of different backgrounds to ensure a better understanding of the experiences of those with whom they will be dealing.[51]

The need to maintain a gender balance within the judiciary is now widely recognised.[52] As Cartwright notes:

> It goes without saying that women start with a better understanding of women's lives because that is our conditioning. It does not mean that women judges are biased in favour of women . . . but because gender means assumptions about men and women . . . it is essential for one half of the population to have one half of the judiciary understand something of their lives while the other half strive to learn more about them.[53]

Much remains to be done for the number of women in the judiciary at all levels remains disappointingly low with only South Africa, Zimbabwe and Zambia in the region having women sitting in their apex courts. The position is particularly serious at the local court level where the indications are that women are grossly under-represented, this despite the fact that no formal professional qualifications are required and that the majority of cases involve the family and domestic relations.[54] Encouraging equality requires states to identify and tackle the factors that inhibit the entry of women and minorities onto the bench: for example, not imposing the duty upon women to go on circuit or be posted away from their home areas. The 'fast-tracking' of appropriate candidates is also necessary

[51] See, for example, paragraph 7 of the Bloemfontein Statement of 1993: '. . . it is fundamental to a country's judiciary to enjoy the broad confidence of the people it serves: to the extent possible, a judiciary should be broad-based and therefore not appear (rightly or wrongly) beholden to the interest of any particular section of society'.

[52] One of the Principles enshrined in the *Latimer House Guidelines* states: 'It is recognised that redress of gender imbalance is essential to accomplish full and equal rights in society and to achieve true human rights. Merit and the capacity to perform public office regardless of disability should be the criteria of eligibility for appointment'. The *UN Basic Principles on the Independence of the Judiciary* state that in the selection of judges there shall be no discrimination against a person on grounds of sex (para 10).

[53] Cartwright, 'The Judiciary', p. 45.

[54] For example, a report on Zambia found that there were only sixteen female local-court justices out of a total of 907 (1.6 per cent). See 'The Dilemma of Local Courts in Zambia', Report of the Inter-African Network for Human Rights and Development, 1998, http://afronet.org.3a/reports/Lcourts.htm.

although this should not be at the expense of applying less rigorous qualification requirements on them, for the principle that judicial appointments are made on merit is inviolable. Arguably, the appropriate approach to redressing existing imbalances is for all levels of the judiciary to have, as an objective, a selection system based on 'merit with bias', i.e. that where two candidates are of equal merit the bias should be to appoint a woman or member of an under-represented minority. But encouraging more women to seek appointment to the bench is only part of the story. It is crucial that steps are taken to ensure equality of men and women entering the legal profession itself. This must start with law schools adopting a 'merit with bias' approach towards the admission of students until effective parity is achieved. This is already occurring in some law schools, but must be regarded as a universal norm.

Financial autonomy

Probably the most impressive collective statement by countries of the Commonwealth on judicial funding is contained in the 1998 *Latimer House Guidelines.*[55] Paragraph II(2) states:

> Sufficient funding to enable the judiciary to perform its functions to the highest standards should be provided. Appropriate salaries, supporting staff, resources and equipment are essential to the proper functioning of the judiciary. As a matter of principle, judicial salaries and benefits should be set by an independent commission and should be maintained. The administration of monies allocated to the judiciary should be under the control of the judiciary.

Financial autonomy is fundamental. Without it, the executive can seriously impact upon judicial independence by limiting the judiciary's access to the funds voted to it by parliament and/or by assuming control of the services and staff upon which the judiciary depends. Two aspects require particular attention.

Providing for judicial self-accounting

Providing budgetary independence enables the judiciary to control its own funds and to make use of them according to its own priorities.[56]

[55] *Guidelines on good practice governing relations between the executive, parliament and the judiciary in the promotion of good governance, the rule of law and human rights to ensure the effective implementation of the Harare Principles.*

[56] Ideally a constitution should also provide for a judiciary that is self-accounting. See, for example, s.118(3) Constitution of Lesotho.

This is not the case in many ESA countries where the judiciary is required to go 'cap in hand' to the relevant government ministry with a request for funds. This results in the decision whether to grant any or all of the funds requested resting with the executive according to its own policy or priorities or presidential dictates.

Terms and conditions of service

The UN Basic Principles on the Independence of the Judiciary state that 'the term of office of judges, their independence, security, adequate remuneration, conditions of service, pensions and the age of retirement shall be adequately secured by law'.[57] As Kirby puts it:

> A decision-maker who must examine and weigh up evidence and submissions fairly, and reach conclusions affecting powerful and opinionated interests, must be put beyond the risk of retaliation and retribution . . . That is what the tenure of judges and other independent office-holders is about. It concerns giving substance to the promise that important decisions will be made neutrally: without fear or favour, affection or ill-will.[58]

Here the constitutional provisions in some ESA states need reinforcing.

Remuneration Given the earnings enjoyed by most successful legal practitioners, taking up a judicial appointment almost inevitably leads to a considerable reduction in income. Whilst it is probably impossible to equate judicial remuneration with that of senior legal practitioners, a realistic income is necessary, both to attract and retain capable candidates and to reduce the chances of judges becoming vulnerable to corruption or even going on strike.[59]

Invariably, and rightly, the remuneration of judges is voted by Parliament and paid out of the Consolidated Revenue Fund[60] and cannot be reduced whilst a judge remains in office. With the ongoing rampant inflation in many of the ESA states, judicial salaries rapidly lose their value. Whilst there is certainly a case for insisting upon all-round 'belt-tightening' in times of economic hardship, judicial salaries must never be allowed to fall too low and a regular review of the position by the Judicial

[57] Para 12.

[58] Michael Kirby, 'The Abolition of Courts and Non-Reappointment of Judicial Officers in Australia', Ronald Wilson Lecture, Perth, Australia, 28 November 1994.

[59] In June 1998, magistrates in several parts of Zambia went on strike over pay. As the Law Association chairman reportedly noted, the pay for magistrates 'can neither instil confidence nor alleviate corruption', *Times of Zambia*, 20 June, 1998.

[60] This is the central fund for government income and expenditure.

Services Commission or even an independent statutory review body is eminently desirable.[61]

The retired judge Providing satisfactory retirement benefits for judges also strengthens judicial independence and can help combat corruption. This is particularly so because pension rights are limited as appointment to the Bench often comes comparatively late in life whilst future 'employment' prospects are limited. There are seemingly no constitutional restrictions *per se* upon retired judges taking up other constitutional or official positions such as an ambassadorial posting. Even so, the acceptance of such an appointment requires careful consideration for this might fuel public concern that a judge's previous decisions, especially in cases involving government, may have been affected by the promise of an attractive appointment upon retirement.[62]

In principle, whilst retired judges may accept an appointment as a consultant to a law firm, it is not acceptable for them to return to legal practice where this would entail them appearing in court. Embarking on a career in politics is also a sensitive matter, especially as this may provide ammunition to political opponents out to attack perceived bias within the judiciary. Similarly, and for similar reasons, becoming actively involved with non-governmental organisations that have political affiliations should also be discouraged.

Maintaining the status of the judiciary

Protection for and accountability of judges

Judicial independence and judicial accountability are closely related. A society must support and protect the judiciary for, as the 2000–1 Zimbabwe crisis demonstrates, judges remain an easy target for those wishing to make partisan political capital. In return, society can expect judges to accept fair and temperate criticism of judgments and to maintain appropriate standards of ethical behaviour.

[61] In Malawi judicial salaries and allowances must be increased periodically so as to retain their original value (s.114(2) Constitution of Malawi).

[62] A particularly unacceptable practice occurred on several occasions in Zambia under the presidency of Kenneth Kaunda where judges were removed from the bench and appointed to the executive and sometimes to the ruling party, UNIP, and then back to the bench. This created great insecurity among the judges and significantly decreased their ability to withstand government pressure.

To help retain the sensitive balance between independence and accountability, several ESA states have developed codes of judicial ethics. These are an extremely desirable means of establishing the parameters for public expectations and criticism of judicial conduct. The method of creation of such codes varies. Providing a statutory code, as in the case of Zambia, raises concern that the legislature or Minister may have too much input into determining the appropriate conduct for judges. In any event a statutory code is arguably inappropriate in that ethical rules are seldom absolute and it is preferable to set out standards of conduct rather than to lay down legally enforceable rules. This has led to the development of codes by members of the judiciary themselves.[63] These have the advantage of ensuring that the code has judicial support although, of course, it runs the risk of being viewed from the outside as being a self-serving document. Given its potential relevance to so many, the development of a code is best undertaken as a result of a co-operative effort on the part of judges, the legal profession, legal academics and civil society,[64] preferably based on internationally agreed standards.[65]

Ideally, such a code should deal with both the exercise of judicial duties and extra-judicial activities and, in particular, require judges to disclose their assets: this to check against potential corruption. Whilst many lay down rules that are seemingly straightforward and obvious to lawyers, they provide the public with a clear statement as to what they can expect from their judges. It is extremely useful, for example, to know that judges who cause undue delay in the hearing of cases, or serve in a politically sensitive capacity are justifiably open to public criticism. The effectiveness of such codes largely depends upon their wide public dissemination and much more effort is required in this respect.[66]

Curiously, there is rarely any formal procedure for the taking of disciplinary action for any breach of the code of ethics where the complaint

[63] The *Latimer House Guidelines* call for the development and adoption by each judiciary of a code. Such codes exist in Tanzania, Namibia and South Africa.

[64] A suitable body for drafting, revising and overseeing the working of the code is therefore a fully representative Judicial Service Commission.

[65] See, for example, the *Bangalore Principles of Judicial Conduct* which were drawn up by the *Judicial Group on Strengthening Judicial Integrity* in February 2001 and whose drafting committee included senior judges from Uganda, Tanzania and South Africa. The Code highlights six values: *Propriety* (propriety, and the appearance of propriety, are essential to the performance of all of the activities of a judge); *Independence*; *Integrity*; *Impartiality*; *Equality* (ensuring equality of treatment to all before the courts); *Competence and diligence*.

[66] For example, ensuring a copy of the code in all the major languages is readily available to all litigants.

does not involve the possibility of removal. In practice such matters are usually dealt with as an internal matter by the Chief Justice with no public admonition of the judge. This is not adequate. To maintain public confidence it is necessary to develop an effective method of upholding judicial accountability as well as offering appropriate protection for judges against unfounded criticism. A suitable approach is the establishment of an independent Judicial Ombudsman that is the link between the judges and the public. This might be a separate institution or an additional responsibility given to the Judicial Service Commission. For example, in Uganda the JSC is mandated to receive recommendations and complaints concerning the judiciary and the administration of justice from members of the public, and to investigate complaints and to take 'appropriate action' in collaboration with the judiciary. This is useful so far as it goes, but the lack of a requirement to make public the results of its enquiries is a serious shortcoming. There is a need for transparency in such matters and there is no reason why details of disciplinary action against any judicial officer should not be made public.

Few ESA states follow the Ugandan lead of expressly providing for judicial immunity from prosecution.[67] This is a serious omission as this protection 'enables judges to act fearlessly and impartially in the discharge of their judicial duties as it will be difficult for the judges to function if their actions in court are made subject to legal proceedings either civil or criminal'.[68] The President himself/herself enjoys such immunity and the position of the judges is undoubtedly strengthened if such a protection is extended to them by the constitution.

The limits on the criticism of judges

Legitimate criticism of judges arising from the discharge of their duties, even if somewhat emphatic and unhappily expressed, is permissible as being the exercise of the freedom of expression.[69] Unjustified and unreasonable attacks on judicial integrity strikes at the judiciary's constitutional role and, in extreme cases, a court may cite its critics for contempt of court.[70] Unless resorting to this extreme action, inevitably judges

[67] Art 128(4) of the Constitution of Uganda provides: 'A person exercising judicial power shall not be liable to any action or suit for any act or omission by that person in the exercise of judicial power.'

[68] Statement of Objects and Reasons in the Judges (Protection) Act 1985 (India).

[69] See, for example, Ogilvie Thompson C. J. in *S v van Niekerk* 1972 (3) SA 711 (A) at 720.

[70] There are two modes of conduct that fall within the scope of criminal contempt. One is contempt in the face of the court. The other is conduct calculated to bring a court, a judge or the administration of justice through the courts generally into contempt. It is sufficient

themselves and their families must 'suffer in silence'. As Gubbay has put it: 'Unlike other public figures, judges have no proper forum in which to reply to criticisms. They cannot debate the issue in public without jeopardizing their impartiality.'[71] This is why providing public support for the judiciary is essential, particularly on the part of the Attorney-General[72] and Minister of Justice. Speaking out in defence of judicial independence is also a prime duty of legal professional bodies in fulfilment of their commitment to uphold the rule of law and the protection of human rights. Law teachers in their writings must expose flawed judgments but this must never extend to personal attacks on judges.

The relationship between parliament and the judiciary remains a potentially tense and acrimonious one. Paragraph I of the Executive Summary to the *Latimer House Guidelines* emphasises the need to apply the doctrine of 'mutual restraint', i.e.:

> Relations between parliament and the judiciary should be governed by respect for parliament's primary responsibility for the making of legislation and for the judiciary's role in interpreting legislation and in ensuring its compatibility with the constitution.

Yet experience has shown that the judicial role of interpreting legislation (as well as the constitution itself) can bring it into conflict with both parliament and the executive and make it the subject of harsh and bitter criticism.[73] Constitutional adjudication is inherently controversial and political disputes inevitably enter the judicial arena. Yet it is inimical to the rule of law if political pressure is directed towards the judges by those who have not succeeded in the judicial adjudication or who wish to influence future decisions. Parliamentarians and ministers, like everyone else, must accept court decisions until they are either overturned by a

'if it is a scurrilous attack on the judiciary as a whole, calculated to undermine the authority of the courts and endanger public confidence, thereby obstructing and interfering with the administration of justice. See *Chokolingo v A-G of Trinidad and Tobago* [1981] 1 All ER 244 (PC) at 248' per Gubbay C. J. *In re Chinamasa* [2001] 3 LRC 373 at p. 384.

[71] A. R. Gubbay, 'The Independence of the Judiciary: Judicial Autonomy and Budgetary Control and Administration,' in Hatchard and Slinn, *Parliamentary Supremacy*, p. 49.

[72] Regrettably, in many countries the politicisation of the post has effectively removed the Attorney-General from playing any meaningful supportive role for the judiciary. See generally the unpublished paper by Charles Goredema, 'The Attorney-General in Zimbabwe and South Africa: Whose weapon, whose shield?' in which he argues that the politicisation of the post of Attorney-General means that the incumbent cannot perform his/her functions in an independent manner with the result that the institution is 'emasculated' (at p. 25).

[73] See, for example, the experience of the Zimbabwe Supreme Court discussed in chapter 3.

superior court or through a constitutionally authorised process. They are entitled to criticise a ruling but what is never acceptable is the making of vague allegations of improper motives for decisions, personal attacks on the integrity of individual judges or threats against their personal safety. As East puts it, the relationship between parliaments and the courts 'should be marked by mutual respect and restraint'.[74]

Sadly, as the 2000–1 crisis in Zimbabwe demonstrated, judges of an internationally renowned apex court, not forgetting several principled High Court judges, were harassed and threatened both verbally and physically simply for carrying out their constitutional duties. In consequence, the much-admired Chief Justice was forced to take early retirement. Damaging to the judiciary, certainly. But even more damaging to society and especially those who seek the protection of their constitutional rights.[75] We must also remember that the crisis did not develop overnight but came as a result of a gradual undermining of constitutional safeguards and the accumulation of presidential power, often through the use of constitutional amendments.

Removal proceedings

Given that judges and magistrates hold office during 'good behaviour', invariably misbehaviour is a ground for removal. Equally, removal for mental incapacity is unexceptional. 'Incompetence' is sometimes an additional ground for removal. This is a somewhat vague concept but can perhaps be judged against the criteria for judicial performance set out in a Judicial Code of Conduct.[76] The protection of judicial security of tenure means strictly limiting the grounds for removal.[77] Accordingly

[74] Paul East, 'Free Speech: Parliamentary Privilege and the *sub judice* rule' in Hatchard and Slinn, *Parliamentary Supremacy*, 117 at p. 119.

[75] Another example comes from Zambia where the decision by Evans, J. in the politically sensitive case of *Silva and Freitas* [1969] ZR 121, led to physical attacks on the judge and the Chief Justice. President Kaunda himself added fuel to the fire by denouncing the judge stating 'I think Justice Evans should have known that in taking up the case like that in a sensitive situation he was playing with fire' (Interview with the *Times of Zambia* 29 September 1969). The attacks led to the departure of several senior judges and the affair undoubtedly undermined the independence of the judiciary for some years. See further John Hatchard, *Individual Freedoms and State Security in the African Context: the Case of Zimbabwe*, Ohio State University Press, Athens, Ohio, 1993, p. 132.

[76] See art. 144 Constitution of Uganda. A poor legal knowledge might perhaps fall into this category. Kahn refers to several South African judges who were known amongst practitioners as 'Old Necessity' because either 'Necessity knows no law' or 'Necessity is the mother of invention' (see Kahn, *Law, Life and Laughter*, Juta, Cape Town, 1984, p. 15).

[77] Although there seems to be no bar to a president 're-assigning' a serving judge, with their consent, to another position within the public service. See, for example, s.119(7)

there is serious cause for concern when such removal can be for 'any other cause'.[78]

A transparent and independent removal procedure is also essential. A fundamental constitutional issue here concerns who has the right to initiate such proceedings. Whilst any person or body is entitled to call for removal, arguably the initiation is best left to an independent Judicial Service Commission (or Judicial Ombudsman) or the Chief Justice. If left in the hands of the President, Cabinet or Parliament, it provides a potential weapon through which to intimidate judges and thus help create or maintain a pliant judiciary. In effect, it undermines the separation of powers and the independence of the judiciary. Yet article 119(3) of the Constitution of Malawi provides:

> The President may by an instrument under the Public Seal and in consultation with the Judicial Service Commission remove from office any Judge where a motion praying for his removal on the ground of incompetence in the performance of the duties of his office or misbehaviour has been-
> (a) debated in the National Assembly
> (b) passed by a majority of the votes of all the members of the Assembly;
> (c) submitted to the President as a petition for the removal of the judge concerned;
>
> Provided that the procedure for the removal of a judge shall be in accordance with the principles of natural justice.

The danger was highlighted in 2001 with the moving of a parliamentary motion for the removal of three High Court judges and a resultant petition to the President (apparently made under article 119) for their removal from office. This was seemingly in response to decisions made by the three judges that were unacceptable to certain members of Parliament and which were perceived as being biased in favour of political opponents.[79]

In practice it is a common constitutional requirement for the President to establish a tribunal of inquiry acting on the advice of the Chief Justice or the JSC, to investigate the allegations.[80] Here it is essential that neither the Chief Justice nor the JSC make any public statement or

Constitution of Malawi. Whilst in the past this may have been necessary as a means of making the best use of scarce human resources, the provision now poses a potential threat to judicial independence. Of course this does not apply to the secondment of a judge to a senior international judicial posting, such as to the International Court of Justice.

78 E.g. s.87(1) of the Constitution of Zimbabwe.

79 Parliament went so far as to issue summons to the judges to appear before the House and state their case: this despite a High Court restraining order.

80 This would also be an important function for a Judicial Ombudsman.

comment concerning the merits of the grounds for the possible removal of a judge(s).[81] This is the more so in that several ESA constitutions place a duty on the Chief Justice or JSC to advise the President on whether or not to suspend a judge whilst the matter is before the tribunal.[82] The tribunal's recommendations are then binding on the President. As regards magistrates, Uganda provides an excellent model in that the JSC appoints and exercises disciplinary control over magistrates including the power to remove them from office.[83]

The judiciary and the promotion and protection of constitutional rights

Maintaining an effective and ethical judiciary

The judiciary's effectiveness in protecting and promoting constitutional and other rights also depends upon the judges having the necessary training and 'tools' with which to do the job. It was once a widely held view that judges did not require any training although how elevation to judicial office gave them sufficient knowledge and wisdom to deal with every legal issue that might come their way was never explained. As Cartwright forcefully puts it, the belief by judges that any form of compulsory study:

> . . . would interfere with their own independence to determine cases impartially has given way to an appreciation that this was a recipe for stagnation or for the idiosyncratic decision-making that arises from isolation.[84]

Today providing continuing judicial education is almost universally seen as being a necessary and integral part of strengthening the judiciary. Key areas include the development of judicial skills, IT skills and social context education. Sensitising judges to the social setting in which decision-making occurs is particularly desirable as they may have little familiarity

[81] This includes publicly pressurising judges to resign or face having their case referred to a tribunal of inquiry.

[82] See, for example, art. 84(5) Constitution of Namibia and s.62(6) Constitution of Kenya. To avoid any consititutional problems here, it is surely advisable to provide for the suspension of the judge as soon as the case has been referred to the tribunal of inquiry: see, for example, art. 144(5) Constitution of Uganda.

[83] In large jurisdictions, such a responsibility may overburden a JSC and hence the creation of a separate Magistrates' Commission with similar powers as a JSC is worth considering.

[84] 'The Judiciary', at p. 42.

with gender issues, customary-law matters or comparative Commonwealth jurisprudence. How such training is organised varies from state to state. In Uganda, for example, the JSC is tasked with preparing and implementing judicial education programmes. In Zimbabwe the Judicial Studies College[85] provides similar training although significantly, this is not only for judges and magistrates but for others involved in the administration of justice. This emphasises that improving the quality of judicial performance also involves developing appropriate training for all those in the administration of justice with the aim of improving the efficiency of the entire system. In the absence of any formal training body, this is an area in which human rights commissions might consider involvement, perhaps working with law schools to develop suitable courses and/or materials and engaging law teachers to assist with the running of the programmes.

A judiciary committed to judicial activism and social justice is particularly necessary where the failure of other state organs to address problems adequately means that the rule of law will be substantially impaired if the courts fail to secure fundamental rights to the poor and the disadvantaged.[86] As Baxi puts it:

> . . . an activist judge will consider herself perfectly justified in resorting to law-making power when the legislature doesn't bother to legislate. Whatever may be said in the First World concerning this kind of law-making by judges . . . , it is clear that in almost all countries of the Third World such judicial initiatives are both necessary and desirable.[87]

If judges are to fulfil this role effectively, they must have exposure and access to local, regional and international human rights developments and comparative Commonwealth jurisprudence. Since 1988 the series of *Judicial Colloquia on the Domestic Application of International Human Rights Norms* have had a significant impact in this respect. Organised by the Commonwealth Secretariat and Interights,[88] the series has brought together judges from ESA countries (and beyond). Paragraph 9 of the 1988 *Bangalore Principles* states as follows:

[85] Established by the Judicial Studies College Act 1998.

[86] See Bhagwati J. in *Gupta v President of India* AIR 1982 SC 149, at p. 189.

[87] Upendra Baxi, 'On the Shame of not being an Activist: Thoughts on Judicial Activism', in N. Tiruchelvam and R. Coomaraswamy, *The Role of the Judiciary in Plural Societies*, London, Inter, 1987, p. 173.

[88] The International Centre for the Legal Protection of Human Rights, an NGO based in the United Kingdom.

> It is essential to redress a situation where, by reason of traditional legal training which has tended to ignore the international dimension, judges and practising lawyers are often unaware of the remarkable and comprehensive developments of statements of international human rights norms. For the practical implementation of these views it is desirable to make provision for appropriate courses . . . ; provision in libraries of relevant materials; . . . better dissemination to judges, lawyers and law enforcement officials; and meetings for exchanges of relevant information and experience.

The 1989 Harare Colloquium further emphasised the need to develop a culture of respect for international human rights norms 'which would see these norms applied in the domestic law in national courts'.[89] Together with the holding of several national training programmes, the impact has been remarkable with apex courts in the ESA region (and throughout the Commonwealth) regularly referring to and obtaining guidance from international and regional human rights norms as well as comparative Commonwealth jurisprudence.[90] This still requires further development and the use of law interns to assist judges undertake research is an area in which law schools can help make a useful contribution. The development of IT skills amongst the judiciary to enable them to take advantage of the wealth of legal materials on the Internet would further enhance their performance.[91]

The most effective way of gauging the effectiveness and competence of judges is through examining their judgments. Until recently in many ESA jurisdictions, this task was virtually impossible due to the wholly inadequate system of law reporting. In fact the development of law reporting is one of the recent 'success' stories, with an increasing number of states establishing or re-establishing their own series of law reports and key decisions becoming available on the Internet. As well as enabling other Commonwealth jurisdictions to utilise such decisions, international exposure (and often acclaim) for them has also been helpful in strengthening the

89 Lord Lester of Herne Hill, 'The Challenge of Bangalore: Making Human Rights a Practical Reality' (1999) 25 CLB 50.

90 This has also led to judges throughout the common-law world using decisions from courts in the ESA states, and in particular decisions of the Zimbabwe Supreme Court and the South African Constitutional Court.

91 This implies that judges have access to the appropriate hardware. In practice, foreign donors have readily supplied the necessary equipment but the challenge has been to persuade some judges to use it. For example, every judge of the Zimbabwe Supreme Court was supplied with a computer in the mid-1990s. Little use was ever made of them as the judges viewed them with suspicion and continued to write their judgments in longhand. This situation may resolve itself as younger and more computer-literate individuals are appointed to the bench.

position of judges against presidential, ministerial and parliamentary criticism of 'unpopular' decisions. Certainly condemnation by international jurists of the attacks on members of the Zimbabwe judiciary in 2000–1 were spurred by their high regard for the Supreme Court's judgments.

In terms of training and resources, magistrates remain the poor relations. Whilst some cases go on review to higher courts, the fact that the decisions of magistrates are seldom, if ever, reported and the difficulties in obtaining their written judgments, mean that there remains scope for considerable abuse of power and corruption. In-service training is certainly a partial answer. But the decisions and activities of magistrates need to be thoroughly analysed and researched. Surprisingly, there is little literature on this area and the need for in-depth research on the magistracy is urgent.

There is also a need to assist legal practitioners improve the quality of legal arguments on constitutional matters before the courts, a problem often exacerbated by their having inadequate access to relevant comparative case law and other research materials.[92] In practice, it may be that the court has access to decisions and other material that raises a point not dealt with by counsel. Here it is essential that the court gives both sides an opportunity to submit arguments on the point. This was emphasised by Dumbutshena AJA in the Namibian Supreme Court in *Kauesa v Minister of Home Affairs & Others*:[93]

> It would be wrong for judicial officers to rely for their decisions on matters not put before them by litigants either in evidence or in oral or written submissions. Now and again a judge comes across a point not argued before him by counsel but which he thinks material to the resolution of the case. It is his duty in such circumstances to inform counsel on both sides and invite them to submit arguments either for or against the judge's point. It is undesirable for a Court to deliver a judgment with a substantial proportion containing issues never canvassed or relied on by counsel.

In addition, it is quite unacceptable (and arguably unethical) for a Court to make no mention of, or merely passing reference to, significant issues and decisions relied upon by counsel in arguing a constitutional matter.

It follows that to assist counsel, the development of compulsory continuing legal education courses as well as access to adequate research facilities, including the Internet, are essential. Here the pooling of library and IT resources or maintenance of a well-stocked court library or university law

92 On several occasions senior judicial figures have complained privately to the authors about the frequency of poorly presented constitutional cases.

93 1996 (4)SA 965 (NmSC) at pp. 973–4; [1995] 3 LRC 528 at pp. 533–4.

library has much to commend it.[94] It is also essential to include international, regional and comparative Commonwealth human rights jurisprudence in the law curriculum. This calls for a commitment on the part of all law schools to incorporate such topics into their teaching at all levels.[95]

Interpreting the constitution

Adopting a liberal approach to the rules of locus standi and other procedural requirements in constitutional cases is essential; for those whose rights 'are allegedly trampled upon must not be turned away from the court by procedural hiccups'.[96] This is especially necessary where poverty, illiteracy and governmental abuse of power is so prevalent.[97]

Refreshingly, courts in many ESA states have adopted this liberal approach. As Lugakingira J. in the Tanzanian case of *Mtikila v Attorney General* has noted, the

> . . . notion of personal interest, personal injury or sufficient interest over and above the interest of the general public has more to do with private law as distinct from public law. In matters of public interest litigation this court will not deny standing to a genuine and bona fide litigant even when he has no personal interest in the matter . . . where the court can provide an effective remedy.[98]

This enlightened approach has enabled civil society groups, in particular, to take up the cases of vulnerable groups and individuals.[99] It remains to

[94] For example, in Zimbabwe the Leo Baron Library is operated by a local NGO, the Legal Resources Foundation. This provides access to local, comparative and international legal materials that is unrivalled outside of the Supreme Court library and one that is open to all legal practitioners.

[95] There are moves to address this problem. In particular the Commonwealth Legal Education Association has developed a model human rights curriculum and related materials that is freely available to all legal educators (see www.ukcle.ac.uk/clea).

[96] Per Harper J. A. in *Att-Gen v Alli* [1989] LRC (Const) 474 (Court of Appeal of Guyana) approved by Egonda-Ntende J. in *Rwanyarara v S* (Court of Appeal of Uganda, unreported, 1998).

[97] Cappelletti argues convincingly that in modern societies a single action can be beneficial or prejudicial to a large number of people. This makes the traditional two-party adversarial approach inadequate and thus there is a need to develop new procedures and remedies: (M. Cappelletti 'Access to Justice: the Judicial Process in Comparative Perspective,' 1922 *TSAR* 256, at pp. 268–308).

[98] High Court of Tanzania, unreported, 1994, at p. 11.

[99] See, for example, *Catholic Commission for Justice and Peace v Attorney General* 1993 (2) ZLR 442; *Unity Dow v Attorney General* [1992] LRC (Const) 623 and *Ferreira v Levin* 1996 (1) BCLR 1 (CC).

be seen how far the courts are prepared to extend the locus standi rules although it is likely that they will refuse to grant it in cases when activists seek to raise purely political issues for judicial determination.[100]

On the issue of constitutional interpretation, this turns upon the ability and willingness of judges to tease from a series of written clauses a political philosophy upon which to base society. This provides a range of options from a strictly legalistic approach:

> This court has always stated openly that it is not the maker of laws. It will enforce the law as it finds it. To attempt to promote policies that are not found in the law itself or to prescribe what it believes to be the current public attitudes or standards in regard to these policies is not its function;[101]

to adventurous judicial activism:

> The Constitution-makers have given us one of the most remarkable documents in history for ushering in a new socio-economic order and the Constitution which they forged for us has a social purpose and an economic mission and therefore every word or phrase in the Constitution must be interpreted in a manner which would advance the socio-economic objective of the Constitution.[102]

The role of constitutional interpretation means that judges are the co-architects in the building of a society based on the rule of law and respect for fundamental rights. For some, this is disturbing: the liberal approach to constitutional interpretation introduces into the legal system uncertainty and unpredictability and a situation where the law is non-static and never finally settled. It also raises the 'counter-majoritarian difficulty' described by Bickel as follows:

> [W]hen the Supreme Court declares unconstitutional a legislative act . . . it thwarts the will of the . . . people of the here and now; it exercises control, not on behalf of the prevailing majority but against it.[103]

[100] See *United Parties v Minister of Justice, Legal and Parliamentary Affairs* 1997 (2) ZLR 254; [1998] 1 LRC 614.

[101] Pickard C. J. in *Bongopi v Chairman of the Council of State, Ciskei* 1992 (3) SA 250, at p. 265.

[102] Bhagwati J. in *People's Union for Democratic Rights v Union of India* AIR 1982 SC 1473, at p. 1478.

[103] A. M. Bickel, *The Least Dangerous Branch*, Yale University Press, New Haven, 1962, pp. 16–17.

This attack centres on the view that unelected and unaccountable judges,[104] can nullify the actions of a democratically elected legislature and ministers who are accountable to the people. The vast body of literature emanating from the United States, in particular, bears witness to the convoluted efforts that many have made to develop an appropriate constitutional theory on the issue.[105] For the ESA states there are several specific considerations to support such activism.

Firstly, it is the court's express constitutional duty to interpret fundamental rights provisions. This is not unlimited, however, for it must be remembered that 'there are functions that are properly the concern of the courts and others that are properly the concern of the legislature. At times these functions may overlap. But the terrains are in the main separate and should be kept separate'.[106] Secondly, given the enduring weakness of legislatures, the reality is that the judges are often, albeit perhaps reluctantly, seen as the 'guardians of the Constitution' and are bound by their oath of office to uphold the Constitution and 'fearlessly administer justice to all persons without favour or prejudice . . .' Thirdly, executive lawlessness remains a fact of life. Legislation, both primary and secondary, is passed or approved by compliant legislatures and used to enhance unduly presidential power and to thwart the will of the people. The judiciary therefore has the duty to protect the basic structure of the constitution. Fourthly, the development of an appropriate appointment, promotion, training and accountability regime for judges means that they can expect the people's respect, trust and support in carrying out their duties. Fifthly, judges follow certain basic principles of interpretation, some of which are laid down in the constitution itself. Thus the South African Constitution

[104] Although, see the earlier discussion on judicial accountability.

[105] For a useful overview see Dennis Davis, Matthew Chaskalson and Johan de Waal, 'Democracy and Constitutionalism: the Role of Constitutional Interpretation', in Dawid van Wyk *et al. (eds.) Rights and Constitutionalism: the New South African Legal Order*, Clarendon Press, Oxford, 1995, p. 7–10.

[106] Chaskalson P. in *S v Makwanyane* 1995 (6) BCLR 665 at para. 104. As Chaskalson has also put it: '. . . government of a modern state cannot be undertaken without regulating the affairs of the inhabitants in various ways. Regulation which differentiates rationally between categories of persons but does not discriminate unfairly between them, does not infringe the equality clause of the Constitution. But unfair discrimination is not permissible and constitutes a breach of the Constitution: see *Prinsloo v van der Linde* 1997 (6) BCLR 759 (CC) at para. 25; and *National Coalition for Gay and Lesbian Equality v Minister of Justice* 1998 (12) BCLR 1517 (CC) at paras. 15–19.' A. Chaskalson, 'The Role of the Judiciary in Translating Human Rights Law into Practice', in *Developing Human Rights Jurisprudence, Volume 8* 2001, Interights/Commonwealth Secretariat, pp. 252–3.

provides that when interpreting the Bill of Rights a court, tribunal or forum, 'must promote the values that underlie an open and democratic society based on human dignity, equality and freedom'.[107] In the absence of any express provision, courts can rely on the Privy Council decision in *Minister of Home Affairs v Fisher* where Lord Wilberforce noted that constitutions, 'call for a generous interpretation avoiding what has been called "the austerity of tabulated legalism", suitable to give individuals the full measure of the fundamental rights and freedoms referred to'.[108] Based on this approach, the Zimbabwe Supreme Court, for example, has developed a series of basic principles that have guided its approach to fundamental rights cases.[109] These have proved helpful from an analytical point of view and for ensuring consistency in constitutional interpretation. During the judicial crisis of 2000/1, they also helped negate presidential and ministerial accusations of bias or favouritism on the part of senior judges and showed that such attacks were no more than political posturing of the very worst kind.

Of course the making of subjective choices is an inevitable part of constitutional interpretation. As the Namibian Supreme Court noted in the *Corporal Punishment* case:[110]

> [T]he decision which this court will have to make in the present case is based on a value judgment which cannot primarily be determined by legal rules

[107] S.39(1)(a). They must also consider international law and may consider foreign law: s.39(1)(b)(c). Section 11 of the Malawian Constitution challenges the courts to develop 'appropriate principles' for constitutional interpretation to 'reflect the unique character and supreme status' of the Constitution. In doing so courts shall, amongst other things 'promote the values which underlie an open and democratic society' and 'where applicable, have regard to current norms of public international law and comparable foreign case law'.

[108] [1980] AC 319 at p. 328. The jurisprudence of the Supreme Court of Canada on the Canadian Charter of Human Rights has also been referred to regularly by courts in the SEA states, particularly the case of *R v Big M Drug Mart Ltd* (1985) 18 DLR (4th) 321. This is partly because the jurisprudence reflects modern thinking, partly because Canada, like most SEA states, had a justiciable Bill of Rights grafted onto an older Westminster model and partly because the Charter served as one of several precedents examined when later constitutions in the region were being drafted.

[109] See, in particular, *In re Munhemeso* 1994 (1) ZLR 49 and *Retrofit (Private) Ltd v PTC* 1995 (2) ZLR 422. See also *S v Zuma* 1995 (4) BCLR 401 the very first case of the Constitutional Court of South Africa: 'A Constitution embodying fundamental rights should as far as the language permits be given a broad construction' (per Chaskalson P. at p. 412); and the judgment of Aguda J. A. in *Unity Dow Attorney-General* [1992] LRC (Const) 623, at p. 668.

[110] *Ex parte Attorney-General, Namibia in re Corporal Punishment by Organs of State* 1991 (3) SA 76; [1992] LRC (Const) 515.

> and precedents, as helpful as they may be, but must take full cognizance of the social conditions, experiences and perceptions of the people of this country.

Courts must therefore adopt the 'always speaking' approach to constitutional interpretation. As Aguda J. A. explained in *Unity Dow v Attorney General*:[111]

> The Constitution is the Supreme Law of the land and it is meant to serve not only this generation but also generations yet unborn. It cannot be allowed to be a lifeless museum piece; on the other hand the Courts must continue to breath life into it from time to time as the occasion may arise to ensure the healthy growth and development of the State through it . . . We must not shy away from the basic fact that whilst a particular construction of a constitutional provision may be able to meet the designs of the society of a certain age such a construction may not meet those of a later age . . . I conceive it that the primary duty of the judges is to make the Constitution grow and develop in order to meet the just demands and aspirations of an ever developing society . . .[112]

In making what are in effect value judgments, one key issue is the extent to which a court should take into account the public's views. According to the court in *S v Vries*:[113]

> There may be a need for an 'evidentiary enquiry' into public opinion in determining current community values and norms. The words of the Constitution alone will not always be a sufficient indicator of the underlying values and objectives of a constitutional guarantee.

Thus in the Tanzanian case of *Republic v Mbushuu*[114] the Court of Appeal was faced with the issue of the constitutionality of the death penalty. Whilst accepting that it constituted a 'cruel or degrading punishment', the court considered that the issue of its retention was a matter of proportionality i.e. was the death penalty reasonably necessary? The court considered that it was for society to decide. It therefore took into account newspaper articles suggesting continued considerable public support for

[111] [1992] LRC (Const) 623, at p. 668.

[112] See also the judgment of Manyindo D.C.J. in the Ugandan Constitutional Court case of *Tinyefuza v Attorney General* (1997, unreported) where he stated, 'while the language of the Constitution does not change, the changing circumstances of a progressive society for which it was designed may give rise to a new and fuller import to its meaning' (at p. 16).

[113] 1996 (12) BCLR 1666 (High Court of Namibia).

[114] [1994] 2 LRC 335.

capital punishment and held that in the circumstances the 'reasonable and necessary' standard for upholding the constitutionality of the provision had been met. In *State v Makwanyane*, a case involving the same issue, Kentridge J. in the Constitutional Court of South Africa also commented that 'Public opinion . . . could not be ignored. The accepted mores of one's own society must have some relevance to the assessment . . .'.[115]

Bowing to popularist demands is a dangerous course for any court to take and is an imprecise and unsatisfactory means of proceeding. Given the sometimes wide social, ethnic, religious and economic disparities within a country, it is not clear just how a court can determine 'contemporary community standards'. Relying on newspaper articles to glean public opinion is surely an abrogation of judicial responsibility for constitutional interpretation. More worrying still is the potentially disastrous effect such an approach can have on the protection of minority rights. As Chaskalson P put it in *Makwanyane* itself:

> The very reason for establishing the new legal order [in South Africa], and for vesting the power of judicial review of all legislation in the courts, was to protect the rights of minorities and others who cannot protect their rights through the democratic process. Those who are entitled to claim this protection include the social outcasts and marginalised people of our society . . . .'[116]

Herein lies the nub of the issue. Constitutional interpretation requires courts to take a broad approach that promotes the 'values that underlie an open and democratic society based on human dignity, equality and freedom'. As Chaskalson P has emphasised:

> This Court cannot allow itself to be diverted from its duty to act as an independent arbiter of the Constitution by making choices on the basis that they will find favour with the public.[117]

The task of interpreting a constitution is a difficult, and sometimes dangerous exercise. Inevitably, decisions will not satisfy everyone. The development of clear principles by the courts based upon international and Commonwealth norms will both help ensure that there is a consistent approach to constitutional interpretation and act as a justification for judicial activism.

[115] [1995] 1 LRC 269, at p. 352 (CC). [116] Ibid., at p. 311.

[117] Ibid. at para 88. See the discussion by J. Hatchard, 'Constitutionality of the Death Penalty and Penal Policy' (1995) 39 *Journal of African Law* 192, at pp. 193–4.

Overview

Judicial independence is best maintained by its formal constitutional entrenchment backed up by a commitment by all state organs to respect the rule of law and 'accord such assistance as the Courts might require to protect their independence, dignity and effectiveness'.[118] As this chapter has demonstrated, it is precisely when the rule of law is ignored that judicial independence is most at risk.

Ongoing political and public support for judges can help ensure judicial independence. When problems emerge, only the maintenance of effective safeguards can enable judges to continue to carry out their constitutional functions. As the Zimbabwe experience has demonstrated, factors such as weaknesses in the appointment system of judges, politicisation of the Attorney General's office, the willingness of some judges to identify themselves too closely with political controversy and the unwillingness of governors and legislators, from the President downwards, to accept court decisions, all contributed to the undermining of judicial independence.

To provide real protection for the judiciary, we must examine the 'nuts and bolts' of the system. This involves ensuring the maintenance of an effective, transparent and independent appointment and removal process for judges and magistrates, an appropriate procedure for judicial funding, the development and maintenance of satisfactory conditions of service and the development of effective judicial accountability mechanisms. In return, society has a right to expect judges and magistrates to be dedicated, honest and courageous and amenable to adequate and ongoing training. Further that they will keep:

> ... the scales even in any legal contest between the rich and poor, the mighty and the weak, the State and the citizen. As much injustice can be done by keeping the scales weighted in favour of the citizen against the State, as it can be by keeping the scales weighted in favour of the State against the citizen.[119]

This means that fair, temperate and constructive criticism of judgments and judicial conduct is not only justified but eminently desirable as a means of improving judicial performance. Here judicial codes of conduct have an important role to play. However, threats and malicious personal attacks on judges merely bring the perpetrators into disrepute and

[118] See art. 78(3) Constitution of Namibia and s.165(4) Constitution of South Africa.

[119] H. R. Khanna, *Law, Men of Law and Education*, Tripathi, Bombay, 1981, p. 9.

both the local and international legal community must roundly condemn those who attack judicial officers for seeking to uphold their oaths of office. We must not overlook the fact that the effectiveness of the judiciary in upholding and defending constitutional rights also depends on courageous legal practitioners being prepared to take on governments and argue contentious and unpopular cases. For individual lawyers, the support of their professional association is vital as is that from fellow practitioners in other jurisdictions.

A point of potential friction between the judiciary and the other organs of state and civil society concerns constitutional interpretation. Judicial activism is an integral part of constitutionalism but it needs to be approached carefully and systematically. This calls for clear principles of interpretation either enshrined in the constitution itself and/or developed by the judges based on internationally recognised norms. Today the influence of the *Bangalore Principles*, the development of judicial training and the resultant cross-pollination of ideas between judges throughout the Commonwealth has led to an unparalleled vibrancy in constitutional interpretation that has rightly earned some apex courts in the ESA region an international reputation.

Overall, only an independent judiciary committed to appropriate judicial activism can play the role set out at the beginning of this chapter. This is to recognise that:

> ... ordinary men and women need support in their fight to claim and protect their liberties. And their natural protectors are courts, not governments. After all, most governments think they know best what the public interest requires, and are inclined to play down, if not ignore, the rights of those opposed to their policies. Courts need the power, as well as the will, to help governments resist such temptations.[120]

[120] A. Chaskalson quoted in Lord Lester of Herne Hill "The Challenge of Bangalore: Making Human Rights a Practical Reality" (1999) *Commonwealth Law Bulletin* 47 at p. 50.

9

The devolution of power to local communities

Introduction

There are typically three levels of government: national, sub-national (regional), and local government. Decentralisation stresses the attribution of central government functions to lower levels of government (regional or local units), to which may then be granted a sphere of autonomy protected against the supremacy of national government. In answer to the demands for a greater self-determination and influence in decision-making, many countries worldwide are devolving political, fiscal, and administrative powers to sub-national tiers of government. This trend can be seen in countries with a long tradition of centralist government, as well as in federalist systems, and in developing as well as industrialised countries.

This chapter provides a more general analysis of the subject-matter than others in this book because the issue of the devolution of power is one that many of the ESA states have yet to address adequately. The ESA independence constitutions did not provide for elected governments accessible to the people at the local level. Rather the local government systems that were established were centrally controlled by the Ministry of Local Government and power remained consolidated in the central government. With the exception of South Africa and Uganda, this situation still largely remains the same.

In this chapter we examine the arguments for devolution; the powers sub-national tiers of government should enjoy; the relationship between sub-national tiers of government and the central government; and the critical elements that must be addressed if devolution is to succeed. Devolution seeks to transfer political, administrative and economic authority from the centre to local communities and seeks to promote popular participation, empower local people to make decisions, enhance accountability and responsibility and aims to introduce efficiency and effectiveness in the generation and management of resources. Because of this it is important that the means adopted to devolve power have a realistic possibility of achieving the objectives of devolution. This chapter also highlights the key issues relevant to the process of devolution of power to local communities. In the discussion concepts like 'federalism' are avoided since they are not conducive to productive analysis. What framework the devolution of power takes in individual states depends on the political and economic conditions that prevail in the country.

The shift towards devolution is largely a reflection of the political evolution towards more democratic and participatory forms of government that seek to improve the responsiveness and accountability of political leaders to their electorates. It is premised on the fundamental belief that once they are entrusted with their own destiny through the medium of popular local democratic institutions, human beings can govern themselves in peace and dignity in pursuit of their collective well-being. The general arguments to support devolution are therefore clear. It is only through participatory and representative democracy that any forum of government can legitimately formulate its priorities and programmes. In economic terms, devolution permits governments to match the provision of local public goods and services with the preferences of recipients. Competition between sub-national tier governments can also lead to the introduction of innovative social and regulatory policies that can then be adopted nationwide. In political terms, devolution provides local minorities with greater opportunities to preserve their distinctive cultural and linguistic identities. As Ortega y Gasset has observed:

> Devolution of power to regions will serve not only to satisfy historical, cultural and linguistic aspirations, but also, and above all, will draw the average citizen closer to the centres of power and increase his [or her] capacity to control and participate in the decisions of government.[1]

Further, throughout history, societies have attempted to reconcile diversities of culture, religion and language through devolution, particularly in large countries where a unitary and central administration is difficult. Yet, even with smaller nations, where such an administration might be feasible, devolution has proved attractive by being able to accommodate local interests within the stability of a strong central authority. Not surprisingly, then, history shows that the balance of power between central and sub-national tier authorities tends to flow back and forth in response to changing conditions and leadership. Devolution of power to local communities is, therefore, a critical element of good governance for it

[1] Discussed in J. Rodden and S. Rose-Ackerman, 'Federalism Preserves Markets' (1997) 83 Va. LR 1573, at p. 1580.

provides additional checks and balances on central government and a degree of security for constitutional order and social stability that are vital for economic order and development.[2]

Good governance and the devolution of power

Developing the legitimacy and credibility of the government in the eyes of the people is closely related to government conduct and the institutions it puts in place for popular participation at all levels. This requires the effective devolution of government.[3] Before discussing some of the elements required for effective devolution, it is important to understand the case for devolution itself. It is equally important to be clear about the possible dangers that are inherent in the establishment of a sub-national tier system of government. Devolution does not automatically ensure good governance. It means, therefore, that care must be taken to structure devolution in such a way that it is effective if its positive contributions are to be maximised and its negative potential minimised.

The political benefits

With regard to the positive contribution on the political side, a well-constructed sub-national system can enhance good governance. As a South African study[4] has observed, devolution can deepen democracy by bringing government closer to the people. By creating a number of governments below the national level, it multiplies the opportunities for political participation and thus helps to foster the creation of a democratic culture in a country. Locally elected leaders know their constituents better than authorities at the national level, and so are potentially well positioned to provide the public services that local communities need. When things go wrong, physical proximity also makes it easier for citizens to hold local officials accountable for their performance. Further, when a country finds itself deeply divided, especially along geographic or ethnic lines, which is the case in most of the ESA states, devolution provides an institutional mechanism for bringing opposition groups into a formal, rule-bound

[2] See Preamble, *European Charter of Local Government*, Council of Europe Treaties, ETS No. 122.

[3] Report on 'Regions in South Africa: Constitutional Options and Their Implications for Good Governance and a Sound Economy', Report Prepared by the Consultative Business Movement, (unpublished) Johannesburg, SA, 1993, p. 2.

[4] Ibid., at p. 11.

bargaining process. For example, in Uganda and South Africa devolution has served as a path to national unity.[5] In Uganda the task Yoweri Museveni faced when he assumed power in 1986 was to reunite a country that had splintered into hostile factions during years of turmoil. The broad-based politics of 'Resistance Councils' and committees that had developed during the years of civil war helped pacify most of the country.[6] In South Africa the adoption of a political system that gave substantial powers to the provinces was crucial to bringing the Inkatha Freedom Party into the 1994 electoral process which ushered in a democratic South Africa.[7] In both Uganda and South Africa, then, political participation at the local level laid a stronger foundation for stable national governance.

Another important political advantage of devolution is that sub-national authorities can reduce the concentration of power at the centre and thus hinder its arbitrary exercise. In other words, they form an additional accountability mechanism and help to allay the fear of the 'tyranny of the majority'. Further, a devolved system can provide channels for the expression of regional sentiments, and encourage national policies to become more sensitive to regional variations within a particular country. Devolution can also provide scope for regional interests on the political stage, and provide an opportunity for minority parties, which might otherwise be excluded from political power, to exercise an influence and to make their voice heard. In short, a regional system of government can be more, rather than less, 'inclusive' than a purely central government system.

The economic benefits

On the economic side, a devolved system allows the opportunity to formulate and implement regional or sub-regional economic development plans within the context of national goals. This enables development strategies to be targeted more accurately towards the specific needs of particular communities and areas of the economy. Regional plans also permit and encourage a greater sense of involvement in the work of economic development by bringing that work closer to the people. Devolution can

5 World Bank, 'Entering the Twenty-First Century', World Development Report 1999/2000, Washington, DC, p. 109.
6 Y. Museveni, 'What is Africa's Problem?', NRM Publications, Kampala, 1992, p. 48.
7 Final Report of the United Nations Observer Mission in South Africa (UNOMSA) to the Secretary General, 'A Democratic Non-Racial and United South Africa', 1994.

also play a vital role in creating the conditions for balanced growth within the different areas of the country. Regional formations can help maximise the benefits to be derived from intra-national comparative advantages, backward and forward linkages, and economies of agglomeration, and enhance the optimal utilisation of resources. Inequalities between regions can also be counteracted by a deliberate national policy of inter-regional transfers. For example, in Uganda, the Constitution provides for an 'equalisation grant', payable from the Consolidated Revenue Fund, and based on the level of development of the sub-national region and the degree to which the region is 'lagging behind the national average standard for a particular service'.[8] Finally, regional formations provide an institutional framework for coherent and balanced development, and for targeted interventions where needed.

Drawbacks to devolution

There are, however, political dangers in the devolution of power to sub-national units. For example, wrongly structured sub-national entities such as regions can provide an opportunity for political mobilisation on the divisive base of ethnicity or religion, with potential consequences of political oppression, intolerance and, at the extreme, secessionist movements. A related danger is that a regional system might frustrate the task of 'nation-building'. As noted in chapter 6, such concerns have encouraged some states to prohibit the formation of regional political parties. Further, regions have the potential to undermine democracy by inappropriately segmenting or compartmentalising political functions at levels where there is no financial responsibility or policy-making power. Two additional dangers exist. Firstly, regional systems may make government less transparent and accountable by creating a mass of interlocking bureaucracies or 'intergovernmental organisations'. Secondly, devolution can create a mushrooming bureaucracy or sets of bureaucracies. Government departments can be multiplied unnecessarily which is likely to fragment government functioning and services even further. Where this happens devolution can in fact act as an impediment to development.

There are also some potential negative economic effects which need to be taken into consideration when creating or demarcating a country into a system of sub-national entities. Firstly, such an arrangement can

[8] See Constitution of Uganda, art. 193(4).

create an exorbitantly expensive government. By unnecessarily multiplying government departments, regions can become costly and inefficient. Secondly, a devolved system might tend to preserve or shore up the existing economic inequalities between regions, and frustrate the redistribution of wealth that is needed to create a balanced and united nation. Thirdly, devolution can frustrate the implementation of a coherent national economic development programme by creating a host of competing policies relating to economic matters. Further, different regional incentives relating to investments can create undesirable distortions in the economy.

Decentralisation can also entail significant costs in terms of distributional equity and macroeconomic management. This can be especially important in large countries where the economic differences among regions are substantial and can lead to undesirable internal migration, as well as social and political pressures. Decentralisation can also be costly if, because of inequalities in capacity to govern among the sub-national entities that are created, it results in the substandard provision of certain public goods, such as primary education or basic health care, as this can affect productivity and the long-term growth prospects of the economy.

Accordingly, for a system of devolution of power to be successful, it must address a number of key issues. One is to institutionalise the balance of power between the national government and the sub-national governments created. This requires clear rules on devolution, and particularly those concerning the distribution of political power. A second is to develop rules dealing with the way sub-national governments are structured, what they do at each level, and how they are funded. These rules need to be determined as a system, taking into account the interaction between fiscal, political and administrative institutions. This leads to perhaps the most difficult and controversial issue of all: deciding which tier of government controls which resources. The ability of sub-national authorities to act independently of the centre depends on whether they have access to independent tax bases and sources of credit. The third key issue requires the development of rules governing relations between local officials and their constituents, for this, in particular, determines whether devolution produces the intended benefits.

The task of constitution-makers is to ensure that all of the above issues are adequately dealt with and that different levels of government do not compete but are complementary and further the process of good governance and development. In planning and execution, the positive sides of devolution must be encouraged and the negative sides minimised.

The colonial and post-colonial legacy

Traditional African society was highly devolved.[9] Gluckman, for instance, writing about the Lozi of Zambia, observed their complex economy which required many people to co-operate in various productive activities. The village was the basic unit of organisation in the structure of the Lozi economic, political and domestic system. This was the centre from which they exploited gardens and parcels of land. Villages ran their own affairs, had their own judicial systems, conducted their own external relations with other villages and ran their day-to-day affairs without any interference from the Chief. The village was headed by a headman who was responsible for the village to the King in Council and represented the village at the Council. The Chief headed Council and governed with the assistance of councillors.[10]

With the advent of colonialism, African societies experienced protracted economic and social changes. Colonial rule was philosophically and organisationally elitist, centrist and absolute and distorted or destroyed pre-colonial governance systems. Culturally, colonialism divided states into two societies: the traditional culture found in the rural areas where the great majority of the people lived and which was largely outside of the colonial elitism, and the 'modern' culture found in the urban areas. The result was that the colonial state was characterised by a huge gap in the standard and quality of life between the rural and the urban areas. Power was centralised in the governor who, however, had an elaborate system of provincial and district commissioners (all appointed by the governor) that gave considerable discretion to the officers mostly in the field of law and order and the adjudication of local disputes.[11] Indeed, the colonial legacy has endured long after independence.[12]

[9] See generally E. Colson, *Seven Tribes of Northern Rhodesia*, Manchester University Press, Manchester 1957: M. Gluckman, *Politics and Ritual in Tribal Society*, Manchester University Press, Manchester. 1965; I. Dore, 'Constitutionalism and the Post-Colonial State in Africa: a Rawlisian Approach' (1997) 41 *St Louis University Law Journal* 1302.

[10] M. Gluckman, *The Judicial Process amongst the Barotse of Northern Rhodesia*, Manchester, University Press, Manchester 1967, p. 7. See also M. Mainga, *Bulozi under the Luyana Kings*, Longmans, London, 1973.

[11] See Zambian Cabinet Office Circular No. 13 of 1969, 1 February 1969. The circular was an attempt to reorganise the colonial system by the Kaunda government.

[12] B. O. Nwabueze, 'Our March to Constitutional Democracy,' *Guardian Lecture*, 24 July, 1989. Also published in *Law and Practice*, (August 1989), 19–38. R. B. Seidman, 'Perspectives on Constitution-Making: Independence Constitutions for Namibia and South Africa' (1987) 3 *Lesotho Law Journal* 45.

After independence, the degree of centralisation in many ESA states increased especially with the establishment of one-party systems of government. This trend was accompanied by attempts to transfer influence away from the public service towards ruling parties. In 1975, the Zambian President, Kenneth Kaunda, in his address to the National Council of the United National Independence Party (UNIP) stated:

> UNIP is supreme over all institutions in our land. Its supremacy must not be theoretical nor is it enough to merely reduce it to a constitutional provision. More than ever before, our task now is to translate party supremacy into something much more meaningful in the life of our beloved nation.[13]

Zolberg has observed a similar trend in West Africa. He notes that the cumulative effect has been to concentrate and personalise power at the centre, i.e. in the office of the President, and adds:

> The major trend suggested a steady drive to achieve greater centralization of authority in the hands of a very small number of men who occupy top offices in the party and the government, and even more in the hands of a single man at the apex of both institutions.[14]

These moves were primarily concerned with political consolidation and integration. It was often argued that a strong central government was necessary to advance integration and economic development. Kaunda himself argued:

> In formulating proposals for decentralizing action in Zambia we need to bear in mind that Zambia is still a very young state – less than a single decade in age – so that we must be conscious of the dangers of learning to run before we can walk by putting burdens on the relationships within our infant state which may prove too much for our capacity to carry.[15]

In the name of nation building, reversing the colonial structure and bringing about more relevant structures, many ESA governments destroyed the decentralisation that existed under the colonial system of provincial and district administration. This was seen as necessary since it was at the provincial and district level that the extraordinary autocratic powers of the colonial government were most visible. It was therefore

[13] See B. C. Chikulo, 'Decentralisation in Centralism: an Analysis of the Zambian Experience 1964–1981', in K. Osei-Hwendie and M. Ndulo (eds.), *Issues in Zambian Development*, Omenana, Rosbury, MA, 1985, p. 341.

[14] Referred to by Chikulo, ibid., at p. 348.

[15] Ibid., p. 350.

decided that the local administration system should lose its power and its distinctive autocratic identity, which had so alienated the population. As a result, local authorities were stripped of most of their powers which were transferred to newly created central government departments and ministries. As Chikulo has observed, the primary issue which concerned the political leadership at this stage was one of establishing political control over the public service and the country as a whole.[16]

Predictably, political monopolies led to corruption, nepotism and abuse of power. Presidents replaced the colonial governor but like them they became the sole embodiment of the social will and purposes of the countries they ruled. This led to the increased dominance of the repressive one-party system of government[17] which ensured that power not only became centralised but also came to be concentrated in the person of the President. The result was unprecedented economic decline and mismanagement, resulting in unimaginable poverty and a growing economic divide between the urban and rural areas. The dreams of prosperity following independence and self-rule became the nightmares of insecurity and poverty.[18]

Challenges to providing effective devolution of power

The rural/urban divide inherited from the colonial period continues today and has in fact grown. The rural areas continue to be largely neglected, marginalised and impoverished with an extremely weak state presence that is almost completely irrelevant as a provider of services. A large percentage of the people, many of whom live in the rural areas, remain outside the formal structures of the state and rely on self-help and self-reliance for their survival. There is also mounting evidence that the International Monetary Fund (IMF)/World Bank stabilisation and economic structural adjustment programmes that are in place in many of the ESA states have worsened the situation.[19] These programmes have, for example,

[16] Ibid., at p. 341.

[17] C. Gertzel, C. Baylis and M. Szeftel, *The Dynamics of the One Party State in Zambia*, Manchester: Manchester University Press, 1984, and A. Yusuf, 'Reflections on the Fragility of State Institutions in Africa' (1994) 2 *African Yearbook of International Law* 1, at pp. 2–8. See also L. Zimba, 'The Origins and Spread of One-Party States in Commonwealth Africa and their Impact on Personal Liberties; a Case Study of the Zambian Model', in M. Ndulo (ed.), *Law in Zambia*, East African Publishing House, Nairobi, 1984, p. 113.

[18] T. M. Shaw, *Alternative Futures for Africa*, Westview Press, Boulder, Co, 1982, p. 93.

[19] T. Mkandawire and C. Soludo, *Our Continent Our Future: African Perspective on Structural Adjustment* CODESTRIA, Trenton, NJ, African World Press, 1999, p. xi.

undermined the position of the poor rural farmers, in that, through high interest rates, they have restricted their access to credit for production and marketing. Withdrawal of state marketing agencies has also exposed these farmers to exploitation by large traders. The duality of the rural/traditional and the modern/urban sector finds its legal underpinning in the dualism of European-inspired law and customary law.[20] It is further reinforced by the lack of popular participation in governance, and is exacerbated by the lack of effective devolution of power to local communities.

There is thus a critical need for the devolution of power to be undertaken in a manner that will not only improve governance and enhance the accountability of leaders but also make the state a participant in people's lives. In the institutional sense, this means addressing the issue of the centralisation of power. This refers to the constitutional concentration of power in the hands of a few executive offices (and therefore a few people) that undermines the constitutional importance of courts, legislatures and sub-regional governments. This is usually reinforced by the tendency of governments to concentrate the most critical human and financial resources at the headquarters, while leaving rural administration with a lean administrative structure that lacks adequate resources or discretionary authority. A further major feature of any centralised state is a preoccupation with bureaucracy and planning and, hence, the preference for concentrated structures rather than diversified and devolved institutions that emphasise the grassroots empowerment of the people. Another feature is financial centralisation. The central state collects all of the most important and buoyant tax resources and makes scarce funds available to sub-national authorities. Compounding this problem is the fact that financial transfers to sub-national authorities are often done via grants, which are given on a sporadic, rather than on a regular and systematic basis.

Effective devolution of power should mean that the delivery of most government services is devolved to the local level, be it a regional or sub-regional government thus taking the burden off the already

[20] See generally R. B. Seidman and A. Seidman, 'The Political Economy of Customary Law in the Former British Territories of Africa' (1984) 28 *Journal of African Law* 44; V. Palmer and S. Poulter, *The Legal System of Lesotho*, Michie Company Law Publisher, Charlottesville, VA, 1972; M. Ndulo, 'Customary Law and the Zambian Legal System,' in P. Tikarambudde (ed.), *The Individual under African Law: Proceedings of the First All-Africa Law Conference*, 11–16 October 1981, University of Swaziland, Kwaluseni, 1982, p. 121; A. Allott, *New Essays in African Law*, Sweet and Maxwell, London, 1970.

over-extended central government.[21] It entails the existence of local communities endowed with democratically constituted decision-making bodies and possessing a wide degree of autonomy with regard to their responsibilities, the ways and means by which those responsibilities are exercised and the financial resources required for their fulfillment. The right of citizens to participate in the conduct of public affairs is more directly exercised at the local levels. The existence of devolved authorities that are given real responsibilities can provide an administration that is both effective and close to the citizen. Unlike more centralised systems, this provides for more flexible responses attuned to local needs. It opens opportunities for innovation and experimentation in policy formulation and delivery. It can alleviate the workload of an over-stretched central government, something that is especially important to ESA states in view of the numerous tasks of development and transformation that face a typical government.[22]

Even after the wave of democratisation of the 1990s, very few ESA states have made any serious efforts to decentralise power and even among those that profess commitment to it, there is often a wide gap between political rhetoric and reality.[23] There has been little devolution of power on both substantive matters (policy and development programmes) and administrative (budget and personnel) matters to enable sub-national governments to undertake their functions effectively. The results of the current arrangements are not only a waste of resources but also encourage corruption in central government institutions and lower the ability of lower-level government institutions to expand or even maintain existing infrastructures. In addition, because power is not devolved, the struggle to control the central government becomes a matter of life (and sometimes death) among the political leadership. As a result, states tend to be strong in those areas in which they ought to be weak (repressive power) and weak where they ought to be strong (popular mobilisation and responsiveness).[24]

[21] M. Stoddard, 'South Africa's Elections: Establishing Democracy at the Grassroots', (1997) 21 Fletcher F World Affairs, 83, at p. 85.

[22] R. Simeon, 'The Structures of Intergovernmental Relations', paper presented at the International Roundtable on Democratic Constitutional Development Conference, 1995 July 17–20, Pretoria, South Africa.

[23] B. C. Chikulo, 'Decentralisation in Centralism: an Analysis of the Zambian Experience (1964–1981)', in Kwaku Osei-Hwedie and Muna Ndulo (eds.), *Issues in Zambian Development*, Omenan, Roxbury, MA: 1985, p. 341.

[24] James Paul, 'Developing Constitutional Orders in Sub-Saharan Africa: an Unofficial Report', in *Building Constitutional Orders in Sub-Saharan Africa* (1988) *Third World Legal Studies*, p. 5.

The process of democratisation must therefore go hand in hand with that of the devolution of power to local communities. It is not enough to have democracy at the national level; it must be complemented at the sub-national and community levels. Societal and state institutions must exist as partners in social engineering and must seek to empower the ordinary people in matters of governance. Democracy itself implies self-governance, and local community-based social and political institutions ought to be the building blocks of a new and effective polity. South Africa and Uganda are the only two ESA states that have made serious efforts to decentralise power. South Africa is divided into nine provinces with the legislative authority being vested in their provincial legislatures. Within the provincial system, there exists a local government level consisting of municipalities whose executive and legislative authority is vested in their municipal councils. The Local Government: Municipal Structures Act 1998 calls for three main types of municipality – metropolitan councils, local councils and district councils. The provinces and municipalities have the right to govern the affairs of their communities, subject to any national legislation,[25] whilst the central government retains primary fiscal responsibility for expenditure that has a major redistributive impact, such as health and education.[26] The Constitution thus provides considerable space for local communities to play a part in the national development process. In the case of Uganda, the system entails giving power to the people within a village to freely choose their leaders within the forty-six districts, which are subdivided into smaller units down to the village level, which likewise hold substantial responsibilities for education, health and local infrastructure.[27]

[25] Constitution of South Africa, s.151(3).

[26] Constitution of South Africa, ss.213–14. The relationship between national and provincial governments, competence of provincial legislatures in respect of regional planning, local government and development and local government registration of land-tenure rights were considered by the South African Constitutional Court in *DVB Behuising (Pty) Limited v North West Provincial Government and Another*, 2000(4) BCLR 347.

[27] See generally the Constitution of Uganda, chapter 11. In particular, article 176(3) enumerates the principles that apply to the local government System as follows: (a) the system shall be such as to ensure that functions, powers and responsibilities are devolved and transferred from central government to local government units in a coordinated manner; (b) decentralisation shall be a principle applying to all levels of local government and in particular, from higher to lower government units to ensure people's participation and democratic control in decision-making; (c) the system shall be such as to ensure the full realisation of democratic governance at local-government levels; (d) there shall be established for each local government unit a sound financial base with reliable sources of income; and (e) appropriate measures shall be taken to enable local-government units to

The other ESA states' constitutions typically have in place local-government systems whose powers and functions are limited. In Namibia the Constitution provides for regions whose power and duties are as may be assigned to them by an Act of Parliament and may be delegated to them by the President.[28] Similarly the Malawi Constitution establishes local government authorities whose powers include: the promotion of infrastructure and economic development; the presentation to central government authorities of local development and plans; the consolidation of local democratic institutions and democratic participation.[29] The powers do not include the capacity to enact legislation. In fact there is no transfer of political power in the arrangement.[30]

When it comes to finance, the local authorities are almost completely dependent on the central government. For example, section 150 of the Malawi Constitution provides that Government is under a duty to ensure that there is adequate provision of resources necessary for the proper exercise of local government functions. The budget for local government authorities is prepared by the National Local Government Finance Committee which prepares a consolidated budget for all local government authorities and presents it to the National Assembly through the Minister of Local Government.[31] The Tanzanian Constitution in article 145 provides for the establishment of local government authorities and states that the purpose of local government authorities is to transfer authority to the people and to consolidate legislative powers and democracy at the local level.[32] Here again the authorities are not provided with adequate powers to raise revenue. In a decentralised system, for the transfer of power to be meaningful sub-national tier governments have to share in political power and be empowered to raise funds and draw up their own budgets. Also, the governing councils or parliaments of the regions or sub-regions must approve the budgets. Taxpayers, either through their representatives or through interest groups should be able to express their views at various levels of local governance, and to influence public decisions. This in turn should increase the accountability of government. The empowerment of

plan, initiate and execute policies in respect of all matters affecting people within their jurisdiction. Article 176(3) then provides that: 'The system of local government shall be based on democratically elected councils on the basis of universal adult suffrage'.

[28] Constitution of Namibia, art. 108. [29] Constitution of Malawi, s.146(2).

[30] Section 146(3) makes it clear that: 'Parliament shall, where possible, provide that issues of local policy and administration be decided on at local levels under the supervision of local government authorities'.

[31] Constitution of Malawi, s.149(d).

[32] Constitution of Tanzania, arts. 145(1) and 146(1).

local authorities to raise revenue also creates many possibilities for the generation of local economic initiatives.

In order to achieve effective devolution of power from the central government to sub-national governments, the principle of local governance should be recognised and provided for in the national constitution. It is important that the powers belonging to the sub-national tier of governments have as their origin the national constitution, for then these powers may not be removed, except by the procedure prescribed for constitutional amendments. It should clearly be provided and explained that local governance denotes the right and ability of local institutions, within the limits of the law, to regulate and manage a substantial share of public affairs under their own responsibility and in the interests of the local population. The right should be exercised by sub-national assemblies composed of members freely elected on the basis of direct, equal and universal suffrage and, where they are relevant, for example in rural areas, these should allow the participation of traditional leaders. Powers given to sub-national governments should generally be full and exclusive and clearly defined.[33] They should not be undermined or limited by the central government except as provided by law. To enable sub-national governments to function effectively, the national economic policy should entitle them to adequate financial resources of their own, of which they should dispose freely within the framework of their powers. Sub-national governments should also have the power to levy local taxes and charges.[34] The protection of financially weaker sub-national entities calls for the implementation of financial equalisation procedures or equivalent measures that are designed to correct the effects of the unequal distribution of potential sources of finance.

In demarcating regional or sub-regional units that are to form the basis of sub-national governments, great care is needed to ensure that the resulting units are viable and do not lead to divisiveness. As ethnicity is one of the potential causes of instability, it would be unfortunate if regionalism were to have the effect of promoting these ethnic divisions and of heightening the potential for conflict. The overriding goal in the demarcation of regions therefore must be to avoid the creation of exclusive ethnically homogeneous units. There are a number of criteria to consider when demarcating regions. Boundaries should be drawn in such a way

[33] A good example is the South African approach where the Constitution provides for provinces and a system of local government created with their own legislatures and clearly defined powers: see chapters 6 and 7.

[34] In both Uganda and South Africa, local authority structures enjoy revenue-raising powers: see Constitution of Uganda, art. 191 and Constitution of South Africa, ss.228–9.

that the requirements for effective development can be met. The logistics of transport, flows of labour, goods and services, as well as planning and administration need to be met by both the shape and size of the regions created. This involves consideration of the need to include one or more modes for administration in each region, i.e. identification of regional centres, as well as centres for sub-regional administration. It is important that regions or sub-regions should be compact and not fragmented. In terms of administrative coherence, regions should not be so large as to be unmanageable, or so small as to lead to their proliferation. Institutional capacity within regions or sub-regions will be crucial to effective planning and development. Regions or sub-regions which lack the necessary institutional capacity will be at a serious disadvantage in relation to those regions which are well endowed in this respect. Improving local services requires an effective local administration. Even a well-meaning political team cannot overcome incompetent administration.

The role of traditional institutions

Any examination of the modalities affecting the devolution of power in ESA states must address the issue of the future of traditional institutions of governance.[35] There is now a general consensus that traditional leaders, such as chiefs, should have a role in the governance of the state. Yet their exact role is a source of ongoing disagreement and as a result it remains largely undefined. In the South African constitutional negotiations, the question of what to do with traditional institutions was a major point of discussion. In the end, the South African Constitution states that national legislation may provide for the role of traditional leadership as an institution at the local level on matters relating to traditional leadership, the role of traditional leaders, customary law and the customs of communities observing a system of customary law.[36] Even so, this does not really integrate them into the mainstream South African post-apartheid political system. They are not, for instance, integrated into the provincial or local government structures. The Ugandan Constitution adopts the same approach, merely providing: 'Subject to

[35] Nana Wereko Ampem II, 'The Role of Chiefs and Chieftaincy in the Development of a Democratic Constitution in Ghana', paper presented to the International Roundtable on Democratic Constitutional Development, 17–20 July 1995, Pretoria, South Africa.

[36] See Constitution of South Africa, s.211(1)–(3) and 212(1)(2). Even this has proved controversial with ongoing conflict being reported between elected local structures and traditional leaders, with some local structures refusing to recognise traditional leaders.

the provisions of this Constitution, the institution of traditional leader or cultural leader may exist in any area of Uganda in accordance with the culture, customs and traditions or wishes and aspirations of the people to whom it applies.'[37] Hence neither South Africa nor Uganda integrates the traditional rulers into the sub-national tier government system.[38]

Constitutional arrangements need to accommodate traditional leaders or, at least, face up to their existence. Their incorporation into any decentralised government system could, quite conceivably, enhance its legitimacy in the rural areas where traditional leaders provide the link between the people and the external world (the government). Reaching those communities effectively requires us to confront this reality. If colonial powers were shrewd enough to use traditional institutions in administering the colonial state,[39] why should modern African political systems not make use of them in an effort to reach out to small communities and to help build national consensus and cohesion?[40] In any event, it makes sense to find a place in the national political system for structures and institutions that cannot be wished away. Since democracy means involving the various communities in a country in the governance of their affairs, it is imperative that rural communities should not be ignored in any democratic arrangement. Every effort should be made to integrate traditional institutions into the modern political structures so that all institutions are made accountable and responsive to the people. The state's vital interests in public order and stability, it would seem, are enhanced, rather than diminished, by the accommodation of traditional governance within the modern political systems of governance.

In advocating the accommodation of traditional structures in modern political systems, we should not ignore the fact that aspects of these institutions are often oppressive, exploitative, discriminatory and intolerant,

[37] Constitution of Uganda, art. 246(1).

[38] Botswana is considered one of the few countries that has made use of its traditional leaders. See Mamadou Dia, *Africa Management in the 1990s and Beyond*, World Bank, Washington, DC: 1996, p. 105–09. The position in Zambia is also disappointing with the Powers of the House of Chiefs nowhere clearly defined. The Constitution merely provides that the House of Chiefs shall be an advisory body to the government on traditional, customary and any other matters referred to it by the President.

[39] See, for example, F. D. Lugard, *The Dual Mandate in British Tropical Africa*, Blackwood, Edinburgh, 1922, esp. pp. 149–50.

[40] N. Nhlapo, 'Accommodating Traditional Forms of Governance in a Constitutional Democracy: a Motivation', paper presented at the International Roundtable on Democratic Constitutional Development, 17–20 July 1995, Pretoria, South Africa.

especially to women and children.[41] The argument, however, is not that traditional institutions are perfect; rather, that it is more effective to build democracy and effective governance through familiar institutions. Since the goal is to establish a democratic order, the need to incorporate traditional institutions into the modern political system cannot take precedence over the needs of a democratic society.[42] With regard to objections that these institutions are gender discriminatory, governments and the courts must address the areas that need reform and discard the discriminatory aspects of traditional institutions and, more importantly, confront the traditional values that underpin gender discrimination and authoritarianism. Much of this discrimination is underpinned by customary law norms. This problem is neatly addressed in South Africa and Namibia which both have constitutional provisions that render invalid customary-law norms which are in conflict with the constitution, and give the courts the power to declare gender insensitive customs and practices illegal and unenforceable. This practice should be emulated elsewhere.[43]

Devolution and its relationship to the centre

A major question that arises in any discussion on the devolution of power is how to design institutions to manage the intergovernmental institutions. Although there are many different approaches to devolution in place in different parts of the world, two broad models can be identified: the model of shared, or integrated governance; and the model of divided governance.[44] In the shared model a vast range of power is shared or concurrent. This model stresses not so much the autonomy and freedom of action of the individual devolved sub-national entities, but rather their collective influence over decisions made at the centre.

[41] M. Ndulo, 'Liability of a Paramour in Damages for Adultery in Customary Law,' (1981) 28 *African Social Research* 179; N. Nhlapo, 'The African Family and Women's Rights: Friends or Foes?' (1991) *Acta Juridica* 135.

[42] See the views of Thabo Mbeki, *Debates of the Constitutional Assembly*, 24 January 1995, no. 1, 11.

[43] See Constitution of South Africa, s.211(3); Namibian Constitution, art. 66(1). Cf. s.23(3) Constitution of Zimbabwe and the case of *Magaya* v *Magaya* [1999] 3 LRC 35.

[44] Richard Simeon, 'The Structures of Inter-governmental Relations', paper presented at International Roundtable on Democratic Constitutional Development, 17–20 July 1995, Pretoria, South Africa, p. 7. See also A. W. Johnson, 'Fiscal Arrangements in a Multi-tier State: the Canadian Case and how it Relates to South Africa's Interim Constitution', paper presented at the International Roundtable on Democratic Constitutional Development, 17–20 July 1995, Pretoria, South Africa, p. 2.

The chief advantages of the shared model are maximum uniformity and application of national norms and standards, and maximum collective influence of devolved entities. Its chief challenges are how to gain some local autonomy for the sub-national entities, how to achieve the flexibility for sub-national governments to meet local needs, and how to make clear decisions when most responsibilities are shared.

In the divided model, the powers are allocated among devolved governments that have relative autonomy. The divided model maximises the autonomy of each government, and so provides the widest room for variations in provincial policy, for experimentation and innovation. It increases the sub-national governments' ability to set their own priorities. To the extent that responsibilities are clear the model may also facilitate accountability and transparency for citizens. However, the divided model makes it more difficult to ensure common standards, common policies and harmonisation in such areas as taxation or social policy. Another issue to resolve is where devolved government will fit into the intergovernmental picture. In most ESA states local government is provided for in the Constitution but little autonomy is given to the local authorities.[45] The exceptions, as noted above, are South Africa and Uganda whose Constitutions provide substantial powers to local authorities.

The division of power between the sub-national governments and the centre needs to be spelled out clearly, and mechanisms for the resolution of conflicts in the exercise of such power must be established. There are several common types of arrangements with regard to the division of power between the central government and sub-national government.[46] Exclusive powers are those reserved for the sub-national entities and in those areas the centre has no power. For example, under the South

[45] In Namibia, Regional Councils have power within the regions as may be assigned to them by Act of Parliament and may be delegated to them by the President. See Constitution of the Republic of Namibia, article 108.

[46] The Canadian Constitution for instance allocates each power exclusively to the federal or provincial level of government. Section 91 of the Constitution Act 1867 sets out the federal government's exclusive powers, and section 92 sets out the exclusive powers of the provinces. In theory, these powers do not overlap. Sometimes, however, one aspect of a particular activity may come within a head of federal power, while another aspect of the same activity comes within a head of provincial power. In the case of direct conflict or preemption, the exercise of federal power prevails, but ordinarily either the federal or provincial legislature has exclusive power over a particular activity. Because of the exclusive allocation of power in Canada, a law or governmental action is always open to constitutional challenge on ultra vires grounds. See Robert A. Sedler, 'Constitutional Protection of Individual Rights in Canada: The Impact of the New Canadian Charter of Rights and Freedoms' (1984) 59 *Notre Dame L R* 1191, at pp. 1196–7.

African Constitution, the provinces have exclusive legislative competence in provincial planning, veterinary services excluding regulation of the profession; provincial sports; cultural matters and licensing matters relating to such things as parks and markets.[47] Concurrent powers exist where different responsibilities are allocated with regard to one function to different levels of government. In the South African Constitution, provinces have concurrent powers in agriculture, airports, animal control, health services, housing, transport, consumer protection, education, language policy, media, police matters, and population control.[48] The modern growth of government functions and the complex linkages and interdependence that have developed, particularly in the economic and social spheres, have made it unrealistic to think of allocating all, or even most, functions exclusively. In certain circumstances, the central government is given overriding powers. This is the right of the central government to act as the higher legislative authority in an area allocated to a region or sub-region where the national interest demands such action. A problem that often arises is what to do with residual powers. In this context, residual power embraces all those powers not specifically designated in the Constitution as being either the exclusive or concurrent preserve of the various levels of government. What powers remain unallocated in a given jurisdiction depends on whatever the national constitution leaves unregulated. An example in most jurisdictions would be traditional authority such as chiefs.

Typically a decentralised system of government has to decide on what to do with any powers not expressly delegated to the sub-national levels of government. Approaches to this vary. One approach is that any powers not expressly assumed by the autonomous communities in their statutes will continue to be exercised by the central government. This is just the opposite of the case of the United States where the powers of the federal government are only those specifically outlined in the US Constitution. Another approach is that if the government to which the subject has been entrusted does not act, the subject goes unregulated. In the United States, by contrast, the norm is that the non-exercise of federal power to regulate increases the area for state regulation; there are few if any separate spheres in which it is constitutionally permissible only for states to regulate.[49]

[47] South African Constitution, schedule 5, Functional Areas of Exclusive Provincial Legislative Competence.

[48] South African Constitution, schedule 4, Functional Areas of Concurrent National and Provincial Legislative Competence.

[49] Martha A. Field, 'The Differing Federalisms of Canada and the United States' (1992) 55 *Law and Contemporary Problems* 108. Field points out further: 'Even if in both the USA

There are several principles that need to be taken into account when deciding the allocation of legislative powers.[50] First, there is the imperative of national government responsibility for nation building, including the promotion of national well-being and the celebration of the nation's diversity. Secondly there is the imperative of regional or sub-regional responsibility and autonomy for the development and the differentiation of regional public services to suit the particularities, the needs and the cultural identities of the different regions or sub-regions created. Thirdly, there is the imperative of recognising that there are 'national aspects' of many of the matters that are assigned to regions or sub-regions, which must be taken into account in devising constitutional competencies and arrangements and equally in recognising that there are regional or sub-regional interests in many of the matters where national legislation and/or financing is called for. The Constitution should provide for a system in which both central government and sub-national tier governments complement each other. The objective should be to develop a 'co-operative model' of government that will enable greater co-operation between various tiers of governments.

Fiscal arrangements and revenue sharing measures

Perhaps the most important and controversial matter in the division of powers concerns revenue collection and other fiscal matters since these impact on the ability of the sub-national governments to function effectively. At present, in most ESA states, local governments are funded by direct grants from the central government. Section 150 of the Malawi Constitution, for example, provides that the central government is under a duty to ensure that there is adequate provision of resources necessary for the proper exercise of local government functions. This approach is unsuitable where it is intended to achieve effective devolution of power to

and Canada the constitutions were written to give the central government more power, the interpretation of the powers of the central government has been different under both systems. For example, in relation to the 'power to regulate commerce,' in the USA 'the clause has been read to allow Congress to regulate any activity that could have any impact at all on interstate commerce, leaving Congress free to regulate any economic activity it wishes and displacing any separate sphere for state legislative control of the economy. In Canada, by contrast, the clause giving the central government control over trade and commerce has been interpreted to allow regulation of only international or inter-provincial trade. The narrow interpretation of the commerce power is part of a more general cutback on the powers of the central government'. See pp. 109–10.

50 See Simeon, 'Structures of Inter-governmental Relations'.

local communities. A better approach is to authorise sub-national governments to raise funds by a variety of taxes. Thus, for example, provinces in South Africa are allowed to impose taxes, levies, duties other than income tax, value added tax, general sales tax, or customs duties.[51]

Rye discusses three key questions concerning the allocation of fiscal measures.[52] The first concerns what is the best allocation, between levels of governments, of revenue-raising powers and of expenditure responsibilities. He suggests a number of relevant considerations. First is the geographical incidence of each service or tax. Thus the benefits of defence against external threats accrue to the nation as a whole and it is hard to see how it could be other than a national responsibility. At the other extreme, garbage collection and waste disposal is usually a local matter. There are, of course, many public services, such as education and health, where the division is not so clear. On the tax side, the incidence of company tax is likely to fall well outside its notional geographic source, so this tax may be collected properly by central government. Property taxes, by contrast, seem to lie naturally at the local level. A second consideration is the need for the national government to be able to run an effective fiscal policy. One implication of this is that the national government might wish to retain a high degree of control over taxation. A third consideration is the need to provide financial resources for ironing out horizontal imbalances between the various regions that are created pursuant to decentralisation.[53] Typically, arrangements are made to provide assistance to regions or sub-regions that are economically behind others.

The second question in the allocation of fiscal measures concerns the best structure of fiscal transfers from central to sub-national governments. This is a question of whether such transfers should be through tied grants (specific purpose payments) or untied (general) grants. An example of a tied grant would be money given to build a road and a general grant would be money not tied to a specific project. As Rye points out, sometimes the objective of the 'specific purpose payment' is to provide a mechanism whereby the central government may achieve national

[51] Constitution of South Africa, art. 228.

[52] Dick Rye, 'Intergovernmental Relation Structures Responsible for Financial and Fiscal Management' paper presented at the International Roundtable on Democratic Constitutional Development, 17–20 July 1995, Pretoria, South Africa.

[53] See, with respect to Canada, Federal Provincial Fiscal Arrangements and Federal Post Secondary Education and Health Act, 1976–77. Section 3 authorises the Minister of Finance to pay fiscal equalisation funds to provinces.

objectives in particular areas.[54] For example, if there are perceived problems in education provision by the regions, the central government may provide grants on condition that they are used to tackle those problems. However, in any transfer system designed to provide a measure of equalisation, some general revenue grants are likely to be needed. In particular, it does not seem that specific purpose payments can effectively compensate for inequalities in revenue-raising capacity.

The third question in this area concerns the extent to which grants from the central government are untied and intended for equalisation purposes. This raises issues as to what is the best mechanism, and the best institutional framework, for deciding on the allocations.[55] It is probably best to allocate such responsibility to an independent Commission charged with that responsibility. It is important that such a Commission functions in a transparent manner in order to instil confidence in the people that political considerations are not paramount in decisions relating to the allocation of funds to sub-national governments. For example, under the South African Constitution a statute must provide for the equitable division of revenue raised nationally among the national, provincial and local spheres of government[56] and that a Financial and Fiscal Commission must be consulted on the division of revenue.[57] The division of the revenue should take into account the population, income per capita, indicators of backwardness, and the local authorities' own tax effort.

Resolving disputes between sub-national governments and the centre

Clearly sharp differences of opinion, and sometimes conflicts, are going to arise as to whether or not certain powers are vested in the central government or the sub-national governments. Typically, disputes might concern conflicts between national legislation and sub-national tier government legislation or between national legislation and a provision of a sub-national government constitution. There is also the fact that there

[54] Ibid.

[55] Compare section 162(2) of the 1999 Constitution of Nigeria which provides: 'The President, upon the receipt of advice from the Revenue Mobilisation Allocation and Fiscal Commission, shall table before the National Assembly proposals for revenue allocation from the Federation Account, and in determining the formula, the National Assembly shall take into account, the allocation principles especially those of population, equality of States, internal revenue generation, land mass, terrain as well as population density . . .'

[56] Constitution of South Africa, s.214(1) and (2). [57] Ibid.

is often resistance by the organs of the central bureaucracy to relinquish their powers to the sub-national governments. This results in continuous conflicts which weaken the efficiency of the intergovernmental arrangements. This can be minimised by ensuring that the division of roles is as unambiguous as possible and making adjudication correspondingly easier. However, no matter how much care is taken to demarcate power there are bound to be numerous difficulties. This is almost inevitable given the complex system of the apportionment of powers in a state based on the devolution of powers to the sub-national governments. Typically these difficulties will include long lists of competencies attributed to the state or to the autonomous sub-national governments, which often affect both legislative and executive powers and which often seem to belong to both the central government and the autonomous sub-national governments. Clearly there is a need for dispute-resolution mechanisms.

Courts play an important role in arbitrating and resolving differences as this would mean the resolution of conflicts between the central government powers and the sub-national governments in legal and judicial terms rather than in political terms. For example, in the South African arrangement, a provincial legislature is bound only by the Constitution and, if it has passed a constitution for its province, also by that provincial constitution, and must act in accordance with, and within the limits of, the Constitution and that provincial constitution.[58] Disputes are to be resolved by the courts[59] although if a dispute cannot be resolved in this way, national legislation prevails over the provincial legislation or provincial constitution. But other supervisory bodies can also be established to resolve disputes. For instance, national forums, committees or commissions could be used to bring together the different levels of government in relation to specific fields of shared competence (e.g. education and health) where collisions and conflicts could be forestalled and/or arbitrated. To resolve differences of grey areas which inevitably arise in the field of concurrent powers, it is not necessary to have constant recourse to the courts. In fact the South African Constitution requires an organ of state involved in an intergovernmental dispute to make every reasonable effort to settle it by means of mechanisms and procedures provided for that purpose

[58] S.104(3) Constitution of South Africa. Article 104(1) provides: 'The legislative authority of the province is vested in its provincial legislature, and confers on the provincial legislature the power to pass a constitution for its province or to amend any constitution passed by it in terms of sections 142 and 143.' Most of the provinces are still working on their constitutions.

[59] S.146(4) Constitution of South Africa.

and to exhaust all other remedies before it approaches a court to resolve the dispute.[60] At the same time care must be taken to ensure that the organs established to co-ordinate the different levels of government do not proliferate, and do not escape accountability.

Overview

Devolution can raise levels of participation and involvement of the people and can provide them with an increased opportunity to shape the context of their lives. This can then result in more responsive and efficient local governance. The ultimate purpose of devolution is to place decision-making in the hands of the people through representation, which is closer and more directly accountable, thereby promoting democracy and good governance. Devolution enhances equitable development through mobilisation of local resources, increased efficiency and effectiveness. However, when poorly designed, devolution can result in over-burdened local governments without resources or the capacity to fulfil their basic responsibilities of providing a local infrastructure and services. The objective should be to ensure policy development that addresses the political will to decentralise and delineate the types of devolution suitable to a country's circumstances. Such policy should specify the necessary financial, legal institutional and organisational changes to effect devolution. It should also restructure relative responsibility and authority between the central and sub-national governments. For decentralisation to succeed it requires strong institutions and trained personnel to run it.

[60] Constitution of South Africa, art. 41(3).

10

Developing autochthonous oversight bodies: human rights commissions and offices of the ombudsman

Introduction

In the Harare Commonwealth Declaration, Commonwealth Heads of Government recognised that developing appropriate 'institutional structures which reflect national circumstances' is a key element for promoting and protecting human rights, good governance and the rule of law. This reflects Nwabueze's warning that a major cause of the failure of constitutional government in Africa is the lack of understanding and acceptance of its principles and institutions by the populace. Institutions do not have an independent existence but survive only if they are capable of serving their society in a meaningful fashion. Therefore states must develop autochthonous oversight bodies designed to provide *in practice* meaningful protection to those seeking administrative justice and/or the enjoyment of their constitutional rights.

This chapter examines the organisation, functions and powers of two of the main oversight bodies, i.e. offices of the ombudsman and human rights commissions (collectively referred to as national institutions) and assesses their contribution towards furthering the aims of the Harare Commonwealth Declaration. A separate note on anti-corruption commissions is also included.

Offices of the ombudsman

The 1974 resolution of the International Bar Association sets out concisely the traditional functions of an ombudsman:

> An office provided for by the constitution or by action of the legislature or parliament and headed by an independent high-level public official who is responsible to the legislature or parliament, who receives complaints from aggrieved persons [alleging maladministration] against government agencies, officials and employees or who acts on his/her own motion, and

who has the power to investigate, recommend corrective action and issue reports.[1]

The importance of offices of the ombudsman for the region was noted as early as 1965 by the Presidential Commission on the Establishment of a Democratic One-Party State in Tanzania which stated that:

> In a rapidly developing country, it is inevitable that many officials, both of Government and of the ruling party, should be authorised to exercise wide discretionary powers. Decisions taken by such officials can, however, have the most serious consequences for the individual, and the Commission is aware that there is already a good deal of public concern about the danger of abuse of power. We have, therefore, given careful thought to the possibility of providing some safeguards for the ordinary citizen.[2]

The result was the establishment of the Permanent Commission of Enquiry in 1966. This lead was followed by Zambia (1974) (known as the Commission for Investigations), Zimbabwe (1980) and Uganda (1986) (known as the Inspector-General of Government). The 1990s then saw a further increase in their number: Namibia (1990); Malawi (1995); South Africa (1995, known as the Public Protector[3]); Lesotho (1996); and Botswana (1998). An Office of the Ombudsman operated in Swaziland between 1983 and 1987 before being scrapped and, as discussed later, the reasons for its demise well illustrate the challenge of organising and running an effective and demonstrably independent institution.

Human rights commissions

The 1990s saw the establishment of human rights commissions in South Africa,[4] Uganda, Malawi and Zambia.[5] Whilst human rights commissions,

[1] The title of the institution varies from country to country. For the sake of convenience, the word 'ombudsman' is used in this chapter.

[2] At p. 32.

[3] This to avoid the apparent gender bias in the word 'ombudsman'. In fact the word comes from Swedish and has no gender connotation whatsoever.

[4] A series of other 'State institutions supporting constitutional democracy' are also provided for in chapter 9 of the 1996 Constitution including the Commission for Gender Equality and Commission for the Promotion and Protection of the Rights of Cultural, Religious and Linguistic Communities. A statutory Independent Complaints Directorate is tasked with investigating complaints against the police.

[5] In 1996 the Kenya Human Rights Standing Committee was formed by President Moi. Members were appointed by him, it reported to him, action was decided by him and

as such, exist elsewhere,[6] this 'new breed' of institution is very different, having wide powers to investigate, protect and promote human rights. In many respects they have evolved from the ombudsman model although structurally the two institutions differ in several key respects:

* Human rights commissions are multi-member bodies whilst the traditional office of the ombudsman is headed by a single individual;
* Human rights commissions base their jurisdiction specifically on human rights norms whilst the prime concern of an ombudsman is to investigate complaints of administrative injustice;
* An office of the ombudsman investigates complaints against 'public officials' whilst the jurisdiction of a human rights commission also often extends to the private sector;
* Unlike an office of the ombudsman, a human rights commission has a specific mandate to promote human rights;
* Some human rights commissions also undertake a variety of other human rights-related functions, such as reviewing proposed legislation for compliance with international human rights obligations;
* Whilst an ombudsman is traditionally restricted to making recommendations to resolve a complaint, human rights commissions generally enjoy somewhat wider remedial powers.

'Quasi' human rights commissions also operate in Namibia and Zimbabwe where the Ombudsman can also investigate allegations of human rights violations. From the practical point of view, this type of body is probably less effective than a full-blown human rights commission in that the lack of a collegiate body can negatively impact on the independence of the institution itself and may also lead to an excessive workload.

The desirability of developing an autochthonous oversight body or bodies means that there is no 'model' national institution and as de Smith has pointed out, they 'cannot be bought off the peg [but] must be made to measure'.[7] Thus whilst the *United Nations Principles Relating to the*

members could be removed by him. In the circumstances, the rationale for its existence was hard to see and it is clearly inappropriate to refer to it as a national institution.

6 Although most are restricted to dealing with anti-discrimination issues, e.g. the human rights commissions in Canada and New Zealand. Commissions operating along similar lines to the SEA states include those in Australia, Ghana, Sri Lanka and India. For details of each see J. Hatchard, *National Human Rights Institutions in the Commonwealth*, Commonwealth Secretariat London 3rd edn, 1998.

7 Mauritius Legislative Assembly Sessional Paper No. 2 of 1965, para. 39.

Status of National Institutions (the *Paris Principles*)[8] and the 2001 Commonwealth Secretariat *Best Practice Guidelines* provide a recommended framework for their organisation and powers, much still depends upon, amongst other things, the scope of constitutional rights and the size, structure and history of the state itself.

Ensuring the independence of national institutions

Developing an institution aimed at securing effective, accountable and responsible government is a considerable challenge. It requires a legal framework that explicitly protects the national institution's independence and impartiality. Entrenching it in the Constitution is the ideal as this provides a measure of protection against any attempt to undermine its activities or even to legislate it out of existence.[9]

The institution must enjoy operational independence. The Constitution of Malawi recognises this by providing that the Office of the Ombudsman 'shall be completely independent of the interference or direction of any other person or authority'.[10] Similarly, in the Constitution of South Africa 1996, national institutions are to be:

> . . . independent, and subject only to the Constitution and the law, and they must be impartial and must exercise their powers and perform their functions without fear, favour or prejudice.[11]

Based on the *Paris Principles*, the independence of a national institution depends on three key conditions. These are, whether (i) it is composed of demonstrably independent appointee(s); (ii) its members enjoy satisfactory conditions of service, including adequate protection against arbitrary removal from office; and (iii) it enjoys adequate funding and resources.

[8] Adopted by the United Nations as an Annex to General Assembly resolution 48/134 of 20 December 1993.

[9] For example, in November 1997 the Ombudsman Act in Vanuatu was repealed apparently as a result of concern on the part of some parliamentarians that the ombudsman was investigating (perhaps rather too effectively) some of their own activities.

[10] Art. 121 Constitution of Malawi.

[11] S.181(2). See also article 54 of the Constitution of Uganda which provides that the Commission 'shall be independent and shall not, in the performance of its duties, be subject to the direction or control of any person or authority'.

Independent appointees

Providing for a demonstrably fair and open appointment procedure

The appointment procedure is essentially a confidence-building exercise for government officials, citizens and civil society alike in the integrity, independence and ability of the ombudsman or human rights commissioners. It follows that undue executive influence over the appointment process can undermine public confidence in the institution's independence. This is why the original Scandinavian model provided that the ombudsman should be appointed by, and answerable to, the legislature. South Africa has adopted this approach. Here a committee of the National Assembly proportionately composed of members of all the political parties represented in the Assembly nominates human rights commissioners. Once nominees have received the support of a majority of the members of the Assembly, or in the case of the Public Protector at least 60 per cent of the membership, the State President must then make the formal appointments.[12]

Elsewhere, executive involvement in the appointment process remains common. Thus the appointment of the commissioners of the Permanent Commission of Enquiry in Tanzania remains the sole responsibility of the head of state. In Zambia, Namibia and Zimbabwe the President is merely required to consult with or to act on the recommendation of the Judicial Service Commission. This is disappointing in that the *Paris Principles* recommend that the appointment procedure involves the 'pluralistic representation of the social forces (of civilian society) involved in the protection and promotion of human rights . . .' including representatives of non-governmental organisations and universities, as well as Parliament.[13] Only in Malawi is any effort made to formally involve civil society, for here nominations for ombudsman come solely from the

[12] See s.193 Constitution of South Africa 1996. The fact that there is no special parliamentary majority required for human rights commissioners means that their appointments are essentially left in the hands of the ruling party. Compare this to the position under section 115(2) of the 1993 Constitution where a majority of 75 per cent of the National Assembly and the Senate was required. It is not clear as to why this requirement was dropped in the final Constitution.

[13] See *The Paris Principles*, 'Composition and guarantees of independence and pluralism' para. 1. *The Principles of Best Practice for Commonwealth Human Rights Institutions* adopted in 2001 suggest the desirability of forming a steering committee to guide the process comprising of, for example, ministers, MPs, officials of government departments, members of major political parties, relevant government agencies, human rights NGOs,

public.[14] The successful candidate is then appointed by the all-party parliamentary Public Appointments Committee[15] with the President having no formal role to play.[16] The Malawi Human Rights Commission, consists of the Law Commissioner[17] and Ombudsman *ex officio* with the other commissioners being nominated by

> Those organisations that are considered in the absolute discretion of both the Law Commissioner and the Ombudsman to be reputable organisations representative of Malawian society and that are wholly or largely concerned with the promotion of the rights and freedoms guaranteed by [the Constitution of Malawi].[18]

The President is then required to formally appoint such persons as commissioners.

Overall, the *formal* endorsement of an ombudsman and/or commissioners by the head of state is probably useful in that it may enhance the profile and status of appointees. Even so, the process itself must closely involve the potential 'customers' and this is best achieved through a Malawi-style procedure. One further point is that no ESA state specifically requires the filling of any vacancies within a set period following the expiry of the term of office, retirement, death, resignation or removal of an ombudsman or human rights commissioner. This is a serious omission for any unwarranted delay in making new appointments can significantly affect operational efficiency.[19]

judges and jurists, trades unions and professional groups, human rights experts and academics. See *National Human Rights Institutions: Best Practice*, London: Commonwealth Secretariat, 2001, p. 9 (hereinafter Commonwealth Best Practice Guide). Whilst a potentially unwieldy group, the process has the advantage of making appointments a national issue.

[14] Here the Clerk to the National Assembly must place public advertisements inviting nominations.

[15] The all-party Public Appointments Committee is appointed by the National Assembly: s.56(7) Constitution of Malawi.

[16] See s.122(1) Constitution of Malawi.

[17] A permanent, salaried official appointed by the President on the recommendation of the Judicial Service Commission who must be a legal practitioner or a person qualified to be a judge: s.133(a) Constitution of Malawi.

[18] S.131 Constitution of Malawi.

[19] For example, in 2001 in Malawi, the term of office of all Commissioners came to an end simultaneously and none sought renewal of their contract. This resulted in a lengthy hiatus before the appointment of new commissioners and seriously affected the work of the institution (personal communication to one of the authors).

Providing for suitably qualified appointees

There is no consensus as to the qualification(s) needed for appointment as an ombudsman or human rights commissioner. In the case of an ombudsman, commonly legal qualifications or experience in the public service is required.[20] Sometimes the qualifications for appointment are so wide as to be virtually meaningless.[21] It is questionable whether specific qualifications for appointment are either necessary or desirable. Certainly ready access to legal expertise within the institution is essential, but the real need is to appoint demonstrably independent, able persons who possess public credibility. Thus it is *who*, not *what* the appointees are that is crucial. This is recognised in, amongst other countries, South Africa where the Human Rights Commission must reflect broadly the country's race and gender composition and in Uganda where commissioners must be of 'high moral character and proven integrity'. The point is also neatly illustrated by the case of the Swaziland ombudsman. Here the incumbent, who was appointed by the King, also held the post of Secretary to the *Liqoqo* (the Supreme Council of State). This position was incompatible with his position as ombudsman and seriously tarnished the public image of the office. The failure to establish an unquestionably independent office significantly contributed to the eventual failure of the office and led to its subsequent abolition.[22]

Being multi-member bodies, human rights commissions have the great advantage of being able to appoint commissioners from a variety of different backgrounds and ensure that there is a satisfactory gender balance. This concern was particularly evident in the establishment of the Uganda Human Rights Commission for, as the Oder Commission noted, one cause of Uganda's past troubles was the lack of tolerance and mutual suspicion amongst the different ethnic and religious groups in the country.[23]

[20] For example, the Inspector-General of Government in Uganda must possess considerable experience and have demonstrated competence and be of high calibre in the conduct of public affairs. See art. 223(5)(c) Constitution of Uganda.

[21] For example, the Zimbabwean ombudsman must have legal qualifications; experience as a Permanent Secretary of a Ministry or as a regional magistrate; or is, in the opinion of the President, 'a person of ability and experience and distinguished in the public life of Zimbabwe'. In Malawi the ombudsman must fulfil seven specific conditions before being eligible for appointment: see s.122(2) Constitution of Malawi.

[22] See J. Ayee, 'The Ombudsman Experience in the Kingdom of Swaziland: A Comment' [1988] *Verfassung und Recht in Ubersee* 8, at p. 14.

[23] '*The Pearl of Blood' Report of the Uganda Commission of Inquiry into the Violation of Human Rights* (The Oder Commission Report), Government of Uganda, Kampala: 1994, p. 10.

Whilst the Constitution provides that the commission must consist of a legally qualified chairperson[24] and not less than three others,[25] it was decided to appoint a chairperson and six commissioners. This was the minimum number thought necessary both to ensure that commissioners were drawn from all parts of the country and to help reassure all Ugandans that their views and concerns would receive due consideration by the Commission. In addition, regard was had to the ages, religious beliefs and professional background of commissioners as well as the need for a gender balance.[26] In practice, there remain concerns about gender bias and other discriminatory practices in some commissions themselves, and as a Commonwealth Human Rights Initiative report argues, before human rights commissions can adequately promote and protect the human rights of all citizens, they must correct the internal imbalances and biases that they themselves reflect.[27]

Providing satisfactory conditions of service

The effectiveness of a national institution also depends upon its ability to maintain public confidence and develop appropriate links with those bodies subject to investigation.[28] This takes time and patience and

[24] The Chairperson must be a Judge of the High Court or a person qualified to hold that office: see art. 51(3)(4) Constitution of Uganda.

[25] Art. 51(2) Constitution of Uganda.

[26] In the event, the first set of commissioners comprised a former magistrate, two lawyers, a former government minister, an educationalist and a former senior civil servant. Three commissioners, including the chairperson, were female. For a detailed account of the Commission see J. Hatchard, 'A New Breed of Institution: The Development of Human Rights Commissions in Commonwealth Africa with particular reference to the Uganda Human Rights Commission' (1999) 32 *Comparative and International Law Journal of Southern Africa* 28–53.

[27] For example the results of a study of African and South Asian human rights commissions by Aurora revealed that women are discriminated against in many commissions with regard to their internal composition and/or the fact that women generally occupy lower paying and lower status positions within the institutions. See S. Aurora, *Balancing the Scales: an Analysis of Gender Representation within Commonwealth National Human Rights Institutions*, Commonwealth Human Rights Initiative, 2000, at www.humanrightsinitiative.org/Programmes/hrcommission/humanrightspublic.htm).

[28] The importance of this link is illustrated by the story told to one of the authors by an SEA ombudsman. He had spent several years developing an excellent working relationship with the head of the civil service which enabled him to get many complaints swiftly resolved through unofficial channels. Whilst he was away on leave, the deputy ombudsman had quarrelled with the civil service chief who, as a result, became extremely unco-operative. According to the ombudsman, it took him several months to re-establish a good working relationship during which time it was not possible to settle several complaints expeditiously.

emphasises the need for incumbents to enjoy an appropriate term of office. This was recognised in Zambia where the Commission for Investigations consisted of the Investigator-General (Ombudsman) and three Commissioners. Originally the latter served for three years and were then automatically replaced. This was found unsatisfactory in that commissioners were required to relinquish office just when they had come to grips with the position and as a result, a constitutional amendment increased their term of office to six years.[29]

In most states the ombudsman and human rights commissioners enjoy fixed term appointments ranging from three years (e.g. Tanzania) to seven years (e.g. the Public Protector in South Africa). Certainly reasonably long mandates provide incumbents with greater security whilst retaining the necessary expertise and experience within the institution. It follows that terms of office of commissioners should not come to an end at the same time. In most states the appointment is renewable. In effect, this means the incumbents are in a similar position to contract judges and may suffer the same concerns over re-appointment.[30] On the face of it, this favours making appointments non-renewable, although an alternative approach is to provide for a career post, such as that in Namibia where the Ombudsman holds office up to the age of sixty-five years.[31]

Investigations may well involve delving into sensitive and potentially embarrassing affairs of government and government officials and thus carry the potential for the exertion of political pressure on office holders and staff. This calls for establishing adequate safeguards. These include, firstly, providing that when acting in the course of their official duties, members and staff of national institutions enjoy immunity from suit.[32] Secondly, an ombudsman and human rights commissioners must enjoy, as far as possible, the same terms and conditions of service as a senior judge. Indeed recognising the need to provide adequate protection, drafters of the 1996 South African Constitution were specifically charged with developing an appropriate safeguard on the 'independence and impartiality' of the Public Protector.[33] The removal procedure proposed envisaged a finding by a National Assembly committee that grounds of misconduct,

[29] Constitution of Zambia (Amendment) Act 1986. Curiously, the term of office of Commissioners of the Permanent Human Rights Commission in Zambia was reduced to three years (Human Rights Act 1996, s.7(1)).

[30] See Chapter 8 for a full discussion.

[31] In Namibia the President may extend the retiring age to seventy years. Arguably this is a matter that should be left to the incumbent to decide.

[32] This would not preclude an action for judicial review.

[33] See Constitutional Principle XXIX contained in the interim Constitution.

incapacity or incompetence existed and that this finding was adopted by a resolution of a majority of National Assembly members. Thereafter the President would remove the Public Protector from office. However, the Constitutional Court[34] did not consider that this adequately safeguarded the office-holder's independence and impartiality and the draft Constitution was amended to require a two-thirds majority of National Assembly members.[35]

To avoid possible conflicts of interest, an ombudsman and human rights commissioners are generally required to relinquish certain public offices upon appointment.[36] Given that many human rights commissions can investigate complaints against private enterprises, it is particularly important that commissioners are required to declare publicly both their public and private interests to avoid any possible conflicts of interest.

Obtaining adequate funding and resources

Operational independence is a prerequisite for any national institution. This includes enjoying financial autonomy and access to adequate and secure funding so as to retain appropriate staffing levels, premises and resources. This is reflected in Uganda where the Inspectorate of Government is constitutionally entitled to enjoy:

> An independent budget appropriated by Parliament and controlled by the Inspectorate ... It shall be the duty of the State to facilitate the employment by the Inspectorate of such adequate and qualified staff as are needed to enable the Inspectorate to perform its functions effectively and efficiently.[37]

[34] The court was required to certify that the 1996 Constitution complied with certain Constitutional Principles. See its judgment in 1996 (10) BCLR 1253.

[35] Curiously, the removal of a human rights commissioner requires only a majority of the members of the National Assembly.

[36] For example, membership of Parliament; membership of a local government council; membership of the executive of a political party or political organisation; or employment as a public officer.

[37] See art. 229 Constitution of Uganda. This approach is reflected in other national institutions. For example, in Malawi and South Africa major expenses are charged on the Consolidated Fund whilst the Ugandan Human Rights Commission is self-accounting, with all expenses charged on the Consolidated Fund and with salaries and other allowances being prescribed by Parliament. Compare the position in Ghana where the budget of the Commission for Human Rights and Administrative Justice is subject to ministerial vetting. As the Commissioner has emphasised: 'I wish to express my view once again that the independence of the Commission can be fully realised only if its budget is submitted direct to Parliament for vetting and approval.' *CHRAJ Second Annual Report*, 1995, 2–3. By late 2003, this position had still not changed.

With the continuing economic constraints, the ability (and willingness) of many governments to provide adequate funding is becoming increasingly uncertain. The fact that it is only normally provided on an annual basis is also potentially problematic given that national institutions may require medium and long-term financial support for projects such as the development of human rights promotional programmes. External funding provided from both civil society and from international aid agencies is an obvious way of alleviating the problem and, indeed, some make good use of it.[38] Whilst such funding may well raise concerns, particularly on the part of government, over its possible effect on the independence of the recipient institution, there is no evidence to support this[39] and it can only help facilitate the effectiveness of a national institution. This means that the question of whether or not to accept external funding is entirely a matter for the institution itself and any requirement for ministerial approval is both unnecessary and unacceptable.[40] Perhaps the one caveat to external funding is the practical point that the institution's recurrent expenditure should remain covered by its 'secure' government funding in case of the withdrawal, non-renewal or non-availability of donor funds.

Accountability of national institutions

Protecting the independence of a national institution does not mean insulating it from regular review (although not *supervision*) of its performance. This is needed in order to maintain both public confidence in the institution and high operational standards.

Gaining media interest in reporting on, and critically analysing, the institution's activities is particularly helpful and can complement the

[38] For example, the Uganda Human Rights Commission received a sizeable grant from a Canadian donor to purchase its office complex in Kampala. External funding has also proved invaluable in the development of human rights promotional programmes by the Commission on Human Rights and Administrative Justice (CHRAJ) in Ghana. See E. Short, 'The Commission on Human Rights and Administrative Justice', paper presented at a workshop organised by the UHRC, Kampala, November 1997, p. 21 and the 1997 Annual Report of CHRAJ, Accra, pp. 3–4. Denmark (Danida, Danish Centre for Human Rights), the UK (DFID), USA (USAID), the European Union and Norway (NORAD) have also contributed to similar programmes.

[39] Certainly the Ghanaian Human Rights Commissioner and Chair of the Uganda Human Rights Commission have both publicly stated that such funding has in no way compromised the operations of their commissions (see Short, 'Commission', p. 21).

[40] Compare the position in Uganda where the Minister responsible for justice acting in consultation with the Minister responsible for finance must approve any external funding offered to the Uganda Human Rights Commission.

formal accountability mechanisms. At present, most national institutions are required to send a copy of their annual report to parliament and/or to the head of state/government and this supposedly provides a detailed account of its performance. In practice such reports are frequently disappointing with little meaningful data on, or information about, the institution's operation. Furthermore, there are often lengthy delays in publication resulting in reports often being out of date before they are even published. Even then, there is no obligation on parliament to debate the report and it appears that almost invariably they are effectively ignored.

This is quite unsatisfactory and calls for the development of effective parliamentary scrutiny. As a minimum, a national institution should be under a legal obligation to submit its annual report to the legislature within a specific time with parliament then being required to debate the document. The ombudsman or commissioners should also be required to appear annually before the appropriate parliamentary committee to discuss the report and the institution's performance. Inviting civil society groups to testify before the committee should also be implemented. As an alternative, parliament might consider establishing a formal advisory committee on national institutions whose responsibilities would include holding regular consultations with civil society groups and with members of the institution itself as well as providing advice, support, encouragement and, where necessary, criticism as to its operations.[41]

Scope of investigations

In general the prime role of offices of the ombudsman is to investigate complaints from members of the public involving 'maladministration' on the part of public officials.[42] The *Paris Principles* call for human rights commissions to have the power to investigate 'any situation of violation of

[41] The legislature in Uganda goes some way towards this goal in that it is required to make laws to regulate and facilitate the performance of the Uganda Human Rights Commission (art. 58 Constitution of Uganda). Such a provision is particularly useful if viewed as placing an obligation on Parliament to monitor the work and functioning of the Commission and to take appropriate action to support and strengthen it.

[42] A former Investigator-General in Zambia has provided a useful list of examples of such conduct: 'The abuse of authority or maladministration . . . may take various forms, for example, corruption, favouritism, bribes, tribalism, harshness, misleading a member of the public as to his rights, failing to give reasons when under a duty to do so, using powers for the wrong purposes, failing to reply to correspondence or causing unreasonable delay in doing desired public acts' (see *Annual Report of the Commission for Investigations 1975*, 3).

human rights which it decides to take up'. Coupled with their extensive investigatory powers, this makes national institutions extremely powerful oversight bodies. However, the effectiveness of an individual institution depends greatly upon the types of cases it is mandated to investigate.

Who can be investigated?

In most ESA states national institutions are precluded from investigating the actions of certain office holders. These include the head of state and/or government and members of the judiciary. This is not the position in Uganda where there are no express limitations upon who can be investigated by the Human Rights Commission and therefore it is seemingly able to investigate complaints of human rights violations against even the most senior officials in the country, including the President. This position is problematic in that it effectively places the Commission above the other organs of government. Assuming that there are alternative constitutional and other procedures available, such as impeachment powers, it is probably preferable to preclude investigations into the President and the judiciary.

What can be investigated?

Despite the *Paris Principles'* strictures, many national institutions are precluded from investigating key areas of public life, such as complaints against security forces personnel.[43] Again the Uganda Human Rights Commission provides the best model in that it is empowered 'to investigate, at its own initiative or on a complaint made by any person or group of persons against the violation of any human right'.[44] The sole restriction is that the matter should not be pending before a court or judicial tribunal.[45]

[43] For a critique of this position, see the discussion in chapter 11.

[44] Art. 52(1)(a). The legislation of most human rights commissions leaves undefined the scope of the term 'human rights'. It is thus arguable that the jurisdiction extends not only to those rights protected by the Constitution but also to those enshrined in international and regional human rights instruments to which the country is a party. Such a reading is likely to radically extend the scope of investigations.

[45] Even so, this should be interpreted in a restrictive manner so as, for example, to enable a national institution to investigate allegations of police brutality against suspects during interrogation although not, of course, the merits of any subsequent criminal proceedings brought against those persons.

Even in cases where complaints are 'outside jurisdiction', a problem particularly associated with offices of the ombudsman, some are still able to offer advice and assistance in an effort to informally resolve the matter.[46] The power to 'informally conciliate, amicably resolve, stipulate, settle or ameliorate any grievance' when the complaint is outside jurisdiction[47] offers a means of resolving misunderstandings and removing unnecessary tension and animosity when other avenues of redress are closed. Such a function is certainly not a substitute for a more formal legal-advice scheme but it does represent a useful alternative approach to dealing with the problems of access to justice particularly for the poor and rural dwellers.

Facilitating accessibility

A compelling features of national institutions is that an aggrieved person may lodge a complaint and (if it is accepted) have it investigated free of charge.[48] Most institutions impose a time limit for receipt of complaints of one or two years from the date on which the complainant first knew of the facts which gave rise to the problem although, in practice, out-of-time complaints are often accepted. This reflects the objective of national institutions to make their services accessible to all those needing advice and assistance.

That this objective remains largely unfulfilled reflects the acute practical operational problems that both human rights commissions and offices of the ombudsman continue to encounter. As a result, their activities are often confined to a few urban areas. This is exacerbated by a general lack of ready access to any electronic means of communication on the part of many people, especially those in the rural areas. The challenge for national institutions is to facilitate accessibility.[49] This was emphasised by the then President of Tanzania, Julius Nyerere, who noted that

[46] Indeed such cases often constitute a significant percentage of complaints received (see J. Hatchard, *National Human Rights Institutions* (2nd edn 1992), p. 69).

[47] As in Pakistan (see art. 33 Establishment of the Office of Wafaqi Mohtasib (Ombudsman) Order No 1 of 1983).

[48] In practice, even oral complaints are accepted. There are seemingly no restrictions on the language used for making complaints.

[49] This challenge was highlighted in the first Annual Report of the Permanent Commission of Enquiry in Tanzania which noted that only privileged individuals were obtaining significant practical benefits from the Commission. There is little to suggest that the Commission has resolved this problem.

> . . . we must not forget the Permanent Commission [of Enquiry] receives complaints only from the most literate, aware or energetic and courageous of our citizens.[50]

The importance of accessibility is further illustrated by the situation in Swaziland where few people knew of the office of the ombudsman and fewer still sought to utilise its services. Indeed in the three years of operation, it received just forty complaints. As one writer has remarked:

> This might suggest some disappointment with or apathy to the institution. It is therefore tempting to say that knowledge and use of the office was very much the preserve of a tiny minority, the urban and literate population.[51]

Developing plans to tackle the problem is also made much more difficult because many national institutions have little or no detailed statistical information on the background of complainants or even adequate case-management systems. This is explained away by some as being due to a shortage of staff and/or resources.[52] Yet it means that scarce resources are not necessarily being directed towards the most important areas and issues, and this is particularly the case where an institution is empowered to undertake its own investigations, especially through the holding of public inquiries into systemic human rights problems.[53]

There are several useful strategies being used by some national institutions to improve accessibility. One is to carry out regular nationwide tours to help create greater awareness of the office amongst the general populace and to foster positive links with local officials.[54] Similarly, the mounting of advertising campaigns and encouraging media coverage of activities provides a higher public profile for the institution.[55] In addition, some institutions have embarked on publicity campaigns targeted at young people. For example, human rights commissioners in Uganda have frequently addressed school children because they are perceived as an

[50] J. Nyerere, *Freedom and Development/Uhuru na Maendeleo: a Selection from Writings and Speeches 1968–73*, Oxford University Press, Nairobi, 1973, p. 182.

[51] See Ayee, 'Ombudsman Experience', p. 14

[52] See J. Hatchard, *National Human Rights Institutions* (2nd edn, 1992), p. 69.

[53] The computerisation of many national institutions has undoubtedly improved matters but the issue still remains to be adequately addressed by all national institutions.

[54] The offices of the Ombudsman in both Tanzania and Zambia have both reported that this method has proved helpful.

[55] For example, in Zimbabwe all courts and government offices have a general information leaflet on the Ombudsman written in the three national languages, whilst regular reports on the investigation of cases appear in the press.

articulate group who can influence their parents and other adults and can tell them what matters are handled by the office. Workers' and employers' groups have been similarly targeted. Although electronic access for the majority of people remains a somewhat distant prospect, the development of websites by national institutions, both as a mechanism for the promotion of human rights and a means for lodging complaints, is now underway and should prove an increasingly useful mechanism for enhancing accessibility.[56]

In larger jurisdictions, a more structured approach is to decentralise the office. This is epitomised in Ghana, where the Constitution *obliges* the Commission on Human Rights and Administrative Justice to establish regional and district branches and this has enabled it to lobby successfully for increased government funding to establish a nationwide presence.[57] Decentralisation does raise some problems, particularly over the delegation of powers and may be unsuitable for smaller jurisdictions.[58] Even so, it is a policy that ESA states should consider adopting.

Another mechanism is to permit third parties to lodge complaints on behalf of complainants. This focuses attention on the nature of a complaint and is a particularly useful protection for the more vulnerable members of society who may find it difficult, if not impossible, to lodge complaints personally, for example, children, those in institutions and the mentally disabled, as well as those living in the rural areas. *A fortiori* for those who may not wish to be seen contacting the institution through fear of possible reprisals.[59]

[56] Both the South African Human Rights Commission and the Ugandan Human Rights Commission have developed excellent websites (see www.sahrc.org.za and www.uhrc.org).

[57] Art. 220 Constitution of Ghana 1992. By the end of 2002 the Commission had established ten regional offices. It was also well on its way to establishing a full complement of 110 district offices. The Commonwealth Best Practice Guide states that offices 'should, where possible, be located away from other government and military offices' (at p. 31). This rightly recognises that national institutions must emphasise their independence by being physically separate from government offices. In practice, cost and availability of suitable premises may make this impossible.

[58] The Ghanaian Commissioner has addressed this by issuing policy guidelines allowing Regional and District Offices to investigate and settle specific types of cases without reference to Headquarters. Where such a matter is not amicably settled, the Regional Office may hold a formal hearing but its decision must be sent to Headquarters for approval before being divulged to the parties.

[59] In all such cases the national institution should satisfy itself that there is some substance in the allegation and it is in the public interest to carry out an investigation.

Instigating investigations

An investigation should not be dependent upon receipt of a complaint for an 'ombudsman [or human rights commission] must not wait for complaints to be brought to him [or her], but must go out to unearth corruption and maladministration whether the public complains or not'.[60] This is particularly necessary in the ESA states where many people remain susceptible to governmental abuse of power but do not complain either through ignorance of their rights or through fear of reprisals if they seek to do so. This has proved a very useful, if sometimes controversial, power.[61]

The power to pursue long-term investigations into systemic problems of administration was and remains an important part of the original Swedish model. It encompasses the power to 'identify legislative, policy and procedural deficiencies, and encourage systemic improvements to overcome those deficiencies; and contribute advice to the Government on the adequacy, effectiveness and efficiency of the various means of review of administrative action'.[62] A useful example again comes from Uganda where the Human Rights Commission responded to a series of individual complaints concerning unlawful detention by undertaking a study of problems within the criminal justice system and thence working with the police and prison authorities on a review of detention procedures.

An integrated institution?

There is no agreement as to whether or not the protection and promotion of human rights and administrative justice is best served by the creation of a single integrated institution. In South Africa, Malawi and Uganda, human rights commissions operate independently of offices of

[60] General Information on the Office of the Inspector-General of Government (Kampala, n.d.), p. 7. On a personal note, in 1993, John Hatchard headed a team of experts from the Commonwealth Secretariat to The Gambia to advise the government on establishing a national institution. Broad agreement was reached on the body and consequently a Bill was drafted. Hatchard was later informed privately by a high-ranking government official that the commission would never see the light of day because it was empowered to investigate allegations of corrupt practices by government officials. The Bill later inexplicably got bogged down in Parliament. Shortly afterwards, a military coup occurred and was justified on the grounds of, amongst other things, 'government corruption'.

[61] For example (and perhaps not surprisingly given its subject matter), the South African Human Rights Commission was subjected to considerable media criticism following its decision to question newspaper editors over alleged racial bias in the press.

[62] Commonwealth and Defence Force Ombudsman, 'Annual Report 1989–90', 2.

the ombudsman, whilst the offices of the ombudsman in Namibia and Zimbabwe operate as 'one-stop' institutions.[63] As noted below, some countries have gone further and chosen to establish, in addition, a separate anti-corruption commission.

Although national circumstances will inevitably dictate the most appropriate or politically acceptable institutional structure, there are a number of factors which lend support for an integrated approach. These include the fact that firstly, administrative costs are reduced which is a major consideration given the parlous financial state of some institutions. Secondly, focusing attention on a single body can raise its public profile and better counter executive attempts to weaken or undermine its operation. In particular, it cannot be assumed that government is fully committed to the development of a powerful and effective national institution and one way to dissipate its strength is to ensure its functions are fragmented. Thirdly, expertise can be concentrated in a single institution: again this is of considerable importance given resource constraints. Finally, it avoids both uncertainty as to which institution(s) has jurisdiction and the possible duplication of powers and work.

Investigative and remedial powers

On occasions an investigation will meet with a defensive, even hostile, response from an agency or enterprise and this may include the deliberate delaying of a response to communications or refusal to provide accurate information and documentation. The 'teeth' enjoyed by national institutions is that they enjoy the power of a court to (i) issue summons or other orders requiring any person to appear before it; (ii) question any person in connection with an investigation, including the holding of a formal hearing; (iii) compel the production of any relevant document or record; and (iv) enter and search buildings and compel the giving of information. Any person can be committed for contempt for failing to comply with any such order. Another useful power is the setting of specific time limits within which agencies are required to respond.

All national institutions have the power to reach a decision on the merits of a complaint and to make such recommendations for remedial action as appropriate. In practice, the vast majority of cases are settled through conciliation or by a positive response by the offending person or

[63] Although the Zimbabwean ombudsman can only deal with complaints against public officials.

body to such recommendations.[64] In some cases, a formal report on an investigation may be published.[65]

In the case of many offices of the ombudsman, where a recommendation is not complied with, the matter is generally referred to another body (in most cases the President) who then determines the appropriate action. It has been argued that limiting the office to recommending remedial action is fundamental to its operation. This is based on the view that it allows an ombudsman to proceed at a more informal level and to manage a very much larger case load because the ultimate decision rests with the agency and not with the ombudsman.[66] Such a limitation has long been criticised as being the real weakness of the offices and has led to them being branded 'toothless bulldogs'. In response, a range of additional powers are now available to some offices of the ombudsman and, arguably, these powers should extend to all such bodies. The Namibian Ombudsman provides a useful example. Here the ombudsman can bring proceedings for an interdict or other suitable remedy 'to secure the termination of the offending action or conduct or the abandonment or alteration of the offending procedures'.[67] This provides complainants with a direct, speedy and potentially effective protection from abuses of power by intransigent government officials and is especially useful in cases requiring urgent action. In addition, the ombudsman may challenge the validity of any statutory provision if the offending action or conduct 'is sought to be justified by subordinate legislation or regulation which is

[64] These might include reviewing the relevant procedure; making an ex gratia payment to recompense the complainant for expenses incurred or financial loss suffered; paying compensation to the complainant; or sending him/her an apology. National institutions should also have the power to issue Guidelines on Best Practice in an effort to improve administrative practices (see Commonwealth Best Practice Guide, p. 25).

[65] A good example of this is the March 1998 Report by the Permanent Human Rights Commission in Zambia on allegations of the torture of detainees following the 1997 coup attempt which in the public interest recommended the compulsory retirement of officers accused of torture. This led to the establishment of a formal Commission of Inquiry under the Inquiries Act, Cap. 41 (see SI No 94 of 1998). Of course the whole exercise begs the question as to why the recommendations of the Human Rights Commission alone were not acted upon by government and demonstrates the weakness of a Commission that has no enforcement powers.

[66] See, for example, Commonwealth Ombudsman in Australia, 'Annual Report 1989–1990', p. 3. One of the resolutions of a sub-regional conference on the office of the ombudsman also states tersely: 'The Ombudsman should *not* have enforcement mechanisms and/or powers'. See E. Kasuto and A. Wehmhorner (eds.), *The Ombudsman in Southern Africa: Report of a Sub-regional Conference*, Windhoek, 1995, p. 5.

[67] Art. 91(e)(dd) Namibian Constitution.

grossly unreasonable or otherwise ultra vires'.[68] The wide-ranging investigations by the institution may also uncover criminal conduct on the part of some government officials. In such circumstances the Namibian Ombudsman may refer the matter to the Prosecutor-General with a view to prosecuting the offender(s).[69]

As regards human rights commissions, the scope of their remedial powers following a human rights violation also remains a matter of some debate. Some, such as the Zambian Human Rights Commission, only have the power to recommend action. This is quite unsatisfactory and other commissions go much further by seeking to enable complainants to enforce their rights. For example the Malawi Human Rights Commission is empowered to give advice and assistance to complainants in bringing their cases to court. Even so, in practice the courts are often hampered in handling such matters due to, amongst other things, procedural complexities, wide-ranging rules on state privilege and strict rules of evidence. These restrictions rarely affect human rights commissions.[70] As a result, two other approaches are being used. The first is to empower a human rights commission to enforce its own orders.[71] This is the position in Uganda where the Human Rights Commission may:

> . . . if satisfied that there has been an infringement of a human right or freedom, order –
> (a) the release of a detained or restricted person;
> (b) payment of compensation; or
> (c) any other legal remedy or redress.

Commission decisions have the same effect as those of a court, are enforced in the same manner and it is also empowered to commit persons for contempt of its orders.[72] In effect, this creates another avenue of legal redress with complainants having a choice of forum through which to pursue their grievances, the main restriction being that the Commission cannot hear a case that is pending 'before a court or judicial

[68] Art. 91(e)(ee) Namibian Constitution. This power is of particular interest because it means that subordinate legislation becomes subject to critical review.

[69] Art. 91(e)(cc). See also the powers of the Malawian Ombudsman (s.126 Constitution of Malawi).

[70] Although commissions must observe the rules of natural justice and procedural fairness.

[71] The possibility of giving an office of the ombudsman the power to make binding decisions is discussed below.

[72] S.8(4) Uganda Human Rights Commission Act and art. 53(2) Constitution of Uganda. Any person or authority dissatisfied with any such order has a right of appeal to the High Court.

tribunal'.[73] Given the ease of access for complainants, the fact that the entire process is undertaken free of charge, the Commission's wide-ranging investigatory powers and the relative informality of the proceedings, it is not surprising that it has attracted many complainants eager to enforce their rights. These enforcement powers emanated from the desire of the Ugandan Constitution drafters to create a Commission with 'teeth' as a safeguard against any failure by the courts to protect human rights, as had occurred previously. In this sense it is very much a 'made to measure' institution. Its powers certainly create major, albeit not insurmountable, procedural problems but, even so, political and public support for the Commission's work remains strong.[74]

Adopting a 'partnership' approach between a human rights commission and the courts is the other possibility. Here the Commission utilises its wide-ranging powers to investigate a complaint and to make any necessary order for redress. If this is not complied with, rather than having its own enforcement powers, the order of the Commission is then 'adopted by the courts as judgments and decrees of such courts for the purposes of enforcement or execution'. This is the position in Ghana where the Commission on Human Rights and Administrative Justice can ask the Court to enforce its decision and recommendations if they are not complied with within three months from the submission of the decision.[75] This creates a working partnership between the Commission and the courts by utilising the investigatory advantages enjoyed by the Commission but retaining the court's enforcement role. In practice, the Ghanaian Commission has resorted to the procedure in only a tiny proportion of cases but it is seen as an essential part of its armoury.[76] It also provides a useful deterrent against the refusal of an agency to comply with the Commission's order. The one real difficulty with this procedure is that it is unclear whether a court is required merely to enforce the Commission's judgment or whether it must satisfy itself as to the merits of the decision. The matter is yet to be finally resolved in Ghana but to enjoy the full protection of the system, the former view should prevail.[77]

[73] Art. 53(4)(a) Constitution of Uganda.

[74] See Hatchard, 'A New Breed of Institution', pp. 41–6.

[75] S.18(2) Commission for Human Rights and Administrative Justice Act.

[76] Out of 8,775 cases disposed of, in only thirteen was the Commission compelled to institute court action to enforce its recommendations: see Short, 'Commission', pp. 5–6.

[77] In such cases the need for Commissioners who hear such cases to have legal qualifications (or at least have legal advice readily available) is overwhelming. Administrative justice will also require that reasons for decisions are provided (and published) and that there is provision for judicial review.

Overall, given the 'bespoke' nature of national institutions, there is no one 'right' answer as to the remedial powers each should enjoy. What is clear however, is that some countries are making significant efforts to improve the effectiveness of their national institutions by introducing imaginative ways of upholding the rights of complainants. These efforts are most welcome and hopefully will encourage others to do likewise.

Promoting human rights

All the human rights commissions in the ESA states are tasked with promoting respect for and observance of human rights. This is a heavy responsibility for it involves developing a culture of understanding of human rights issues that extends to people at work and at school, in families and in public life, including government officials, parliamentarians and security forces members. Its importance is emphasised by the Oder Commission's findings that a key factor in the perpetuation of the cycle of violence in Uganda prior to 1987 was the ignorance of human rights by both law enforcement officers and their victims. It noted that in consequence, 'officers and agents of the state regularly abused the rights of those who fell into their hands and the victims and the public often aided the process by being passive'.[78] Further, it also remarked that there was a pervasive lack of 'internal democracy' in all Ugandan institutions including the family. In its view, this 'breeds people, who from childhood, are nurtured to violently repress other people's rights'.[79]

The role of human rights commissions in the development of human rights education programmes for specific groups is mentioned elsewhere in the book.[80] Overall the aim must be to impart the message to all public servants that sensitivity to human rights issues is required for effective job performance. In doing so, national institutions must have as their aim the development of a culture of respect for human rights that permeates throughout government. In carrying out this task, national institutions should work, in particular, with legal educators and NGOs in the design and delivery of training courses.[81]

Promoting human rights is not just about education, and three related issues require discussion.

[78] Oder Commission Report, p. 10. [79] Ibid., At p. 10.

[80] See chapters 7, 8 and 11 on human rights education for parliamentarians, judges and members of the security forces respectively.

[81] See further the Commonwealth Best Practice Guide at pp. 22–3.

Taking a position on national human rights issues

It is widely accepted that a human rights commission should be free to comment on national human rights issues[82] and indeed it must do so if it encounters evidence of human rights violations.[83] How it should respond to national debates on controversial human rights issues is more problematic. For example, in a debate on the death penalty or abortion or euthanasia, should a commission merely provide information and facilitate public discussion or should it seek to lead public opinion by taking a specific position? The Commission on Human Rights and Administrative Justice in Ghana faced this dilemma on the death penalty issue. Commissioners found it extremely difficult to adopt a detached attitude, particularly because the media was continually seeking their views, apparently (and somewhat encouragingly) regarding the Commission as the 'conscience of the nation'.[84] National circumstances mean that it is not possible to adopt a hard and fast rule although the prime role of a human rights commission in such matters is to facilitate debate, provide information and ensure that all views on the topic are widely disseminated. In addition, the independence of the commission may be adversely affected if it does take sides and, in any event, as a multi-member body, it may well be impossible for commissioners to reach any consensus.

Overseeing the state's compliance with international human rights obligations

With many ESA states failing to fulfil fully their obligations under international and regional human rights instruments, it is useful to provide national institutions with the role of overseeing their compliance with these obligations. The Uganda Human Rights Commission is specifically tasked with doing this[85] although it is arguably impliedly included in

[82] Compare the *Paris Principles*, para 3(a)(iv).

[83] This makes all the more inexplicable and regrettable the failure of the Zimbabwean Ombudsman to seemingly make any public statement or take any action in the face of the appalling human rights violations that were witnessed in the country both in the early 1980s and at the beginning of the new millennium. Its abysmal record makes it a suitable candidate for abolition in the same way as its Swazi counterpart.

[84] For example, the Commissioner regularly appeared in televised debates on capital punishment. The Commission eventually publicly proclaimed its support for the abolition of the death penalty.

[85] See art. 52(1)(h) Constitution of Uganda. This led to the setting up of a Monitoring and Treaties Department tasked with monitoring government's compliance with its international treaty obligations.

the promotion of human rights mandates of other commissions. Such a power is potentially extremely significant in that a broad interpretation of 'monitoring' would require government to report to a commission on steps taken to comply with its international human rights obligations.[86]

The monitoring role could also extend to overseeing the preparation of national reports required under regional and international human rights instruments and, where necessary, providing appropriate training in their preparation for government officials. The importance of retaining its independence means that a commission should not take responsibility for compiling such reports. Indeed it should be free to provide a separate, 'alternative' report if necessary.

Reporting on the state of human rights in the country

The Uganda Human Rights Commission also provides a useful model here. In line with the *Paris Principles*[87] it is required to prepare reports both on the state of human rights in Uganda and, where necessary, on specific issues. Civil society can also play a key role by following-up the Commission's reports and endeavouring to ensure that any recommendations for action are duly implemented. The preparation of such reports is a potentially valuable 'stock-taking' exercise and if widely disseminated, could be an effective means of promoting and strengthening human rights.

The Ugandan Human Rights Commission is also required to submit an annual report to Parliament on the state of human rights and freedoms in the country. This, in itself, is unusual for an annual report normally merely provides an overview on the Commission's work. The obligation is significant as it emphasises the importance of providing Parliament with an objective, reliable, properly structured[88] and 'user-friendly' assessment of the human rights situation in the country. There is no statutory duty on parliaments to debate such reports and this is a major oversight since there remains a danger that the report will otherwise have little impact.

[86] Presumably, a Commission could then recommend, or take, action to remedy any shortcomings. This is an area that requires specialist knowledge and is one in which input from organs of civil society, such as human rights non-governmental organisations, could prove invaluable.

[87] Para 3(iv) of the *Paris Principles* states that human rights commissions have the responsibility for drawing the attention of the Government to violations of human rights in any part of the country and to propose initiatives to remedy them.

[88] The development of model Guidelines on reporting by national institutions should be considered, along similar lines as adopted by UN human rights agencies.

However, wide publicity of the report in the media may persuade parliamentarians of the importance of debating it.[89]

New challenges

The work of national institutions must evolve to take into account new challenges, such as dealing with the human rights implications of the AIDS pandemic or anti-terrorism laws. There is also a need to adopt fresh approaches towards tackling some existing challenges. Here the issues of privatisation and cross-border co-operation require particular attention.

Privatisation and non-state actors

The radical privatisation programmes by many governments have had significant consequences for oversight bodies as non-state actors become increasingly the focus of administrative injustice and human rights concerns.[90] Such changes require a re-appraisal of the domestic human rights and administrative justice protection mechanisms where the key assumption remains that the principal violators[91] are states. There are those who believe that privatisation means less regulation. This is not the case: in reality, it means a different type of regulation. Indeed the need for an even more acute type of regulation or oversight is necessary, not least because the increasing globalisation of business provides increased opportunities for abuse of power and corrupt practices.

These developments have particularly impacted upon offices of the ombudsman whose jurisdiction is based on the assumption that administrative justice/injustice lies in the hands of public servants. But privatisation means that in the new millennium the private sector may well overtake the State as a focus of administrative injustice and human rights concerns.[92] Privatisation means that public servants are 'transformed' into employees of privatised enterprises and fall outside the ombudsman's traditional jurisdiction. The result of this is that in many key areas

[89] A duty to provide copies of all annual and other reports to the appropriate Minister(s) and requiring a public response thereto within a specific time would also be useful.

[90] As Fraser has noted: 'Many governments would have conducted policies designed to see that workers gained a fair share of the returns of an enterprise. . . . such policies are no longer possible' (M. Fraser, 'The Nation State and Globalisation' (1999) 2 *Commonwealth Currents* 18).

[91] And, paradoxically, the chief defenders as well!

[92] See the discussion by R. L. Barsh, 'Changing Forces and Non-State Actors in the Struggle for Human Rights', in *The Universal Declaration of Human Rights: Fifty Years and Beyond*, Yoel Danieli, Elsa Stamatopoulou and Clarence T. Dias (eds.), New York, 1999, pp. 403–10.

aggrieved citizens are precluded from pursuing their claims for administrative justice.

On the face of it the simplest remedy is to extend the jurisdiction of offices of the ombudsman to non-state actors. This is already the case with human rights commissions where complaints against privatised industries involving human rights issues, such as breaches of trade-union rights, environmental rights and cultural rights, as well as allegations of discriminatory treatment are already routinely heard. This is the approach in Namibia where the Ombudsman has a duty to investigate complaints concerning 'practices and actions by persons, *enterprises and other private institutions* where such complaints allege that violations of fundamental rights and freedoms under this Constitution have taken place . . .' (our emphasis).[93] Even so, doubts remain as to whether the traditional office of the ombudsman is appropriate for dealing with complaints involving the private sector. For example, the legal or public service background of many incumbents is not necessarily appropriate for dealing with complaints involving the commercial operations and practices of a private enterprise.[94] Further, the traditional office of the ombudsman is required to report to Parliament (or the President) on the work of the office. It can also seek parliamentary (or presidential) assistance in resolving a case where there is a refusal on the part of a public servant to accept and implement a recommendation. This procedure is not appropriate when the recalcitrant party is a non-state actor. Creating a multi-member institution might resolve some concerns although this would change the traditional view of the office as being 'headed by an independent high-level public official' and might meet resistance on this score.[95]

An alternative approach is developing separate private sector offices of the ombudsman. These are well established in several western countries and are themselves largely the product of the 1980s privatisation process and the widespread recognition of the need for 'good governance' in both the private and public sector.[96] Whilst retaining many of the

[93] Constitution of Namibia, art. 91(a).

[94] This is a weakness of the Namibian model in which the ombudsman must be either a judge of Namibia or 'a person possessing the legal qualifications which would entitle him or her to practise in all the Courts of Namibia' (art. 89(4) Constitution of Namibia). A move to make the office a multi-member body would help overcome this problem.

[95] This perhaps is another argument in favour of developing a single unified institution.

[96] In the United Kingdom, for instance, separate private sector ombudsman-style bodies handle complaints from the public concerning, amongst others things, telecommunications, the water, gas and electricity industries, banks, and insurance and pension companies. Whilst some, such as the Legal Services Ombudsman and the Building Societies Ombudsman, are statutory bodies, most are non-statutory and exist by virtue of a voluntary

features of the traditional office, there remain several significant differences. Firstly, unlike public officials who fall under the jurisdiction of the traditional ombudsman by virtue of their office or post, members of an industry must voluntarily submit to the jurisdiction of a private-sector ombudsman. This is often linked to the development of a *voluntary* Code of Conduct/Practice for the particular industry. The voluntary nature of the arrangement remains a potential weakness in the system, although peer, economic and government pressure may well persuade enterprises to join up.[97] Certainly, to be effective a large majority of industry members must be subject to the jurisdiction of the ombudsman and, ideally, the aim should be to have 100 per cent industry coverage. Secondly, a private-sector ombudsman is responsible for the oversight of a particular industry and this requires him/her to have specialist knowledge and expertise in that area that is unlikely to be held by a traditional ombudsman. Further, the investigation powers of a private-sector ombudsman are inevitably different in that s/he will not normally be entitled to demand information, to summon witnesses and question them on oath, nor be in a position to obtain access to information that is subject to privilege.[98] This will inevitably limit the scope and effectiveness of some inquiries. Thirdly, remedial powers are also an issue. Arguably, the power to recommend remedial action is not sufficient for a private-sector ombudsman because, unlike the traditional ombudsman, there is no 'higher body' to whom a report can be made with a request for further action. If the process is to have any credibility, the only realistic answer is to make the decision of the private-sector ombudsman binding on the parties.[99] Another potential remedial power is to publicly 'name and shame' any offending party who refuses to comply with the ombudsman's decisions or recommendations. This will involve another significant departure from the traditional ombudsman model where the identity of all the parties remains confidential. The 'name and shame' approach is surely justified on the basis that disclosure of 'maladministration' by

agreement within the particular industry. See P. Birkinshaw, *Grievance, Remedies and the State*, Sweet and Maxwell, London, 2nd edn, 1994, pp. 242–4.

[97] Likewise, an enterprise may withdraw its consent to accept the jurisdiction of the ombudsman.

[98] In addition, in the case of multi-national corporations, such information may not necessarily be locally available.

[99] In some cases, this is already possible. For example, the Insurance Ombudsman in the United Kingdom may make a binding financial award up to a specific amount to a successful complainant. Above that amount, compliance with the decision becomes a voluntary matter.

employees of an enterprise will result in adverse publicity and, depending on its seriousness, a possible consequent loss of business, income and profits for the enterprise. This will certainly be of interest to shareholders!

To date, no ESA state has established a private-sector ombudsman's office. Yet in areas such as power supply, telecommunications and financial services the establishment of industry-specific institutions could provide a flexible and realistic response to the need to provide suitable oversight bodies for the privatised twenty-first century.

Transnational and cross-border co-operation

Increasingly national institutions are facing matters that include a transnational or cross-border dimension, such as those relating to refugees, asylum cases and the investigation of corrupt practices in international business transactions. However, at present, offices of the ombudsman, human rights commissions (and anti-corruption commissions) are generally ill-equipped to deal with such issues in that they are still regarded as being *national* bodies whose task is to tackle *national* issues.[100] They can no longer afford to retain this limited focus.

Certainly some institutions have developed 'networking' capacities with similar bodies elsewhere, sometimes through the establishment of a regional association or through the work of the Commonwealth or the International Ombudsman Institute. Yet there has been little work on the development of mutual co-operation and assistance regimes *inter se* to facilitate cross-border and transnational investigations.[101] A useful starting point would be the signing of a Memorandum of Understanding between such institutions. An example of this kind of arrangement is the 1995 Memorandum of Understanding between the Canadian Human Rights Commission and the National Human Rights Commission in India. This provides for the sharing of information and documentation, staff exchanges between the two commissions and the development of

[100] See, for example, the 'Report of the Commonwealth Regional Workshop on Strengthening National Ombudsman and Human Rights Institutions' where at a four-day workshop in 1998, involving participants from institutions from fourteen countries, no mention is made either of any transnational aspect to the work of the Ombudsman nor the impact of privatisation and non-state actors.

[101] For example, exchanges of information between institutions in different countries to facilitate investigations into allegations of the systematic bribery of public officials in those countries by a multi-national corporation based elsewhere. Other examples include addressing the problem of refugees, migrant workers or the trafficking in women and children as well as environmental issues.

stronger links between human rights centres in universities in their respective countries aimed at enhancing the quality of information available to them.

A Memorandum of Understanding is a useful device already used by other investigative agencies, such as the police and customs authorities in dealing with cross-border crime. In the case of oversight bodies, such a Memorandum might include an agreement that the human rights commission in country A will investigate complaints originating in country B that have a transnational element and *vice versa*. Further it might provide for staff exchanges leading to closer professional ties between staff from different institutions. In this way co-operation and trust is facilitated, knowledge of the transnational aspect of the problem clarified and efficiency enhanced. The use of universities and other higher-learning institutions to play a research role is also attractive, especially as time and staffing constraints often make this almost impossible for the institutions themselves.

A Memorandum of Understanding is not the sole mechanism for developing transnational and cross-border co-operation between oversight bodies, but it does illustrate a potentially effective method of doing so. It also highlights the crucial fact that national institutions must respond to new challenges in a positive and effective manner. In doing so, they must shed their tag as *national bodies* and operate as *transnational bodies.*

Anti-corruption commissions

'Acts of Corruption'[102] in the public sector are now regarded as a serious governance problem for ESA states.[103] In response some states have

[102] The Southern African Development Community Protocol against Corruption signed in August 2001 by the Heads of State of Government of ten of the eleven SEA states includes in its definition of 'Acts of Corruption' '(a) the solicitation or acceptance, directly or indirectly, by a public official, of any article of monetary value, or other benefit, such as a gift, favour, promise or advantage for himself or herself or for another person or entity, in exchange for any act or omission in the performance of his or her public functions; (b) the offering or granting, directly or indirectly, by a public official, of any article of monetary value, or other benefit, such as a gift, favour, promise or advantage for himself or herself or for another person or entity, in exchange for any act or omission in the performance of his or her public functions; (c) any act or omission in the discharge of his or her duties by a public official for the purpose of illicitly obtaining benefits for himself or herself or for a third party.'

[103] For example, the Transparency International Corruption Perceptions Index 2002 ranks them as follows (out of a total of 102 states worldwide): Botswana 24th, Namibia 28th, South Africa 36th, Malawi 68th, Tanzania and Zimbabwe 71st equal, Zambia 77th, Uganda 93rd, Kenya 96th. Lesotho and Swaziland are not included in the list.

made the investigation and prevention of corruption a specific function of national institutions: for example the Public Protector in South Africa, the Inspector-General in Uganda and the Namibian Ombudsman. Others have established separate anti-corruption commissions (ACCs): for example Zambia (Anti-Corruption Commission), Botswana (Directorate on Corruption and Economic Crime), Kenya (Kenyan Anti-Corruption Authority (KACA)), Tanzania (Prevention of Corruption Bureau), and Malawi (Anti-Corruption Bureau). Anti-corruption commissions are organised and have similar investigatory powers as human rights commissions and offices of the ombudsman. Thus much of the earlier discussion in this chapter applies equally to them.

The development of ACCs has much to do with the institutional anti-corruption mechanisms demanded by international donors as part of economic structural adjustment programmes. For instance, in Kenya the KACA was created in 1997[104] primarily as the result of pressure from the International Monetary Fund and World Bank. Its functions reflected the general powers and functions of ACCs namely:

(a) To take necessary measures for the prevention of corruption in the public, parastatal and private sectors;
(b) To investigate, and subject to the directions of the Attorney General, to prosecute for offences under this Act and other offences involving corrupt transactions;
(c) To advise the Government and the parastatal organisations on ways and means of preventing corruption;
(d) To inquire into and investigate the extent of liability of any public officer in the loss of any public funds and to institute civil proceedings against the officer and any other person involved in the transaction which resulted in the loss for the recovery of such loss;
(e) To investigate any conduct of a public officer which is connected with or conducive to corrupt practices and to make suitable recommendation thereon;
(f) To undertake such further or other investigations as may be directed by the Attorney General;
(g) To enlist members of the public in fighting corruption by the use of education and outreach programmes.

The importance attaching to such bodies by donors was highlighted following the 2000 decision of the High Court of Kenya in *Gachiengo and*

[104] Through an amendment to the Prevention of Corruption Act, Cap. 65.

Kahura v Republic[105] in which the High Court of Kenya surprisingly ruled the body unconstitutional.[106] As a result, donors promptly froze all lending.[107] It was no surprise therefore that following the 2002 presidential and parliamentary elections, the creation of a new anti-corruption body was one of the first promises made by the newly elected Kenyan president, Mwai Kibaki.

The effectiveness of ACCs remains unclear. Certainly the Directorate on Corruption and Economic Crime in Botswana has reported some success[108] although others remain less sanguine about the position elsewhere.[109] Of course, it must be remembered that ACCs form just a part, albeit an important part, of anti-corruption mechanisms and strategies and that the priority for states is to develop a holistic approach towards tackling the problem of corruption.[110]

Overview

Maintaining and developing powerful and effective oversight bodies is a challenging task. Certainly the record of national institutions has been the subject of severe criticism and some see them as merely 'window dressing' by governments.[111] That governments treat such institutions

[105] High Court of Kenya, unreported, 2000.

[106] On the ground that it was contrary to the separation of powers for a serving High Court judge to head the KACA.

[107] See Gitau Warugi, 'East and East-Central Africa', in Robin Hodess (ed.), *Global Corruption Report 2001*, Transparency International, Berlin, 2001, p. 69.

[108] See the DCEC *Annual Report 2001*, chapter 1.

[109] See Penny Dale, 'Southern Africa', in Hodess (*Global Corruption Report*, pp. 58–9). See generally Constance Kunaka, Noria Mashumba and Philliat Matsheza, *The SADC Protocol against Corruption*, Human Rights Research and Documentation Trust of Southern Africa, Harare, 2002, p. 62.

[110] These include developing regional initiatives such as the Southern African Forum Against Corruption (SAFAC) and the African Parliamentarians Network Against Corruption. The 2002 conviction for bribery of a major international construction company by the Lesotho High Court in connection with the Lesotho Highlands Water Project (LHWP), a project billed as the biggest construction and engineering scheme in Africa, also raises expectations that courts will also play an increasingly significant role. See *R v Acres International* (2002, High Court of Lesotho, unreported, CRI/T/2/2002). The company was fined more than US$2 million. See also *R v Sole* (2002, High Court of Lesotho, Unreported, CRI/T/111/99) where the head of the LHWP was convicted of corruption in respect of the taking of bribes from Acres International and sentenced to eighteen years in prison.

[111] See in particular the detailed analysis undertaken by Binaifer Nowrojee, *Protectors or Pretenders: Government Human Rights Commissions in Africa* (2001, Human Rights Watch, www.hrw.org/rreports/2001/africa/overview/conclusion.html).

with suspicion is perhaps inevitable given the strong tradition of executive control within the ESA states and the lack of commitment to independent institutions. The challenge therefore remains to make them effective. To do so, six fundamental elements must be in place. These are (i) demonstrable independence; (ii) provision of adequate resources; (iii) accessibility for all citizens; (iv) power to inquire into the widest possible range of complaints; (v) adequate investigatory powers; and (vi) appropriate remedial powers. Without them, a national institution is likely to become a 'front and a facade' that should be consigned to history, as was the case in Swaziland.

The potential 'benefits' accruing from the development of 'successful' national institutions are considerable. It means that citizens can enjoy administrative justice and the protection of their human rights. This can also strengthen the Constitution itself by demonstrating that the people can and do derive meaningful benefits from the Constitution and it is thus worth defending it against those who would undermine or abrogate it. National institutions can also act as a link between government and civil society. Their task is not only to highlight, and where appropriate, to take action to prevent administrative injustice and abuses of human rights, but also to defend those who are unfairly accused of such practices. It is crucial therefore to ensure that national institutions are not (and are not regarded as) 'super-NGOs' or 'pro-Government' bodies but are instead demonstrably independent, even-handed in their operation and enjoy the support of all sections of society. Even so, non-governmental organisations, the media and other organs of civil society can make a significant contribution to the operational effectiveness of such bodies and it is therefore important to develop appropriate relations with them.

11

Seeking constitutional control of the military

> The military should always be kept in subjection to the laws of the country to which it belongs, and he is no friend of the Republic who advocates the contrary.[1]

The relationship between civilian government and the military

The most prized right of any political community is the right to govern itself. It follows that good governance and undue military involvement in the political process are incompatible and that a civilian government must retain supremacy over the military. In essence this means that the military must have sufficient power and autonomy to carry out its constitutional role but that it must not dominate or unduly influence other aspects of governance or enjoy an excessive share of national resources.[2] As the ANC in South Africa declared in its seminal 1992 policy statement *Ready to Govern*, the security forces should be:

> Bound by the principles of civil supremacy and subject to public scrutiny and open debate . . . [and] be accountable and answerable to the public through a democratically elected parliament.[3]

The principle of 'civil supremacy' was also considered by the Sub-Council on Defence and the Joint Military Co-ordinating Council during the 1993 constitutional negotiations in South Africa. In doing so, it noted:

> There is a fundamental division between the military and civilian spheres whatever the level of interaction between them. The essence of the division is that armed forces should refrain from involvement in politics other than through constitutionally approved channels whilst civilians refrain from

[1] Taft C. J. in *Dow v Johnson* (1879) 100 U.S. 158, at p. 169.
[2] See OECD Report, *Participatory Development and Good Governance*, Paris: OECD, 1995, paras 53–65 and IBRD, *Governance: the World Bank's Experience*, Washington, 1994.
[3] Ibid., at p. 71.

interfering in operational matters, and with the military chain of command and the military discipline code.[4]

How to maintain civilian supremacy over the military is the focus of this chapter. In it, the 'military' is used as an omnibus term to describe the various arms of the security services,[5] i.e. the defence forces (army and/or air force/navy), para-military bodies, and the intelligence services.[6] The chapter is divided as follows. The first part considers undue military involvement in government in the ESA states and some of the reasons therefor. The next examines the mechanisms employed in the new constitutions to keep the military in barracks. The third discusses the role of civil society in protecting the constitution against military intervention, whilst the fourth section considers the sensitive issue of how a state deals with its history of human rights violations by the military or previous authoritarian regimes.

Undue military involvement in government

Coups

The most familiar assertion of military power comes in the form of a coup that overthrows the civilian government and replaces it with military rule. In this situation usurpers usually claim that the action was taken in the name of the 'People', 'Motherland' (or 'Fatherland?'), 'Democracy' or the like. This is then accompanied by a pledge to return the country to constitutional government as soon as possible. In reality the ousting of the civilian administration almost inevitably leads to a lengthy period of authoritarian rule. During this time constitutional provisions are undermined or abrogated and the normal democratic process terminated, for at the heart of military government is the fact that power is sustained through the use (or threat) of force rather than by popular consensus.[7]

[4] JMCC, *Post-election Civilian Control*, p. B-3, cited in G. Cawtra, *Securing South Africa's Democracy: Defence, Development and Security in Transition*, Macmillan, London, 1997, p. 61.

[5] This is based on the definition of 'security services' in the Constitution of South Africa 1996, s.199(1).

[6] State 'intelligence' bodies are the least visible but potentially the most threatening to constitutionalism of all the security services. For a fascinating insight into the operation of the Rhodesian Central Intelligence Organisation, see K. Flower, *Serving Secretly*, Murray, London, 1987.

[7] See A. C. Bundu, 'Recognition of Revolutionary Authorities: Law and Practice of States' (1978) 27 ICLQ 18 and T. O. Elias, 'The Commonwealth in Africa' (1968) 31 MLR 284.

Africa abounds with examples where the military has usurped power and suspended the constitution in whole or in part.[8] Nigeria epitomises the military in government. Between independence in 1960 and 1999, the country experienced eight military rulers, six military-inspired changes of government – five of which were successful military coups, four constitutions (one of which was never used), at least four unsuccessful coup attempts, two civilian regimes that lasted a total of ten years, and one civil war. On the face of it, compared to West Africa, the ESA region is something of a 'coup-free' zone. Even so, both Uganda and Lesotho have experienced successful coups, attempted coups have occurred in Tanzania, Zambia and Kenya and the military still plays a disturbingly powerful political role in several states. Whilst it may be true that sometimes the 'military has its own reasons for its periodic eruptions on the political scene which we may not always understand',[9] attempting to identify the causes, both external and internal, for military intervention can assist constitution-makers in devising ways of addressing these issues.

External causes are characterised by the reasons given for the 1971 military coup in Uganda by Idi Amin. He announced eighteen points justifying the action that were based largely on assertions of political and economic mismanagement, tribalism and widespread corruption amongst the national leadership. As the people of Uganda quickly discovered, his promised return to an elected civilian government that would uphold and protect the Constitution was soon forgotten as he declared himself President for life and ruled by decree. During this period thousands lost their lives and there was political and economic chaos and the complete breakdown of the rule of law. The return of former President Milton Obote and his Uganda People's Congress Party (UPC) to power following the controversial and hotly disputed 1980 elections did little to stabilise the country, and, according to Mukholi:

For a useful compilation on the impact of military decrees on fundamental rights, see B. Owasanoye and C. Nwanku, *Suppressed Rights: Constitutional Rights Violations in Military Decrees 1984–1999*, Constitutional Rights Project, Lagos 1999.

[8] For example, between 1956 and 1983 no less than sixty successful coups and seventy-one attempted coups occurred in thirty-seven African states: P. McGowan and T. Johnson, 'African Military Coups d'Etat and Underdevelopment: a Quantitative Historical Analysis' (1984) 22 Journal of Modern African Studies 633. See also B. Agyeman-Duah, 'Military Coups, Regime Change and Interstate Conflicts in West Africa' (1990) 16 *Armed Forces and Society* 547.

[9] Chief Emeka Anyaoku (Secretary-General of the Commonwealth) in a speech at the Opening of the Roundtable of Heads of Government of Commonwealth Africa on Democracy and Good Governance in Africa, Kasane, Botswana, 24 February 1997.

> Poll-rigging, oppression by UPC functionaries, the abuse of office and the gross violation of human rights provided a 'just cause' for the armed struggle against the UPC government.[10]

Ironically, it was not until the National Resistance Army, under the leadership of Yoweri Museveni, seized power in January 1986 that the cycle of violence in the country came to an end. Uganda's experience thus contains many of the factors identified as common causes for military intervention, namely, the lack of regime legitimacy; absence of adequate dialogue between rulers and ruled; economic crises and chronic instability;[11] and allegations of corruption within the civilian government.[12]

The personal ambitions of the military are the 'internal' factors that can lead to military intervention. Thus Nwabueze asserts that, at least in the case of Nigeria, individual officers' personal ambition for political power is such that 'every soldier sees himself as a potential president'.[13] This becomes an attractive prospect when coupled with the knowledge that the risk of failure is low, the gains from success high and the fact that usurpers can expect to remain in power for a lengthy period.

We must also not overlook the situation where the military publicly pledges its support to the incumbent President at the expense of other potential presidential hopefuls. This may include threats not to recognise any election results in which the President is defeated.[14] Such conduct must be recognised as a coup-like scenario and condemned as another example of an illegitimate exercise both of military power, and where orchestrated by the President, of presidential power.

Despite continuing examples of 'bad governance' in some of the ESA states, as of late 2003 none of them had an overtly military government. Several have successfully maintained civilian rule since independence whilst the others have seemingly made a satisfactory transition from military to civilian rule. So it is useful to explore Finer's question

[10] David Mukholi, *A Complete Guide to Uganda's Fourth Constitution: History, Politics and the Law*, Kampala, Fountain Publishers, 1995, p. 45.

[11] E. Luttwak, *Coup d'Etat: a Practical Handbook*, Knopf, New York, 1968, 6. See also J. Krause, 'Ghana 1966', in W. G. Andrews and U. Ra'anan (eds.), *The Politics of the Coup d'Etat: Five Case Studies*, Reinhold, New York, 1969, 89, at p. 100.

[12] B. O. Nwabueze, *Military Rule and Constitutionalism in Nigeria*, Spectrum Books, Lagos, 1992, p. 331.

[13] Ibid., p. 334.

[14] For example, in Zimbabwe prior to the 2002 presidential election, security chiefs reportedly publicly stated that they would not 'accept' an electoral defeat for Robert Mugabe. See *The Times* 10 January 2002.

as to why, given its organisational superiority and monopoly of arms, the military ever obeys its civilian masters.[15] Writing in 1986 at the height of the one-party state era, Goldsworthy argued that 'personal rule' was the paramount determinant of successful civilian control of the military.[16] This is unconvincing given the fact there often remained a close relationship between the military and 'the Party and its government'.[17] Others have pointed out that some of the ESA states have significant historical differences compared to the rest of Africa since many gained independence more recently. Other explanations have rightly focused on the fact that the military in much of the region received political education through their involvement in the various liberation struggles and this included the acceptance of civilian political control and supervision.[18]

Whatever the validity of these possible explanations, the challenge is to elicit and maintain popular support for civilian rule through the development of effective mechanisms and institutions that promote and protect good governance and the rule of law. This includes addressing issues of 'bad governance' such as corruption and economic maladministration, perversion of the constitutional system and an unacceptable accumulation of political power in the hands of a ruling elite. This is then supported by the knowledge that the international community will not recognise the legality of military regimes, but will bring diplomatic and economic pressure on the usurpers to hand power back to civilian rule at the earliest possible moment.[19]

[15] S. E. Finer, *The Man on Horseback: the Role of the Military in Politics*, Praeger, New York, 1962, p. 5.

[16] D. Goldsworthy, 'Armies and Politics in Civilian Regimes', in S. Baynham (ed.), *Military Power and Politics in Black Africa*, St Martin's Press, New York, 1986, p. 97.

[17] For example in Tanzania during the time of the one-party state, the ruling CCM party had branches in all army barracks and all officers were party members. The de-linking of the military from political parties after the restoration of multi-party democracy is therefore a key element in maintaining an appropriate civilian–military relationship.

[18] Excellent examples being South Africa and Namibia but not Zimbabwe. In contrast, in West Africa the military were not involved in the liberation struggles and developed on essentially elitist lines: see the discussion by Karl P. Magyar, 'Military Intervention and Withdrawal in Africa: Problems and Perspectives', in Constantine P. Danopoulos, *From Military to Civilian Rule*, Routledge, London, 1992, chap. 12.

[19] See, for example, the work of the Commonwealth Ministerial Action Group (CMAG). A difficult situation will still arise where an ostensibly corrupt government is replaced at the polls by the only viable rival political party that itself then proves to be thoroughly corrupt. Hence, the military might argue that it is the only body left to resolve the crisis. It will be left to groups such as CMAG as well as the courts (perhaps through the sensible use of the doctrine of necessity: see for example the case of *Syed Zafar Sali Shah v General*

The military and 'internal security'

Whilst coups are the most obvious example of undue military intervention in government, the thorny issues of the involvement by the security services in internal-security matters merits attention. For example as Cawthra notes, with the downfall of the apartheid regime in South Africa, the primary security concerns of the SEA states are not usually military threats from other states but arise from the fact that their economic, social and political weaknesses make them vulnerable to other internal threats.

Internal security itself is constitutionally a matter for the police and justifiable concerns arise when the security services become involved. This is particularly so where an ostensibly civilian government becomes increasingly dependent on such forces to retain political power and/or uses the military against the civilian population. Almost inevitably this provides the military with excessive influence on decision-making and significantly weakens civilian control.[20] Similarly, the use of internal intelligence-gathering bodies to provide information and advice to the government on national security issues is commonplace and, subject to appropriate controls, is entirely proper. Again, concern arises if such bodies are used to target political rivals or otherwise seek to influence the political life of the country. As the Uganda Constitutional Commission noted, during both periods in which Milton Obote headed an ostensibly civilian administration, the army was allowed to become a law unto itself and 'caused terror and abused people's human rights to a horrifying extent. Instead of fighting external enemies it has been principally dealing with "internal" enemies . . .'[21]

One of the best-documented examples of the use of the military to deal with 'internal enemies' concerns the activities of 5 Brigade in Zimbabwe.[22] Between 1980 and 1987 the country experienced serious security problems, particularly in Matabeleland and parts of the Midlands – areas that were the stronghold of the main minority party PF-ZAPU. The Government claimed that these problems were the result

Pervaiz Musharraf, Chief Executive of Pakistan PLD 2000 SC 869 discussed below) to steer the country back to civilian rule.

20 See the discussion by Magyar, 'Military Intervention', pp. 154–6.

21 Uganda Constitutional Commission, *Guidelines on Constitutional Issues*, Government Printers, Kampala; 1991, p. 71.

22 See Catholic Commission for Justice and Peace, *Breaking the Silence; Building the Peace*, CCJP, Harare, 1997 (the CCJP Report).

of 'dissident' activity and deployed in the affected areas the infamous 5 Brigade, whose members were trained by foreign instructors specifically for so-called 'internal defence purposes'. Significantly, it was not an integrated part of the Zimbabwean National Army (ZNA) and it was not answerable to the normal ZNA command structure nor to its disciplinary procedures. It used a different communications system to other brigades, members wore a different uniform and used different weapons. In reality it was answerable directly to then Prime Minister, Robert Mugabe.[23]

During the period in question, widespread human rights abuses occurred against the rural population in particular and 'it is indisputable that thousands of unarmed civilians died, were beaten, or suffered loss of property . . . most as a result of the action of Government agencies [i.e. 5 Brigade, the Central Intelligence Organisation and a police special unit]'. Indeed a Report on the troubles concluded that almost 80 per cent of the 1,437 killings recorded between 1982 and 1987 were perpetrated by members of 5 Brigade[24] with 'dissidents' being responsible for less than 5 per cent.[25] For the purposes of the present discussion what is alarming is that these events took place whilst the Constitution of Zimbabwe remained in operation, yet the constitutional safeguards were not only incapable of preventing the atrocities but could not even penetrate the Government's veil of secrecy that was drawn over the activities of the security forces. As the Report pertinently asks: 'Why was it that these human rights violations could occur on our very doorstep without most of us knowing about it? Why is it that it has taken so long for victims to be heard?'[26]

The examples of Uganda and Zimbabwe highlight the need for every state to develop effective constitutional and other safeguards to counter abuses by the military. These are considered in the following sections.

[23] See J. Alexander, 'Dissident Perspectives on Zimbabwe's Post-Independence War' (1998) 68(2) *Africa* 151, at p. 158. In 2001 so-called 'war veterans', who were fiercely loyal to the President, were enrolled into the Zimbabwean army, apparently in order to facilitate their campaign of intimidation and violence against the civilian population. This is another stark reminder of the danger of involving the military in internal affairs.

[24] The CCJP Report also places prime responsibility for the torture of civilians and the destruction of property on 5 Brigade, see pp. 171–87.

[25] See also Lawyers Committee for Human Rights report *Zimbabwe: Wages of War*, LCHR, New York, 1986. In 1987 a Unity Accord between the ruling party ZANU(PF) and PF-ZAPU led to the ending of the unrest.

[26] Ibid., at p. 213. The mechanisms for dealing with such questions are considered below.

Constitutions and coups

The 'Snow White' factor

The fate of a constitution following a coup is depressingly familiar. Military usurpers abrogate, suspend or significantly amend the document and then rule by decree. When eventually there is a handover of power, they oversee the replacement of the old constitution with a brand new document that provides them with immunity from prosecution and sufficient benefits for them and their families to enjoy a comfortable 'retirement'. Worse still, the military leader may also seek election as the new 'civilian' President, thus perpetuating the undue influence of the military in national life.[27]

To avoid such scenarios, constitutions must include deterrents to potential usurpers by demonstrating that *the risk of failure is high and the gains from 'success' low*. First and foremost the constitution must retain its validity no matter what the military usurper may decree. This is the 'Snow White' factor. In the fairy story, Snow White is happily living with her seven vertically challenged friends when the wicked queen poisons her. Apparently dead, a handsome prince later awakens her from sleep, the wicked queen is destroyed and Snow White and the prince live happily ever after. This powerful story of good and evil can be applied to attacks on constitutions and indeed a 'Snow White' clause is included in the Constitution of Uganda.

In Uganda, the Constitutional Commission recommended such a provision in order to avoid any repetition of the gross constitutional dislocation the country had experienced. Clearly acutely aware of the role the military had played in that dislocation, the Commission considered ways of providing:

> Strict juridical measures against those who disrespect or try illegally to overthrow the Constitution. This would apply even to those who carry out a successful revolution and subsequently suspend the Constitution.

As a result, article 3(3) provides:

> This Constitution shall not lose its force and effect even when its observance is interrupted by a government established by the force of arms; and in any case, as soon as the people recover their liberty, its observance shall be re-established . . .

[27] A useful constitutional provision might be to prohibit members of the security forces from standing for political office except after an appropriate period has elapsed following their resignation.

The article is important for several reasons. Firstly, it emphasises that a constitution is a 'tough' resilient trans-generational document that is capable of withstanding an attack by a military usurper. Secondly, it proclaims that the Constitution is the supreme law and that even though the military may regard themselves as 'guardians of the state', the reality is that they are always subordinate to the Constitution. Thirdly, it emphasises that the Constitution can only be replaced or amended by constitutional means. Fourthly, it ensures that the 'coup punishment' provisions (discussed below) come into operation by preventing usurpers providing themselves with immunity from prosecution. Finally, it encourages civil society to take steps to defend the Constitution.

Judicial response to coups

As few constitutions contain an express 'Snow White' clause, the issue of the legality of a usurper's regime and the subsequent fate of the constitution has fallen to the courts for determination. Given the enormous amount of literature on the subject, it is intended here merely to provide an overview of the various judicial approaches.

In some cases courts have held that a successful revolution creates a new legal order so that its government and laws are valid. Thus in *Uganda v Commissioner of Prisons ex parte Matovu*[28] the court, following the decision of the Pakistan Supreme Court in *S v Dosso*,[29] applied Kelsenite principles[30] in ruling that the 1962 Constitution had been abolished as a result of a victorious revolution which deprived it of its *de facto* and *de jure* validity. A somewhat similar issue was raised in Lesotho in 1986 when a military council set up after a coup d'etat annulled the general elections. In *Mokotso and Others v HM King Moshoeshoe II & Others*,[31] and again relying heavily on Kelsen, the court held that a successful coup d'etat was legitimate *ab initio*. Such reasoning was based on the recognition that (i) the government was firmly established without a rival government;

28 [1966] EA 514. 29 PLD 1958 SC 533.

30 The principles identified by the court were that (a) a coup d'etat is recognised in international law as a proper and effective legal means of changing government or constitutions in sovereign states; and (b) that the new order must be efficacious. The court accepted affidavit evidence of eight senior officials from the public service and the army that the new 1966 Constitution had been accepted without opposition and that the machinery of government was functioning smoothly.

31 [1989] LRC (Const) 24.

and (ii) its administration was effective, in that the majority of the people are behaving 'by and large' in conformity with it.[32] In these cases, the key factor for the courts was the *effectiveness* of the new regime.

The concept of revolutionary legality was much debated in the case of *Madzimbamuto v Lardner-Burke*[33] which revolved around the 1965 Unilateral Declaration of Independence by the civilian Rhodesian government and the validity of the 1965 Constitution of Rhodesia, which purported to replace the 1961 document. After considerable disagreement between the Rhodesian judges themselves, the Privy Council finally ruled that the judges functioned under the authority of the 1961 Constitution. The matter was well put by Fieldsend J. A. in the Rhodesian Appellate Court:

> A court created by a written constitution can have no independent existence apart from that constitution; it does not receive its powers from the common law and declare what its own powers are; it is not a creature of Frankenstein which once created can turn and destroy its maker. It is a matter of the supremacy of the constitution . . . It is my firm conviction that a court created in terms of a written constitution has no jurisdiction to recognise [another] constitution.[34]

The weight of judicial and academic opinion is now firmly against revolutionary legality.[35] The result is that in recent years courts throughout the Commonwealth have taken the view that a military coup is illegal from the outset. In other words, what the 'Snow White' provision expressly provides in article 3(3) of the Ugandan Constitution is *implied* elsewhere and accordingly courts must uphold the validity of the existing constitution.

[32] See the views of Cullinan C. J., p. 133. The Court of Appeal in Lesotho later approved the decision in *Makenete v Lekhanya* [1993] LRC 13. See also the decision of the Court of Appeal in the Seychelles in *Valabhati v Controller of Taxes* (1981) CLB 1249.

[33] 1966 RLR 756 (GD); 1968 (2) SA 284 (AD); [1968] 3 All ER 561 (PC).

[34] 1968 (2) SA, p. 430.

[35] See, in particular, the two most recent decisions: *Republic of Fiji Islands v Prasad* 2001 2 LRC 743 (text available on www.vanuatu.usp.ac.fj) and *Syed Zafar Sali Shah v General Pervaiz Musharraf, Chief Executive of Pakistan* PLD 2000 SC 869. For a useful overview of revolutionary legality see J. Smart, 'The Legality of Revolutionary Regimes in the New Commonwealth', unpublished paper, esp. p. 53–55. For a critical review of the Commonwealth jurisprudence see John Hatchard and Tunde Ogowewo, *Tackling the Unconstitutional Overthrow of Democracies: Emerging Trends in the Commonwealth*, Commonwealth Secretariat, London, 2003.

Whilst adopting the 'Snow White' approach by implication, the reality of military rule has led some judges to adopt the principle of necessity. Lord Pearce in *Madzimbamuto* formulated it in this way:

> I accept the existence of the principle that acts done by those actually in control without lawful validity may be recognised as valid or acted on by the court, with certain limitations namely: (a) so far as they are directed to and reasonably required for the ordinary orderly running of the State; and (b) so far as they are intended to and so do in fact directly help the usurpation and do not run contrary to the policy of the lawful sovereign.[36]

The principle is a potentially vital mechanism for resolving a constitutional crisis for, in effect, it allows the courts to uphold the constitution's validity whilst at the same time enabling them to 'negotiate' with the usurpers as to the scope of their powers and the process for their final withdrawal. This is well illustrated by the Pakistan Supreme Court in *Shah*[37] which strictly circumscribed the powers of the military usurpers, including protecting the 'basic features' of the 1973 Constitution, and declared that a general election must be held within three years: i.e. placing a strict time limit on the length of the military intervention. Of course, some might object to this approach on the basis that it both places the courts in the political arena (the 'political question') and gives some kind of judicial blessing to a blatant illegality. This overlooks the essence of 'necessity': i.e. the political reality that constitutional office-holders must take all necessary steps, which may well include interacting with the military, to end the intervention and return the country to constitutional rule.

[36] [1968] 3 All ER 561, at p. 579. In *Attorney-General of the Republic of Cyprus v Mustapha Ibrahim* (1964) CLR 195, Josephides J., after undertaking a comparative review of judicial approaches summarised the position as follows: 'I interpret our Constitution to include the doctrine of necessity, which is an implied exception to particular provisions of the constitution; and this in order to ensure the very existence of the state. The following prerequisites must be satisfied before the doctrine may become applicable: (a) an imperative and inevitable necessity or exceptional circumstances; (b) no other remedy to apply; (c) the measure must be proportionate to the necessity; (d) it must be of a temporary character, limited to the duration of the exceptional circumstances' (at pp. 264–5). As the *Ibrahim* case itself and the later decision of the Malawi Supreme Court of Appeal in *Attorney-General v Malawi Congress Party and Others* (unreported, MSCA Civil Appeal No. 22 of 1996) (*the Press Trust* case) both demonstrate, the doctrine is not restricted to matters involving the military, but extends to situations where constitutional government has become impossible.

[37] *Syed Zafar Sali Shah v General Pervaiz Musharraf, Chief Executive of Pakistan* PLD 2000 SC 869.

Making the military accountable

Finer has identified three massive advantages enjoyed by the military over civilian organisations.[38] Firstly, a marked superiority in organisation and resources, secondly, a monopoly of arms, and thirdly, a highly emotionalised symbolic status that supposedly invests the military with the status of 'guardianship' of the state (and thus superiority over the constitution). In view of this, he concludes that the wonder is not why the military rebels against their civilian masters but why they ever obey them.[39] Part of the answer lies in developing effective constitutional mechanisms designed to protect 'civil supremacy'.

Defining the constitutional role of the military

A constitution must establish a sound and acceptable civilian–military relationship that reflects the overriding principle of civilian supremacy and the need for the accountability of the military to democratic institutions. Defining the constitutional parameters for the military also helps to limit opportunities for it to legitimate any expansion of its functions into areas that are normally considered as civil matters. This recognises that the various component parts of the military undertake different constitutional functions. So far as the army/defence forces are concerned,[40] their prime role is to defend the constitution and the sovereignty and territorial integrity of the state against *external* aggression, leaving internal security matters to the police. It follows that the involvement of the defence forces in *internal* security matters is exceptional and requires very clear constitutional parameters and safeguards.

Some constitutions also envisage members of the military engaging in productive activities for 'the development of the country'.[41] This is seemingly based on the view that their hierarchical organisation is particularly suitable for implementing development programmes.[42] This is an

[38] Finer, *Man on Horseback*, does not overtly include the police force nor the intelligence service in his discussion. However, the para-military duties of the current police in many SEA countries and their historical military duties makes it important to include them in the discussion.

[39] Ibid., p. 5 [40] I.e. the army, air force and navy (if any).

[41] See, e.g. Constitutions of Uganda, art. 209(d); Zambia, art. 101(d).

[42] This echoes the argument of Nyerere that the military should serve as a socio-economic militia with national development as its central duty: see A. Mazrui, 'Anti-Militarism and Political Militancy in Tanzania', in J. Van Doorn (ed.), *Military Profession and Military Regimes*, Mouton, The Hague, 1969, p. 227. See further A. Kornberg et al., 'Representative

unattractive proposition. The military is organised in a way that makes its use in such ventures as farming very expensive and inefficient.[43] Besides, involving the armed forces in development projects potentially undermines their military readiness. Equally unattractive is the situation where youth are organised initially for development purposes and then militarised for political purposes.[44]

Providing for the political accountability of the military

The military must carry out its functions under the political direction of an elected government. This is symbolised by the subordination of military to civil power, with the Head of State or Government holding the constitutional position of Commander in Chief and empowered to appoint the chief of the defence force as well as the heads of the other services.[45]

As with other constitutional appointments, the need to ensure transparency and accountability is paramount. Perhaps more than in any other case, it is necessary to limit the opportunity for a president to appoint senior military officers, including intelligence chiefs, based purely on their personal loyalty to him/her. This approach is reflected, to some extent, in several constitutions. In Malawi the appointment and removal from office of senior Defence Force officers is done by the President on the recommendation of an Army Council, which includes the Minister responsible for Defence and the High Command of the Defence Forces. The exercise of such powers is then subject to scrutiny by the Defence

and Military Bodies: their Roles in the Survival of Political Systems of New States', in J. Smith and L. Musolf (eds.), *Legislatures in Development: Dynamics of Change in New and Old States*, Duke University Press, Durham NC, at p. 80.

43 Certainly in Zambia, the system of National Service was a disaster.

44 For example, in Malawi the Malawi Young Pioneers (MYP) were organised initially for development objectives and then militarised to act as violent 'enforcers' of President Banda's reign: see Harvey J. Sindima, *Malawi's First Republic*, University Press of America, Lanham, MD 2002, p. 152. It was left to the Malawi Army to launch Operation *Bwezani* (Operation Return All) with the goal of disarming the MYP and forcing the government to formally disband it. See Kings M. Phiri, 'A Case of Revolutionary Change in Contemporary Malawi: the Malawi Army and the Disarming of the Malawi Young Pioneers' (2000) 1(1) *Journal of Peace, Conflict and Military Studies* 1.

45 See, for example, Constitutions of Zambia (art. 33(1)), Namibia (art. 118(2)), Malawi (art. 160(1)) and South Africa (s.202(1)). The need for senior military personnel to eschew political activity, including membership of a political party, is also fundamental to good governance. See further the discussion in chapter 7.

and Security Committee of the National Assembly (DSC).[46] In the case of the Inspector-General of Police, whilst appointed by the President, the Public Appointments Committee enjoys important oversight functions.[47] Elsewhere, appointments are made on recommendation of an ostensibly independent Security Commission[48] or the like.[49]

There is also a need to distinguish between political control and operational control. Political control must always remain the preserve of the civilian authorities. This is made clear in South Africa where command of the Defence Force must be exercised in accordance 'with the directions of the Cabinet minister responsible for defence, under the authority of the President'. In addition, there must be a civilian secretariat for defence.[50] Civilian oversight of the military also carries with it political responsibility for any wrongdoing. Hence it is not open to the President, as Commander in Chief, nor the relevant Minister, to feign ignorance of human rights violations by members of the military nor to claim that these were the independent actions of their subordinates.

Accountability to the legislature

In a functioning multi-party democracy, the legislature should play a significant oversight role. Whilst it should not normally intervene in operational matters *per se*, there is a fine line between matters of policy and matters of operational practice. For example, defence procurement is sometimes controversial since choice of weaponry or other equipment is

[46] See Constitution of Malawi arts. 161/2. The DSC is discussed later in this chapter. Of course this begs the question as to the meaning of 'scrutiny'. In its normal sense, the word means no more than a power to critically examine appointments. Even here, a public hearing by the DSC on the appointment of senior defence force officers could, at the very least, provide a useful forum for raising public and media interest in the matter.

[47] See Constitution of Malawi art. 154(2).

[48] For example, article 114 of the Namibian Constitution provides for a Security Commission. This comprises the Chairperson of the Public Service Commission, the Chief of the Defence Force, the Inspector-General of Police, the Commissioner of Prisons and two members of the National Assembly appointed by the President on the recommendation of the National Assembly and is tasked with recommending to the President the appointment of the Chief of the Defence Force and the Inspector-General of Police.

[49] Cf. Lesotho where responsibility for appointing the Commander of the Defence Force lies with the Defence Commission of which the Prime Minister is the chairperson (Constitution of Lesotho, s.146(3)). The Defence Commission is responsible for the appointment, discipline and removal of members of the Defence Force, Police Force and Prison Service.

[50] Constitution of South Africa ss.202(2) and 204.

often sensitive from a political or policy standpoint.[51] Of course, accusations of human rights abuses against members of the military during 'operations' are always a matter for the legislature.

Oversight by the legislature takes a number of forms such as through the exercise of budgetary control, the work of a specialist all-party parliamentary committee on security and parliamentary questions to ministers.[52] These should focus on issues of operational and financial accountability.

Operational accountability

Whilst witholding detailed information on military operations is normally justified on grounds of national security, this is certainly not the case with regard to the deployment of the military and the reasons for doing so. However, in practice, obtaining such information continues to prove a major problem with some governments reluctant even to inform parliament of the situation, except perhaps as an afterthought. For example, in 1998 in both Uganda and Zimbabwe there were significant delays in ministers reporting to the respective legislatures on the involvement of their troops in the Democratic Republic of Congo, and then in only the barest detail.[53]

This riding roughshod over parliament is neither acceptable nor, in some cases, constitutional.[54] The South African approach to the issue is instructive. Here national security is subject to the authority of Parliament,[55] and in certain specific circumstances,[56] the President must report to Parliament 'promptly and in appropriate detail' the reasons for deployment of the defence forces, the place of deployment, the number

[51] See generally K. Kemp and C. Hudlin, 'Civil Supremacy over the Military: its Nature and Limits' (1992) *Armed Forces and Society* 7.

[52] See chapter 7 for a full discussion.

[53] For example, in his 1998 address to Parliament, President Museveni stated: 'Our involvement in Congo, indirectly last year and a bit more directly this year, is mainly because of the threats to our security . . .', Address to Parliament, 15 September 1998 (mimeo). In the case of Zimbabwe, the Minister of Defence informed Parliament in the broadest possible terms of the deployment of troops in the Congo one month after the event, a fact that a handful of members severely criticised: see *Parliamentary Debates*, 16 September 1998, especially columns 329–45.

[54] Section 210 of the Constitution of Uganda provides: 'Parliament shall make laws regulating the Uganda Peoples' Defence Forces, and in particular providing for . . . (d) the deployment of troops outside Uganda'.

[55] Constitution of South Africa, s.198(d).

[56] The specific circumstances when the defence forces may be deployed are: (a) in cooperation with the police service; (b) in defence of the Republic; or (c) in fulfilment of an international obligation (s.201(2) Constitution of South Africa).

of troops involved, and the expected duration of their deployment.[57] It is then beholden on Parliament, including the relevant parliamentary committee, to maintain a close watch on the situation.[58]

Financial accountability

Military expenditure places an enormous financial strain on national resources and economic development because sophisticated equipment and weaponry is expensive and demands for its replacement and/or upgrading constant. Sometimes it seems as if such expenditure is used by governments to 'keep the military happy' (and thus, hopefully, out of politics or at least supportive of the government). Financial accountability for military expenditure is therefore essential, as is a recognition that in the absence of an emergency situation, the military is subject to the same budgetary constraints as other government departments.

In theory, legislatures must approve all military expenditure, including the cost of research, development and procurement of new weapons or equipment.[59] Further, an increasingly common constitutional provision requires parliamentary approval of any international arms agreements entered into by the government.[60] Yet 'national security' concerns are often used as a pretext for preventing proper parliamentary oversight. Here the Westminster tradition has assisted governments in that the authorisation of expenditure is carried out with a broad brush, which gives parliament little opportunity for effective scrutiny. For instance, expenditure on the intelligence services and 'special projects' may be concealed within the presidential vote which is traditionally never debated in the legislature.[61]

[57] Constitution of South Africa, s.201(3).

[58] To ensure ongoing scrutiny of the situation, it is vital to ensure the relevant parliamentary committee remains 'in post' throughout the period of the military operations, notwithstanding that parliament stands adjourned. See the discussion on the DSC in Malawi, p. 256.

[59] See J. A. G. Griffith, M. Ryle and M. A. J. Wheeler-Booth, *Parliament: Functions, Practice and Procedures*, Sweet and Maxwell London, 1989, p. 9.

[60] This is part of a general requirement for parliamentary approval of any international treaty, convention or agreement that imposes fiscal obligations upon it. See, for instance, Constitution of Zimbabwe s.111B and Constitution of South Africa s.231(2).

[61] See chapter 7 for further discussion on this issue. Griffith et al. (*Parliament* at 9) note that for several years no mention was made to Parliament of the original decision to develop a British atomic bomb, the relevant expenditure being buried under the broad headings of weapons research and development.

The need for a meaningful oversight process has led to the establishment of specialist parliamentary committees and other committees on defence matters made up of parliamentarians with a special interest in and/or expertise on such matters. The power to order the relevant Minister and his/her staff to appear before the committee to face the kind of detailed questioning on defence matters that is often not possible in the parliamentary chamber represents a potentially powerful accountability mechanism. A useful example is the Defence and Security Committee (DSC) of the National Assembly of Malawi.[62] This has several interesting characteristics. Firstly, it is an all-party body.[63] Secondly, it may meet at any time, even when parliament is adjourned or stands dissolved. Thirdly, the DSC may scrutinise both the appointment and removal of members of the Defence Forces and the operational use of those Forces.

The military and the courts

The trial of civilians in military courts should be prohibited at any time. The consequences of not doing so are starkly illustrated by the situation in Uganda when the civilian courts came to a virtual standstill in 1972 following the abduction and murder of the Chief Justice, Benedicto Kiwanuka, by army personnel and the arrest of many magistrates.[64] The army then took over the work of the courts. Cases of alleged 'economic crimes' as well as treason were dealt with by military tribunals staffed by military officers who had neither legal training nor experience in handling such cases and whose loyalty lay with the military government.[65] As the Oder Commission noted, persons convicted by these tribunals were denied a fair trial and many were wrongly convicted and sentenced to long terms of imprisonment or even death.[66]

[62] Established by art. 162 Constitution of Malawi.

[63] Given the fact that Malawi has three well supported political parties in Parliament, the committee has a potentially particularly useful function to play.

[64] *The Pearl of Blood: Report of the Uganda Commission of Inquiry into the Violation of Human Rights* (The Oder Commission Report) Kampala, 1994, pp. 40–1.

[65] Established by the Trial by Military Tribunals Decree No 12 of 1973. The Oder Commission chronicles some cases where even the most basic procedural requirements were overlooked by the tribunal.

[66] Similarly the tragic case in Nigeria of Ken Saro-Wiwa who, along with eight others, was tried by civil disturbance tribunals in Nigeria established under the Civil Disturbances (Special Tribunal) Decree. The only appeal was to the Special Appeal Tribunal controlled by the military: see the discussion of the case in (1997) 42 JAL 215, 217. Emergency powers provisions are sometimes used to extend the jurisdiction of military courts to the civilian

It follows that the use of military courts must be strictly limited to trying military personnel accused of military offences. Even here, they must be subject to the constitution and a final appeal available to a court comprising civilian judges.[67]

The military and national institutions

As noted in chapter 10, national institutions, i.e. offices of the ombudsman and/or human rights commissions, are firmly established in many ESA states. There are several reasons why these hold out the promise of an effective investigative and oversight role over the activities of the military. Firstly, their wide-ranging investigative powers, including the right to inspect documents and to question officials, are often more appropriate for the handling of complaints involving state security than are those of the courts.[68] Secondly, practice has shown that national institutions are even-handed in their consideration of cases and determine each complaint objectively. Thus the military need have no fear of a vendetta against it. Indeed the patient development of a sound working relationship with military officials enhances the potential for the carrying out of meaningful investigations. Thirdly, national institutions can reinforce public confidence that an impartial and independent examination of complaints concerning the military will be undertaken. Finally, and perhaps most important of all, the power to investigate also sends an important message to members of the military that they are never above the law and remain accountable for their actions. For example, investigating allegations of the torture of detainees by members of the security services must always be within the jurisdiction of a national institution. It is precisely in such dark corners of government activity that they must operate,

population but this is only if military operations make it impossible for the courts to function in a particular area: see *Duncan v Kahanamoku* 327 US 304.

[67] Thus in the Canadian case of *R v Genereux* [1992] 1 SCR 259, the Supreme Court of Canada held that courts martial were not a 'fair and independent tribunal' as required by the Canadian Charter of Rights and Freedoms because military judges were appointed by superior officers and were therefore not independent. The point is important as, for example, the National Resistance Army Statute 1992 in Uganda provides for a wide range of military offences, several carrying the death penalty. Cases are heard before a Unit Disciplinary Committee comprising five persons none of whom need have any legal qualification whilst membership of the Courts Martial Appeal Court does not specifically provide for the appointment of civilian judges.

[68] See L. Gering, 'Legal Institutions and Human Needs' (1974) 37 *Tydsk Rif Vir Hededaagse Romeins-Hollandse Reg* 274, at pp. 287–9.

for if they cannot then there is little chance of any real accountability at all.

The effectiveness of this safeguard depends both upon maintaining their independence and the extent to which government is prepared to permit investigations into the activities of the military. As regards the latter, it is disappointing that only a bare majority of national institutions in the ESA states are permitted to investigate complaints by members of the public against the security forces.[69] The main justification for this restriction is seemingly that such an investigation 'might have the result of inhibiting the activities [of the security forces], much to the detriment of the State'.[70] Such a view is unconvincing and leaves a government open to charges that it is prepared to countenance potentially unlawful behaviour by members of the military. It is also regrettable because members of the military are frequently responsible for some of the worst human rights violations.[71]

Perhaps the Constitutional Commission in Ghana expressed the point best when it noted that the inclusion of the security forces in the jurisdiction of the Office of the Ombudsman was 'because the Constitution . . . contemplates a State in which the democratic rights of every citizen are legally guaranteed and protected.'[72] Without such a body, many are not able to exercise those rights.

Supporting the Constitution: the role of civil society

Even when the allegations by a military usurper of corruption, mismanagement and oppression on the part of the former civilian regime have some validity, the fact is that the military lacks the right to govern.

[69] On the other hand, a national institution can normally investigate complaints from members of the security forces concerning their terms and conditions of service.

[70] See the statement of the Zimbabwean Minister of Justice in *Parliamentary Debates*, 18 June 1982, col.113. Interestingly, the objection was later withdrawn and the Zimbabwean Ombudsman now has the power to investigate complaints against the security forces. Regrettably, there is little evidence of the exercise of such power, despite the persistent allegations of ongoing human rights abuses by members of the security forces against civilians.

[71] The importance of such a jurisdiction is illustrated by the fact the in Zambia, for example, complaints against the security forces (including the police) have sometimes accounted for over 25 per cent of all complaints: see J. Hatchard, *National Human Rights Institutions in the Commonwealth*, Commonwealth Secretariat, London, 1992, p. 81.

[72] Proposal of the Constitutional Commission for a Constitution for Ghana to the Members of the Constituent Assembly, 1968, no. 495.

Certainly in some cases the intervention of the military has seemingly received enthusiastic public support, at least at the outset, although this is arguably more often the result of just plain fear on the part of civilians to do otherwise. Finer has argued that none of the opportunities for military intervention arise at random and that the 'greater the public attachment to civil institutions' the less opportunity and the less likelihood of success will the military enjoy.[73] It is here that the development and impact of an ethos of constitutionalism amongst the people and in civil society, as well as in the military, must make itself felt.

Civil society and the duty to resist

Perhaps the greatest bulwark against military rule is the determination on the part of all sections of civil society to make their Constitution 'work' and to defend it against those wishing to undermine it. This includes accepting that protecting the Constitution is the responsibility of everyone. This was emphasised by the Oder Commission which noted that 'officers and agents of the state regularly abused the rights of those who fell into their hands and the victims and the public often aided the process by being passive'. It added that the 'assumptions that those who do not oppose are safe and that only those who had "offended" the regime in power or belonged to the "wrong" ethnic groups were wanted by the regime, proved disastrous . . .'[74]

To emphasise the point, article 3(4) of the Ugandan Constitution places a legal right and duty on Ugandan citizens to defend their Constitution by resisting the overthrow of the established constitutional order and 'doing all in their power to restore the Constitution'. Any person or group of persons who resists the suspension, overthrow, abrogation or amendment of the Constitution in such circumstances is declared to have committed 'no offence'. Further, 'upon the restoration of the Constitution' those punished for such action are entitled to be absolved from all 'liabilities arising out of the punishment'.[75]

Resistance can take many forms. Armed resistance is certainly one course of action contemplated by the article. Nwabueze argues that to make such resistance effective requires constitutional measures directed

[73] *Man on Horseback*, p. 75. [74] P. 10.
[75] This follows closely the wording of article 3(4)–3(6) of the Constitution of Ghana 1992 although the Ghanaian provisions are rather more generous in that those resisting are entitled to receive 'adequate compensation' as determined by the Supreme Court (art.3(7)).

at the source of the military's power, i.e. their monopoly of arms and their training in their use. He asserts that the citizenry:

> should no longer continue to make itself hostage to the political ambitions of members of the armed forces by denying itself the ability to defend its constituent power against armed usurpation[76]

and suggests a constitutional right for every person to bear arms together with a scheme of compulsory military training for all school-leavers and university graduates. The practicality of such a move is dubious. For one thing, an armed citizenry is unlikely to be a match for the military and, in any event, making arms more readily available would in all probability simply create intolerable law-and-order problems in societies already experiencing high levels of violent crime.

In practice, the real value of the provision is that it places a right and a duty on those in civil society to resist usurpers in whatever manner is appropriate: for example, through civil disobedience or non-co-operation. Such action denies the military usurpers any semblance of the popular support that has, in many cases, provided a justification for continued military rule.

Public servants have a particular responsibility, for every military regime depends upon its civilian collaborators to help secure its position. Without them, its ability to hold on to power is greatly diminished, for, whilst the military may possess the expertise to take over government, the running of the country is another matter entirely. As Janowitz notes, 'it is difficult, if not impossible, for the military to manage the politics of a nation in the process of rapid economic development'.[77] Certainly in Nigeria it appears that at times the senior members of Public Service not only fully co-operated with the military, but were also often the dominant element in policy-making. As a result, the public servants gained considerable power as the military took over key areas of the economy.[78]

The challenge is to develop and maintain a well-trained, independent, loyal and professional public service that is overseen by an independent

[76] *Military Rule*, at p. 334.

[77] M. Janowitz, *The Military in the Political Development of New Nations: an Essay in Comparative Analysis*, University of Chicago Press, Chicago, 1964, pp. 103–4. The Amin regime in Uganda co-opted a large number of civilians (fifteen out of a Cabinet of eighteen) to join the military in governing the country: see A. G. Gingyera-Pinycwa, 'The Militarisation of Politics in an African State: the Case of Uganda', in W. O. Oyugi (ed.), *Politics and Administration in East Africa*, East African Educational Publishers, Nairobi 1993, p. 215.

[78] Nwabueze, *Military Rule*, at p. 136.

Public Service Commission, and which can serve as a hedge in times of conflict amongst politicians. Easier said than done certainly; but a goal that must be worked towards.

Providing human rights training for all members of the security forces

The Oder Commission found that a key factor in the perpetuation of the cycle of violence in Uganda was the ignorance of human rights by the army, law enforcement officers and their agents. This was highlighted by the admission in 1988 before the Uganda Human Rights Commission, by Mustafa Adrisi, the Ugandan Vice-President that during the period of military rule (1970–9) he had not known about the existence of the Constitution of Uganda.

Given such an experience, it is unfortunate that education on the Constitution and human rights still plays relatively little part in the training programmes for members of the military in the ESA states. Only the South African and Ugandan constitutions make such training a specific constitutional requirement.[79] Since 1995–2005 is the United Nations Decade of Human Rights Education, it is appropriate that real efforts are made to provide training in human rights and constitutionalism to all members of the security forces. Here human rights commissions, working with and through civil society groups and Commonwealth organisations, such as the Commonwealth Legal Education Association, can play a vital part in developing and running such programmes with a view to making them an integral part of all training programmes for the military.

Dealing with the past

How does a country come to terms with a past in which the military (or authoritarian government[80]) has perpetrated or been involved in serious human rights violations? For many, the matter is not necessarily one of seeking to punish those responsible through the judicial process. Rather it

[79] Constitution of Uganda arts. 221 and 4(b). Section 199(5) of the South African Constitution provides: 'The security services must act and teach and require their members to act in accordance with the Constitution and the law . . .'

[80] Similar issues arise when a country is seeking to come to terms with a past in which an authoritarian government has perpetrated serious human rights abuses. See, for example the work of the Truth and Reconciliation Commission in South Africa discussed below and the compensation tribunal established in Malawi in 1994 to hear and compensate those whose rights were violated by the Banda regime.

is about establishing the 'truth' for it is said that only this can bring about 'the healing of a traumatised, divided, wounded, polarised people'[81] and help them come to terms with an 'atrocious history'.[82] The mechanisms adopted to deal with the past by several ESA states well illustrate the choices to be made.

Drawing a line through the past

In his book *Serving Secretly*, Ken Flower, the former head of Rhodesian intelligence, describes how, at independence in 1980, Prime Minister Robert Mugabe invited him to remain as head of Zimbabwe's internal security body, the Central Intelligence Organisation, with these words:

> . . . we were trying to kill each other; that's what the war was about. What I am concerned with now is that my public statements should be believed when I say that I have *drawn a line through the past*.[83]

Drawing a line through the past and granting automatic amnesty to all those involved in human rights violations is mainly justified on grounds of national reconciliation. It is said that states emerging from conflict are fragile and may be unable to withstand the prosecution of those allegedly involved in the abuses.[84]

In fact, by itself this approach is likely to prove ineffective and even represents a hindrance to such reconciliation, as evidenced in the case of Zimbabwe itself. Here the amnesty policy goes back to 1975 when the then Rhodesian security forces took increasingly repressive measures against the black civilian population. In 1975, the Catholic Commission for Justice and Peace published a booklet entitled *The Man in the Middle* which alleged that members of the security forces had tortured innocent civilians and destroyed property with the aim of extracting information about the movement of guerrillas, and of intimidating the African

[81] The words of Archbishop Desmond Tutu concerning the work of the Truth and Reconciliation Commission in South Africa. See also M. Ensalaco, 'Truth Commissions for Chile and El Salvador: a Report and Assessment' (1994) 16 *Human Rights Quarterly* 656.

[82] A. B. de Brito, 'Truth and Justice in the Consolidation of Democracy in Chile and Uruguay' 46 *Parliamentary Affairs* 579, at p. 580.

[83] K. Flower, *Serving Secretly*, Murray, London, 1987, p. 3 (our emphasis).

[84] It may be that prosecutions might also seriously affect the position of the judiciary. For instance, in the case of South Africa it was argued that had prosecutions proceeded against those accused of involvement in the apartheid regime, the overwhelmingly white judiciary would have been engulfed in controversy, especially if their decisions did not meet with general public agreement.

populace into co-operating with the security forces. The government refuted these allegations although it rejected a call for an independent inquiry on the ground that any aggrieved person had a perfectly adequate remedy through the ordinary courts. Categorical assurances were given that the courts would remain open for individuals to air their grievances. Accordingly, a number of civil claims were brought against the state alleging human rights violations by members of the security forces.

In response, the Indemnity and Compensation Act 1975 was passed, ostensibly because the government took the view that the claims were being brought for purely political reasons. The Act banned the bringing of civil or criminal proceedings against the state in any court in respect of acts done in good faith while acting for the purpose of, or in connection with, the suppression of terrorism or the maintenance of public order. This enabled the Rhodesian security forces to carry out human rights violations including large numbers of extra-judicial executions of prisoners and civilians, not only in clear violation of international human rights standards but also of the laws of war. The perpetrators remained protected from prosecution by the 1975 Act and, as part of the 1979 Lancaster House settlement, an amnesty was declared for all acts carried out in the course of the war with the War Victims Compensation Act providing for the payment of compensation to victims.

The decision by Mugabe at independence in 1980 to draw a line through the past was essentially politically motivated since national reconciliation was viewed as the paramount consideration.[85] This meant that human rights violators were not only not brought to justice but that several were retained within the security apparatus itself. From shortly after independence serious security problems were again experienced in certain parts of the country, with the Zimbabwean Government claiming that these were the result of 'dissident' activity. As noted earlier, it is now well documented that members of the military perpetrated the majority of the resultant widespread human rights abuses. With the repeal of the Indemnity and Compensation Act 1975,[86] emergency regulations based on the

[85] Thus Mugabe also reportedly said to Flower: 'From now on we must trust each other if we are to work together for the benefit of the majority. I want people to believe in my policy of reconciliation and to respond accordingly' (Flower, *Serving Secretly*, p. 3).

[86] It had been successfully invoked by a senior government minister, Edgar Tekere, when facing a charge of murdering a white farmer. As a result of public concern, the government was forced to repeal the statute: see J. Hatchard, *Individual Freedoms and State Security in the African Context: the Case of Zimbabwe*, Baobab Books, Harare, 1993, p. 131.

1975 Act were made under the Emergency Powers Act.[87] These operated both retrospectively and prospectively, thus effectively placing the security forces above the law.[88] In 1987 a Unity Accord between the two major political parties ended the unrest and another amnesty followed in 1988 under which every member or former member of the security forces was granted a free pardon in respect of any offence committed during 'anti-dissident' operations. Unlike the 1980 amnesty, there was no provision for compensation for the victims of such operations. The government also refused to publish two judicial reports on the events in Matabeleland and it was left to two local NGOs to reveal the extent of abuses against civilians.[89] Even this provoked a hostile government response.[90]

The use of the presidential pardon

The presidential power to pardon members of the military for human rights violations is another mechanism for drawing a line through the past. The power itself is a worldwide phenomenon[91] and exists because:

> it has always been thought essential . . . to vest in some authority other than the courts the power to ameliorate or avoid particular criminal judgments.[92]

Yet the granting of a pardon strikes at the heart of the whole criminal justice process in that its effect is to expunge the conviction from the record.[93] This means that the exercise of the power must be accompanied

[87] Emergency Powers (Security Forces Indemnity) Regulations 1982 SI 487/82.

[88] The Supreme Court later ruled that the regulations breached the constitution. See *Granger v Minister of State Security* 1984 (2) ZLR 92. Government dominance of the legislature ensured that there was there was no parliamentary debate on the regulations.

[89] The matter was pursued by two local NGOs, the Catholic Commission for Justice and Peace and the Legal Resources Foundation. In 1997 they submitted their joint CCJP report to the government but refrained from publishing it instead urging government to respond to the report by offering compensation to the victims of the human rights violations cited therein. With no response forthcoming, the report was then published. This accused the government and the security forces of widespread human rights violations in Matabeleland. For details, see the discussion above, p. 245.

[90] In a television interview in December 1997, President Mugabe bitterly criticised the CCJP and its report stating that although the Rhodesian forces had committed 'worse atrocities' the Commission had not condemned those acts. He had seemingly conveniently overlooked the *Man in the Middle* publication (discussed above).

[91] For a useful survey see L. Sebba, 'The Pardoning Power – a World Survey', 68 *Journal of Criminal Law and Criminology* 83 and K. D. Moore, *Pardons*, Oxford: Oxford University Press, 1989.

[92] Taft C. J. in *Ex parte Grossman* 267 US 87

[93] See C. H. Rolph, *The Queen's Pardon*, Oxford University Press, Oxford, 1967, at p. 35.

by adequate checks otherwise it is liable to be used for improper political purposes.

The problems surrounding the exercise of the presidential pardon is again well illustrated by the experience of Zimbabwe. Section 31I of the Constitution of Zimbabwe empowers the President to grant a pardon to any person concerned in or convicted of a criminal offence against any law. In 1993 concerns over the exercise of such powers were raised in the cases of Kizito Chivamba, a member of the Central Intelligence Organisation (CIO) and Elias Kanengoni, an official of the ruling party, ZANU(PF). Both were convicted in the High Court of attempted murder and sentenced to seven years imprisonment. Their victim was a leading opposition candidate whom they had shot and seriously wounded whilst he was campaigning for the 1990 general election. Following the dismissal of their appeals by the Supreme Court, the two men were granted a presidential pardon[94] and released.[95] The decision gave rise to considerable criticism from legal and human rights bodies, especially as this was not the first time that persons committing violence against members of other political parties had been granted a pardon.[96]

There are three pre-conditions for the exercise of the power. Firstly, because of the danger it poses to the operation and credibility of the criminal justice system, the exercise of a pardon must be undertaken in consultation with others who are in a position to give objective advice.[97] Secondly, a pardon is justified only as a means of preventing injustice, so it is possible to specify in advance the type of reasons for clemency.[98] These should be on legal grounds or where there is a later ascertainment

[94] There was considerable doubt over whether the men were actually pardoned or had had their sentences remitted. This merely emphasised the lack of transparency over the issue.

[95] Indeed it appears that Chivamba went straight back to work.

[96] See L. Mhlaba, 'The Presidential Pardoning of Dr Shava' (1989) 1(6) *Legal Forum* 25. It is not just members of the military who can benefit from presidential favours. Thus in 1988 Sheila Hove, the wife of the influential Zimbabwean Minister of Mines avoided a three-month prison term thanks to a presidential pardon. The grounds for the action were given as ill-health and the fact that there was no one to look after her children. Prison overcrowding might be eliminated if every convicted person could rely on this excuse to escape incarceration.

[97] As noted in chapter 5, in Zimbabwe the President must act on the advice of the Cabinet, s.31H(5) Constitution of Zimbabwe. However, it is interesting to note that with regard to the Chivamba case the Minister of Justice reportedly said that the President 'has absolute power to pardon whoever he wishes' which is perhaps an insight into the decision-making process within the administration: see (1994) 6(1) *Legal Forum* 4.

[98] J. Bentham, *Works XI*, London, 1962, 37.

of innocence or a real doubt as to guilt,[99] or, as Taft C.J. neatly puts it

> . . . relief from undue harshness or evident mistake in the operation or enforcement of the criminal law. The administration of justice by the courts is not always wise or certainly considerate of circumstances which may properly mitigate guilt.[100]

This view differs significantly from that taken in Zimbabwe where the presidential decision to pardon Chivamba and Kanengoni was based on so-called 'social' grounds (see below). This is defensible only if, as Bentham has pointed out, a pardon is the exercise of 'free grace' and can thus be granted on any ground the executive may regard as sufficient. Given the potential for abuse, such a view is untenable.

Thirdly, in order to assuage public disquiet and speculation over its use, there should be a duty to disclose the reasons for the granting of the pardon. In the Chivamba case, for example, the Minister of Justice stated that the decision was taken on 'social grounds'. There was no elaboration on the meaning of this term and one is left with the uneasy suspicion that the pardon was granted simply because the perpetrators were government supporters whilst the victim was a political opponent.

Although the constitutions of the ESA states all provide the head of state with a power of pardon, they adopt a variety of safeguards on its exercise. In Malawi the power is exercisable in consultation with the Advisory Committee on the Granting of Pardon.[101] A similar procedure is adopted in Zambia and Lesotho.[102] In South Africa the President is required to consult the Executive Deputy President(s). The composition of such a review body is crucial in ensuring an objective assessment of individual cases and, in this respect, the approach in Lesotho merits particular attention. Here the three members of the Pardons Committee on the Prerogative of Mercy are appointed 'by the King acting in accordance with the advice of the Judicial Service Commission from among persons who are not public officers or members of the [legislature]'.[103] The broad-based membership of the JSC means that it has the capacity to be relatively

[99] A formulation based on a UK Home Office memorandum number 33391 of 1874.
[100] *Ex parte Grossman*, at p. 92.
[101] Art. 89(2). The composition and formation will be determined by a future statute.
[102] Constitutions of Zambia arts. 59 and 60 and Lesotho ss.101–102.
[103] S.102(1).

objective.[104] An alternative approach in Namibia also seeks to provide for an independent assessment of the case. Here the exercise of the presidential power or pardon can be reviewed, reversed and corrected following a resolution passed by a two-thirds majority of all the members of the legislature.[105]

The recognition in at least some states that the granting of a pardon must be based on objective advice to the head of state goes a long way towards avoiding the controversy engendered by the Chivamba case. Given the widespread executive domination of legislatures it is suggested that the approach in Lesotho is preferable. Even so, it is regrettable that none of the constitutions provide for either of the two other points discussed above.

Overall, the effect of amnesty laws and the improper use of the power of pardon is to send a clear message that members of the security forces are above the law and that the state is prepared to cover up its own crimes by granting itself immunity. This was recognised by the 1990 Report of the UN Working Group on Enforced or Involuntary Disappearances that noted:

> Perhaps the single most important factor contributing to the phenomenon of disappearances may be that of impunity. The Working Group's experiences over the past ten years has confirmed the age-old adage that impunity breeds contempt of the law. Perpetrators of human rights violations will become more brazen when they are not held to account before a court of law.[106]

As Carver points out, the amnesty for the Rhodesian human rights violators did not 'cause' the continuation of abuses in Zimbabwe but, 'it did provide the environment, and the means, for new human rights violations . . . for it allowed a culture of abuse and impunity to permeate the security structures'.[107] It means that seeking to draw a line through

[104] Section 132 of the Constitution provides that the Commission will consist of the Chief Justice, Attorney-General, Chairman of the Public Service Commission, and a member from amongst persons who hold or have held high judicial office.

[105] Art. 32(9). This has the advantage of requiring an explanation to be given to Parliament although the ever-present problem of government-dominated legislatures makes this safeguard less attractive than it might otherwise seem.

[106] Para 344.

[107] R. Carver, 'Called to Account: How African Governments Investigate Human Rights Violations' (1990) 89 *African Affairs* 391.

the past, without more, is arguably 'immoral and counterproductive'[108] and is an affront to those who suffered at the hands of the military. As Oloka-Onyango comments on the granting of immunity by the Ugandan government to prominent members of previous regimes:

> Few of the victims of any of the past violations are ever treated with the same courtesy, nor have they been compensated for the losses (physical and otherwise) that they suffered.[109]

Bringing usurpers to trial

A very different approach is to ensure military usurpers face the prospect of both being confronted with their actions before a criminal court and losing any financial gains made from their actions.

On the first issue, article 3(2) Constitution of Uganda provides:

> Any person who singly or in concert with others by any violent or other unlawful means, suspends, overthrows or abrogates this Constitution or any part of it, or attempts to do any such act commits the offence of treason and shall be punished according to the law.

Putting military usurpers on trial sends out an important message that the supremacy of the Constitution is being maintained and reinforces the illegitimacy of any military inspired 'constitution' or decree aimed at providing them with an all-embracing immunity clause. Even in the absence of a specific constitutional provision, as discussed earlier, there is a strong argument that a constitution survives a military coup, that what is made explicit in the Ugandan Constitution is implicit elsewhere and that the courts must make this clear. Thus such a provision sends a message to any future usurpers that, even if they succeed in taking power in a coup, at some future time they will be brought to justice.[110] Punishment is only deferred, not avoided.[111]

[108] J. Kollapen, 'Accountability: the Debate in South Africa' (1993) 37 *Journal of African Law* 1, at p. 6.

[109] J. Oloka-Onyango, 'Uganda' in P Baehr et al. (eds.), *Human Rights in Developing Countries Yearbook 1996*, Kluwer, The Hague, 1996, p. 380.

[110] As Yaqub Ali J. put it in *Jilani v Government of the Punjab* PLD SC 1972, 139: 'As soon as the first opportunity arises, when the coercive apparatus falls from the hands of the usurper, he should be tried for high treason and suitably punished. This alone will serve as a deterrent to would be adventurers' (p. 243).

[111] See D. F. Orentlicher, 'Settling Accounts: the Duty to Prosecute Human Rights Violations of a Previous Regime', in F. Newman and D. Weissbrodt (eds.), *International Human Rights: Law, Policy and Process*, Little, Brown, Boston, MA, 1996, p. 135.

There are several potentially difficult issues here, not least being the fact that any possibility of their being tried for treason and other offences may well disincline the military to relinquish power, at least peacefully. A further problem, highlighted by the experience of countries in Latin America, is that membership of the military is normally continuous, despite changes in the civilian government. Thus criminal trials may be seen as a threat to the military, especially as they may implicate serving officers. As a result, Argentina, for example, had only modest success in bringing those responsible for the 'dirty war' of 1976–83 to justice and the government was eventually forced to enact legislation ending large-scale prosecutions to avoid further unrest in the army.[112] To date, the trials of military personnel have so far proved ineffective.[113]

However, the 'deterrent' approach is increasingly receiving support from the international community. In particular the *Pinochet* ruling[114] demonstrates that there are fewer and fewer hiding-places for military usurpers, as many states now incorporate their international human rights obligations into domestic law.[115] Such an approach inevitably encounters practical difficulties, including the identifying and tracing of alleged perpetrators, obtaining their extradition and adducing credible and admissible evidence against them. However, improved international co-operation in extradition matters and the obtaining of evidence for trial purposes may persuade states of the desirability and practicability of pursuing usurpers through the courts.

The second issue concerns removing the financial benefits from staging a coup. To complement the 'no hiding-place' approach, states must adopt a 'no financial gain' approach. This requires them to put in place

112 See generally W. C. Banks and A. D. Carrio, 'Presidential Systems in Stress: Emergency Powers in Argentina and the US' (1993) 15 *Michigan Journal of International Law* 1 and P. K. Speck, 'The Trial of the Argentine Junta: Responsibilities and Realities' (1987) 18 *University of Miami Inter-American Law Review* 491.

113 In Uganda, eighteen security officers named in a 1974 report of commission of inquiry into human rights violations were tried by a military tribunal but all were acquitted. Who tries the cases is also problematic for the judges may themselves be identified with the previous military regime. A forthright judicial stand against legal recognition of coups would make this less of a concern.

114 *R v Bow Street Metropolitan Stipendiary Magistrate ex Parte Pinochet Ugarte* [1999] 2 All ER 97

115 Indeed some of those accused of human rights violations in the former Yugoslavia and Rwanda were brought to trial at two United Nations war-crimes tribunals. A third, on Sierra Leone, was established in December 2002. In addition, the establishment of the International Criminal Court demonstrates worldwide support, albeit with the exception of the United States of America, for the approach.

mechanisms designed to ensure that usurpers and their families do not derive any financial benefit from their unlawful actions as their assets will be traced, frozen and confiscated *no matter where in the world they seek to deposit them.* This is potentially an invaluable deterrent in that it hits where it hurts most: in their pocket.[116]

Making this a reality requires close international and regional co-operation between governments, police and financial institutions. In the past this was immensely difficult given, for example, the strict bank secrecy laws of many of the key countries. This is now becoming a thing of the past.[117] Increased mutual co-operation means that it is possible for a country to enlist the assistance of other states to trace the funds hidden away by usurpers, freeze them and eventually have them returned.[118] A significant obstacle to the effectiveness of these measures lies in the continuing lack of expertise on the part of many government lawyers on how to operate the system. The need for suitable training is paramount. To address this problem, the Commonwealth Legal Education Association has developed, in co-operation with the Criminal Law Unit of the Commonwealth Secretariat, a training programme for law students, legal practitioners and judges on the law and procedural aspects of extradition, mutual assistance and proceeds of crime.[119] This has been introduced into the professional legal training programmes of several ESA states. In this way, it is hoped that the dramatic changes to international and regional co-operation regimes will be complemented by the development of a requisite pool of legal expertise.

Learning from the past

Holding a formal judicial commission of inquiry into past human rights abuses gives those victimised an opportunity to be heard and ensures that

[116] An additional benefit of the 'Snow White' approach is that it prevents usurpers from incorporating into a new constitution financial advantages for themselves and their families.

[117] Much of the credit for this goes to the work of the Financial Action Task Force set up following the 1989 G7 summit to tackle money laundering. Its 'Forty Recommendations' provide a blueprint for the development of national laws and procedures designed to facilitate anti-money laundering measures and mutual cooperation. See generally W. Gilmore, *Dirty Money* (2nd edn), Council of Europe, Strasbourg 1999 and at www.oecd.org/fatf.

[118] The East and Southern Africa Anti-Money Laundering Group (ESAAMLG) was established in 1999 and includes as members all the SEA states. One of its aims is to strengthen the legislative and regulatory framework within member states to reflect the aims of the Forty Recommendations: see http://www.oecd.org/fatf.

[119] For details see (2001) 86 *Commonwealth Legal Education* 24.

their experiences are recorded for posterity. It also assists constitution-makers to develop safeguards designed to prevent future military interventions. In Uganda, this approach was attempted on two occasions.

The Saied Commission of 1974 was remarkable in that it sat whilst the military were still in power. Despite this, it concluded that the special security bodies, the Public Safety Unit and the State Research Bureau, established by Amin, bore the major responsibility for the disappearances of thousands of people and criticised army officers, intelligence services and military police for abuse of their powers. It also found that the military decrees made by the Amin government giving powers to soldiers to arrest and detain had facilitated disappearances. The Commission made a number of detailed recommendations providing, amongst other things, for improved training in human rights and strict rules of accountability for members of the military. Given the continuing reign of terror being perpetrated by the Amin regime, it was hardly surprising that the recommendations were never implemented. Even so, the Commission's work at least provided a useful historical record and supplied the international community with an insight into the workings of the regime.[120]

The second commission, *Uganda Commission of Inquiry into the Violation of Human Rights* (the Oder Commission), was established by the National Resistance Movement (NRM) in 1986 upon its assumption of power. The Commission, consisting of a Supreme Court judge, Justice Arthur Oder, as chairperson, and five other Commissioners,[121] was tasked with inquiring into the violation of human rights from independence in 1962 until the take-over of power by the NRM in 1986 and to make recommendations for the implementation of safeguards against future human rights abuses. It was not intended to have a role of bringing human rights violators to justice and it was quickly decided that any evidence gathered would not be used directly in any subsequent criminal investigations.[122] Its report, entitled *The Pearl of Blood*, runs to some 700 pages with a verbatim record of proceedings of over 13,000 pages and provides a frightening

[120] For a useful account of the work of the Commission see Richard Carver, 'How African Governments Investigate Human Rights Violations', paper presented at the African Studies Association conference, 1989, pp. 5–8.

[121] The other commissioners were a university law professor, a medical doctor, a university lecturer, a lawyer in private practice and a 'farmer/writer'. Two were members of the National Resistance Council.

[122] This was on the basis that it might otherwise deter people from testifying. However, public transcripts of the hearings were made available to the police.

account of the systematic abuse of human rights by successive regimes and highlights the reasons that underlay 'Uganda's violent and bloody post-independence history'.

The Oder Commission provides a useful model in that it was demonstrably independent, sat in public, enabled victims to give a full account of their experiences and issued a detailed report, including a series of wide-ranging recommendations, that was made widely available.[123] In doing so it sought to assist the people of Uganda both to confront and understand their past and to devise a new constitutional structure taking into account the lessons of the past. The Constitution of Uganda 1995 stands as a testament to its work.

Whilst the Oder Commission indicates that establishing a formal commission of inquiry serves a useful purpose, in two respects its work did not go far enough. Firstly, there was no mechanism to compensate victims of human rights violations. Secondly, there was no incentive for those allegedly responsible for the violations to give evidence before the Commission, thus potentially depriving the country of knowledge of the full facts.

Seeking truth and reconciliation

This approach is based on the view that determining the 'truth' leads to national reconciliation and to some kind of national healing process. Its underlying basis is the need not for vengeance, but for the truth for with this comes forgiveness. In the words of Pope John Paul II:

> Forgiveness, in its truest and highest form, is a free act of love. But precisely because it is an act of love, it has its own intrinsic demands: the first of which is respect for the truth.[124]

Ignatieff has questioned this approach as it assumes that 'the truth is one, not many; that the truth is certain, not contestable; and that when it is known by all, it has the capacity to heal'. He adds that this assumption is essentially an article of faith about human nature: i.e. 'that the truth is one and if we know it, it will make us free'.[125] That this is still a worthwhile

[123] Commissions of inquiry are often required to report directly to the President who is under no legal obligation to publish its report. This was the fate of the reports of two commissions established by President Mugabe in 1983 and 1984 to investigate the activities of the security forces in Matabeleland.

[124] Quoted in the CCJP report, *Breaking the Silence*, p. 1.

[125] M. Ignatieff, 'Truth, Justice and Reconciliation', paper delivered at the Commonwealth Law Conference, Vancouver, Canada, 1996, p. 3. See the similar view of Wilson who also questions the meaning and scope of 'reconciliation' in this context: Richard A. Wilson,

exercise is evidenced by the establishment of the Truth Commissions in Chad, Chile, El Salvador, Argentina and Brazil that documented the fate of the thousands of innocent persons killed or tortured by the military juntas.

It also inspired the establishment of the Truth and Reconciliation Commission (TRC) in South Africa[126] whose main objective was to 'promote national unity and reconciliation in a spirit of understanding which transcends the conflicts and divisions of the past' and which was enjoined to pursue that objective by 'establishing as complete a picture as possible of the causes, nature and extent of the gross violations of human rights' committed between 1 March 1960 and 11 May 1994. The decision to develop a process of truth-telling was explained by the Minister of Justice as follows:

> I could have gone to parliament and produced an amnesty law – but this would have ignored the victims of violence entirely. We recognised that we could not forgive perpetrators unless we attempt also to restore the honour and dignity of the victims and give effect to reparation.[127]

The importance of the TRC in this context is demonstrated through the work of its three committees. The Human Rights Violations Committee was tasked with investigating human rights abuses, establishing the identity of the victims, their fate or present whereabouts and the nature and extent of the harm they had suffered. Further, it sought to establish whether the violations were the result of deliberate planning by the state or any other organisations. On the issue of compensation, victims so identified were then referred to the Reparation and Rehabilitation Committee. The third committee, the Amnesty Committee, could hear applications from those seeking an amnesty for any act, omission or offence associated with a 'political objective' committed between 1 March 1960 and 11 May 1994.[128]

Overall, the establishment of a culture of good governance and respect for human rights requires a country to undertake an honest and frank

The Politics of Truth and Reconciliation in South Africa: Legitimizing the Post-Apartheid State, Cambridge University Press, Cambridge, 2001, esp. Part II.

[126] See the Promotion of National Unity and Reconciliation Act 34 of 1995.

[127] Dullah Omar, South African Minister of Justice in opening the parliamentary debate on the establishment of the Truth and Reconciliation Commission.

[128] The final date for submission of applications was 30 September 1997. This cut-off date 'encouraged' perpetrators to seek an amnesty but carried with it the threat of the prosecution of those who did not do so.

acknowledgment of its past, however 'atrocious'[129] this may be. This is not achieved through the use of indemnities. Commissions of inquiry have succeeded in shedding some light on past human rights abuses and their reports, as official documents, can also have the effect of officially recognising that such abuses occurred. The experience in the ESA states suggests that there is much agreement on some of the requirements for dealing with the past, i.e. (i) giving victims a forum in which to recount their experiences; (ii) preparing an accurate historical record, for only by understanding the reality of past abuses, and their causes, can future abuses be prevented; and (iii) providing redress to individual victims as well as to whole communities.[130] As the Oder Commission has suggested: 'Families or relatives of victims of murders and arbitrary deprivation of life at the hands of state organisations should be adequately compensated and assisted with legal aid to pursue their claims'.[131]

The main area of debate is between the 'amnesty in exchange for the truth' approach of South Africa and the 'deterrent' approach. Given the introduction of the *gacaca* courts in Rwanda, which will try many of those accused of genocide in that devastated country and worldwide support leading to the rapid establishment of the International Criminal Court in 2002, the bringing to trial of military usurpers and other perpetrators of human rights abuses is now increasingly likely to become the accepted norm.[132]

Overview

Has the 'Day of the Man on Horseback' finally ended in the ESA region? At independence in 1961, Tanzania reportedly considered abolishing its army or placing it under the direct command of the United Nations. The repercussions of such a policy for both the country and the region must

[129] See J. Sarkin, 'The Development of a Human Rights Culture in South Africa' (1998) 20(3) *Human Rights Quarterly* 628. See also N. Roht-Arriaza, 'Combating Impunity: some Thoughts on the Way Forward' (1996) 59 *Law and Contemporary Problems* 93 and R. Teitel, 'Transitional Justice: the Role of Law in Political Transformation' (1997) 106 *Yale Law Journal* 2009.

[130] Human rights abuses by the security forces directly or indirectly affects whole communities and not just individuals. In view of this the CCJP Report recommends 'communal reparation' through the establishment of the 'Reconciliation/*Uxolelwano* Trust' designed to raise funds from governments and donors to implement 'reconciliation projects' in affected communities (p. 212).

[131] Oder Commission, Recommendation 13.5(i).

[132] For a useful discussion see J. Sarkin, 'The Tension between Justice and Reconciliation in Rwanda: Politics, Human Rights, Due Process and the Role of the *Gacaca* Courts in Dealing with the Genocide' (2001) 45 *Journal of African Law* 143, pp. 161–9.

remain a matter of conjecture. Certainly all the ESA constitutions provide for the military and it is idealistic to expect its abolition.[133]

On the question of obedience to the civilian government, there are grounds for guarded optimism. No longer can a collection of case studies on civilian control of the military exclude African countries on the basis that they 'have yet to establish means of civilian control that have stood the test of time'.[134] In fact in recent years many ESA states have seriously addressed the issue of developing an acceptable civilian–military relationship based on subordination and accountability of the military to the civilian government. As the Ugandan Constitution puts it,[135] the Peoples' Defence Forces must be 'non-partisan, national in character,[136] professional, disciplined, productive and subordinate to the civilian authority'.

This chapter has examined some of the constitutional and other legal mechanisms needed to retain an acceptable civilian–military relationship. Part of the strategy lies in adopting 'anti-coup' provisions. In particular, these should include the 'Snow White' approach, and the placing of a duty on civil society to resist unconstitutional activities by the military. Whilst few constitutions contain express provisions to this effect, they apply, by *implication*, in every state that is committed to good governance and the rule of law. Further, the judicial response to a coup must be to firmly reject the concept of revolutionary legality. This means that potential usurpers know in advance that the risk of failure is high and the opportunity for gains is low. There is also the need to provide ongoing education on good governance and human rights to all members of the military, as well as ensuring that law officers have the requisite expertise to facilitate the extradition of usurpers and to seek the return of looted property.

Overall, the matter is perhaps best summarised by Nwabueze, who asserts that there is no viable alternative to a government freely elected by the people and limited in its powers by a supreme constitution.[137]

[133] Even a reduction in military spending seems unlikely.

[134] Claude E. Welch (ed.), *Civilian Control of the Military: Theories and Cases from Developing Countries*, State University of New York Press, Albany, NY, 1976, xi.

[135] Art. 208(2).

[136] If important groups or sub-groups are under-represented in the officer corps in particular, the military may be identified with the values and interests of the dominant group(s). This point was identified by the Oder Commission as one of the problems in Uganda. The deliberate policy in Tanzania of drawing members of the military equally from all regions of the country has ensured the development of a *national* force that has tended to promote stability.

[137] Nwabueze, *Military Rule*, p. 330.

12

Constitutionalism and emergency powers

There may come a time in the life of a nation when a situation arises that seriously threatens its security or stability. In response, a government may legitimately declare a state of emergency and make emergency regulations designed to counter the danger. Article 4 of the International Covenant on Civil and Political Rights (ICCPR) recognises that 'in time of public emergency which threatens the life of the nation' a state may take measures derogating from its obligations under the Covenant. The real concern arises from the potential abuse of emergency powers: for example, where an unscrupulous government declares a state of emergency in order to maintain itself in power, then suspends or abrogates key constitutional provisions and effectively rules by decree, for an indefinite period. This is a scenario that is aptly called the 'permanence of the temporary'[1] and calls for the development of effective constitutional safeguards against such abuse of power. This issue is examined in the first part of the chapter.[2] A frequent companion of a state of emergency is the use of preventive detention and this area is considered in the second part of the chapter.

States of emergency

During the colonial period, states of emergency were imposed in Kenya, Northern Rhodesia, Southern Rhodesia and Nyasaland[3] as efforts were made to retain political and economic control and to stem the tide of

[1] A phrase used by A. Mathews and R. Albino, 'The Permanence of the Temporary: an Examination of the 90 and 180 Day Detention Laws' (1966) 83 *South African Law Journal* 16.

[2] For a full analysis see John Hatchard, *Individual Freedoms and Emergency Powers in the African Context: a Case Study of Zimbabwe*, Ohio University Press, Athens, Ohio and James Currey Publishers, London, 1993.

[3] For example, in 1952 in Kenya, and following the onset of the *mau mau* rebellion, a state of emergency was declared. Emergency regulations were then made which ousted the jurisdiction of the courts in some cases, reduced judicial safeguards in others and imposed detention without trial. Emergency regulations also empowered the courts to impose the death sentence: see e.g. *Kuruma v R* [1955] AC 197.

African nationalism. Regrettably, the usefulness of emergency powers was not lost on the leaders of the newly independent states and several used them, sometimes for lengthy periods, to entrench political power and to curtail the legitimate exercise of constitutional rights and freedoms.[4] Similarly, during the prolonged struggle for Namibian independence, the South African authorities used a wide array of emergency powers against its nationalist opponents whilst in *apartheid* South Africa itself the use of emergency laws was commonplace.[5] It follows that it is vital to provide effective constitutional and other safeguards to deal with an otherwise very effective method of undermining a constitution by constitutional means.

Determining the basis for the declaration of a state of emergency

Given the variety of situations encompassed and the differing political circumstances in which the declaration is made, it is probably not practical to define exactly what constitutes a state of emergency. Rather we need to focus on the basic criteria that justify such a declaration. The African Conference on the Rule of Law mentions several. Firstly, '. . . the regular operation of authority [is] impossible, but that so long as a situation exists where the authorities can operate and the problems arising can be overcome, a state of emergency may not be declared'.[6] Secondly, a state of emergency and measures taken thereunder are of an exceptional and temporary nature and may only last as long as the life of the nation is threatened,[7] i.e. an exceptional situation of crisis or emergency that

[4] For example, in Lesotho in 1970, Chief Leabua Jonathan and his ruling party were defeated in a general election. Unwilling to renounce power, he declared a state of emergency and detained without trial leading members of the successful Basotho National Party.

[5] See generally A. Mathews, *Freedom, State Security and the Rule of Law* Juta, Cape Town, 1986.

[6] *African Conference on the Rule of Law 1961 Report on the Proceedings*, p. 162. This is also the view of Marks who states that an emergency situation is one which places 'institutions of the state in a precarious position and which leads the authorities to feel justified in suspending the application of certain principles': S. Marks, 'Principles and Norms of Human Rights Applicable in Emergency Situations: Underdevelopment, Catastrophes and Armed Conflict', in K. Vasak and P. Alston (eds.), *The International Dimension of Human Rights*, UNESCO, 1982, vol. 1 p. 175.

[7] Four elements are contained here: (i) the public emergency must be actual and imminent; (ii) its effects must involve the whole nation, although arguably the emergency may apply to events of a more localised nature; (iii) the continuance of the organised life of the community must be threatened; (iv) the crisis must be exceptional. See the decision of the European Court of Justice in *Denmark, Norway, Sweden and Netherlands v Greece* (3321–3/67; 3344/67) Report: November 5 1969.

affects the whole or part of the population and constitutes a threat to the organised life of the community of which the state is composed.[8] This is a fundamental principle in that one of the major problems in practice is that a threat to the *government* is sometimes treated as being a threat to the *state*.

Thirdly, the reasons for the emergency declaration must be clearly articulated. In general these will include: (i) a state of war or preparations to meet its imminent outbreak (here extremely wide powers are required and these will almost inevitably affect major areas of national life); (ii) armed internal rebellion or subversion (this situation is sometimes linked with (i) above but does not necessarily require the taking of such wide-ranging powers concerning, for example, external relations or restrictions on non-nationals); (iii) civil unrest on a localised scale (here additional law and order provisions, applicable only to those areas affected by the unrest, are all that are normally required; (iv) an economic emergency (for example the parlous state of the national economy may require the taking of emergency powers aimed at preventing the economic collapse of the country);[9] or (v) natural disasters (*force majeure*).[10]

The Westminster export model constitution contained no requirement to give reasons for the declaration of a state of emergency and its influence still pervades the Constitutions of Zambia, Zimbabwe, Kenya and Botswana. Even here, whilst the President is not required to fit the 'emergency' into a constitutional formula, in practice the need to obtain the legislature's approval for such action means that some reasons purporting to justify the introduction or continuation of a state of emergency are required, however vague and unhelpful these may be. Elsewhere,

8 For a useful example of the application of this term see the decision of the European Court of Human Rights in *Re Lawless* 1 EHRR 15. In addition, many unproclaimed states of emergency exist when the ordinary law-making procedures are used to pass 'quasi' emergency laws in the shape of wide-ranging security legislation: see the discussion below.

9 Some writers assert that a serious economic crisis should also be covered by an emergency proclamation. See, for instance, A. Mathews, *Law, Order and Liberty in South Africa*, Juta, Cape Town, 1971, p. 39. In Ghana, section 26 of the Second Republican Constitution (1969) defined a state of emergency as one which was 'calculated to deprive the community of the essentials of life, or which renders necessary the taking of measures which are requisite for securing public safety, the defence of Ghana and the maintenance of public order and supplies and services essential to the life of the community'.

10 For a brief but helpful examination of this point see H. Groves, 'Emergency Powers' (1961) (Winter) *Journal of the International Commission of Jurists* 1 and C. Rossiter, *Constitutional Dictatorship: Crisis Government in the Modern Democracies*, Princeton University Press, Princeton, NJ: 1948, p. 6.

providing reasons for the action are a constitutional necessity. For example, article 26(1) of the Namibian Constitution 1990 states that the President may only declare a state of emergency at a time of national disaster; during a period of national defence; or during a public emergency threatening the life of the nation or constitutional order. In Tanzania, the grounds include 'a definite danger of great magnitude, to the extent that peace will be disrupted and public safety will be endangered [so that] the situation can only be contained by resorting to extraordinary steps' and 'other dangers that are obviously a threat to the country'.[11] Although the terminology remains uncomfortably vague, the requirement to provide reasons at least restricts the declaration (or renewal) of a state of emergency to situations when the very foundations of society are threatened. For the sake of clarity it is certainly preferable to impose a constitutional requirement upon the head of government/state to publicly provide detailed reasons for the proclamation of a state of emergency.

Providing safeguards on the declaration of a state of emergency

Given its serious constitutional implications, it is imperative to provide effective safeguards on the declaration or renewal of a state of emergency. In most ESA states, the sole constitutional safeguard is one that requires the legislature to approve the declaration or its renewal, failing which the declaration lapses. In practice this has proved hopelessly inadequate. In Zimbabwe, for example, between independence in 1980 and 1990[12] successive Ministers of Home Affairs produced an extraordinary assortment of reasons for retaining the state of emergency including: increasing crime; security threats from South Africa; civil unrest; the need to restructure the economy; economic problems; and industrial unrest. There is no doubt that based on article 4 of the ICCPR (which was the declared basis of the state of emergency in Zimbabwe), these reasons did not justify the retention of the state of emergency for such a lengthy period, if at

[11] Section 32(2) Law of the Fifth Amendment of the State Constitution of 1984. In South Africa the relevant provision covers situations where '(a) the life of the nation is threatened by war, invasion, general insurrection, disorder, natural disaster or other public emergency; and (b) the declaration is necessary to restore peace and order, (s.37(1) Constitution of South Africa 1996).

[12] The state of emergency was originally declared in 1965 just prior to the Unilateral Declaration of Independence by the Rhodesian government. Successive parliaments meekly agreed to its continuance.

all.[13] At best reliance on them demonstrated a lack of understanding as to the grounds for making and maintaining an emergency proclamation. At worst they illustrated a desire on the part of government to use emergency powers to circumvent the normal constitutional process and to rule by decree. Despite these concerns, the ruling party's domination ensured that every six months members of Parliament meekly obeyed their political masters and voted to approve the renewal of the state of emergency with little or no meaningful debate.

The weakness of the parliamentary safeguard is further demonstrated in the Zambian context. In June 1992 in a speech at a Commonwealth human rights conference, the then Vice-President (now President) Levy Mwanawasa condemned the previous government of Kenneth Kaunda for 'perpetuating a state of emergency for 27 years during which time thousands of people were detained without trial' and pledged to ensure that this would not recur.[14] Just a few months later, the then Zambian President, Frederick Chiluba, accused members of UNIP, the former ruling party, of plotting to overthrow the government by unconstitutional means through a plan known as the 'Zero Option'. He proceeded to proclaim a state of emergency and ordered the detention of several persons (including one of the participants at the aforementioned June conference). No convincing case was ever established for the declaration[15] and there was a real hope that the National Assembly would refuse to approve the proclamation. However, following strong presidential pressure, members meekly approved it.

In fact, no legislature in any ESA state has ever refused to approve the declaration or renewal of a state of emergency even when, as highlighted by the Zambian case, there was no compelling evidence placed before parliamentarians to support such action. Perhaps in recognition of this reality, constitutional drafters have sought to strengthen the safeguards. In South Africa and Namibia, for example, a specially enhanced

[13] See the discussion in Hatchard, *Individual Freedoms*, at pp. 17–23. A similar situation occurred in Lesotho in 1988 where the reasons for the declaration of a state of emergency were given as being 'due to the sudden increase in the incidence of . . . armed robbery, house-breaking, theft of motor vehicles and stock-theft': see the judgment of Cullinan C. J. in *Law Society of Lesotho v Minister of Defence* [1988] LRC (Const) 226, at p. 229.

[14] Speech delivered at the official opening of the Commonwealth Workshop on Setting Zambian National Human Rights Strategies, Livingstone, Zambia, 25 June 1992.

[15] Indeed all those charged in connection with the 'Zero Option' incident were later acquitted.

parliamentary majority is required.[16] This at least demands a degree of unanimity on the matter but the procedure still suffers from the same drawbacks concerning special majorities as discussed earlier in chapter 3. It is curious that once again legislatures are seen as being the 'guardians of the constitution' when all the evidence points to the fact that currently they are generally ill equipped to act as an effective safeguard on such important matters.

There are alternative approaches. In Malawi, the declaration requires approval of the National Assembly's all-party Defence and Security Committee.[17] Since the move to multi-party government, no party has enjoyed an overall parliamentary majority and the committee could be useful in the event of an emergency situation arising. However, it has limited value as a model for the numerous states where one party largely dominates the legislature.

Another approach is to establish a separate body specifically tasked with making an objective assessment of the need for a state of emergency or its continuance. A possible model is one based on the Council of State in Lesotho where the Prime Minister may revoke the declaration of a state of emergency at any time acting in accordance with the Council's advice.[18] The Council comprises up to fourteen persons with a majority being non-government appointees and which must include two judges, two National Assembly members, a traditional Chief and a private legal practitioner.[19] To enhance its objectivity, it is essential that such a body has access to other sources of information beyond that coming from government security agencies. It follows that it must be entitled to take evidence from the public and to summon members of the security forces or other public servants to give evidence (in camera if necessary). Whilst security considerations may well preclude full public debate on the issue, the requirement for such a body to approve the original declaration and provide a continual monitoring of the situation could prove to be a most effective safeguard.

The judiciary also has a crucial role for it is well established that a court may review the validity of an emergency declaration. For example, in 1988 the High Court of Lesotho held that the Declaration of a State of Emergency and the emergency regulations made thereunder were null

[16] In South Africa this only applies to an extension of the state of emergency: s.37(2) Constitution of South Africa.

[17] S.162 Constitution of Malawi.

[18] S.23(3) Constitution of Lesotho. [19] Ibid., s.95.

and void because they were not made in accordance with the procedure prescribed by the Emergency Powers Act 1982.[20] Arguably, this power should also extend to reviewing whether the proclamation of a state of emergency is necessary based on the statements made by government justifying its introduction or retention.[21]

Dealing with the 'permanence of the temporary' is also necessary. The Constitutions of South Africa, Uganda and Zambia provide that a state of emergency can remain in force for up to three months without renewal, whilst in Kenya, Namibia, Zimbabwe and Lesotho the period is six months. Of course although it is rarely possible to predict the duration of an emergency situation, the shorter period is preferable as it emphasises the temporary nature of the declaration and provides for a frequent public re-assessment of the need for its retention.

Overall, there is a clear case for establishing a body organised along similar lines to the Council of State in Lesotho but with powers similar to the Malawian Defence and Security Committee. This would have several advantages including (i) helping to ensure that the declaration is in compliance with the state's international human rights obligations; (ii) preventing the continuation of the state of emergency based on spurious grounds; (iii) ensuring an objective monitoring of the emergency; and (iv) removing (or at least reinforcing) the role of the legislature.

The use and abuse of emergency powers regulations

Even when a declaration of an emergency is justified, it does not necessarily mean that the use of wide-ranging emergency measures is warranted. Article 4 of the ICCPR provides that such measures must be limited 'to the extent strictly required by the exigencies of the situation'.[22] For, as the Human Rights Committee has noted, it is precisely during times of emergency that the protection of individual freedoms becomes

[20] See *Law Society of Lesotho v Minister of Defence.* In both South Africa and Malawi, the courts are competent to inquire into the validity of an emergency declaration (and any extension) and any action taken thereunder, including the making of any emergency regulations.

[21] See the approach of the Pakistan Supreme Court in *Leghari v Federation of Pakistan* PLD 1999 SC 57 and the Indian Supreme Court in *Minerva Mills Ltd v Union of India* AIR 1980 SC 1789.

[22] Further the emergency must have been officially proclaimed, the measures must not be inconsistent with the State's other international obligations or must not involve certain forms of discrimination.

all important and this is especially true for those rights not subject to abrogation.[23]

A nexus is therefore required between the reasons for the emergency and the measures chosen to deal with it. This is emphasised in the European Convention for the Protection of Human Rights and Fundamental Freedoms which provides that although individual governments may decide the scope of the emergency powers, the European Court of Human Rights can determine whether any action has gone beyond that which is strictly required by the exigencies of the situation.[24] This is a vital safeguard in that one very real danger to constitutional rights and freedoms is the use/abuse of emergency powers in circumstances that have little or no connection with the stated reasons for the declaration of the emergency. This is well illustrated by the experience of Zimbabwe.

Here the Emergency Powers Act empowers the President to make emergency regulations having nationwide or local effect which 'appear to him necessary or expedient' for, amongst other things, the public safety, the maintenance of public order; the maintenance of any essential services, and the preservation of the peace.[25] The term 'essential services' includes hospital services; transport and distribution services; electricity, water and sanitary services; communications; and 'any other service declared by the President, by notice in the *Gazette* to be an essential service for the purposes of the Act'.[26] In effect an essential service is any 'service' if the President so determines. In *Stubbs v Minister of Home Affairs*[27] a person held under a thirty-day detention order on suspicion of violating the exchange control laws applied for a writ of habeas corpus. In the Supreme Court, Beck J. A. admitted that his first impression was that the reasons

23 GC 5/13, HRC 36, 110.

24 This approach is substantially repeated in other regional documents such as the American Convention on Human Rights and the European Social Charter. See also B. Mangan, 'Protecting Human Rights in National Emergencies: Shortcomings in the European System' (1988) 10 *Human Rights Quarterly* 376, who argues that an emergency situation does not, by itself, justify systematic human rights violations and that a government must consider the magnitude of the emergency and whether the deprivation of human rights can be avoided.

25 The other situations cover (a) making adequate provision for dealing with any circumstances which (i) have arisen or, in his opinion, are likely to arise whether such circumstances relate to the maintenance of any essential or other services or otherwise; and (ii) in his opinion, will interfere with the peace, order and good government; or (b) making adequate provision for terminating the state of emergency (s.3 Emergency Powers Act).

26 S.2 Emergency Powers Act.

27 Supreme Court of Zimbabwe (unreported, 1981).

for the detention order did not fall within any of the areas detailed in the Emergency Powers Act and added that the concept of exchange-control laws seemed entirely remote from the wording of any of the various purposes enumerated in the Act. But he continued:

> [Counsel] has drawn our attention to the Emergency Powers (Declaration of Essential Service)[28] which declared that 'finance, commerce and industry' are to be included within the phrase 'an essential service' for the purposes of the Exchange Control Act. That declaration is still extant. . . . Clearly, the effect of that declaration is to bring the concept of the nation's finance, and hence the protection of its foreign currency reserves for which, in turn, Exchange Control laws are designed, within the ambit of . . . the Act, which both refer to 'the maintenance of any essential service'.

The detainee also contended that the investigation of a criminal complaint was something very different from the purposes contemplated in the Emergency Powers Act. Thus it was improper to detain a person merely to facilitate the investigation of a criminal charge. It was further argued that the ordinary criminal law already provided for adequate investigatory powers and that this was strengthened by the ministerial power to deny bail in such cases. The court rejected these arguments because:

> Once it is appreciated . . . that an offence against the Exchange Control laws is such a matter for which it has appeared to the President to be necessary and expedient to make regulations for the maintenance of the country's financial interests, including regulations which empower the police to arrest and detain persons suspected of having contravened such laws, the submission, so it seems to me, loses all its force. How can it be said that the investigating officer has used his power of detention for an improper purpose in this case when he is using it to investigate suspected Exchange Control offences and when he is specifically and lawfully authorised to do so in relation to offences of this kind?[29]

The drafters were certainly intent on providing a 'catch-all' scenario in that the Act specifically states that emergency powers regulations may make provision for, amongst other things: detention without trial; deportation of aliens; control of movement of persons within the country; control of business and industry; compulsory acquisition of property and the

[28] Rhodesia *Government Notice* 798A of 1965. See also Emergency Powers (Maintenance of Essential Services) Regulations 1989 SI 160A/89.

[29] P. 3.

searching of premises.[30] This list is supplemented by a presidential power to make such regulations as appear 'to him to be necessary or expedient', whether or not they relate to any of the matters specified in the Act. The almost limitless scope of these powers means that unless in violation of the Constitution,[31] few emergency regulations will ever be *ultra vires* the Act.

Under the Act's most far-reaching provision the President may, by regulation, amend or suspend any law, or declare the application of any law with or without any modification.[32] The accepted use of regulations and other subordinate legislation is to permit a minister to take certain action derived from powers devolved by Parliament and contained in an enabling Act. Accordingly any other action is *ultra vires*. However, the Emergency Powers Act provides for what may be termed 'legislative' regulations which permit the minister to legislate by regulation without the need to follow the parliamentary process. This 'Henry VIII' style clause is a major deviation from the accepted use of regulations and is a provision which can effectively lead to rule by the executive.[33] Indeed fourteen statutes were amended or modified in this manner between 1980 and 1990.

Overall, the Zimbabwe experience highlights the manner in which emergency regulations can be used to impose limits and controls on almost every aspect of national life, even though many may have little or no connection with the reasons for the state of emergency.[34] The potential for the misuse of such powers is immense and emphasises the need for effective safeguards on the making of emergency regulations. This means that they must be (i) limited to areas directly connected with the publicly stated reasons for the emergency; (ii) have a limited life span; and (iii) require specific parliamentary approval for both their making and renewal.

[30] S.3(2) Emergency Powers Act.

[31] And some significant constitutional rights can be abrogated or suspended during the state of emergency: see below.

[32] S.4(2).

[33] For a full discussion of this topic see C. K. Allen, *Law and Orders*, Stevens, London, 1965, p. 169–73.

[34] See Hatchard, *Individual Freedoms*, especially at chapter 9. The considerable scope for executive action in the most unlikely of situations was well illustrated in 1981 when a dispute arose between the Minister of Health and the Family Planning Association over the supply of a certain kind of contraceptive. Unhappy with the reluctance of the Association to supply the device, the Minister made emergency regulations which permitted him to take possession of the entire assets of the Association: see Emergency Powers (Family Planning) Regulations 1981 SI 643/81.

Emergency powers and the suspension of constitutional rights

The protection of constitutional rights is particularly important during a state of emergency. Whilst there are some that are internationally recognised as being non-derogable at any time, the right to suspend or abrogate other fundamental rights is well established, albeit with appropriate safeguards. An immediate problem is identifying which rights are considered 'dangerous' enough as to merit possible suspension. As the following Table indicates there is little agreement on this issue.

Fundamental rights provisions liable to suspension during a state of emergency

Access to court: SA
Access to information: SA
Arbitrary arrest and detention: N
Freedom from discrimination: Z; L; K; Zim
Freedom of assembly: M; N; Z; SA; K; Zim
Freedom of conscience: Z
Freedom of expression: M; Z; SA; K; Zim
Freedom of information: M
Freedom of movement: M; N; Z; SA; K; Zim
Protection of young persons from exploitation: Z
Right of a child to parental care, security, basic nutrition and basic health and social services: SA
Right of personal liberty: N; Z; L; SA; K; Zim
Right to administrative justice: SA
Right to collective bargaining: SA
Right to education: N; SA
Right to engage in economic activity: SA
Right to equal protection of the law: L; SA
Right to a fair trial: SA
Right to a healthy environment: SA
Right to participate in cultural activity: SA
Right to political activity: N; SA
Right to privacy: N; Z; SA; K; Zim
Right to property: N; Z; SA
Right to withhold labour: N

Key K = Kenya; L = Lesotho; M = Malawi; N = Namibia; SA = South Africa; Z = Zambia; Zim = Zimbabwe

The list raises several points. Firstly, there is clearly no agreement as to which rights are liable to suspension. Secondly, the number of rights liable to suspension differs considerably. Thus the Constitution of Lesotho permits the suspension of just three whereas in South Africa the number is nineteen. Thirdly, it is often difficult, if not impossible, to find any link between an emergency situation and the need to suspend some rights. For example, there is no justification for suspending the rights to education, a healthy environment and freedom of conscience. *A fortiori* the power to undermine the right to a fair trial. In some cases the provisions contravene the ICCPR: for example in Zambia suspending the freedom of conscience is in direct contravention of article 18 of the ICCPR. Fourthly, there are some curious inconsistencies. For example, the right of young persons to protection from exploitation can be suspended in Zambia, but not in South Africa nor Malawi, whilst the right of young persons to basic health care can be suspended in South Africa but not in Malawi. One is thus left with the feeling that insufficient thought has gone into the list of suspensions. The danger is that the wider the list, the greater the power of the executive to rule by emergency decrees and regulations, with the result that key constitutional rights have little or no meaning at a time when they are most needed.

Overall, the constitutional safeguards on the use of emergency powers are disappointing. With human rights abuses commonplace during periods of states of emergency, it is essential to provide for effective safeguards, rather than rely on those that failed so miserably in the past. This means placing strict limits on the power to suspend or derogate from fundamental rights. The present chaotic situation needs a complete re-appraisal.

Dealing with quasi-emergency powers

The influence of the colonial legal order also remains much in evidence through the retention (and even strengthening) of 'quasi' emergency laws which operate without the need for a state of emergency. These include the Preventive Detention Act in Tanzania that provides for indefinite detention without trial and the infamous Law and Order (Maintenance) Act (LOMA) in Zimbabwe, which even the government publicly described as a piece of 'draconian' legislation.[35] In addition, vague criminal laws

[35] For many years the Government was urged to repeal LOMA. Finally, in 1998 a new Public Order and Security Bill was published. According to the Memorandum accompanying the

on sedition and criminal libel and restrictive laws on political activity, the registration and regulation of political parties and trade unions all play their part in providing the executive with a vast array of security powers. Other quasi-emergency measures are of more recent origin. For example, in Botswana, the National Security Act 1986 prohibited the carrying out of acts which are considered prejudicial to the safety or interests of Botswana, this vague offence being punishable by up to thirty-years imprisonment.[36] Further, the Presidential Powers (Temporary Measures) Act 1986 permits the Zimbabwean President to make regulations for up to six months to deal with urgent situations that arise or are likely to arise when he/she considers it necessary or expedient to do so 'in the interests of defence, public order . . . economic interests or the general public good'. This extraordinarily wide provision, that also permits the modification or amendment of statutes, continues to play a significant role in presidential attempts to undermine the rule of law in the country.

The fact is that many countries are in the same position as Tanzania, where the Nyalali Commission found that some forty colonial and post-colonial laws remained in force which restricted the freedom of citizens to express themselves freely, organise or participate freely in state affairs or criticise those in authority. Many such laws probably contravene constitutional rights: indeed in Tanzania the coming into force of the Bill of Rights was delayed supposedly to allow government to bring such laws into line with the Constitution. That this has not occurred suggests that the government is content to retain such laws for as long as possible. From time to time, courts have struck down specific provisions contained in security legislation, although inevitably this is an inefficient and piecemeal exercise. It is therefore beholden upon each state to undertake an in-depth review of their quasi-emergency laws with a view to repealing them, or bringing them into line with the constitution and its international human rights obligations.

draft legislation it would 'replace the draconian Law and Order (Maintenance) Act'. The Bill was duly passed by Parliament and was then sent to the President for signature. In July 1999 he refused to do so intimating that the Bill had 'inadequacies'. Parliamentarians then resolved to let the Bill lapse. For details see John Hatchard, 'The Sad Tale of the POSB' (2000) 44 JAL 132. A much strengthened Public Order and Security Act [Cap 11:17] was enacted in 2002.

[36] The Act further provided: 'Where it appears to a police officer of or above the rank of Sergeant . . . that the case is one of great emergency and that in the interests of Botswana immediate action is necessary, he may search [any premises] without a warrant': see s.11(2).

Overview

It is only right and proper that when a public emergency threatens the life of the nation, the necessary legal powers to combat that threat are readily available. It is the potential for the abuse of emergency powers that is the cause for concern and although some ESA states have sought to strengthen the relevant safeguards, much remains to be done.

Similarly, states must seriously re-examine their current security legislation with a view to ensuring its compliance with the constitution. There is little doubt that if done properly, this will lead to the repeal of many of these 'colonial relics'.[37]

Preventive detention

The right to personal liberty is invariably subject to preventive detention laws and several ESA states have a long and lamentable history on the use and abuse of such laws.[38] Indeed the abuse of the detention laws by successive Ugandan governments led the Oder Commission to recommend that the new Ugandan Constitution should prohibit detention without trial.[39] That the recommendation was not accepted perhaps reflects the widespread perception that preventive detention laws remain necessary for the protection of national security, the more so following the events of 11 September 2001.

Preventive detention describes a situation where a person is detained on political grounds or in 'the interests of national security, public safety or public order' or the like. In theory, this is justified on the basis that the criminal-justice system is an inadequate weapon where action of a preventive nature is necessitated by terrorism, subversion, civil war or the like and that safety comes first in times of emergency: *salus populi suprema lex*. This inadequacy may be substantive, in that the criminal law is incapable of dealing with such matters, or procedural in that it may be impossible to adduce admissible evidence that will satisfy a court

[37] For an excellent discussion of this area see J. Stevens, 'Colonial Relics: the Requirement of a Permit to Hold a Peaceful Assembly' (1998) 42 *Journal of African Law* 118.

[38] See generally Hatchard, *Individual Freedoms*, chapter 6; and the chapters by J. Sarkin-Hughes on South Africa, C. M. Peter on Tanzania and M. Mbao on Zambia in Andrew Harding and John Hatchard (eds.), *Preventive Detention and Security Law*, Martinus Nijhoff, Dordrecht, 1993.

[39] Recommendation 13.3. This was not accepted by the Constituent Assembly and preventive detention is provided for in the new Constitution, although at least some thought was given to providing detainees with meaningful safeguards (see below).

of law beyond reasonable doubt as to the guilt of the detainee because, for example, such evidence cannot be produced for security reasons, or because witnesses are too frightened to give evidence.

Preventive detention (or detention without trial) has several distinct differences from detention under the criminal-justice system. Firstly, its purpose is often ostensibly to prevent *future* conduct rather than to detain until trial or to punish for an offence that has already been committed.[40] Secondly, there is no expectation that the grounds for the detention will be tested in a criminal trial. Thirdly, the process by which detainees come under suspicion and become the subject of detention orders is essentially secret, bureaucratic and intimately connected with the political process. This raises the prospect of detentions being based upon political expediency and the narrow interests of those in power masquerading as the public interest. For this reason persons detained without trial are often regarded as (and often regard themselves as) political detainees. Finally, preventive detention is potentially of unlimited duration.

In practice the regime of preventive detention is quite similar in the ESA states with its main features being readily identifiable. Firstly, preventive detention is normally provided for in the constitution and is often linked to the declaration of a state of emergency.[41] Secondly, a specified high executive authority may make a detention order if satisfied that the detention is necessary to prevent a named person from acting in a manner that is considered prejudicial to state security, public order or public safety.[42] Often law enforcement and other state officials are also empowered to detain individuals without trial for 'investigative purposes' for a specified period that is far in excess of their powers under the ordinary criminal-justice system.

Thirdly, certain safeguards are normally offered to detainees. These cover the right to be informed of the grounds of detention and a right of access to a legal representative of their choice. There is no right to appear before a court of law but instead it is common to permit representations to a separate review body. Fourthly, judicial review of the decision to detain is generally available. Granted that the detention is effected through an administrative procedure rather than by court order, the question arises

[40] This is likely to become an increasingly significant issue as states seek to use detention laws in an effort to combat 'terrorist' activities.

[41] The exceptions are discussed below.

[42] The formula is expressed in different ways but there is essentially little difference in substance.

as to whether the courts can nonetheless review the detention by way of habeas corpus or similar application. The answer to this question tells us a great deal about the constitutional theory prevailing in a particular country, as well as about the practical efficacy of its laws. Often preventive detention law is the battlefield *par excellence* in which the delineation of the separation of powers is determined.

Given the reality of preventive detention laws, the constitutional imperative is to provide meaningful safeguards to protect detainees against the abuse of such laws.

Restrictions on using detention laws

Preventive detention laws must be regarded as irregular and their use justified only for a temporary period and in the face of a clear and present danger to the state (and again *not* just to the government). It follows that such laws should operate only during a declared state of emergency for otherwise they become a permanent feature of the legal landscape. This principle is reflected in most ESA constitutions although Tanzania, Swaziland and Kenya still seemingly utilise ordinary legislation.[43]

Providing a right of access to detainees

> Any person can be picked up at any time once there is an order to that effect signed and sealed with the public seal and get locked up or detained for an indefinite period. I am afraid that even 'disappearances in the night', that dreaded phenomenon of the police state, could find fertile soil and be made a reality . . .[44]

These words of Mr Justice Kalunga on the situation in Tanzania graphically emphasise the importance of imposing on the state a duty to provide meaningful information about the detention, and for the detainee to have access to outside assistance at all times, and in particular to a legal representative and medical practitioner. This is particularly critical during the early stages of the detention for all the evidence points to the fact that detainees are most at risk of torture or mis-treatment during this

[43] See Preservation of Public Security Act (Cap 57) (Kenya); Preventive Detention Act 1962 (Tanzania); Detention Order 1987 (Swaziland).

[44] Referred to by C. M. Peter, *Human Rights in Africa*, Greenwood Press, Westport, 1990 p. 249.

period.[45] Several safeguards are necessary, although regrettably they do not appear in all the ESA constitutions.

Right of a detainee to have his/her next of kin informed promptly of the detention

This is well illustrated by the approach in Malawi where the state must notify an adult family member or friend of the detainee of the detention order as soon as reasonably possible, and in any case, not later than forty-eight hours after the detention.[46]

Right of access to a legal representative of the detainee's own choice

This is a well-established right[47] although its scope has yet to be fully explored by the courts. Arguably it must incorporate a prohibition on the questioning of any detainees prior to consulting with their legal representatives (except with their express and informed consent). In addition, such representatives must be informed of the precise whereabouts of their clients and have the right to enjoy immediate access to them.[48] The need for such provisions is highlighted by the Air Force 6 case in Zimbabwe.[49]

Following a devastating attack on a Zimbabwe Air Force base, six Air Force personnel were charged with assisting the saboteurs. There was effectively no evidence against them save for their confessions in which each admitted their involvement in the sabotage. The preliminary question for the trial judge, Dumbutshena J. P. (as he then was) was whether these statements, which had previously been confirmed by magistrates, were admissible, failing which the state had no case. The evidence which was accepted by the court revealed several disquieting aspects: (a) all the accused were denied access to their legal representatives until after their

[45] See, for example, the report of the Zambia Human Rights Commission *Report, Findings and Recommendations of the Human Rights Commission's Visits to Prisons and Places of Detention made between November 1997 and February 1998*, Lusaka, 1998, pp. 8–9.

[46] Constitution of Malawi, s.45(6). See also article 47(b) of the Constitution of Uganda which permits next of kin to have access to the detainee within seventy-two hours of the commencement of the detention.

[47] A significant constraint in some countries is the unavailability of legal aid. In view of the seriousness of the matter, arguably the right of a detainee to adequate legal representation is an absolute one with states being under an obligation to pay all necessary legal expenses. Alternatively, local professional bodies should undertake to provide senior legal practitioners to assist on a *pro deo* basis.

[48] The South African Constitution comes closest to doing so by permitting such access 'at any reasonable time': see s.37(6)(d).

[49] *S v Slatter* [1986] LRC (Crim) 66. Although not a preventive detention case, it illustrates starkly the lengths to which government officials will go to prevent access to legal representatives.

incriminating statements were recorded; (b) they were constantly moved from place to place as their lawyers increased pressure on the police to gain access to them (as the trial judge noted, the police action was undertaken 'in order to put off their lawyers until after statements had been obtained and confirmed');[50] (c) the statements were made as a result of fear after sustained mental and physical torture perpetrated both by police officers and by members of the security services. Thus the statements were challenged not only on the grounds that they were not voluntary, but also because the accused were denied access to their legal representatives at all material times. The court accepted that a breach of the constitutional right of access to a lawyer in itself rendered the statements inadmissible by reason of undue influence. The trial judge made the position very clear:

> In my judgment, if an accused person wants a legal practitioner before, or during, interrogation, the police investigators must stop their investigations and only resume after the accused has had consultations with his legal practitioner . . . If the police, in spite of the accused's request to have his lawyer present, continue with their interrogations thus denying him the protection of his constitutional rights and professional advice, it cannot be said that the police have not brought to bear upon the will of the accused by external impulses undue influence. The denial of access to a lawyer is in itself a form of psychological coercion and inducement which is brought to bear on the will of the accused.

Thus on this ground alone, he held the statements inadmissible and all six accused were acquitted.

To ensure their continued well-being, a right for legal representatives to make unannounced visits to detainees would be useful although regrettably this is not provided for in any of the ESA constitutions. In practice, given the likely reluctance on the part of government officials to co-operate, this might prove difficult to enforce and is perhaps a role better undertaken by human rights commissions.[51]

[50] The police action was later described in the Supreme Court as 'a calculated course of conduct that was persisted in for improper motives': see *S v Slatter* (unreported, Supreme Court of Zimbabwe, SC-49-84).

[51] For example, the Uganda Human Rights Commission has the express right to visit places of detention unannounced. Even here, the difficulty of such access is well illustrated by the experience of the human rights commissioners in Zambia who made concerted efforts to gain access to persons detained following the failed coup attempt in October 1997 but were continually rebuffed by state security officials. It was several weeks before they were able to gain access and later reported evidence of physical torture perpetrated against several of the detainees: see Zambia Human Rights Commission, *Report*, n.45 at paras. 4–5.

Right of access to a medical practitioner of the detainee's own choice

The constant risk of physical and mental abuse whilst in detention means that detainees must enjoy the right of access to a medical practitioner of his/her own choice *at all times*,[52] and at the state's expense. The responsibilities of medical practitioners are set out clearly in the 1975 World Medical Association Tokyo Declaration:[53]

> 1. [A] doctor shall not countenance, condone or participate in the practice of torture or other forms of cruel, inhuman or degrading procedures, whatever the offence of which the victim of such procedures is suspected, accused or guilty, and whatever the victim's beliefs or motives, and in all situations, including armed conflict and civil strife . . .

Duty to publicise the making of a detention order

The duty to publish the names of all detainees within a fixed period is a potentially useful safeguard against the 'disappearance' of detainees. In the ESA states the period varies between five days and thirty days,[54] although clearly the shorter period is eminently desirable. Rather than restricting the duty to publish the names of detainees to the *Government Gazette* as is the norm, details of the use of detention powers must be widely circulated. Thus the Constitution of Uganda requires the publication of the detainees names 'in the media',[55] and for the responsible Minister to inform Parliament every month in which it is sitting of the number of persons detained without trial.[56]

Overall, one glaring weakness is that none of the Constitutions place a specific duty on the detaining authority to inform detainees of their rights. As is discussed below, it falls to the courts to oversee the enjoyment of these rights.

[52] Cf. the less satisfactory phrase 'visited at any reasonable time' found in section 37(6)(d) of the South African Constitution. The other SEA Constitutions are largely silent on the matter.

[53] *Guidelines for Medical Doctors Concerning Torture and Other Cruel, Inhuman and Degrading Treatment or Punishment in Relation to Detention and Imprisonment.*

[54] The exception is Swaziland which provides no time limit. A further useful provision in the Constitutions of Uganda s.47(c) and South Africa 1996 s.37(6)(b) is the requirement to give particulars of the provision of law under which the detention is authorised.

[55] Article 47(c) requires the responsible Minister to publish in the *Government Gazette* and 'in the media' the number and names of the persons restricted or detained.

[56] Art. 49(1). Given the fact that a legislature may meet relatively infrequently, there is surely no justification for restricting such a report to the period when Parliament is sitting. A body similar to the Defence and Security Committee in Malawi that continues its work 'notwithstanding that Parliament stands adjourned' would provide a suitable model.

Justifying the need for detention

The need to justify detention is paramount for there is always the danger that the process is used as a purely investigatory tool or as a weapon to intimidate political opponents. A related problem is that vague grounds are often offered as justifying detention with terms such as suspicion of 'acting in a manner prejudicial to state security' or of being a 'danger to peace and good order' being particularly popular. It follows that justifying the need for detention is the state's fundamental obligation and it must therefore provide detainees with detailed reasons for their detention. Quite untenable is the argument that providing a specific time limit for the giving of reasons is unrealistic because the authorities need sufficient time to investigate a detainee's case thoroughly. Without a strict time limit it is possible for state officials to detain persons for periods far in excess of that allowed under the ordinary criminal justice system without furnishing any reasons for this and to then release them without them ever knowing the reasons for their detention. In view of its importance, it is disappointing to find considerable variations as to the appropriate time frame for providing reasons. These range from the quite unacceptable 'as soon as reasonably practicable'[57] or within fourteen days,[58] to the far more satisfactory requirement that reasons be given 'in writing within twenty-four hours'.[59]

The duty to give sufficient information to enable detainees to prepare their case and to make effective representations is also necessary. For example, in both Namibia and Kenya detainees are entitled to receive a statement in writing in a language that they understand specifying *in detail* the grounds upon which they are detained.[60] Of course what constitutes adequate reasons is contentious, for the state is normally anxious to disclose as little information as possible 'in the interests of security' or in order to protect its sources of information. For example, in the case of *Austin and Harper v Minister of State (Security)*[61] Blackie J. in the High Court of Zimbabwe neatly summarised the situation as follows:

[57] S.21(2) Constitution of Lesotho. [58] E.g. Constitution of Zambia, art. 26.

[59] A detainee must be given a statement in writing specifying the grounds for detention within twenty-four hours: see Constitution of Uganda art. 47(a).

[60] Constitutions of Namibia art. 24(2)(a) and Kenya s.83(2). In the case of Namibia, the Constitution helpfully adds that 'at their request this statement shall be read to them' (art. 24(2)(a)).

[61] 1986 (2) ZLR 28.

> (a) the applicants have had to make repeated approaches to the authorities and to the court for adequate reasons for their detention to be supplied to them; (b) such reasons as have been supplied have only been supplied at the last possible moment, often after the deadline set by the court, and then, repeatedly, in inadequate form; (c) that when they were released from detention and placed on remand pending a prosecution under the Official Secrets Act, the State was unable to produce sufficient information to satisfy the Supreme Court that there was a reasonable suspicion that the applicants had committed the offence of which they were charged; (d) that no meaningful inquiries have ever been made of the applicants as to the matters in which it was alleged that they have participated; (e) that the State has never once produced a set of reasons for detention entirely consistent with those previously given. Some reasons overlap with the previously given reasons, but in no case are such reasons consistent; (f) that even today the reasons supplied are inadequate and are not the reasons relied on at the time of their original detention.

In the event both the High Court and Supreme Court ruled that the reasons were inadequate and ordered the detainees release.

In the absence of a specific constitutional provision to give detailed reasons for detention, it is for the courts to impose the requirement. For example, in *Paweni v Minister of State (Security)*[62] a detention order alleged in general terms that the detainee had engaged in 'acts of economic sabotage against the State and People of Zimbabwe' and: 'It is considered that [his] activities pose a threat to the economic security of Zimbabwe'. It was argued on his behalf that these statements were so vague as to fail to comply with the constitutional requirement to give reasons for his detention. In upholding this argument, the court approved the views of Baron J. in the Zambian case of *Kapwepwe and Kaenga Attorney General* that the 'detainee must be furnished with sufficient information to enable him to know what is being alleged against him and to make meaningful representation'.[63]

What constitutes sufficient information to make a 'meaningful representation' varies from case to case but it is suggested that the reasons must be (i) such as *prima facie* warrant detention; (ii) sufficiently detailed to enable the detainee to make a meaningful representation to the review tribunal; and (iii) based upon information that is considered reliable.[64] This does not mean that it is never appropriate to place the evidence against

[62] [1985] LRC (Const) 612. [63] (1972) ZR 248, at p. 262.
[64] *Austin and Harper v Minister of State (Security)* 1986(2) ZLR 28.

the detainee before the court, for the distinction between the reasons and the evidence upon which they are based is not absolute. However, so long as the above criteria are satisfied, the court need look no further at that stage,[65] for it is not concerned with determining the truthfulness of the reasons for the detention. This is the sole responsibility of the review tribunal. Rather, the court is concerned with *fairness* to the detainee.[66] This means that the detainee must receive the basic facts and material particulars which form the foundation or basis of the detention because together they form the grounds upon which the detention order is based.[67] Thus courts have held that the giving of details concerning the date, time, place and material particulars of the alleged conduct of the detainee are sufficient to satisfy the obligation.[68] Conversely, accusations of 'carrying on subversive propaganda', or describing a person as 'a man of desperate habits and dangerous character'[69] or alleging that a person is a 'South African espionage agent and a threat to the security of Zimbabwe'[70] have been held invalid on the ground of vagueness. Of course, the mere failure to give a specific date for an alleged act in the grounds for detention, or to spell out the nature of the force planned against the state, does not necessarily prevent the making of a meaningful representation. Even so, there may be cases in which a date is significant and a failure to inform the detainee of it might hinder the preparation of his/her defence. For example, when the detainee is alleged to have taken part in an illegal meeting and details of the time, date and

65 *Ibid. See also R v Secretary of State for the Home Department ex parte Hosenball* [1977] 3 All ER 452; *R v Gaming Board ex parte Benaim and Khaida* [1970] 2 All ER 528; and *Bishop v Road Services Board* 1956 R & N 23.

66 *Evans and Hartlebury v Chairman of the Review Tribunal* HC-H-131-86 (High Court of Zimbabwe, unreported, 1986). The various statutory and moral requirements directing the methods and procedures that the tribunal should adopt are all embraced by this term: see *Barlin v Licensing Court of the Cape* 1924 AD 472; *Maxwell v Department of Trade and Industry* [1974] QB 523; and *Crow v Detained Mental Patients Special Board* 1985 (4) SA 83.

67 *Minister of Home Affairs v Austin and Harper* 1986 (1) ZLR 240; 1986 (4) SA 281; [1986] LRC (Const) 567. See also the Indian case of *State of Punjab v Talwandi* [1985] LRC (Const) 600 where Chandrachud C. J. stated: 'His right is to receive every material particular without which a full and effective representation cannot be made. If the order of detention refers to or relies upon any document, statement or other material, copies thereof have, of course, to be supplied to the detenue as held by this court in *Ichhu Devi Choraria v Union of India* (1981) 1 SCR 640 at 650.'

68 *State of Punjab v Talwandi.*

69 *State of Bombay v Atma Ram* 1951 SCR 167; *Sasthi v State of WBA* 1974 SCR 525.

70 *Minister of Home Affairs v Austin and Harper.*

place of the meeting are of such crucial significance that they must be provided.[71]

As only the grounds for detention are relevant at this stage, the detainee is not entitled to know the evidence or source of information upon which the allegations are based.[72] However, where possible, the reasons must set out an assessment by the detaining body as to the reliability of the information upon which the detention is based with such particularity as is consistent with security.[73] Inevitably it falls to the judiciary to ensure adequate protection of detainees by critically examining in each case whether it is possible to make a meaningful representation in response to the allegations.

The importance of such safeguards cannot be overestimated because, in the words of Justice Bhagwati, these 'are the barest minimum which must be observed before an executive authority can be permitted to preventively detain a person and thereby drown his right of personal liberty in the name of public good and social security'.[74]

Reviewing the detention order

Detainees are invariably given the constitutional right to an automatic review of their case by a tribunal or similar body. As this provides the only opportunity for an 'objective' assessment of the merits of the detention order, the review process must fulfil certain criteria.[75]

Firstly, a definite time frame within which a case is heard by the review tribunal is essential.[76] For example, the South African Constitution requires a 'review of the detention as soon as it is reasonably possible but not later than 10 days after the detention'.[77] A detainee must also have the

[71] An example given by Dumbutshena C. J. in *Austin and Harper v Chairman of the Detainees Review Tribunal* [1988] LRC (Const) 532 at p. 535. See also *Puta v Attorney General* (Supreme Court of Zambia, Judgment 25/83 (unreported) and *Musakanya v Attorney General* Supreme Court of Zambia Judgment 35/80 (unreported).

[72] *State of Punjab v Talwandi.* It appears that the detaining authority need not supply the detainee with the name of the informant: *Minister of Home Affairs v Austin and Harper.*

[73] *Minister of Home Affairs v Austin and Harper.*

[74] Bhagwati J. in *Khudram Das v State of West Bengal* (1975) 2 SCR 832, at p. 838.

[75] See further Dumbutshena C. J. in *Austin and Harper v Chairman of the Detainees Review Tribunal.*

[76] Merely providing that this should occur 'forthwith' or 'as soon as possible' is quite unacceptable: see in particular the judgment of Pittman J. in *Hickman and McDonald v Minister of Home Affairs* 1983 (2) ZLR 180.

[77] See s.37(6)(e) Constitution of South Africa.

right to apply for a further review at any stage following the expiration of a specified period after the previous review. The ESA constitutions vary markedly as to the appropriate time period although in principle the provision of a reasonably short period is necessary in order to emphasise the temporary and exceptional nature of the detention.[78]

Secondly, a demonstrably independent body must undertake the review. This is normally done by means of a review tribunal with a majority of its members having legal qualifications. The one exception is in Uganda where in an effort to ensure a wholly objective assessment of each case, the review is carried out by the Uganda Human Rights Commission.[79]

Thirdly, a detainee must enjoy certain rights. In particular the right to receive in advance the reasons submitted by the state to the tribunal justifying the detention (or continued detention).[80] Whilst proceedings are inevitably held in camera, a detainee must also enjoy the right to legal representation (at the state's expense) before the tribunal and to call witnesses on his/her behalf and to have an opportunity of responding to the state's case.

Fourthly, the review body must be empowered to order release if satisfied that continued detention is not necessary. In the past, most review bodies had the power merely to recommend release with the final decision being left to the executive and this remains the case in Kenya, Zimbabwe and Lesotho. This position is quite unacceptable for it ensures that the fate of detainees remains entirely in the executive's hands. It is satisfying to note that most of the new ESA Constitutions provide the review body with the power to order release. Linked with this is a prohibition on re-detention on the same ground(s) unless the state shows good cause to a court of law prior to such re-detention.[81] Finally, detainees must retain the right to seek habeas corpus and judicial review at any stage of their detention.

Consequences of breach of the constitutional safeguards

Given their significance, the constitutional safeguards are certainly mandatory rather than directory.[82] Thus the main issue concerns the

[78] For example every six months (Zimbabwe); every three months (Zambia); every ten days (South Africa); every five days (Malawi).

[79] This reflects concern over the lack of independence of past detention review tribunals.

[80] Again within a specified period. For example, not later than two days before the review: see s.45 (6)(d)Constitution of Malawi and s.37(6)(h) Constitution of South Africa.

[81] See, for example, s.37(7) Constitution of South Africa.

[82] See *York v Minister of Home Affairs* HC-H-218-82, unreported, 1982, at p. 16.

consequences attaching to a breach of one of those safeguards. It is trite to observe that where a detention order is itself unlawful, the detention is invalid *ab initio* and inevitably results in an order for release. This covers the situation where, for example, the maker of the detention order had no reasonable grounds for ordering the detention or the order itself was in the wrong form.[83]

The real controversy centres on where a detention order is validly made, but later a constitutional safeguard is contravened. The leading authority is the Zambian case of *Chipango v Attorney-General.*[84] Here the failure to furnish grounds for detention within the specified period was held to invalidate the detention despite being given only two days after the required date. In the High Court of Zambia, Magus J. referred with approval to the English decision in *Dale*[85] and stated that there was a breach of 'constitutional conditions subsequent to arrest' which were all mandatory and fundamental rights of the individual. Doyle C. J. in the Supreme Court then held that the breach went to the root of the detention and that the constitutional safeguards were:

> Introduced to provide for the protection of the rights and freedoms [of the people of Zambia] and where possible [the Constitution] should be interpreted effectively to protect the rights and freedoms. That the protection given is a limited protection is no reason for cutting down what is given.[86]

Thus was recognised the overriding principle that the executive's failure to comply with a constitutional safeguard renders the detention unlawful and leads inexorably to an order of release. This approach was later applied by the High Court of Zimbabwe in *York v Minister of Home Affairs*[87] for '[t]o hold otherwise it would have to be maintained that the order of the Minister can override a provision of the Constitution with which it

[83] For example, in Zimbabwe a detention order was ruled invalid where the police officer making the arrest was merely obeying orders and did not 'himself have reason to believe there were grounds for detention' as required by the section: *Holland v Commissioner of the Zimbabwe Republic Police* 1982 (2) ZLR 29.

[84] (1970) ZR 31 (HC).

[85] (1881) 6 QBD 376. Here Brett L. J. stated: 'I take it to be a general rule that the courts . . . will not allow any individual in this kingdom to procure the imprisonment of another unless he takes care to follow with extreme precision every form and every step in the process which is to procure that imprisonment', at p. 463.

[86] *Chipango v Attorney General* (1971) ZR 1, at p. 7.

[87] See above fn 82.

conflicts. That cannot be for the Constitution is the highest legal authority we know.'[88]

There remains some authority supporting the executive's right to remedy any failure to comply with the constitutional safeguards.[89] Yet the executive's immense power during a state of emergency cannot be allowed to erode the already limited rights of detainees and it is the courts' duty to protect those rights.[90] This includes requiring the executive to 'follow with extreme precision every form and every step' of the detention process[91] and to order release whenever this is not done.

Conditions in detention

Detainees are immensely vulnerable to mistreatment and, as the Commonwealth Human Rights Initiative has noted, it is essential to develop binding rules which secure the right of a detainee to fair and humane treatment during detention.[92] The fundamental principle is that a detainee retains all the rights of an ordinary citizen except those that are expressly or by implication taken away by law. These include proper housing, the

[88] Applying the words of Malone J. in *Kelshall v Munroe* (1971) 19 WIR 136, at p. 146.

[89] See, for example, the decision of the Supreme Court of Zimbabwe in *Dabengwa v Minister of Home Affairs* 1984 (2) SA 345; [1985] LRC (Const) 581: '. . . the violation of a safeguard relating to continued detention subsequent to the making of an order . . . must, initially be remedied by way of an order to ensure that the safeguard in question is afforded to the detainee', at p. 596. The judgment was based on several dubious authorities, including the cases of *Greene v Home Secretary* [1941] 3 All ER 388, *In re O'Laighleis* [1969] IR 93 and *R v Attorney-General and Brigadier Green, ex parte Olivia Grange and Eric Brown* (1976) 23 WIR 136. The name of the applicant and citation are incorrectly given in the judgment. See also the unsatisfactory Ugandan case of *Uganda v Commissioner of Prisons ex parte Matovu* [1966] EA 514 where it was held, using a contractual analogy, that procedural defects amounted to a condition subsequent and were curable by the appropriate detaining authority.

[90] See Dumbutshena J. in *York v Minister of Home Affairs* and *Hdhibandhu Das v District Magistrate of Cuttack* 1969 AIR SC 63.

[91] Support for this view is found in the judgment of Malone J. in *Kelshall v Munroe* where he stated at p. 140: '. . . in construing an emergency regulation it is necessary to ensure that there has been strict compliance with the terms of the enactment and that the enactment conforms with the Constitution'.

[92] CHRI, *Put Our World to Rights* 1991, London: CHRI, p. 76. For a suitable set of principles see the *Standard Minimum Rules for the Protection of Persons Detained Without Trial* in Harding and Hatchard, *Preventive Detention*, pp. 12–16 (set out at the end of this chapter). On the international position see H. Cook, 'Preventive Detention – International Standards and the Protection of the Individual', in S. Frankowski and D. Shelton, *Preventive Detention Law: a Comparative and International Perspective*, Nijhoff, Dordrecht, 1992.

right to wear one's own clothing, adequate food, protection from torture, adequate exercise and the right not to be kept in isolation.[93]

The appropriate treatment of detainees is also usefully set out in the United Nations *Code of Conduct for Law-Enforcement Officials*[94] which states:

> No law-enforcement official may inflict, instigate or tolerate any act of torture or other cruel, inhuman or degrading treatment or punishment, nor may any law-enforcement official invoke superior orders or exceptional circumstances such as a state of war or threat of war, a threat to national security, internal political security or any other public emergency as a justification of torture or other cruel, inhuman or degrading treatment or punishment.[95]

To enhance these practical safeguards requires that those responsible for detainees must be fully appraised of their obligations. This emphasises the importance of the general principle laid down in article 5 of the UN Declaration on the Protection of All Persons from Being Subjected to Torture and Other Cruel Inhuman or Degrading Treatment or Punishment:

> The training of law-enforcement personnel and of other public officials who may be responsible for persons deprived of their liberty shall ensure that full account is taken of the prohibition against torture and other cruel, inhuman or degrading treatment or punishment. This prohibition shall also, where appropriate, be included in such general rules or instructions as are issued in regard to the duties and functions of anyone who may be involved in the custody or treatment of such persons.[96]

Overview

Preventive detention laws undermine the right to freedom of movement and their gross abuse remains a blot on the human rights record of states throughout the region. Whilst the temptation exists to call for the repeal of all preventive detention laws, the reality is that they remain part of the

[93] This reflects the approach of the United Nations *Standard Minimum Rules for the Treatment of Prisoners* which are specifically stated also apply to persons detained without charge. See also the discussion in *Bull v Minister of State (Security)* HC-H-308-86, High Court of Zimbabwe, 1986, unreported and *Goldberg v Minister of Prisons* 1979 (1) SA 14, especially at p. 40.

[94] In this context, the term also covers state security and prison officials.

[95] Article 5.

[96] See also art. 10(1) UN Convention against Torture and Other Cruel, Inhaman or Degrading Treatment or Punishment.

legal landscape in all the ESA states. Indeed they may well attain a higher profile as states seek to make use of them in their efforts to combat threats of international terrorism.

The experience of gross misuse and abuse highlights the importance of the Zambian Constitutional Review Commission's view that the 'rights and safeguards of detained and restricted persons should be spelt out in the Constitution' and that 'the right to human dignity should never be diminished by [the] circumstances of a person's detention'.[97] The task therefore is to ensure that there are *meaningful* rights which are available to all those unfortunate enough to be detained without trial.

In considering the legal regimes within the ESA states, one is struck by the fact that although the basic detention process is similar, there are significant differences in the strength and scope of basic procedural rights for detainees. This suggests that insufficient attention has been, and is being paid, to providing clear, unambiguous and effective safeguards. Arguably, the development of an appropriate model 'code' dealing with such issues is necessary. The following provides a sound approach.

A model code of preventive detention law[98]

Justification for preventive detention laws

Preventive detention laws should be enacted only under constitutional provisions which set out clearly the situations in which such laws are justified and the limitations to be imposed on such laws, in particular those concerning the rights of detainees. They should be regarded as irregular laws, justified only by clear and present danger to public order or security or other similar emergency, and should remain in force, subject to renewal, for a limited period. The statute itself should recite the reasons for its being enacted, and there must be opportunity for review by the legislature of the necessity for the statute.

Access to judicial review

The constitution should make it clear that the judiciary's power to review preventive detention orders and procedures and the manner of detention is not and may not be ousted or restricted, and is to be exercised, whether

[97] Chapter 10 (2).
[98] This is taken from Harding and Hatchard *Preventive Detention*, pp. 7–10

on habeas corpus application or otherwise, in the same manner as the power to review other administrative acts.

The grounds for detention

The constitution or enabling statute must state as fully as possible, with definitions of key terms, the grounds on which a person may be detained. The grounds must relate to national security and law and order only and not be purely criminal or economic in nature. Where the grounds relate to possible future or anticipated conduct, detention should not be permissible except upon clear evidence that the relevant acts may be committed. Detention should not be permissible where the acts alleged may properly be considered by a criminal court. The statute must expressly provide for the practical carrying into effect of constitutionally guaranteed rights, which must include all those set out below.

Detaining authority

The power to detain must ultimately be vested in a minister, who must be answerable to the legislature for his decision. Any concurrent or preliminary police powers of arrest must be limited as to time.

Detention order procedure

Detention may only be lawful under the terms of a detention order, served on the detainee within seven days of arrest. It must be made by the minister. It must specify the grounds on which it is concluded that detention is necessary, and also the precise allegations of fact which lead the authority to be satisfied that the grounds cited exist. Neither grounds nor allegations may be expressed in the alternative. They must be clearly expressed, and must not be vague, overlapping or inconsistent. Detainees must be communicated with orally and in writing in a language they understand.

The detention order must be made for a period not exceeding six months, and will be invalidated by any failure to comply with the law. On the expiry of the six-month period no re-detention may be permitted except on fresh grounds occurring after release.

Right to counsel

The detainee must have early and regular access to counsel of his choice, or failing any choice, to competent counsel selected by the appropriate legal professional body, and at the expense of the state.

Review

Detainees must be allowed, within two months of the detention order, to make representations against their continued detention to a review body chaired by a person of judicial standing. The review body must have a statutorily prescribed code of procedure which complies with the requirements of natural justice. In particular detainees must be allowed legal representation and must be provided with the state's case, including the detailed evidence against them. Where the production of such evidence is alleged to be contrary to national security, the review body must have power to scrutinize the evidence itself to verify the claim. The review body must be empowered to order detainees' release if it is not satisfied that continued detention is necessary.

Judicial standards

The judiciary should enforce rigorously all procedural restrictions on preventive detention; failure to observe any restriction should be regarded as invalidating the detention. The judiciary should apply an objective, not a subjective, test of the reasonableness of executive satisfaction, and should be prepared to scrutinise the allegations of fact as well as the grounds for the detention.

Judicial inspection

The detaining authority must inform the appropriate judicial authority of the fact and place of detention within twenty-four hours thereof. Judicial authorities must be allowed access to detainees, including the right to speak to detainees in private, and to order medical examination of detainees.

Place of detention

Detainees must be detained in a place designated for the purposes of detention and which is reasonably near to their habitual residence. The place of detention should not be altered during the period of detention except for adequate reasons, on the authority of the minister, and with notification to the appropriate judicial authority.

Conditions of detention

The state must accede to any reasonable request by detainees for reading and writing materials, access to news media, and visits by friends, relatives, legal counsel and independent medical personnel, as well as food, drink, clothes and items of comfort provided by their friends or family. They must be kept in sanitary, light, temperate and airy conditions, with adequate bedding, space and opportunity for adequate daily exercise, and must be given wholesome and nutritious food and drink in sufficient and regular quantities. They must not be subjected to any form of torture, solitary confinement, or inhuman or degrading treatment, threats, or intimidation.

Detainees must not be detained together with convicted persons. They should retain all the legal rights of a citizen, including freedom of correspondence, other than that of personal liberty, and must not be subjected to any punitive measure. Any restraint on their liberty must be proportionate to the circumstances of the case and the factual situation justifying preventive detention measures.

Interrogation

Interrogating officers must keep records of all the times during which the detainee is interrogated, which must not be excessive. Interrogating officers must identify themselves by name or number to the detainee. A complete transcript, or audio or videotape recording, of the interrogation must be made available to the individual detainee or counsel.

Interrogation must be suspended where a judicial officer orders examination by a medical officer, until the medical officer is satisfied that it can continue without injury to the health of the detainee. In the case of a female detainee, a female officer must be continually present during all periods of interrogation.

Publicity

The executive must within seven days publish in the *Government Gazette* notice of the detention order and inform the detainee's nearest relative of the arrest and the place of detention. The state must regularly publish in the *Government Gazette* the names of all detainees and the places of their detention. The executive must also report annually to the legislature the total numbers of persons detained and released.

Time limits

All rights must be granted, and all procedural steps taken, promptly and within the period specified by the statute.

Liability

Failure to comply with any of the above principles should render detention invalid, and individual officers responsible for breaches should be liable to disciplinary proceedings, or criminal proceedings where appropriate. The state must compensate detainees in tort damages for any period of unlawful detention.

Foreigners

Foreign nationals must either be charged under criminal law, detained pending extradition or deportation under immigration law, but must not be otherwise detained.

13

Constitutional governance: the lessons from southern and eastern experience

In our opening chapter, we quoted the words of the Harare Commonwealth Declaration, enjoining the practice of good governance and democracy upon the members of the Commonwealth, eleven of which fall into our eastern and southern African grouping.[1] What lessons can be learned from the study undertaken in this book of the elements of constitutional governance in this regional setting? Underlying this study is the notion that good government in a democratic context is an essential prerequisite of development. This now appears to have acquired the status of received wisdom, although, as Patrick Chabal reminds us, the lesson of East Asia is that democracy is the outcome of, and not the precondition for, economic development.[2]

Constitutions do matter: the problem of constitutionalism

R. H. Green's remark that 'many African constitutions are simply irrelevant' reflects in a stark fashion the hardly controversial proposition that merely studying the constitutional texts may tell us very little about the realities of the political order which governs the daily life of citizens.[3] Writing nearly forty years ago, Stanley de Smith, one of the founding fathers of Commonwealth constitutional scholarship conceded that:

> ... [i]n developing countries constitutional factors will seldom play a dominant role in the shaping of political history. When choosing a particular

[1] See chapter 1, above p. 10.

[2] P. Chabal, 'The Quest for Good Government and Development in Africa: is NEPAD the Answer?' (2002) 78 *International Affairs* 448, at p. 455.

[3] See above, chapter 2, p. 22 n. 36. Green was writing in 1988, when many African states were subject to one-party rule. An obvious example from outside Africa of the irrelevance of a constitutional text is the rights ostensibly guaranteed to Soviet citizens under the 1936 Constitution of the Soviet Union, promulgated as hundreds of thousands went to their deaths in the great purges.

> method of enacting political practice one is merely adopting a tentative assumption that this method will provide the soundest basis for stable, democratic government.[4]

Of course, it is the spirit of the people rather than the text of any constitution, no matter how expertly drafted, which matters most. As Judge Learned Hand once observed:

> . . . I often wonder whether we do not rest our hopes too much upon constitutions, upon laws and upon courts. These are false hopes . . . Liberty lies in the hearts of men and women; when it dies there, no constitution, no law, no court can save it: no constitution, no law, no court can even do much to help it.[5]

However, a recent anthology of writings on constitutionalism in Africa emphasises the crucial value of the process of constitution-making and reform in the shaping of the governance agenda. Its editor describes with 'only slight trepidation' the developments at the commencement of the twenty-first century as constituting a 'new epoch in African history – the epoch of the rebirth of constitutionalism'.[6] Certainly, this study has shown that political change normally takes place through the medium of debate about constitutional change rather than that of constitutional breakdown. The most dramatic change of all, the transition in South Africa, was achieved not through the armed struggle but through a succession of constitutional conventions in which the political hatreds of decades were sublimated into a negotiating text. The changing political dispensation in Kenya, Malawi, Tanzania and Zambia has been signalled by relatively peaceful struggles over constitutional reform.[7] The process

[4] S. A. de Smith, *The New Commonwealth and its Constitutions*, Stevens, London, 1964, p. 83. This quotation began a contribution by James Gathii, a young Kenyan scholar, to a seminar on law and development in Nairobi shortly after the ending of the de jure one-party state. Gathii catalogued the process whereby the constitution was amended almost at will by the government before and during the one-party era so that the document was used as a mere tool to serve the political purposes of the dominant party, KANU. See James T. Gathii, 'Kenya's Legislative Culture and the Evolution of the Kenya Constitution', in Y. Vyas et al., (eds.), *Law and Development in the Third World*, Faculty of Law, University of Nairobi, Nairobi, 1994, p. 74.

[5] L. Hand, *The Spirit of Liberty* (3rd edn) Hamish Hamilton, London, 1960, pp. 189–90.

[6] J. Olaka-Onyango, 'Constitutionalism in Africa, Yesterday, Today and Tomorrow' in J. Olaka-Onyango (ed.), *Constitutionalism in Africa: Creating Opportunities, Facing Challenges*, Fountain Publishers, Kampala, 2001, p. 1.

[7] See chapter 3. The regional exceptions to the pattern are Lesotho (above at p. 93), Uganda between 1966 and 1986 and Zimbabwe since 2000. In the latter case, although a constitutional referendum and parliamentary and presidential elections have occurred, the

is often challenging for, as the Foreword to the 2002 Report of the Kenya Constitutional Review Commission (KCRC) records:

> In the face of extraordinarily difficult circumstances, with attempts internal and external to derail the process, the Commission has focused on its tasks . . .[8]

However, the Report is positive about the role of constitutional reform:

> The Commission considers that the role of a constitution in Kenya's governance is not to consolidate existing power relations and structure. It is to facilitate social and economic changes that the people want and which are necessary to ensure a democratic, participatory and just society.[9]

Even if there are thus grounds for optimism about the management of political change, the experience of the ESA region examined in this book highlights recurring problems in the assurance of constitutional governance. This concluding chapter seeks to summarise these difficulties and indicate some possible solutions.

Political culture

Some scholars, approaching the issues from the perspective of political science and related disciplines have argued that the failure of the good governance project in Africa lies deep in the nature of African political society. An analysis of these issues is beyond the scope of this study, but essentially the argument is that, despite the veneer of constitutional apparatus, African political society remains essentially 'patrimonial' or 'neo-patrimonial'. Patrimonialism may be described as a situation where the ruler and his or her officials are perceived to be above the law and insulated from a rational legal order or from constitutional rule.[10] According to Chabal, contemporary African politics are best understood as the exercise of neo-patrimonial power, so that, despite the formal political structures

level of political violence has been such that Zimbabwe became the first Commonwealth country to be the subject of a report of the Commonwealth Ministerial Action Group on the Harare Declaration (CMAG) in circumstances where there had not been an unconstitutional overthrow of a democratically elected government.

[8] CKRC Report, p. iii. [9] Ibid., p. 13

[10] Grace Patrick Tumwine-Mukubwa, 'Ruled from the Grave: Challenging Antiquated Constitutional Doctrines and Values in Commonwealth Africa', in J. Oloka-Onyango *Constitutionalism in Africa*, p. 302. The analysis is derived from that of Yash Ghai, 'The Theory of the State in the Third World and the Problematics of Constitutionalism', in Greenberg, Katz, Oliviero and Wheatley, (eds) *Constitutionalism and Democracy*, p. 717.

in place, personalised power is exercised essentially as an informal system of patronage, to which administrative and electoral processes are subordinate.[11] Commenting on the removal in August 2002 of Simba Makoni, Zimbabwe's finance minister by President Mugabe, an anonymous former ZANU-PF official is quoted as confirming the personal nature of Mugabe's rule.[12] Hopefully, the solution may lie in the gradual emergence of a new political generation liberated from traditional patrimonial linkages.[13]

Historical legacy: colonial and post-colonial

This study suggests that there are two roots of the 'cultural' problem of constitutionalism: the colonial experience overlaid with the post-colonial imposition of the one- (or dominant-) party system. The legacy of colonialism is frequently offered as an explanation for Africa's current ills and western criticism of Africa's development performance is often branded as 'neo-colonialist'. There was a fierce reminder of this rhetoric in the speeches of Presidents Mugabe and Nujoma at the Johannesburg Earth Summit in September 2002.[14] Undoubtedly, colonial government was not conducive to the development of a culture of the rule of law in a Diceyan sense, although there were hasty and belated attempts to create a framework for constitutional government in the last years of colonial rule.[15] Indeed, for most of its history, colonial government was by nature authoritarian and its legacy provided a tempting basis for similar conduct by the successor rulers of the new states.[16]

[11] Chabal, 'The Quest for Good Government', 450.

[12] 'It's Mugabe and only Mugabe who has the power. Everyone else does what they are told, and you get rewarded on the basis of how noisy you are in supporting the old man. What happened to Makoni shows where being principled gets you', *The Times*, London, 26 August 2002.

[13] Certainly, European democracies are a product of centuries of such evolution. Thus eighteenth century British politics was based on patronage and distribution of spoils and only slowly evolved in the nineteenth century into a 'modern' democratic system based on parties competing for electoral support on the basis of policy, and on administration by an independent public service. 'Western countries are democratic not because some new regime abruptly and arbitrarily put in place the instruments of a democratic order. They are democratic because democracy is the political order which has emerged from several centuries of economic and political change as the most effective and legitimate system of political accountability': see P. Chabal 'A few considerations on democracy in Africa', (1998) 74(2) *International Affairs* 289, at p. 299.

[14] 'Hands off my country, Mugabe tells Blair', *The Times*, London, 3 September 2002.

[15] See chapter 2, p. 15.

[16] See chapter 2, pp. 14 and 19. 'Authoritarian' does not imply there was no acquiescence or collusion on the part of the 'subject peoples'. Evidence of this is provided by the tiny number

Given this inheritance, the next part of the historical legacy can now be identified as the post-colonial period from the 1960s until the beginning of the 1990s. During this period, Kenya, Lesotho, Malawi, Tanzania, Uganda and Zambia all experienced de jure one-party government. The shortcomings of this system were exposed by the 1991 Nyalali Commission in Tanzania, of which the first president Julius Nyerere had been the apostle of one-partyism. In recommending the adoption of a plural political system, the Commission found that the one-party system had concentrated excessive power in the hands of the presidency, undermined the independence of the judiciary and downgraded the role of parliament and the civil service.[17] Moreover, as the Zambian example shows, an understanding of the poor performance of the parastatals, or state-owned monopoly enterprises, which were a particular feature of the one-party state systems, is important to an appreciation of the crisis in African development.[18] The one-party legacy thus has two aspects: the degradation of the political process and the stagnation of the economy. However, as a commentator pointed out shortly before the general transition to multipartism:

> [A] criticism of the one-party system is not necessarily an endorsement of the multi-party system. Africa's political problems are by far too complex to admit of such an easy solution.[19]

This has proved to be a salutary warning. Moreover, it must not be forgotten that the one-party state, now apparently consigned to the dustbin of failed political experiments, was once lauded by international commentators as a prescription for good governance and human rights in Africa:

of British personnel deployed in the government and security services of the African colonial territories. In 1939, there were 515 administrative officers and 585 police and military officers in the British colonial service in the territories which now make up the SEA states (excluding Zimbabwe and South Africa) (A. Kirk-Greene, *On Crown Service: a History of HM Colonial and Overseas Services 1837–1997*, I. B. Taurus, London, 1999, p. 38).

[17] See p. 20. The apostle became the apostate by casually announcing at a press conference in 1990 that the ruling single party, Chama Cha Mapinduzi (CCM), should consider political change: 'The one party is not Tanzania's ideology: having one party is not God's will', Mwalimu reportedly told his startled audience (J. A. Widner, *Building the Rule of Law: Francis Nyalali and the Road to Judicial Independence in Africa*, Norton, New York and London, 2001, p. 296).

[18] Roger Tangri, *The Politics of Patronage in Africa*, James Currey, Oxford, 1999, p. 5. See also pp. 29–31 for the sad story of Zambia's Industrial Development Corporation (INDECO).

[19] Kibuta Ong'wamuhana, 'Party Supremacy and the State Constitution in Africa's One-Party States: the East African Experience' (1989) 17 *Melanesian Law Journal* 67, at p. 80.

> [A] one-party state can afford citizens more genuine opportunities for political choice than the multi-party system it has displaced, and it can also ensure greater popular participation and involvement in public affairs.[20]

The search for popular and durable constitutions in the 1990s and beyond

A common criticism of the independence Constitutions were that they were 'imposed' from outside and were therefore lacking in local roots or popular legitimacy.[21] The one-party state Constitutions contained merely such adaptations as were necessary to entrench the new dispensation.[22] The serious attempts made during the constitution 're-making' period of the 1990s and beyond to achieve autochthony are therefore instructive. As this study has shown, while valuable resources were invested in Constitutional Commissions and elaborate consultative exercises, these processes were often flawed, particularly by the retention of executive discretion to determine the contents of the final draft constitution. Even so, the rejection of the draft Zimbabwean constitution by a national referendum in February 2000, shows that the people's voice may be heard even in the face of the best efforts of an authoritarian regime.[23] In contrast, the process of the legitimisation of the 'final' South African Constitution by a consensual process involving parliament, the constitutional court and a wide measure of consultation played a major role in providing a secure framework for the new political order.[24]

[20] Shridath Ramphal, then Commonwealth Secretary-General, writing a Preface to the publication of the papers derived from a seminar organised in 1977 by the International Commission of Jurists on 'Human Rights in a One-party State'. See ICJ *Human Rights in a One-Party State*, Search Press, London, 1978, p. 8. Another historical irony may be found in the fervent opposition to the introduction of a one-party state in Zimbabwe by Jonathan Moyo, in 2003 a leading member of the ZANU-PF government and scourge of the opposition MDC: see J. Moyo, 'The Dialectics of National Unity and Democracy in Zimbabwe', in I. Manaza and L. Sachikonye (eds.), *One Party State and Democracy*, SAPES, Harare, Zimbabwe, 1991, pp. 83–102.

[21] Although this study has shown that there was a measure of consultation with the local designated leadership during the drafting process, this certainly did not extend to the people as a whole. See p. 16.

[22] Compare, for example, the texts of the Zambian Constitutions of 1964 and 1973.

[23] See p. 40.

[24] See p. 37. The Report of the Constitution of Kenya Review Commission (CKRC), September 2002, is significantly entitled 'The People's Choice', and places great emphasis on the need for wide popular participation in the process of constitution-making: 'The review has provided Kenyans for the first time ever a chance to decide on the values and rules by which they wish to govern themselves', p. 3.

The drafting and adoption of a constitution, however, is only the beginning of the good governance journey. This study shows how the apparently dry and technical subject of constitutional amendment procedures and their use and misuse may shed light on the health of the body politic. As the Zimbabwean experience prior to the parliamentary elections of 2000 shows, where the amendment process is confined to parliament and the government commands the requisite majority, the Constitution can be amended at the whim of the executive. The Constitution is in effect undermined by constitutional means, immune from challenge through the courts.[25]

Excessive concentration of power in the executive

Here the lawyer is confronted with the reality of political power. Personal rule of the 'Big Men' has been the tradition in the ESA states, whether relatively benign – Nyerere, Kaunda, King Mswati III and Museveni, or despotic – Amin, Banda and, in his later years, Mugabe. The Constitution alone cannot act as a brake upon the arbitrary exercise of executive power. As we have seen, in Zimbabwe the Constitution formally obliges the President to act on the advice of his/her Cabinet, but in practice this body acts as a rubber stamp to decisions taken by the President and the ruling party politburo.[26] Even under the 'new democracies', examples of successful 'Cabinet revolts' are rare.[27] Indeed, it has been argued that the re-introduction of multi-party politics and periodic contested elections have served to legitimate the authoritarian behaviour of 'traditional' ruling elites such as Mugabe's ZANU-PF in Zimbabwe.[28] However, the failure of parliament and the judiciary to play their designated constitutional roles has facilitated the abuse of executive power, as is demonstrated by salutary examples where judicial and parliamentary independence have been asserted successfully.[29]

[25] See chapter 4. At the 2000 parliamentary elections ZANU-PF narrowly lost its two-thirds majority required for constitutional amendment.

[26] See p. 70.

[27] One example was the successful opposition of the Zambian Cabinet to President Chiluba's plans to amend the Constitution so as to enable him to stand for a third term: see p. 71.

[28] See, for example, Chabal, 'The Quest for Good Government', 460 et seq.

[29] The vigorously independent stance of the judiciary in Zimbabwe in respect of abuse of executive power is an obvious example. Examples of parliamentary assertiveness are much rarer.

The conclusion to be drawn is that effective constraints on executive power must be derived from a shift in political culture rather than from constitutional devices alone. The formal checks and balances found in the constitutional dispersal of power among state organs have been too easily undermined by the 'imperial' presidencies. An independent media, an effective trade union movement, a vigorous NGO community and other elements of civil society may provide a surer foundation for a true culture of accountability. Another not unfamiliar way of tackling the problem of executive power is suggested by the Constitution of Kenya Review Commission: a division of 'real' power between the President and a Prime Minister. Under this system, the President will become the guardian of the Constitution: the poacher of excessive executive power will now become the gamekeeper of constitutionality.[30]

Lack of parliamentary autonomy and effective political accountability

One of the arguments in favour of the one-party state was that political parties in Africa tend to form on the basis of ethnicity, appealing to a particular tribal or clan grouping rather than on the basis of competing national policies.[31] Thus political parties do not provide access to the political system on the basis of effective popular participation in the political process. Chapter 6 offers an analysis of the key issues relating to the creation of political parties, funding and the holding of free and fair elections so that the competition between parties is fairly conducted so as to reflect the will of the electorate. These problems are not confined to the ESA countries – the 'decline' of political parties and its impact on the democratic process is a constant refrain in western political debate. However, the region exhibits some acute problems and suggests some solutions in terms, for example, of guaranteeing fair access of political parties to the media during election campaigns.[32] The electoral process is an area where the ESA states have almost invariably accepted and welcomed international monitoring. The Commonwealth has played a major role in this activity since the key part played by the Commonwealth Observer

30 CKRC, pp. 56 and 86.

31 This also currently provides President Museveni of Uganda with a justification for 'no-party politics'. See p. 20.

32 For example, the treatment of political parties under the South African Independent Media Commission Act, see p. 113.

Group in observing the 1980 'independence' election in Southern Rhodesia. It has now become routine for a Commonwealth Observer Group to observe elections in ESA states.[33] However, the result of such monitoring is not beneficial to the local democratic process if there has been a failure to 'call' a flawed election, thus conferring international legitimacy on a government whose democratic credentials are highly suspect.[34]

Even a patently transparent and fair electoral process does not ensure that, once elected, parliamentarians will play their essential role in the democratic process by acting as an effective check on the exercise of executive power. As we have seen, the role of parliament was gravely undermined in one-party states, where it was reduced to the role of a sub-committee of the ruling party.[35] The experience of the ESA states shows, however, that, even if parliament is restored to a key position in the constitutional edifice, it may not 'work' as a mechanism of democratic accountability. Various devices have been tried in the states to make the legislature more representative *of* the people. While Members nominated solely at the presidential discretion may thwart the democratic will of the majority,[36] the election of members by special interest groups likely to be otherwise under-represented (such as the young or disabled) has been tried in Uganda.[37] In this context, the most controversial issue is the chronic under-representation of women. Overall in the region, women make up some 18.1 per cent of parliamentarians of all types, but this figure includes all the provincial legislatures and the national assembly of South Africa, where representation in some cases exceeds 30 per cent. The South African record (which compares favourably with the democracies of Northern Europe) suggests that women's representation will be enhanced not only by artificial quotas but by the mobilisation of women in the political process as occurred through the ANC party structures including the Women's League during the transition to democracy.[38]

[33] Since 1990, elections have been observed in Kenya, Lesotho, Malawi, Namibia, South Africa, Tanzania (including Zanzibar) Zambia and Zimbabwe. See A. Sives, 'A Review of Commonwealth Election Observation' (2001) 39 *Commonwealth and Comparative Politics* 132–49. However the Commonwealth was not invited to observe the last presidential election.

[34] See pp. 118–119, regarding the verdict of the Commonwealth Observer Groups on elections in Kenya and Lesotho.

[35] See p. 68.

[36] As came close to happening in the 2000 parliamentary election in Zimbabwe.

[37] See p. 125. [38] See p. 129.

On the fundamental issue of holding the executive accountable to parliament, the record of ESA states generally is not impressive. Parliament is often treated with contempt by the executive, so that, for example, Ministers do not trouble to turn up to answer parliamentary questions or, when they do, they provide inadequate answers.[39] As the Zimbabwean example shows, parliament may prove totally inadequate in the face of systematic human rights violations by agents of the executive.[40] A persistent problem is that parliament lacks the independent resources to fulfil its oversight role. One solution, therefore, is to provide effective mechanisms to ensure parliamentary autonomy. Thus, for example, Kenya, Uganda and Tanzania have each created Parliamentary Service Commissions to help ensure that Parliament controls its own budget, staff and facilities.[41]

The other side of the coin is the need to ensure accountability of parliamentarians to the people. Here part of the problem stems from the fact that the ESA states have generally followed the Westminster-style constituency model of election. However, this may be slowly changing. In South Africa the National Assembly is elected on a party-list basis whilst the mixed member proportional system was used in the 2002 Lesotho elections, so as to combine the MPs' constituency identity with equitable party balance. In the case of Kenya, the CKRC has also recommended the adoption of the Lesotho system.[42] Unfortunately, MPs in the region are often guilty of neglect of their constituents and their interests. Here the Ugandan solution of confering a constitutional right upon the electorate to recall and replace an errant member merits attention.[43]

Threats to the independence and integrity of the judiciary

The independence of the judiciary (including the magistracy) is the cornerstone of the rule of law and constitutes one of the fundamental political values of the Commonwealth.[44] The principle is enshrined in the constitutions of all the ESA states. However the elaborate provisions prescribing the method of appointment of judges and providing for security of tenure

39 See p. 131.
40 See p. 133, referring to the Matabeleland atrocities in the 1980s.
41 See p. 141. 42 CKRC Report, p. 49.
43 See p. 140. This device currently operates in the context of the 'no-party' system.
44 The Harare Commonwealth Declaration, 1991, refers to 'the protection and promotion of the fundamental political values of the Commonwealth: democracy . . . the rule of law and the independence of the judiciary . . .'

and other safeguards do not guarantee effective independence in the face of the aggressive intrusion of the executive and other state organs. Thus between June 2001 and September 2002, the independence of the higher judiciary in Zimbabwe, a model of independence under a succession of courageous chief justices, was progressively undermined by a systematic campaign of intimidation, including the invasion of the Supreme Court building by pro-government activists, and culminating in the arrest and detention of a recently retired judge in a pre-dawn police raid on his residence.[45] Our analysis shows that the independence of the judiciary may be undermined in less spectacular ways: politicising the appointment process; threatening judges on contract terms with non-renewal for improper reasons; and denying the judiciary adequate salaries and resources.[46] A most insidious threat to the independence and integrity of the judiciary is represented by the corruption of judges themselves. This is now increasingly being recognised as a serious problem at all levels.[47] The underlying solution lies in the development of a culture of executive respect for judicial independence, which in turn depends on the existence of a strong and independent legal profession, responsive to the needs of the people as a whole.[48]

One very positive feature of the record of the judiciary in the ESA states is the standard set by their judgments in terms of a purposive and 'living' interpretation of the bare words of the constitution – constitutionalism in action. As a judge of the Botswana Court of Appeal put it in a leading judgment on sex discrimination in citizenship matters:

> . . . [T]he primary duty of the judges is to make the Constitution grow and develop in order to meet the just demands and aspirations of an ever developing society.[49]

Judges in ESA states have produced landmark decisions on issues such as the death penalty, corporal punishment, access to medical treatment

[45] *The Times*, London, 14 September 2002. [46] See chapter 9, *passim*.

[47] As President Mwanawasa of Zambia observed, in swearing in a new Chief Justice whose predecessor had resigned after allegations of the corrupt receipt of a large sum in US dollars from the former President: 'The judiciary has been battered and its levels of integrity has gone down.' The President also announced a substantial increase in judicial salaries in order to attract private practitioners to the bench. (*The Post*, Lusaka, 10 August 2002). The Report of the Kenya Constitutional Review Commission, published in September 2002, records that '[t]he judiciary rivals politicians and the police for the most criticised sector of Kenyan public society today' (at p. 63)

[48] 'An independent, organised legal profession is an essential component in the protection of the rule of law' (*Latimer House Guidelines*, VIII.3).

[49] Quoted above, see p. 180.

and gender equality, making a contribution to constitutional and human rights jurisprudence of Commonwealth-wide and indeed global significance.[50]

The failure to develop effective methods of devolution of power to local communities

The analysis of the ills of the African body politic has long contained references to the alienation of over-centralised state structures from the mass of the people, particularly in the rural areas where most people live, and the absence of elements of genuine local participatory democracy able to foster self-management and empowerment.[51] The ESA region in general has not had an impressive record in this regard. We have observed that South Africa and Uganda are the only two states that have made serious efforts to decentralize power.[52] Even in the case of the latter there is considerable academic debate about the effectiveness of devolution arrangements in the context of Uganda's 'no-party state' system, although there appears to be real competition for political office in much of the local government system.[53]

A return to multi-partyism may enable opposition parties to capture nominal control of local councils, but this may do little to relax the grip of central government.[54] Certainly devolution also carries considerable historical baggage in the ESA region; British colonial attempts at 'indirect rule' devolved power to unelected chiefs who might, or might not, have had traditional legitimacy. At the macro-level of devolution, the attempt at the imposition of federal or quasi-federal structures was swept away

[50] See, for example, *Catholic Commission for Justice and Peace in Zimbabwe v Attorney-General* [1993] 2 LRC 279 and *State v Makwanyane* [1995] 1 LRC 269 (death penalty); *Ex parte Attorney-General Namibia in re Corporal Punishment by organs of State* 1991 (3) SA 76; *Ephrahim v Pastory* [1990] LRC (Const) 757 (gender discrimination); *Minister of Health and others v Treatment Action Campaign and others* [2002] 5 LRC 266 (access to medical treatment).

[51] See for example, the contributions to 'Pluralism, Participation and Decentralization in Sub-Saharan Africa', 1989, *Third World Legal Studies.*

[52] See p. 195.

[53] Ole Therkildsen, 'Uganda's Referendum 2000: the Silent Boycott: a Comment' (2002) *African Affairs* 101, at pp. 231–41.

[54] R. Southall and G. Wood, 'Local Government and the Return to Multi-Partyism in Kenya', *African Affairs* (1996), 95, 501–27. Southall and Wood show that, although opposition parties in Kenya captured notional control of a large majority of local councils, 'virtually nothing changed in local government, as KANU ran rings around the opposition'.

by the first generation of nationalist leaders in Kenya and Uganda. The Federation of the Rhodesias and Nyasaland, although a sensible exercise in functional co-operation, represented to African leaders a device for maintaining the domination of European settlers over the African majority.[55] In South Africa, there was fierce resistance on the part of the ANC negotiators in the transition process to federal structures (tainted with the legacy of *apartheid*), although the present South African Constitution offers the greatest degree of devolved power to provinces in the region, while also providing for a comprehensive tier of local government.[56]

The lessons from the ESA experience are that if devolved institutions are to be effective, they must be adequately resourced and their autonomy must be respected by central government. At the local level, they must involve civil society so as to mobilise those traditionally excluded from political processes. If people have a sense of empowerment, they will impose accountability on their representatives at all levels and be encouraged to take responsibility for the better management of their own affairs. Thus developments at the local level may be seen as the basis for good governance. However, as the experience of the ESA states shows, the realisation of the many admirable ideas about devolution and local government reform which circulate amongst developmentalists, public administration experts and international organisations requires a serious local interest in re-negotiating the state structure in order to provide for greater public participation, rather than simply in capturing it for the loot which it can provide.[57]

Undermining the Constitution by 'constitutional' and 'extra-constitutional' means

By the standards of francophone Africa, the Sudan and Commonwealth West Africa, the ESA region has been a relatively coup-free zone. Overt military intervention in politics has been confined to Lesotho and Uganda.[58]

[55] The partnership between European and African, as one European political leader put it with striking candour, would be that of the rider and horse: see D. Judd and P. Slinn, *The Evolution of the Modern Commonwealth 1902–1980*, London: Macmillan, p. 102.

[56] See p. 195. [57] Southall and Wood, 'Local Government', p. 526.

[58] See p. 242. The army takeover in Lesotho and Idi Amin's copybook military coup during President Obote's absence at the Commonwealth Heads of Government Meeting in Singapore had been preceded by 'prime-ministerial coups' by Chief Jonathan in Lesotho in 1970 and Milton Obote himself in 1966. By a neat symmetry, Jonathan and Obote were themselves the victims of the coups in 1986 and 1971.

However, as chapters 4, 11 and 12 demonstrate, there is still need for constant vigilance against the threat of military intervention or its undue involvement in government. Moreover, there are also ways in which the constitutional order may be undermined without overt breakdown. Chapter 4 demonstrates how, where the amendment process is confined to parliament, the Constitution may become a plaything in the hands of a government with an overwhelming majority, and the constitutional amendment process a mechanism for ousting the jurisdiction of the Courts and undermining the rule of law.[59] Chapter 12 demonstrates that the exercise of emergency powers may be used by the executive to maintain itself in power in defiance of the popular will or to retain powers of detention without trial – a measure commonly directed against political opponents. The longevity of states of emergency in some ESA states is remarkable. For example, in Zambia the state of emergency declared in 1964 by the Governor of Northern Rhodesia to deal with a minor uprising was retained by President Kaunda until 1991 – a period of no less than twenty-seven years. Similarly, the state of emergency proclaimed by the Rhodesian government in 1965 in order to facilitate the illegal declaration of independence was retained by the independent government of Zimbabwe until 1990.[60] Of course such states of emergency are invariably restricted in time as well as being subject to regular review at the behest of parliament. However, no legislature in an ESA state has ever refused to approve the declaration or renewal of a state of emergency. Modern Constitutions must therefore deploy rather more sophisticated devices to deal with potential abuse.[61]

As far as 'orthodox' military coups are concerned, the constitutional order is ultimately at the mercy of the gun. However, the Constitution may contain an anti-coup provision so as to keep the Constitution alive even if there is an interruption of constitutional government as a result of armed intervention. This also provides a basis for judicial intervention and the subsequent reassertion of the rule of law against the coup's perpetrators.[62] A culture of accountability on the part of the military to

[59] See p. 45.

[60] See chapter 12, passim. As pointed out in that chapter, the use and abuse of emergency powers is another legacy of colonialism. In 1959, Nyasaland (later Malawi) was even described as a 'police state' by the report of a commission of inquiry appointed by the British government: see Judd and Slinn, *Evolution of the Modern Commonwealth*, p. 103.

[61] See p. 279.

[62] See p. 247. Judicial decisions from Uganda and Lesotho reflect the ambiguities of the judicial response to coups.

civilian institutions provides the surest innoculation against threats from this source to the constitutional order.[63]

Weakness of civil society and lack of effective independent oversight institutions

We have seen that one of the structural weaknesses of the ESA states has been the failure of the parliamentary accountability mechanisms that are supposedly the bulwark of Westminster-style democracy. Hence the need for alternative independent institutions such as commissions dealing with human rights and the office of the ombudsman. Such institutions are a prominent feature of the body politic in the ESA states and are found in their most elaborate form in chapter 9 of the 1996 Constitution of South Africa which establishes six 'institutions supporting constitutional democracy', including the Public Protector (Ombudsman), the Human Rights Commission, the Commission for the Promotion and Protection of the Rights of Cultural, Religious and Linguistic Communities and a Commission for Gender Equality.[64] The experience of the ESA states provides an instructive basis for assessing the role and value of such institutions in developing countries and highlighting some of the problems impeding their successive operation, such as denial of adequate resources and attacks on their independence by the executive.[65] These institutions can undoubtedly help to foster and sustain autonomous civil society institutions. Thus an effective human rights commission can help facilitate the activities of non-governmental human rights organisations. However, they in turn are dependent upon co-operation with the very civil society institutions such as a free press and an independent trade union movement which are often weak in developing countries.[66]

[63] See, for example, the brave words of the Constitution of South Africa, 1996, section 199: '(5) The security services must act, and must teach and require their members to act, in accordance with the Constitution and the law. . . . (8) To give effect to the principles of transparency and accountability, multi-party parliamentary committees must have oversight of all security services . . .' This issue is examined in detail in chapter 11, p. 251.

[64] Section 181(1). The CKRC (p. 83) cautions against too many independent institutions and proposes a 'Commission for Human Rights and Administrative Justice', which would combine the functions of people's protector and human rights commissioner.

[65] See chapter 10, passim.

[66] Some commentators suggest that the 'patrimonial' nature of African politics, in which the state is not institutionally differentiated from society, prevents civil society from developing as an autonomous foil to the state: 'The currently fashionable view that the impetus for democratic change will come from 'civil society' is . . . based on wishful thinking rather than a proper examination of the evidence on the ground' (Chabal, 'The Quest for Good Government', p. 461).

Conclusion: the Commonwealth path to good governance

It has been too easy for too long for African political leaders to blame failures in the fields of good governance and development on the colonial legacy and to reject international criticism as being merely 'neo-colonialist'.[67] However, African states will not realise their development potential unless problems of governance and of the effective management of resources for the benefit of all their peoples are resolved. In this sense, the ESA states are sharing with the rest of the international community the task of ensuring good governance for their peoples. As this book shows, these states have faced and continue to face acute difficulties in their 'governance journey'. However, they are in no sense especially delinquent compared with other countries both developed and developing. In some matters, indeed, the ESA states have positive lessons to teach the international community as a whole, for example, on issues relating to the realisation of gender balance, the development of national oversight institutions and in pioneering human rights standards in areas such as the abolition of the death penalty and corporal punishment.

As far as the ESA states are concerned, there may be two reasons for optimism in terms of the scope of this book. Firstly, at the Commonwealth level, despite the muted response of Heads of Government to the Zimbabwe crisis in 2002, the organisation is in a unique position to develop and implement principles of good governance, untainted by the ethos of colonialism or imperialism. All fifty-four members, including fourteen from the African mainland, have subscribed to the fundamental political values of the Commonwealth, including democracy, just and honest government, human rights, freedom of expression and the rule of law. Furthermore, in addition to well-established monitoring procedures such as those which relate to the conduct of elections, the Commonwealth has introduced a unique mechanism through the Commonwealth Ministerial Action Group to address serious or persistent violations of the Harare Principles which embody those fundamental political values. These values are, therefore, by the express will of the governments concerned, also African values, mediated through an international organisation in which African countries play an active leadership role.[68] These Commonwealth

[67] See, for example, President Mugabe's speech to the Johannesburg Summit, 2 September, 2002, *The Times*, London, 3 September 2002.

[68] In 2002, Africa provided the immediate past Chairman-in-Office of the Commonwealth (President Mbeki of South Africa), the next Chairman-in-Office (President Obasanjo of Nigeria) and the immediate past Secretary-General (Chief Anyaoku).

processes are reinforced on a pan-African basis by the New Partnership for Africa's Development (NEPAD) which commits African countries to the upholding of global standards of democracy and good governance.[69] Secondly, there are signs that the peoples of the ESA countries themselves are willing to throw off the 'patrimonial' yoke and insist on the shaping of institutions that will provide for effective democratic accountability and real improvement in governance standards.

Such accountability is not ensured by, for example, the mere process of multi-party elections or apparent respect for democratic forms. It has been argued that forms of accountability which African peoples accept as legitimate are of more significance than participation in formal 'rituals' of multi-party democracy.[70] However, the troubled history of the two 'traditional' monarchies of Lesotho and Swaziland does not suggest that rulers with an obvious claim to legitimacy in the traditional sense are better able to deliver good governance to their peoples. Nor does it indicate that African peoples do not 'want' democracy.[71] Further, the rule of the more recently entrenched patrimonial elites no longer appears acceptable. Significantly entitled, 'The People's Choice', the 2002 Report of the Constitution of Kenya Review Commission reveals in a vivid fashion the aspirations of the people of a Commonwealth African country at the beginning of the twenty-first century.

[69] See p. 98.

[70] Chabal, 'A few considerations on democracy in Africa' (1998) 74 *International Affairs* 289, at p. 302.

[71] See p. 93. Significantly, in 2002 even the King of Swaziland's resistance appeared to be crumbling in the face of demands from (technically illegal) political parties, trade unions and human rights organisations for a democratically elected Prime Minister and a constitutional order based on a Bill of Human Rights ((2002) 43(19) *Africa Confidential*, 27 September).

BIBLIOGRAPHY

'A Regrettable Amendment' *Legal Forum* 6, 1994, 1–2.

Abraham, M., 'Judicial Role in Constitutional Amendment in India: the Basic Structure Doctrine', in M. Andenas (ed.), *The Creation and Amendment of Constitutional Norms*, London, British Institute of International and Comparative Law, 2000.

Adedeji, Adebayo, 'The Leadership Challenge for Improving the Economic and Social Situation of Africa', unpublished paper presented at the Africa Leadership Forum, 24 October – 1 November 1988, Ota, Nigeria.

Advisory Panel to the Constitution of Kenya Review Commission, 'Report of the Advisory Panel of Eminent Commonwealth Judicial Experts', Nairobi, Kenya, 2002.

Africa Faith and Justice (Newsletter), Washington, DC: Faith and Justice Network.

African Conference on the Rule of Law, 'Report on the Proceedings', Geneva, International Commission of Jurists, 1961.

Africa Confidential, vol. 41, no. 24, 8 December 2000
vol. 43, no. 19, 27 September 2002.

Agyeman-Duah, B., 'Military Coups, Regime Change and Interstate Conflicts in West Africa' (1990) 16 *Armed Forces and Society* 547.

Aharon, Yair, *Foreign Investment Decision Process*, Cambridge, MA, Harvard University Press, 1966.

Alexander, H. E., 'Money and Politics: Rethinking a Conceptual Framework', in Alexander, H. E. (ed.), *Comparative Political Finance in the 1980s*, New York, Cambridge University Press, 1989.

Alexander, J., 'Dissident Perspectives on Zimbabwe's Post-Independence War' [1998] 68(2) *Africa* 151.

Allen, C. K., *Law and Orders*, London, Stevens, 1965.

Allott, A., *New Essays in African Law*, London, Sweet and Maxwell, 1970.

Ampem II Nana Wereko, 'The Role of Chiefs and Chieftaincy in the Development of a Democratic Constitution in Ghana', paper presented to the International Roundtable on Democratic Constitutional Development, 17–20 July 1995, Pretoria, South Africa.

Anene, J. C., *The International Boundaries of Nigeria 1865–1960*, New York: Humanities Press, 1970.

Anglin, D., 'Conflict in Sub-Saharan Africa 1997–1998', Ottawa: Carleton University, 1998.

Anthony, L. F. G., *The Story of Northern Rhodesia*, New York: Humanities Press, 1953.

Anyaoku, Emeka, Speech at the Opening of the Roundtable of Heads of Government of Commonwealth Africa on Democracy and Good Governance in Africa, 24 February 1997, Kasane, Botswana.

Armstrong, Patricia, 'Human Rights and Multilateral Development Banks: Governance Concerns in Decision Making', 88 *American Society of International Law Proceedings*. 271.

Aurora, S., *Balancing the Scales: an Analysis of Gender Representation within Commonwealth National Human Rights Institutions*, New Delhi, Commonwealth Human Rights Initiative, 2000.

Ayee, J., 'The Ombudsman Experience in the Kingdom of Swaziland: a Comment' [1988] *Verfassung und Recht in Ubersee* 8.

Bagehot, W., *The English Constitution*, London, Fontana, 1963.

Baloro, J., 'The Devolution of Swaziland's Constitution: Monarchical Responses to Modern Challenges' (1994) 38 *Journal of African Law* 119.

Banks, W. C. and Carrio, A. D., 'Presidential Systems in Stress: Emergency Powers in Argentina and the US' (1993) 15 *Michigan Journal of International Law* 1.

Barsh, R. L., 'Changing Forces and Non-State Actors in the Struggle for Human Rights', in Yael Danieli, Elsa Stamatopoulou and Clarence J. Dias (eds.), *The Universal Declaration of Human Rights: Fifty Years and Beyond*, New York, 1999.

Baxi, Upendra, 'On the Shame of Not Being an Activist: Thoughts on Judicial Activism', in N. Tiruchelvam and R. Coomaraswamy (eds.), *The Role of the Judiciary in Plural Societies*, London, Inter, 1987.

Bentham, J., *Works XI*, London, 1962.

Bentsi-Enchil, K., 'Do African Systems of Land Tenure Require a Special Terminology?', Reprint Series No. 7, North Western University Program of African Studies, 1966.

'Civitas De Africana: Realizing the African Political Dream' (1965) 2 *Zambia Law Journal* 65.

Berger, R., *Impeachment: the Constitutional Problem*, Cambridge, MA: Harvard University Press, 1973.

Bickel, A. M., *The Least Dangerous Branch*, New Haven, CT: Yale University Press, 1962.

Birkinshaw, P., *Grievance, Remedies and the State*, 2nd edn, London, Sweet and Maxwell, 1994.

Bogdanor, V., *The Blackwell Encyclopedia of Political Institutions*, Oxford: Blackwell, 1987.

Boutros Boutros-Ghali, *An Agenda for Peace*, New York, United Nations, 1992.

Brandon, Mark 'The "Original" Thirteenth Amendment and the Limits to Formal Constitutional Change', in Sanford Levinson (ed.), *Responding to Imperfection: the Theory and Practice of Constitutional Amendment*, Princeton, NJ, Princeton University Press, 1995.

Brurnell, P. and A. Walre, *Funding Democratization*, Manchester: Manchester University Press and New York: St. Martin's, 1998.

Bundu, A. C., 'Recognition of Revolutionary Authorities: Law and Practice of States' (1978) 27 *ICLQ* 18.

Butler, D., and Ranney, A. (eds.), *Referendums: a Comparative Study of Practice and Theory*, Washington DC.: American Enterprise Institute for Public Policy Research, 1978.

'Building Constitutional Order in Sub-Saharan Africa' *Third World Legal Studies*, 1988.

Camary, Phiroshoaw, and Gordon, Anne (eds.), *Advocacy in Southern Africa: Lessons for the Future*, Johannesburg: Core, 1998.

Campbell, Ian, 'Nigeria's Failed Transition: 1993 Presidential Elections' (1994) 12 *Journal of Contemporary African Studies* 182.

Cappelletti, M., 'Access to Justice: the Judicial Process in Comparative Perspective' 1992 *TSAR* 256.

Cartwright, S., 'The Judiciary: Qualifications, Training and Gender Balance', in J. Hatchard and P. Slinn (eds.), *Parliamentary Supremacy and Judicial Independence: a Commonwealth Approach*, London, Cavendish, 1998.

Carver, R., 'How African Governments Investigate Human Rights Violations', unpublished paper presented at the African Studies Association conference, Boston, 1989.

'Called to Account: How African Governments Investigate Human Rights Violations' (1990) 89 *African Affairs* 391.

Catholic Commission for Justice and Peace, *The Man in the Middle*, Salisbury, Rhodesia, CCJP 1975.

Catholic Commission for Justice and Peace in Zimbabwe/Legal Resources Foundation, *Breaking the Silence: Building True Peace – a Report on the Disturbances in Matabeleland and the Midlands 1980–1988*, Harare, Zimbabwe, CCJP, 1997.

Cawtra, G., *Securing South Africa's Democracy: Defence, Development and Security in Transition*, London: Macmillan Press, 1997.

Chabal, P., 'A few considerations on democracy in Africa' (1998) 74(2) *International Affairs* 289.

'The quest for good government and development in Africa: is NEPAD the answer?' (2002) 78 *International Affairs* 448.

Chaskalson, A., 'The Role of the Judiciary in Translating Human Rights Law into Practice', in *Developing Human Rights Jurisprudence, Volume 8, 2001*, London: Interights/Commonwealth Secretariat.

Chikulo, B. C., 'Decentralisation in Centralism: An Analysis of the Zambian Experience 1964–1981', in K. Osei-Hwendie and M. Ndulo (eds.), *Issues in Zambian Development*, Rosbury, MA: Omenana, 1985.

Colson, E., *Seven Tribes of Northern Rhodesia*, Manchester: Manchester University Press, 1957.

Commission for Investigations (Zambia), *Annual Report*, Lusaka, 1975.

Commission on Human Rights and Administrative Justice, *Second Annual Report*, 1995, Accra, Ghana: CHRAJ.

Commonwealth Best Practice Guide for National Human Rights Institutions, Commonwealth Secretariat, 1991.

Commonwealth and Defence Force Ombudsman Annual Report 1989–1990.

Commonwealth Human Rights Initiative, *Put Our World to Rights*, London: CHRI, 1991.

The Right to a Culture of Tolerance, London: CHRI, 1997.

Commonwealth Observer Group, *Commonwealth Observer Report on the General Election in Lesotho*, Commonwealth Secretariat, 1993.

Report on the 1991 Presidential and National Assembly Elections in Zambia, Commonwealth Secretariat, 1991.

Report on the 1996 General Elections in Zambia, Commonwealth Secretariat, 1996.

The Parliamentary Elections in Zimbabwe, Commonwealth Secretariat, 2000.

The Presidential, Parliamentary and Civic Elections in Kenya, Commonwealth Secretariat, 1993.

Commonwealth Observer Group to the South African Elections, *End of Apartheid*, Commonwealth Secretariat, 1994.

Commonwealth Ombudsman in Australia, *Annual Report 1989–1990.*

Commonwealth Parliamentary Association, *Parliament and the Media: Building an Effective Relationship*, London: CPA, 2000.

Commonwealth Press Union, *The Independence of the Commonwealth Media and Those Working Within It*, London: CPU, 1999.

Commonwealth Regional Workshop on Strengthening National Ombudsman and Human Rights Institutions, Commonwealth Secretariat, 2000.

Consultative Business Movement, 'Report on Regions in South Africa: Constitutional Options and their Implications for Good Governance and a Sound Economy', Johannesburg Consultative Business Movement, 1993.

Cook, H., 'Preventive Detention – International Standards and the Protection of the Individual', in S. Frankowski and D. Shelton (eds.) *Preventive Detention Law: a Comparative and International Perspective*, Dordrecht: Nijhoff, 1992.

Cotran, E., 'Kenyan marriage, divorce and succession law' (1996) 40 *Journal of African Law* 194.

Culliton Report (White Paper on the Proposed Code of Ethical Conduct for Public Office Holders), Ontario, 1986.

Dale, Penny, 'Southern Africa', in Robin Hodess (ed.), *Global Corruption Report 2001*, Berlin: Transparency International, 2001.

Dale, W., 'The Making and Re-Making of Commonwealth Constitutions' (1993) 42 *ICLQ* 67.

Dale, W. *The Modern Commonwealth*, London: Butterworths, 1983.

Davidson, B., *The Black Man's Burden*, London: James Currey, 1993.

Davis, Dennis, Matthew Chaskalson and Johann de Waal, 'Democracy and Constitutionalism: the Role of Constitutional Interpretation', in David van Wyk, John Dugard, Bertus de Villiers and Dennis David (eds.), *Rights and Constitutionalism: the New South African Legal Order*, Oxford: Clarendon Press, 1995.

de Brito, A. B., 'Truth and Justice in the Consolidation of Democracy in Chile and Uruguay' 46 *Parliamentary Affairs* 579.

'Democracy and Good Governance: Challenges, Impediments and Local Solutions in Africa', a paper prepared by the Commonwealth Secretariat for the Roundtable of Heads of Government of Commonwealth Africa on Democracy and Good Governance in Africa, Gaborone, Botswana, 23–27 February, 1997.

de Smith, S. A. *The New Commonwealth and its Constitutions*, London: Stevens, 1964.

de Villiers, B., 'An Electoral System for the New South Africa', in A. Johnson, S. Shezi and G. Brandshaw (eds.), *Constitution-Making in the New South Africa*, Leicester: Leicester University Press, 1993.

der Vyer, J. van, 'Constitutional Options for Post-Apartheid South Africa' (1991) 40 *Emory Law Journal* 745.

Devenish, G., *Commentary on the South African Constitution*, Durban: Butterworths, 1998.

Dia, Mamadou, *Africa Management in the 1990s and Beyond*, World Bank, Washington, DC, 1996.

Dore, I., 'Constitutionalism and the Post-Colonial State in Africa: a Rawlisian Approach' (1997) 41 *St Louis University Law Journal* 1302.

Duxbury, A., 'Rejuvenating the Commonwealth: the Human Rights Remedy' (1997) 46 ICLQ 344.

East, Paul, 'Free Speech: Parliamentary Privilege and the *sub judice* Rule', in J. Hatchard and P. Slinn (eds.), *Parliamentary Supremacy and Judicial Independence*, London: Cavendish Publishing, 1999.

Ebrahim, Hassen, 'The Process of Drafting South Africa's New Constitution', paper delivered to International Roundtable on Democratic Constitutional Development, CSIR Conference Facility, Pretoria, South Africa, 17–20 July 1995.

Elias, T. O., 'The Commonwealth in Africa' (1968) 31 MLR 284.

Ensalaco, M., 'Truth Commissions for Chile and El Salvador: a Report and Assessment' (1994) 16 *Human Rights Quarterly* 656.

Fall, I. *Parliament: Guardian of Human Rights*, Geneva: Inter-Parliamentary Union, 1993.

Fanon, F, *The Wretched of The Earth: a Handbook for the Black Revolution that is Changing the Shape of the World*, New York: First Evergreen Black Cat Books, 1968.

Feltoe, G., 'The onslaught against democracy and rule of law in Zimbabwe', unpublished paper, Harare, 2001.

Field, Martha A., 'The Differing Federalisms of Canada and the United States' (1992) 55 *Law & Contemporary Problems 107.*

Finer, S. E., *The Man on Horseback: the Role of the Military in Politics*, New York: Praeger, 1962.

Flower, K., *Serving Secretly*, London: Murray, 1987.

Franck, T., 'The Emerging Right to Democratic Governance' (1992) 86 *American Journal of International Law* 46.

Fraser, M., 'The Nation State and Globalisation' (1999) 2 *Commonwealth Currents* 18.

Gann, L. H., *The Birth of a Plural Society, the Development of Northern Rhodesia Under the British South Africa Company, 1894–1914*, Westport, CT: Greenwood Press, 1958.

History of Northern Rhodesia, New York: Humanities Press, 1964.

Gathii, James T., 'Kenya's Legislative Culture and the Evolution of the Kenya Constitution', in Y. Vyas et al., (eds.) *Law and Development in the Third World*, Nairobi: Faculty of Law, University of Nairobi, 1994.

Georges, P. T., 'The Court in the Tanzania One-Party System', in A. Sawyerr (ed.), *East African Law and Social Change*, Nairobi: East Africa Publishing House, 1967.

Gering, L., 'Legal Institutions and Human Needs' (1974) 37 *Tydsk Rif Vir Hededaagse Romeins-Hollandse Reg* 274.

Gertzel, C., Baylis, C., and Szeftel, M., *The Dynamics of the One-Party State in Zambia*, Manchester: Manchester University Press, 1984.

Ghai, Yash, 'The Theory of the State in the Third World and the Problematics of Constitutionalism', in Greenberg, Katz, Oliviero and Wheatley, (eds.) *Constitutionalism and Democracy*.

Ghai, Y., and McAuslan, J. P. W. B., *Public Law and Political Change in Kenya*, Oxford: Oxford University Press, 1970.

Gilmore, W., *Dirty Money*, 2nd edn, Strasbourg: Council of Europe, 1999.

Gingyera-Pinycwa, A. G., 'The Militarisation of Politics in an African State: the Case of Uganda', in W. O. Oyugi (ed.), *Politics and Administration in East Africa*, Nairobi: East African Educational Publishers, 1994.

Ginther, K., Denters, E., and de Waart, P. (eds.), *Sustainable Development and Good Governance*, Dordrecht: Kluwer, 1995.

Gloppen, Siri, *South Africa: the Battle Over the Constitution*, Aldershot: Ashgate, 1997.

Gluckman, M., *Politics and Ritual in Tribal Society*, Manchester: Manchester University Press, 1965.

The Judicial Process Amongst the Barotse of Northern Rhodesia, Manchester: Manchester University Press, 1967.

Goldstone, R., 'Do Judges Speak Out?' (1994) 111 *South African Law Journal* 268.

Goldsworthy, D., 'Armies and Politics in Civilian Regimes', in S. Baynham (ed.), *Military Power and Politics in Black Africa*, New York: St Martin's Press, 1986.

Goredema, Charles, 'The Attorney-General in Zimbabwe and South Africa: Whose weapon, whose shield?', unpublished paper, Harare, 1997.

Green, R., 'Participatory Pluralism and Pervasive Poverty: Some Reflections' (1989) *Third World Legal Studies* 21.

Griffith, J. A. G., Michael Ryle and M. A. J. Wheeler-Booth, *Parliament: Functions, Practice and Procedures*, London: Sweet and Maxwell, 1989.

Groves, H., 'Emergency Powers' (1961) (winter) *Journal of the International Commission of Jurists* 1.

Gubbay, A. R., 'The Role of the Courts in Zimbabwe in Implementing Human Rights, with Special Reference to the Application of International Human Rights Norms', in *Developing Human Rights Jurisprudence, Volume 8, 2001*, London: Interights/Commonwealth Secretariat.

Guinier, Lani, *The Tyranny of the Majority*, New York: Free Press, 1994.

Gurr, Ted Robert and Barbara Harff, *Ethnic Conflict in World Politics*, Boulder, Co: Westview Press, 1994.

Hall, R., *Zambia*, New York: Praeger, 1964.

Hamill, J., 'The Crossing of the Rubicon: South Africa's Post-Apartheid Political Process' (1990) 12(3) *International Relations.*

Hand, L., *The Spirit of Liberty*, 3rd edn, London: Hamish Hamilton, 1960.

Harding, A. J., 'When is a resignation not a resignation? The Sabah Constitutional Crisis of 1994' (1995) 335 *The Round Table* 353.

Harding, A., and Hatchard, J., (eds.), *Preventive Detention and Security Law* Dordrecht: Martinus Nijhoff, 1993.

Hatchard, J., 'The Constitution of Zimbabwe: a New Model for Africa?' (1991) 35 *Journal of African Law* 79.

Individual Freedoms and State Security in the African Context: the Case of Zimbabwe Athens, Ohio: Ohio University Press, London: James Currey Publishers; Harare: Baobab Books, 1993.

'Re-establishing a Multi-Party State: Some Reflections from the 1992 Constitutional Developments in the Seychelles' (1993) 31 *Journal of Modern African Studies* 601.

'Reporting under International Human Rights Instruments by African Countries' (1994) 38 *Journal of African Law* 61.

'Constitutionality of the Death Penalty and Penal Policy' (1995) 39 *Journal of African Law* 192.

'Undermining the Constitution by Constitutional Means: Some Thoughts on the New Constitutions of Southern Africa' (1995) 27 *Comparative and International Law Journal of Southern Africa* 2.

'Engendering Political Decision-Making' (1998) 42 *Journal of African Law*, 141.

National Human Rights Institutions in the Commonwealth, 3rd edn, London: Commonwealth Secretariat, 1998.

'A New Breed of Institution: the Development of Human Rights Commissions in Commonwealth Africa with particular reference to the Uganda Human Rights Commission' (1999) 32 *Comparative and International Law Journal of Southern Africa* 28.

'Presidential Removal: Unzipping the Constitutional Provisions' (2000) 44 *Journal of African Law* 1.

'The Sad Tale of the POSB in Zimbabwe' (2000) 44 *Journal of African Law* 132.

Hatchard, J. (ed.), *Directory of Commonwealth Law Schools 2002–2004*, London: Cavendish Publishing, 2002.

Hatchard, J. and Tunde Ogogewo, *Tackling the Unconstitutional Overthrow of Democracies-Emerging Trends in the Commonwealth*, London: Commonwealth Secretariat, 2003.

Hatchard, J., and Ndulo, M., *Readings in Criminal Law and Criminology*, 1994, Lusaka: Multimedia.

Hatchard, J., and Slinn, P., 'Namibia: the Constitutional Path to Freedom' (1990) 10 International Relations 137.

'The Path towards a New Order in South Africa' (1995) 12(4) *International Relations*.

Hatchard, J., and Slinn, P. (eds.), *Parliamentary Supremacy and Judicial Independence: a Commonwealth Approach*, London: Cavendish Publishing, 1999.

Howard, R., *Human Rights in Commonwealth Africa*, Totowa, NJ: Rowman and Littlefield, 1986.

Human Rights Watch, 'Africa, Zambia and Human Rights in the Third Republic', New York: Human Rights Watch, 1996.

Hyden, G., and Bratton, M., *Governance and Politics in Africa*, Boulder, Co: Lynne Reiner, 1993.

Ignatieff, M., 'Truth, Justice and Reconciliation', paper delivered at the Commonwealth Law Conference, Vancouver, Canada, 1996.

IMF Code of Good Practice on Financial Transparency, Washington, DC: IMF, 2001.

International Bar Association, 'Report on the Legal System and Independence of the Judiciary in Kenya', London: International Bar Association, 1997.
International Commission of Jurists, *Human Rights in a One-Party State*, London: Search Press, 1978.
States of Emergency: their Impact on Human Rights, Geneva: ICJ, 1983.
'International Round Table on Democratic Constitutional Development Report', Pretoria CSIR, 17–20 July 1995.
Janowitz, M., *The Military in the Political Development of New Nations: an Essay in Comparative Analysis*, Chicago, IL: University of Chicago Press, 1964.
Johnson, A. W., 'Fiscal Arrangements in a Multi-tier State: the Canadian Case and How it Relates to South Africa's Interim Constitution', paper presented at the International Roundtable on Democratic Constitutional Development, Pretoria, South Africa, 17–20 July 1995.
Johnson, A., Shezi, S., and Brandshaw, G., *Constitution-Making in the New South Africa*, Leicester: Leicester University Press, 1993.
Judd, D., and Slinn, P., *The Evolution of the Modern Commonwealth 1902–80*, London: Macmillan, 1982.
Judicial Group on Strengthening Judicial Integrity, *Code of Judicial Conduct (The Bangalore Draft)*, Berlin: Transparency International, 2001.
Kemp, K., and Hudlin, C., 'Civil Supremacy over the Military: its Nature and Limits' (1992) *Armed Forces and Society* 7.
Khanna, H. R., *Law, Men of Law and Education*, Bombay: Tripathi, 1981.
Kirby, Michael, 'The Abolition of Courts and Non-Reappointment of Judicial Officers in Australia', Ronald Wilson Lecture, Perth, Australia, 28 November 1994.
Kirk-Greene, A., *On Crown Service: a History of HM Colonial and Overseas Services 1837–1997*, London: Taurus, 1999.
Kornberg A., and Pittman, K., 'Representative and Military Bodies: their Roles in the Survival of Political Systems of New States', in J. Smith and L. Musolf (eds.), *Legislatures in Development: Dynamics of Change in New and Old States*, Durham, NC: Duke University Press, 1979.
Kuria, G. K., and Vaquez, A. M., 'Judges and Human Rights: the Kenyan Experience' (1991) 35 *Journal of African Law* 142.
Kahn, E. 'Extra-judicial Activities of Judges' 1980 *De Jure* 188.
Law, Life and Laughter, Cape Town: Juta, 1984.
Kanyeihamba, G. W., *Constitutional Law and Government in Uganda*, Nairobi: East African Literature Bureau, 1975.
Kasuto, E., and Wehmhorner, A. (eds.), *The Ombudsman in Southern Africa: Report of a Sub-regional Conference*, Windhoek: 1996.
Kollapen, J., 'Accountability: the Debate in South Africa' (1993) 37 *Journal of African Law* 1.

Koovadia, Jerry, Speech to the Society of Law Teachers of Southern Africa conference, July 2000, Durban, South Africa.

Kornberg, A. et al., 'Representative and Military Bodies: their Roles in the Survival of Political Systems of New States', in J. Smith and L. Musolf (eds.), *Legislatures in Development: Dynamics of Change in New and Old States*, Durham, NC: Duke University Press.

Krause, J., 'Ghana 1966', in W. G. Andrews and U. Ra'anan (eds.), *The Politics of the Coup d'Etat: Five Case Studies*, New York: Reinhold, 1969.

Kunaka, Constance, Noria Mashumba and Philliat Matsheza, *The SADC Protocol against Corruption*, Harare: Human Rights Research and Documentation Trust of Southern Africa, 2002.

Lardeyret, G., 'Problems with Proportional Representation' (1991) 2 *Journal of Democracy 30.*

Lavrenic, K., 'Food for Africa', (1979) 137 *New African* 90.

Lawyers Committee for Human Rights Report, *Zimbabwe: Wages of War*, New York: LCHR, 1986.

Lee, J. M., *Colonial Development and Good Government: a Study of the Ideas Expressed by the British Official Classes in Planning Decolonisation 1939–1964*, Oxford: Oxford University Press, 1967.

Legum, Colin (ed.), *Zambia, Independence and Beyond: the Speeches of Kenneth Kaunda*, London: Nelson, 1966.

Lewis, W. A., *Politics in West Africa*, London: Allen and Unwin, 1965.

Lord Lester of Herne Hill, 'The Challenge of Bangalore: Making Human Rights a Practical Reality' (1999) 25 *Commonwealth Law Bulletin* 50.

Lugard, F. D., *The Dual Mandate in British Tropical Africa*, Edinburgh: Blackwood, 1922.

Luttwak, E., *Coup d'Etat: a Practical Handbook*, New York: Knopf, 1968.

Magyar, Karl P., 'Military Intervention and Withdrawal in Africa: Problems and Perspectives', in Constantine P. Danopoulos (ed.), *From Military to Civilian Rule*, London: Routledge, 1992.

Mainga, M., *Bulozi Under the Luyana Kings*, London: Longmans, 1973.

Mangan, B., 'Protecting Human Rights in National Emergencies: Shortcomings in the European System' (1988) 10 *Human Rights Quarterly* 376.

Marks, S., 'Principles and Norms of Human Rights Applicable in Emergency Situations: Underdevelopment, Catastrophes and Armed Conflict', in K. Vasak and P. Alston (eds.), *The International Dimension of Human Rights*, vol. 1, Paris: UNESCO, 1982.

Mathews, A., *Law, Order and Liberty in South Africa*, Cape Town: Juta, 1971.

Freedom, State Security and the Rule of Law, Cape Town; Juta, 1986.

Matlosa, K., 'Democracy and Conflict in Post-Apartheid Southern Africa' (1998) 74 *International Affairs* 319.

Malawi Law Commission: Report on the Technical Review of the Constitution, Government Gazette vol. XXXV No. 58, 16 November 1998.

Mazrui, A., 'Anti-Militarism and Political Militancy in Tanzania', in J. Van Doorn (ed.), *Military Profession and Military Regimes*, The Hague: Mouton, 1969.

'Constitutional Change and Cultural Engineering: Africa's Search for New Directions', in J. Oloka-Onyango (ed.), *Constitutionalism in Africa: Creating Opportunities, Facing Challenges*, Kampala: Fountain Publishers, 2001.

McGowan. P., and Johnson, T., 'African Military Coups d'Etat and Underdevelopment: a Quantitative Historical Analysis' (1984) 22 *Journal of Modern African Studies* 633.

Mhlaba, L., 'The Presidential Pardoning of Dr Shava' (1989) 1(6) *Legal Forum* 25.

Mkandawire, T., and Soludo, C., *Our Continent our Future: African Perspective on Structural Adjustment* CODESTRIA, Trenton, NJ: African World Press, 1999.

Ministry of Legal Affairs, *Constitutional Reform 1996: the Public Debate-Adopting the Constitution: Topic 1 The Constituent Assembly*, Lusaka: Government Printer, 1996.

Moore, K. D., *Pardons*, Oxford: Oxford University Press, 1989.

Morgan, D. G., 'The Indian Essential Features Case' (1981) 30 *ICLQ* 307.

Motala, Ziyad, *Constitutional Options for a Democratic South Africa: a Comparative Perspective*, Washington, DC: Howard University Press, 1995.

Movement for Multi-Party Democracy (MMD), *The Third Republic Alternative: a Bulletin for Social-Economic Change*, No.1, Lusaka, Zambia; MMD, 1991.

Moyo, J., 'The Dialectics of National Unity and Democracy in Zimbabwe', in I. Mandaza and L. Sachikonye (eds.), *One Party State and Democracy*, Harare: SAPES, 1991.

Voting for Democracy, Harare: University of Zimbabwe Press, 1992.

Mubako, S. 'The Constitution of the Republic of Zambia', unpublished, Lusaka, 1972.

'Zambia's Single Party Constitution – a Search for Unity and Development' (1973) 5 *Zambia Law Journal* 67.

Mugabi, Kiai 'Presidential Directives vis-à-vis Democracy, Human Rights and the Rule of Law: a Paradox', in K. Kibwana, Chris Maina Peter, and Joseph Olaka-Onyango (eds.), *In Search of Freedom and Prosperity: Constitutional Reform in East Africa*, Nairobi: Claripress, 1996.

Mukholi, David, *A Complete Guide to Uganda's Fourth Constitution: History, Politics and the Law*, Kampala, Fountain Publishers, 1995.

Mukuwa Wa Mukua, M., 'Why Redraw the Map of Africa? A Moral and Legal Inquiry' (1995) 16 *Michigan Journal of International Law* 1135.

Museveni, Y., *What is Africa's Problem?* Minneapolis, MN: University of Minnesota Press, 1992.

Sowing the Mustard Seed: the Struggle for Freedom and Democracy in Uganda, London: Macmillan, 1997.

Mutharika, A. Peter, 'The 1995 Democratic Constitution of Malawi' (1996) 40 *Journal of African Law* 205.

Mwaikusa, J. T., 'Party Systems and Control of Government Powers: Past Experiences, Future Prospects', in J. Oloka-Onyango, Kivutha Kibwana and Chris Menia Peters (eds.), *Law and the Struggle for Democracy in East Africa*, Nairobi: Claripress, 1996.

'The Limits of Judicial Enterprise in the Process of Political Change in Tanzania' (1996) 40 *Journal of African Law* 242.

Mwanakatwe, J. M., *The End of the Kaunda Era*, Lusaka: Multimedia, 1994.

Mwanakatwe Constitutional Review Commission Supplement, Republic of Zambia, Government Paper, No. 1 of 1995.

Mwanawasa, Levy, Speech delivered at the official opening of the Commonwealth Workshop on Setting Zambian National Human Rights Strategies, Livingstone, Zambia, 25 June 1992.

Nadais, Antonia, *Choice of Electoral Systems in New Democratic Frontiers*, Pretoria: National Democratic Institute, 1992.

Nagabhushan Rao, K. M., 'Parliamentary privilege versus the courts', in Hatchard, J., and Slinn, P., (eds.), *Parliamentary Supremacy and Judicial Independence: a Commonwealth Approach*, London: Cavendish, 1999.

National Democratic Institute for International Affairs, *Nation Building: the United Nations and Namibia*, Washington, DC: NDIIA, 1990.

N'Cube, W., and Nzombe, S., 'The Constitutional Reconstruction of Zimbabwe: Much Ado about Nothing?' (1987) 5 *Zimbabwe Law Review* 2.

Ndulo, M., 'Liability of a Paramour in Damages for Adultery in Customary Law' (1981) 28 *African Social Research* 179.

'Customary Law and the Zambian Legal System', in P. Tikarambudde (ed.), *The Individual under African Law: Proceedings of the first All-Africa Law Conference 11–16 October 1981*, Kwaluseni: University of Swaziland, 1982.

Ndulo, M., and Kent, R., 'Constitutionalism in Zambia: Past, Present and Future' (1996) 40 *Journal of African Law* 256.

'The Constitutions of Zambia' (1998) 30 *Zambia Law Journal* 7.

Nhlapo, N., 'The African Family and Women's Rights: Friends or Foes?' 1991 *Acta Juridica* 135.

'Accommodating Traditional Forms of Governance in a Constitutional Democracy: a Motivation', paper presented at the International Roundtable on Democratic Constitutional Development, Pretoria, South Africa, 17–20 July 1995.

Nohlen, D., Krennerich, M., and Thibaut, B., *Elections in Africa: a Data Handbook*, Oxford: Oxford University Press, 1999.

Nowrojee, B., *Protectors or Pretenders: Government Human Rights Commissions in Africa*, New York: Human Rights Watch, 2001.

Nsibambi, Apolo, 'The Interface among the Capable State, the Private Sector and Civil Society in Acquiring Food Security', Keynote paper at the Conference on Building for the Capable State in Africa, Institute for African Studies, Cornell University, 24–28 October 1997.

Nwabueze, B. O., *Constitutionalism in the Emergent States*, London: Hurst, 1973.

Constitutionalism in Commonwealth Africa, London: Hurst, 1974.

'Our March to Constitutional Democracy', Guardian Lecture, 24 July 1989; published in (1989) *Law and Practice, Journal of Nigerian Bar Association (NBA)* August 19–38.

Military Rule and Constitutionalism in Nigeria, Lagos: Spectrum Books, 1992.

Judicialism in Commonwealth Africa, London: Hurst, 1977.

Nwogugu, E. I. *Legal Aspects of Foreign Investment in Developing Countries*, Manchester: Manchester University Press, 1965.

Nyalali Commission, 'Report of the Presidential Commission on Single Party or Multiparty System in Tanzania', Dar es Salaam: Government Printer, 1991.

Nyerere, Julius, *Freedom and Socialism*, Oxford, 1968.

Freedom and Development/Uhuru na Maendeleo: a Selection from Writings and Speeches 1968–1973, Nairobi: Oxford University Press, 1973.

'Africa Exists in the Economic South' (1988) 41(3) *Development and Social Economic Progress.*

Obasanjo, O., 'Africa in Today's World', unpublished paper presented at the Africa Leadership Forum, Ota, Nigeria, 24 October to 1 November, 1988.

OECD Report, *Participatory Development and Good Governance*, Paris: OECD, 1995.

Ojwang, J. B., 'Rural Dispute Settlement in Kenya', (1975–1978) 7–10 *Zambia Law Journal* 63.

Constitutional Development in Kenya: Institutional Adaptation and Social Change, Nairobi: ACTS, 1990.

Okondo, P. H., *A Commentary on the Constitution of Kenya*, Nairobi, Phoenix, 1995.

Okoth-Ogendo, H. W. O. 'Property Systems and Social Organisation in Africa: an Essay on the Relative Position of Women Under Indigenous and Received Law', in P. Takirambudde (ed.), *The Individual Under African Law*, Mbabane: University of Swaziland, 1982.

'Governance and Sustainable Development in Africa', in K. Giuther, E. Denters and P. de Waart (eds.), *Sustainable Development and Good Governance*, Dordrecht: Kluwer, 1995.

Oloka-Onyango, J., 'Uganda', in P. Baehr et al (eds.), *Human Rights in Developing Countries Yearbook 1996*, The Hague: Kluwer, 1996.

'Constitutionalism in Africa, Yesterday, Today and Tomorrow', in J. Olaka-Onyango (ed.), *Constitutionalism in Africa: Creating Opportunities, Facing Challenges*, Kampala: Fountain Publishers, 2001.

Ong'wamuhana, Kibuta, 'Party Supremacy and the State Constitution in Africa's One-Party States: the East African Experience' (1989) 17 *Melanesian Law Journal* 67.

Orentlicher, D. F., 'Settling Accounts: the Duty to Prosecute Human Rights Violations of a Previous Regime', in F. Newman and D. Weissbrodt, *International Human Rights: Law, Policy and Process*, Boston, MA: Little, Brown, 1996.

Organisation for African Unity, *The Lagos Plan of Action for the Implementation of the Monrovia Strategy for the Economic Development of Africa.*

Oruka, H. O., *Punishment and Terrorism in Africa*, Nairobi: East African Publishing House, 1985.

Owasanoye, B., and Nwanku, C., *Suppressed Rights: Constitutional Rights Violations in Military Decrees 1984–1999*, Lagos: Constitutional Rights Project, 1999.

Palmer, V., and Poulter, S., *The Legal System of Lesotho*, Charlottesville, VA: Michie Company Law Publisher, 1972.

Paul, James, 'Building Constitutional Orders in Sub-Saharan Africa: an Unofficial Report', in *Building Constitutional Orders in Sub-Saharan Africa* (1988) *Third World Legal Studies* 1.

Peter, C. M., 'Constitution-making in Tanzania', in K. Kibwana, C. M. Peter and N. Bazaara, (eds.), *Constitutionalism in East Africa: Progress, Challenges and Prospects in 1999*, Nairobi: Fountain Press, 2001.

Phiri, Kings M., 'A Case of Revolutionary Change in Contemporary Malawi: the Malawi Army and the Disarming of the Malawi Young Pioneers' (2000) 1(1) *Journal of Peace, Conflict and Military* Studies 1.

'Pluralism, Participation and Decentralization in Sub-Saharan Africa', *Third World Legal Studies*, 1989.

Porter, B., *The Lion's Share*, 3rd edn, London: Longman, 1996.

Proctor, J. H., 'The House of Chiefs and the Political Development of Botswana' (1968) 6 *Journal of Modern African Studies* 59.

Read, J. S., 'Nigeria's New Constitution for 1992: the Third Republic' (1991) 35 *Journal of African Law* 174.

Reid, Ann, *Conflict Resolution in Africa: Lessons from Angola*, INR Foreign Affairs Brief, Bureau of Intelligence and Research, Washington DC: US Department of State, April 1993.

Report, Citizens Convention on the Draft Constitution, Lusaka, Zambia, 1996.

Report by the Permanent Human Rights Commission in Zambia, March 1998.

Report of the Inter-African Network for Human Rights and Development, 'The Dilemma of Local Courts in Zambia', Lusaka, 1998.

Report of the National Commission on the Establishment of a One-Party Participatory Democracy in Zambia, Lusaka, 1972.

Report of the Zambia Constitutional Review Commission, Lusaka, 1995.

Reynolds, Andrew, 'Constitutional Engineering in Southern Africa' (1995) 6 *Journal of African Democracy* 86.

Reyntjens, F., 'The Winds of Change: Political and Constitutional Evolution in Francophone Africa' (1991) 35 *Journal of African Law* 44.

Roberts-Wray, K., *Commonwealth and Colonial Law*, London: Stevens, 1966.

Rodden, J., and Rose-Ackerman, S., 'Federalism Preserves Markets' (1997) 83 *Virginia Law Reports* 1573.

Roht-Arriaza, N., 'Combating Impunity: some Thoughts on the Way Forward' (1996) 59 *Law and Contemporary Problems* 93.

Rolph, C. H., *The Queen's Pardon*, Oxford: Oxford University Press, 1967.

Rossiter, C., *Constitutional Dictatorship: Crisis Government in the Modern Democracies*, Princeton NJ: Princeton University Press, 1948.

Rotberg, R., *The Rise of Nationalism in Central Africa: the Making of Malawi and Zambia, 1873–1964*, Cambridge, MA: Harvard University Press, 1965.

Rye, Dick, 'Intergovernmental Relation Structures Responsible for Financial and Fiscal Management', paper presented at the International Roundtable on Democratic Constitutional Development, Pretoria, South Africa, 17–20 July 1995.

Sanford, Levinson (ed.), *Responding to Imperfection: the Theory and Practice of Constitutional Amendment*, Princeton NJ: Princeton University Press, 1995.

Sarkin, J., 'The Development of a Human Rights Culture in South Africa' (1998) 20(3) *Human Rights Quarterly* 628.

'The Tension between Justice and Reconciliation in Rwanda: Politics, Human Rights, Due Process and the Role of the Gacaca Courts in Dealing with the Genocide' (2001) 45 *Journal of African Law* 143.

Schabas, W. A., 'Soering's Legacy: the Human Rights Committee and the Judicial Committee of the Privy Council Take a Walk Down Death Row' (1994) 43 *ICLQ* 913.

Sebba, L., 'The Pardoning Power – A World Survey' 68 *Journal of Criminal Law and Criminology* 83.

Sedler, Robert A., 'Constitutional Protection of Individual Rights in Canada: the Impact of the New Canadian Charter of Rights and Freedoms' (1984) 59 *Notre Dame Law Reports* 1191.

Seidman, R., 'Law and Stagnation in Africa', in M. Ndulo (ed.), *Law in Zambia*, Nairobi: East African Publishing House, 1984.

'Drafting for the Rule of Law: Maintaining Legality in Developing Countries' (1987) 12 *Yale Journal of International Law* 85.

'Perspectives on Constitution-Making: Independence Constitutions of Namibia and South Africa' (1987) 3 *Lesotho Law Journal* 45.

Seidman, R. B., and Seidman, A., 'The Political Economy of Customary Law in the Former British Territories of Africa' (1984) 28 *Journal of African Law* 44.

Shaw, T. M., *Alternative Futures for Africa*, Boulder, CO: Westview Press, 1982.

Shivji, I. G., *The State and the Working People in Tanzania*, Dar es Salaam: Codestria Book Services, 1985.

'State and Constitutionalism: a New Democratic Perspective', in I. G. Shivji (ed.), *State and Constitutionalism*, Harare: Sepos, 1991.

Short, E., 'The Commission on Human Rights and Administrative Justice', paper presented at a workshop organised by the Uganda Human Rights Commission, Kampala, November 1997.

Shugart, M., and Cary, J., *Presidents and Assemblies: Constitutional Design and Electoral Dynamics*, Cambridge: Cambridge University Press, 1992.

Simeon, R., 'The Structures of Intergovernmental Relations', paper presented at the International Roundtable on Democratic Constitutional Development Conference, Pretoria, South Africa, 17–20 July 1995.

Simpson, A. W. Brian, *Human Rights and the End of Empire*, Oxford: Oxford University Press, 2001.

Sindima, Harrey J., *Malawi's First Republic*, Lanham, MD: University Press of America, 2002.

Sives, A., 'A Review of Commonwealth Election Observation' 39 *Commonwealth and Comparative Politics* (2001) 132.

Slinn, P., 'Zimbabwe Achieves Independence' 1980 *Commonwealth Law Bulletin* 1038.

'A Fresh Start for Africa? New African Constitutional Perspectives for the 1990s' (1991) 35 *Journal of African Law* 1.

Smart, J., 'The Legality of Revolutionary Regimes in the New Commonwealth', unpublished paper, Freetown, n.d.

Sono, T., *From Democracy to Partocracy: Why a Party System is Undemocratic?*, Pretoria: Via Afrika, 1993.

Stoddard, M., 'South Africa's Elections: Establishing Democracy at the Grassroots' (1997) 21. *Fletcher Forum of World Affairs Journal* 83.

Southall, R., and Wood, G., 'Local Government and the Return to Multi-Partyism in Kenya' (1996) 95 *African Affairs* 501–27.

'Political Party Funding in Southern Africa', in P. Brunell and A. Ware (eds.), *Funding Democratisation* 1998.

Southern African Development Community – USA, *States Direct Investment in Africa*, Trade and Investment publication, 1998.

Speck, P. K., 'The Trial of the Argentine Junta: Responsibilities and Realities' (1987) 18 *University of Miami Inter-American Law Review* 491.

Stevens, J., 'Colonial Relics I: the Requirement of a Permit to Hold a Peaceful Assembly' (1997) 41 *Journal of African Law* 118.

Sunstein, C. R., 'Impeaching the President' (1998) 147 *University of Pennsylvania Law Review* 279.

Tangri, Roger, *The Politics of Patronage in Africa*, Oxford: James Currey, 1999.

Teitel, R., 'Transitional Justice: the Role of Law in Political Transformation' (1997) 106 *Yale Law Journal* 2009.

Therkildsen, Ole, 'Uganda's Referendum 2000: the Silent Boycott: a Comment' 2002 *African Affairs* 101.

Tumwine-Mukubwa, Grace Patrick, 'Ruled from the Grave: Challenging Antiquated Constitutional Doctrines and Values in Commonwealth Africa', in J. Oloka-Onyango (ed.), *Constitutionalism in Africa: Creating Opportunities, Facing Challenges*, Kampala: Fountain Publishers, 2001.

Uganda Commission of Inquiry into the Violation of Human Rights, 'The Pearl of Blood' (1994) Kampala: Government of Uganda.

Uganda Constitutional Commission, *Guidelines on Constitutional Issues*, 1991.

United Nations, *Basic Principles on the Independence of the Judiciary* 1985.

United Nations, *Code of Conduct for Law-Enforcement Officials* 1979.

United Nations Conference on Trade and Development, 'Foreign Investment in Africa', UNCTAD/DTCI/19, Current Studies, Series A, No. 28, Geneva, 1995.

United Nations Economic Commission for Africa, *Africa Alternative Framework to Structural Adjustment Programs for Socio-Economic Recovery and Transformation* (E/ECA/CM. 15/6/Rev.3.)

UNDP, *Women's Political Participation and Good Governance: Twenty-first Century Challenges*, New York: United Nations, 2000.

United Nations Report of the Secretary-General on Mozambique (ONUMOZ) (S/125518) (1993).

United Nations Report of the Secretary-General to the General Assembly at its Forty-sixth Session (A/46/609/Corr/1 and Add. 1–2).

United Nations Secretary-General to the Security Council, 'Causes of Conflict and the Promotion of Durable Peace and Sustainable Development in Africa', New York: United Nations, 1998.

United Nations, *Secretary-General's Report to the United Nations Security Council*, New York: United Nations, 1998.

United Nations Observer Mission in South Africa (UNOMSA), Final Report to the Secretary General, 'A Democratic Non-Racial and United South Africa', New York: United Nations, 1994.

UN Working Group on Enforced or Involuntary Disappearances, 1990.

United Nations System-Wide Special Initiative on Africa, 'Deliberations of African Governance forum', 11–13 July 1997, New York.

United States Direct Investment in Africa, *Southern African Development Community in USA*; *Trade and Investment*, Washington DC: USDIA, 1998.

Van Wyk, D., 'The Making of the Namibian Constitution: Lessons for Africa' (1990) *Comparative and International Law Journal of Southern Africa* 341.

Venter, A., 'The Executive: a Critical Evaluation', in B. de Villiers (ed.), *Birth of a Constitution*, Kenwyn: Juta, 1994.

Vukor-Quarshie G. N. K. 'Developments in the Field of Criminal Justice Administration in Nigeria: Saro-Wiwa in Review' (1997) 42 *Journal of African Law* 215.

WEDO, *Getting the Balance*, New York: Women's Environment and Development Organization, 2001.

Wehner, J., 'Parliament and the Power of the Purse: the Nigerian Constitution of 1999 in Comparative Perspective' (2002) 46 *Journal of African Law* 216.

Welch, Claude E. (ed.), *Civilian Control of the Military: Theories and Cases from Developing Countries*, Albany NY: State University of New York, 1976.

Wheare, K. C., *Modern Constitutions*, London: Sweet and Maxwell, 1966.

Widner, J. A., *Building the Rule of Law: Francis Nyalali and the Road to Judicial Independence in Africa*, Norton and Company, New York and London, 2001.

Wills, A. J., *An Introduction to the History of Central Africa*, Oxford: Oxford University Press, 1973.

Wing, A. K., 'Towards Democracy in a New South Africa, a Review of Ziyad Motala, Constitutional Options for a Democratic South Africa: a Comparative Perspective' (1995) 16 *Michigan Journal of International Law*.

World Bank, 'Accelerated Development in Sub-Saharan Africa: an Agenda for Action', Washington DC; World Bank, 1981.

World Bank, *Sub-Saharan Africa: from Crisis to Sustainable Growth*, Washington, DC: World Bank 1989.

World Bank, *Governance: the World Bank's Experience*, Washington, DC: World Bank, 1994.

World Bank, *Annual Report*, Washington, DC: World Bank, 1997.

World Bank, *Development Report*, Washington DC: World Bank, 1997.

World Bank, 'Entering the Twenty-First Century', World Development Report 1999/2000, Washington, DC: World Bank.

Yansane, A. Y. (ed.), *Prospects for Recovery and Sustainable Development in Africa*, Westport, CT, Greenwood Press, 1996.

Yusuf, A., 'Reflections on the Fragility of State Institutions in Africa', *African Yearbook of International Law*, vol. 2, Dordrecht: Kluwer Law International, 1994, 2.

Zambia, *Report of the National Commission on the Establishment of a One-Party Participatory Democracy in Zambia (the Chona Commission)*, Lusaka, 1972.

Zambia Human Rights Commission, *Report, Findings and Recommendations of the Human Rights Commission's Visits to Prisons and Places of Detention Made Between November 1997 and February 1998*, Lusaka, 1998.

Zimba, L., 'The Origins and Spread of One-Party States in Commonwealth Africa and their Impact on Personal Liberties: a Case Study of the Zambian Model', in M. Ndulo (ed.), *Law in Zambia*, Nairobi: East African Publishing House, 1984.

INDEX